Behavior Analysis for Effective Teaching

Modern teachers increasingly encounter students who enter their classroom with low motivation, learning problems, or disruptive behavior. This book provides teachers and other human service professionals with specific tools they can use to teach more effectively without using the punitive methods that too often become part of educational practices. At the same time, the book explains the behavioral science on which behavioral practices are based.

This text is intended for undergraduate and graduate students in teacher education, special education, physical education, and educational psychology, as well as for practicing teachers who would like to know more about behavior analysis. The book is also appropriate for students in school psychology, school counseling, school social work, and other human service areas. The book addresses many of the topics covered in the credentialing exam given by the Behavior Analysis Certification Board.

Outstanding features include:

- Classroom Focus—The book integrates behavior management with effective instruction in a classroom context. It focuses on practical steps that teachers can take in any classroom setting to improve performance and reduce disruptions. It explains topics that teachers frequently encounter such as functional analysis, functional assessment, and Individualized Educational Plans. It presents recent developments, including TAG teaching, Precision Teaching, and instruction based upon the book *Verbal Behavior*.
- Exercises—The end of each chapter provides quick checks on basic concepts (with answers), as well as more complex analysis problems, some of which have sample answers.
- Presentation—The author writes clearly and uses a wealth of real (not imaginary) classroom examples.
- Pedagogy—The pedagogy follows behavior-analytic principles including clear behavioral objectives and coordinated end-of-chapter exercises. The book contains an end-of-book glossary and bibliography.
- Website—A coordinated companion website for the book, including instructions for student projects, is planned at www.routledge.com/textbooks/9780415990080.

Julie S. Vargas, Ph.D., is a former third and fourth grade teacher. She taught behavior analysis and instructional design to undergraduate education majors and practicing teachers for over 30 years. She is past president of the Association for Behavior Analysis International and one of the founding editors of *The Behavior Analyst*. Dr. Vargas has written three books and many chapters and articles on educational practices. She is currently President of the B. F. Skinner Foundation.

Behavior Analysis for Effective Teaching

Julie S. Vargas

Routledge
Taylor & Francis Group

NEW YORK AND LONDON

First published 2009
by Routledge
270 Madison Ave, New York, NY 10016

Simultaneously published in the UK
by Routledge
2 Park Square, Milton Park, Abingdon, Oxon OX14 4RN

Routledge is an imprint of the Taylor & Francis Group, an informa business

Typeset in Minion by
Swales & Willis Ltd, Exeter, Devon
Printed and bound in the United States of America on acid-free paper by
Edwards Brothers, Inc.

Library of Congress Cataloging-in-Publication Data
Vargas, Julie S.
  Behavior analysis for effective teaching / Julie S. Vargas
    p. cm.
  1. Behavioral assessment of children.   2. Problem children—Education.
  3. Effective teaching.   I. title.
  LB1124.V37 2009
  371.93—dc22

                                     2008043461

ISBN10: 0–415–99007–6 (hbk)
ISBN10: 0–415–99008–4 (pbk)
ISBN10: 0–203–87980–5 (ebk)

ISBN13: 978–0–415–99007–3 (hbk)
ISBN13: 978–0–415–99008–0 (pbk)
ISBN13: 978–0–203–87980–1 (ebk)

To my grandchildren:
Zoie, Emma, Ethan, and Tristan

BRIEF CONTENTS

CONTENTS

PREFACE

Many writers have pointed out that of all the professions, education has least benefited from scientific advances. Where a physician or electrical engineer from a hundred years ago would be lost in a contemporary setting, they say that a teacher from a prior century would fit right in. How hard is it to lecture?

However true that position may have been at one time, the situation has changed and none too soon. The challenges facing today's teachers differ from those of even a few years ago. Modern teachers work with an increasingly diverse population, often including students with special needs or language difficulties. How would a time-warp teacher handle a mainstreamed child with autism, or a playground bully, or a student who tries but cannot master a simple concept, even after repeated explanations and demonstrations? Without understanding the basic science of behavior, a teacher has little to fall back on other than punishment. But punishment usually makes a situation worse, not better. Moreover, laws such as the Individuals with Disabilities in Education Act (IDEA) increasingly restrict the use of punitive techniques. Today's teachers need behavioral solutions based on behaviorological science. Without them, even enthusiasm and a genuine love of students are not enough.

When I was in seventh grade I decided I wanted to become a teacher. Why, I do not know. I was not a good student: I spent afternoons riding my bike, playing tetherball, and practicing basketball shots at a friend's house instead of doing homework. My report cards stated that I "needed to work harder." I remember handing those reports to my father. He would look briefly at what I handed him, mumble "Uh Huh," and hand the report back without further comment. "What," he would ask whenever I talked about school, "did you *learn*?" Judging from my grades, not much. My highest grade in junior high was a B in mathematics.

I was rescued from academic failure by the small boarding school I attended from 10th through 12th grade in Putney, Vermont. Classes were small and discussions intense. I decided that college wasn't such a bad idea after all! I did go to college and majored in music. I still planned to teach, so I took a summer preparatory program in education. With that one course, I headed to New York City to teach third grade in a private girls' school.

I thought I would be a good elementary school teacher. I loved kids and was enthusiastic about every subject except history. I even loved math! That, I thought, was enough. I soon found out that knowing what to teach, explaining clearly, and liking students was not enough to help all of my students succeed as well as I was sure they could. While I used a few behavioral techniques described in this book, I did not have a good understanding of how my students' behavior adapted to what I did in class and I had little idea of what they got out of the exercises I assigned. That lack was even more conspicuous in my next job, teaching fourth grade in a blue-collar neighborhood outside of Pittsburgh, Pennsylvania.

So back to graduate school. My one behavioral course solidified my behavioral leanings. After graduating, my behavioral training was furthered by continued reading and discussions with colleagues and graduate students. But it was the years of interacting with undergraduate education majors and practicing teachers that showed how necessary positive procedures were for solving behavioral problems and improving student achievement in schools.

I wrote this book to provide an understanding of the science that relates everything you do and assign to the behavior likely to result. No matter how good a teacher you already are, there will be times when the performance of one or more of your students will be disappointing. What do you do then? If a specific technique has not worked, you need to find out why. Moreover you need to identify *where* to make changes. Behavior analysis shows how to adjust and to create new procedures for your students and for your teaching situation. It lets you avoid all-too-common punitive techniques that turn off students, and helps you design techniques that are both positive and effective.

Each interaction with your students affects not only their immediate behavior, but also their future. When you embolden a shy student or rescue a failing student, inspire an interested student or encourage a creative student, you not only equip your student with opportunities for a better life, you contribute to a better, more positive society for all.

ACKNOWLEDGMENTS

Many colleagues contributed to this book. I would like especially to thank the following: Andy Bondy, Rhiannon Brown, Julie Koudys, John Eshleman, Michela Figini-Myers, Lauren Troy, Anne Hoffman, Catherine Horton, Nancy Hughes, Jo-Anne Matteo, Theresa McKeon, Mark Sundberg, Vicci Tucci, Jerry Ulman, Jill Waegenaere, and Cathy Watkins. The many students I have taught over the years also deserve thanks for helping me present behavior analysis more clearly, as well as for the examples they provided through their projects. Bill MacKaye gave editorial suggestions that improved many of the chapters and Alexandra Sharp helped with the final editing and permissions. I would also like to thank Caroline Watson and Siân Findley for their help. Lastly, very special thanks go to my patient editor, Lane Akers, and to my husband who, through our many discussions and his editing of draft after draft after draft, co-wrote this book more than he realizes.

TO THE INSTRUCTOR

The sequence of chapters is organized to facilitate student projects. Chapters 4, 5, and 6 address topics for applying behavioral principles in schools where your students are teaching, or in their communities, or in projects done within your college or university setting. Guidelines for such projects are available on the website for this book: www.routledge.com/textbooks/9780415990080. Also planned for the website are:

For students:

1. Timed one-minute quizzes for the fluency objectives in some of the chapters.
2. Sample answers for some of the Analysis Problems.
3. Video clips.

For instructors:

1. Suggestions for having students conduct a research project as part of course requirements.
2. Guidelines for article abstracts to accompany research projects.

Part I

Science and the Art of Teaching

1

ADDING SCIENCE TO THE ART OF TEACHING

"Education . . . marks the most perfect and intimate union of science and art conceivable in human experience."

John Dewey

OVERVIEW

What is teaching? This chapter looks at what teaching consists of and how teachers can benefit from science as well as from art.

OBJECTIVES

By the end of this chapter you should be able to:

A. Identify definitions of teaching consistent with a behavioral analysis.
B. Select characteristic features of behavior analysis that differentiate it from other ways of teaching.
C. Complete definitions of "operant" and "contingencies" by supplying critical words.

THE KEY ROLE OF TEACHERS

If you were asked "What is the most important resource of a country?" what would you answer? It's not uranium or oil. It's not water or timber. It's not diamonds, or coal, or natural gas. The most critical resource of a country is its people, particularly its youth. How the next generation behaves will determine a country's future as surely as any other resource within its borders. In the United States, the responsibility for producing the academic and social skills of the next generation of workers and leaders rests on the

3

educational system. Even at a local level, it is an awesome responsibility. Teachers can rescue a child from a life of misery, help students learn to handle conflict, and inspire them to accomplish things they never dreamed possible. On the other hand, a careless action by a teacher can make a student hate a subject or education in general. Whatever teachers do affects student lives, often in significant ways.

The skills that students need in the twenty-first century differ from those needed in the past. Manufacturing jobs are going the way of agricultural jobs. In the eighteenth century over 90% of Americans were farmers. Today that segment is less than 5%. With the outsourcing of routine manufacturing jobs overseas, along with the increase in productivity per person and the replacement of assembly line workers with robotic systems, fewer Americans are needed to produce products. Good jobs increasingly demand higher levels of literacy and technical skills. The burden of producing those skills falls on the schools, especially on teachers.

At the same time that teachers are expected to teach more, they are receiving students who are more difficult to teach. Today's teachers encounter students who do not speak English, or who have special needs, or arrive at school hungry or sleep deprived, or even high on drugs. Then, too, the twenty-first century presents new challenges. A few years ago I visited an inner city elementary school in Chicago. When I arrived for my appointment, the teacher hurriedly suggested I look around the classroom, saying she had to leave for a "special activity." After a few moments I looked out into the hallway to see what this "special activity" was. To my right the entire school was lined up from the playground doors to a table where two teachers sat going through student backpacks. Other teachers stood around watching. To my left a very young policeman surveyed the scene. I asked him what was going on. "They're checking for firearms," he said in a bored voice. So *that* was the "special activity"! Later I was told that they did find a gun. In an elementary school, no less! Teachers today are asked to look out for potential violence as well as to teach academic skills and appropriate social **behavior**.

WHAT TEACHING IS AND IS NOT

Most people think of teaching as presenting information. This came home to me when I was teaching an undergraduate teacher education course in a major state university. It was a large course of nearly 500 prospective teachers. Early in the semester each student was asked to teach a five-minute lesson to the other 20 or so students in his or her weekly section meetings. The students were asked to teach as if their peers were in the grade for which their lesson was designed. The other students were to act at the appropriate age level (though not to take the part of troublemakers). The students took the assignment seriously. They appeared nicely dressed and all nervous to teach their first lesson. There were lessons on elementary science, high school algebra, English literature, and an amazing variety of subjects that might be taught in a school system. But although the content of each lesson differed, the way they "taught" did not. All but one of these future teachers *lectured* the entire five minutes. Teaching, they evidently thought, was presenting information.

If only it were that simple! Unfortunately, presenting is *not* teaching. You could present a brilliant lecture in an empty room (see Figure 1.1). Explaining and demonstrating is often *part* of the teaching process. Many a lecture has had an effect on those who have heard it. How much students will actually take away from a lecture,

Fig. 1.1 Lecturer delivering a brilliant lecture—to an empty room
Copyright 2008 Dean Grodzins, grodzins@gmail.com. Printed by permission.

however, depends on many factors, including whether or not they are listening. Some colleges have ruled that students cannot bring portable computers to class because, instead of taking notes on what their professors were saying, students were doing email. Without checking on student achievement, you cannot tell what effect a lecture is having.

Preliminary Definition of Teaching

Any definition of teaching must include the effect on student behavior. Otherwise, all any of us would need in order to teach would be expertise in a subject matter. But knowing your subject is only a small part of teaching. In fact, you can define teaching without referring to content at all. If one person's actions affect what another person does or can do, teaching has occurred. You can define teaching as designing circumstances that change the way other individuals behave.

Teaching deals with behavior. All behavior. Do you have students who disrupt class, making it difficult to teach others? Do you have students who volunteer to help clean up? Have you ever encountered students who fail to do homework or to complete in-class assignments? Do any of your students come into class ready to learn, while others have expressions on their face that can only be read as anxiety or hostility? Why do people behave the way they do? These are all questions about behavior. Society places many demands on teachers, but until recently has not provided them with the tools to handle day-to-day problems. Those tools come from the science of behavior.

WHAT IS SCIENCE?

Science is the systematic study of relations between events, and the formulation of those relations into **scientific laws.** Science assumes that basic processes are orderly; that is, they do not operate one way in a New York laboratory, but a different way in a California supermarket. Nor do they operate differently today than they did a thousand years ago. Science begins with *description*: objects and events are classified to make sense of features of the world and how they relate to each other. Modern chemistry can be traced to classifying elements according to atomic weight instead of by wetness, temperature, lightness or darkness. *Explanations*, that is, statements of how categories relate to each other make up *scientific laws*. Scientific laws permit *prediction*. In physics, calculations from Newton's Universal Law of Gravitation enabled a French astronomer, Le Verrier, to predict the presence in the solar system of an object that no one had ever seen.[1] He wrote his colleagues telling them where the object should be found. On September 23, 1846, the day of receiving Le Verrier's letter, the astronomers saw the planet that would be named Neptune, almost exactly where Le Verrier had said it should be. Scientific laws also facilitate *control*. When predictive factors can be arranged, outcomes can be determined. Newton's laws describing the relation between gravitational pull and centrifugal force made it possible to successfully launch satellites that would stay in orbit rather than flying off into space or crashing into Earth.

> Science is the systematic study of relations between phenomena, and the formulation of those relations into **scientific laws** that explain when and why events occur.

Although the way the world works remains constant, our understanding of it can change. Clarification of the concept of "planet," for example, changed the classification of Pluto. When new facts cannot be accounted for by existing laws, the laws are either refined, or shown to operate only within specific parameters. Newton's basic laws are a case in point. While his three laws of motion still hold, Einstein saw that cosmological data accumulated after Newton's death could not be explained using Newton's concepts of *fixed* space and time. Only if space curved and time could be compressed or extended could cosmological observations of the universe be explained and predicted.

For behavior, science provides not only explanation and prediction, but also procedures for control. As Skinner put it, "When we have discovered the laws which govern a part of the world . . . we are then ready to deal effectively with that part of the world. By predicting the occurrence of an event, we are able to prepare for it. By arranging conditions in ways specified by the laws of a system, we not only predict, we control: we 'cause' an event to occur or to assume certain characteristics."[2]

SCIENCE AND BEHAVIOR

We live in three worlds: the physical world, the biological world, and the behavioral world. Each has its own science. Physics is the oldest. Already by the seventeenth century Galileo had formulated laws about the physical motion of objects. But even with the advances in the succeeding centuries and the most advanced physics of today, physics cannot explain how biological species came about or how they evolve. That is a field that physics does not address. It is the province of biology. Biology in turn, even with the latest in genetic research and brain-imaging techniques, will never be able to explain why one of your students walks over to the window instead of to the door when the lunch bell rings, or why a student wears a red shirt to school, or even such an important aspect of behavior as the language he or she speaks. For that, you need a science of behavior (see Chapter 3).

Of course, the three sciences are not independent. Physical properties, such as the pollution from dirty power plants, affect both biology and behavior. Similarly, genetic endowment determines a portion of what people do, such as moving on two limbs instead of four or communicating by talking (see Chapter 2 for the role of genetics). Interactions between different aspects of our universe are the rule, not the exception. They do not invalidate the scientific principles within each arena.

The science of behavior began with the pioneering work of Burrhus Frederic Skinner. He grew up in a small town in Pennsylvania and spent much time roaming the hills and building contraptions like a cart on discarded roller skate wheels and a slide whose splinters ripped open his mother's feather pillows that he and his friends used as cushions. In high school the young Fred had a teacher, Miss Graves, to whom he would later dedicate his book *The Technology of Teaching*. Miss Graves gave the teenager a "love of literature and art."[3] It was because of Miss Graves that the young Skinner read Francis Bacon and encountered the idea that the goodness of a science is revealed by its practical utility. As Bacon put it, "Nature to be commanded must be obeyed." As an adult, Skinner would quote that statement often.

Fig. 1.2 B. F. Skinner around the time of his graduate school days
Reprinted by permission of the B. F. Skinner Foundation: Cambridge, MA: www.bfskinner.org.

After college, and two years failing to write the "great American novel" while living at home, Skinner did what many young adults do when they don't know what else to do: he went back to school. It was during his graduate student days that he made his discovery (see Chapter 3 for more detail).

Before Skinner came along, people thought that you could explain behavior as a response to a stimulus. The Russian physiologist Pavlov had already shown how you could make a dog salivate to the sound of a bell, and his book had just come out in an English translation when Skinner arrived for graduate school. Skinner had bought Pavlov's book and wanted to extend Pavlov's work. He built contraption after contraption, trying to find behavior that could be predicted by an antecedent event. After a year and a half, he made a discovery: most behavior is *not* the reaction to a stimulus. Most behavior depends upon its effect on the environment. The **consequences** of individual actions determine the likelihood of similar behavior in the future.

After getting his doctorate, Skinner spent five years doing further research on behavior, culminating in 1938 in his book *The Behavior of Organisms*. Skinner called the science he began "the experimental analysis of behavior." By the twenty-first century, the term **behavior analysis** had replaced Skinner's original term. Terms keep evolving. Recently the term **behaviorology** has been proposed.[4] Behaviorology specifies the science that relates behavior to its surrounding events following Skinner's original framework. Whatever the name, Skinnerian science has spawned successful practices in all areas of behavior including animal training, business, clinical work, health, and teaching. These practical applications have kept the science alive. That would have pleased Skinner immensely.

All sciences adopt special vocabularies. Ordinary terms carry misleading connotations and new terms are needed for new concepts. Behavior analysis is no exception. To understand the science and its applications, you need to learn a special vocabulary. Two of the primary terms are **operant** and **contingency**.

Operant Behavior and Operant Conditioning

Skinner coined the term *operant* to distinguish behavior that "operates" on the environment from the "respondent" behavior that Pavlov studied. You can explain a *respondent* eyeblink by identifying the stimulus that preceded it: "Joe blinked because dust hit his eye." Operant behavior differs. If you tell a student, "Blink," he or she may or may not blink. You cannot explain an operant blink by the stimulus preceding it. You must look at the consequences your student has encountered in the past for doing what you asked.

> **Operant behavior** is behavior that operates on the environment and is controlled by its immediate effects, in contrast to **respondent behavior** that can be explained as the response to a stimulus.

Most actions are operant. Their causes lie in individual interactions in their environment. Patterns of actions are always changing, adjusting to the kinds of effects encountered. Not everything a person does is repeated. Only some operants are "selected" by consequences to become stronger and more likely to become part of a person's usual behavior. This strengthening of particular actions through their consequences is called **operant conditioning** and it goes on all the time. By the time a child is born, behavior has already begun its constant evolution through the interplay of genetic and environmental factors.

How patterns of behavior come about in the first place, how they change or why they stay the same constitute the laws of the science of behavior. These laws, like the basic laws of biology, apply to all animals, including human beings.

Most reasons for behavior occur out where they can be seen. Behavior analysts do not appeal to "inner agencies" as causes of behavior. A youngster does not hit because he *is a bully* (see Chapter 2). He hits as a result of consequences that have strengthened hitting over better ways of interacting with others. That's good news, because consequences can be changed.

Contingencies of Reinforcement

The relations between operant behavior and its surrounding events are called **contingencies.** The activities you design, the kind of **feedback** you give, the procedures and rules in your classes or school, your lesson materials and exercises, even informal peer interactions are all part of the contingencies over your students' behavior. To understand why behavior is or is not occurring, you must identify the responsible contingencies.

> **Contingencies** are relations between an operant and features of the environment that affect the likelihood of similar behavior occurring in the future.

The contingencies that behavior analysts address start with two terms and their relationship: clearly defined actions and what follows those actions (their postcedents). The antecedent situation in which behavior–postcedent pairing usually occurs must also be considered, making a **three-term contingency** (antecedent–behavior–postcedent). Sounding out a word when reading is an action. One immediate postcedent might be recognizing the word made by the syllables you just uttered. The antecedent situation includes textual material and perhaps the presence of a teacher. Because many postcedents are

> The **three-term contingency** consists of the relationship between an operant, what results from or follows it, and the antecedent situation in which that behavior–postcedent pairing usually occurs.

consequences of behavior, most behavior analysts write C for the last term, making the letters ABC (Antecedent–Behavior–Consequence). The term "consequence" means *the result of* an action. Until you have determined that a postecedent *is* a consequence of behavior, ABP (antecedent-behavior-postcedent), though a less appealing acronym, is more accurate. A **contingency analysis**, like force or acceleration in physics, deals with *processes*: you can identify the component parts and see their sequencing in time, but you can only infer relationships. You can, however, see results in behavior when contingencies are changed (see especially Chapter 7).

Designing or altering contingencies in the classroom has been called **behavior modification**, but it is really **contingency management**. You do not directly modify behavior. You design instructional contingencies and *they* improve student achievement. As Skinner put it, "Teaching is the arrangement of contingencies of reinforcement to facilitate learning."[5]

Not all contingencies produce positive changes. Both "good" and "bad" behavior can be "taught" and both are. A teacher may be responsible for a student loving math, but teachers also can make

> **Teaching** is the arrangement of contingencies that facilitate learning.

students dislike a subject. Many adults can trace a dislike of math to the actions of a particular teacher. Regardless of whether you plan it or not, whatever affect you have on your students is what you have taught them. That makes it critical to understand how contingencies work.

The basic analysis, though following simple principles, becomes complex in the school setting because behavior is always in flux, always adapting to momentary changes in the hundreds of contingencies in any individual's day. Human behavior is sensitive to very subtle aspects of its immediate environment including sensations inside one's own body. Analyzing the most conspicuous contingencies will not always provide quick answers for why a student behaves a particular way, nor will it give a cookbook procedure that works with all students. A contingency analysis will, however, help you discover factors responsible for behavior you observe. It is up to you, then, to design procedures tailored to your particular setting and individual students. If you hit upon critical contingencies, some simple changes may surprise you with how quickly behavior improves.

The only postcedents that build behavior are positive ones, and they are the ones recommended in this book. Positive consequences in turn produce student enthusiasm as well as success, which in turn motivate you to spend the time and effort that good teaching demands.

BEHAVIOR ANALYSIS FOR A MORE HUMANE WORLD

Behavior analysis and its derivative **Positive Behavior Support** improve the way we deal with each other as well as with other species. They move us as a culture towards a more humane world. Here is an example of what needs to be changed.

Training of elephants: Traditional training techniques used over centuries with elephants include hitting or beating them when they do not obey. In this country, one of the country's best zoos, the San Diego Zoo, was fined following a 1988 incident in which it was charged that "five elephant keepers chained an elephant in a zoo, brought it to its knees and beat it severely with ax handles over two days." The city attorney, in reviewing the case, declared that the procedure "while seemingly cruel, was an accepted practice at zoos and circuses."[6]

"*Seemingly* cruel?" Even though the investigation found that the keepers had been falsely charged, the training did follow "accepted practice" of "dominating" through force. The San Diego Zoo and Wildlife Park now use principles of behavior analysis. Eight of their newer elephants have never felt a blow, including a baby born in the zoo. Behavior is controlled with a technique called **clicker training** (clickertraining.com).

Building new behavior, teaching the animal to respond only on cue, and to execute a complex series of actions, requires more than can be explained here, but the basic process relies on operant conditioning. At the precise moment the animal executes an action to be strengthened, an audible click is sounded, followed by food or tickling, or some other strengthening consequence. Complex behavior can be "shaped" in steps by clicking actions that come closer and closer to the final desired performance (see Chapter 8).

Animals in captivity need medical care. How do you get a big animal to hold still for such medical routines as inoculations or drawing blood? In the past, veterinarians have shot anesthetizing darts into animals when it was not practical to catch them and hold them down. That procedure itself was dangerous. Darts sometimes hit the wrong spot, damaging a foot or an eye, and the "darted" animals often hurt themselves as they staggered around and fell while under the influence of the drug. Today, through shaping techniques, animals co-operate with veterinarians. Elephants come to the railings of their enclosure and hold up their feet for inspection or treatment, and walruses stick their flippers out of their cages, and hold still while veterinarians draw blood. Such behavior can be shaped *only* with behavioral techniques. Punishment will not work. Replacing punishment with positive procedures holds promise for schools too.

FROM PUNISHING STUDENTS TO REINFORCING ACTIONS

For hundreds of years, teachers have used punishment as the main method of control to keep students from misbehaving. Pictures of teachers in old drawings often show them with a cane or switch or paddle. But people began to see this treatment as inhumane. In 1783, corporal punishment of students was abolished in Poland, followed in the nineteenth century by the Netherlands and six other European countries. The pace accelerated in the twentieth century with 19 more countries including China and Japan outlawing the practice. The United States and Canada have been slower to eliminate corporal punishment of students. Towards the end of the twentieth century, fresh out of a teacher education masters program, I was hired as a fourth-grade teacher in Pennsylvania. The opening session for new teachers included talks and materials. I got a pile of books and a narrow wooden cutting board with a handle. I was puzzled by the board sitting on top of my books. How nice of them to give us a little gift. But why was the board so skinny? Even French bread was thicker than that! Were we supposed to use it to cut up snacks for indoor recess breaks? Of course, I soon found out that the wooden board was not for cutting bread. It was for paddling students! Did the school district expect me to *hit* students? I thought I was supposed to teach them.

By 2000, Canada, the United States, and Australia were the only remaining industrialized countries that had not totally abolished corporal punishment of students. As late as 2005, in the United States, a whipping tool called "The Rod" was selling a "few a week."[7] The rod was a 22-inch flexible nylon rod with a safety tip and cushioned vinyl grip for the whipper's comfort. It was advertised as the "ideal tool for child training." Horrible.

But there is progress. In the United States, by 2007, 29 states had outlawed corporal punishment for students. (It was already illegal nationwide for people incarcerated in prisons.) The number of students receiving corporal punishment has decreased over the years to fewer than a quarter of a million American children in the 2006–07 academic year.[8] That is still way too many. Even one child is too many!

People punish others when they have lost control. When you can get students to work and learn with positive methods, there is no reason to punish. Behavior analysis provides those positive methods.

BEHAVIOR ANALYSIS IN ACTION

While paddling fortunately is going out of fashion in schools, other methods of punishment are not. For many students, school is still a place where they can expect to be humiliated, insulted, yelled at, placed in detention, or kicked out all together. How humane is that? When behavioral techniques replace traditional procedures of control, everyone benefits.

Example: TAG Teaching Gymnastics

One set of procedures directly derived from Skinner's original work is called **TAG Teaching** (**T**eaching with **A**coustical **G**uidance). Adapted from clicker training, TAG Teaching was first used for teaching dancing and gymnastic (see tagteach.com). One of the developers of TAG Teaching, Theresa McKeon, describes how her lessons were changed when she worked behavioral principles into her teaching. Here is her report:

> A group of competitive gymnasts are trying to prepare for an important upcoming meet. If they do well, they will qualify for state championships; if not, their season is over. The importance of a clean routine is not lost on the athlete or her coach (me).
>
> Each athlete's turn attempting each skill is scanned for possible errors by the coach creating a no-win environment for both. To be fair, this is how they are judged at competition. Four judges watch a routine and methodically tick away at the gymnast's performance with deductions for the slightest imperfections.
>
> Nicki does a handstand. I call out, "Nicki, every time you go into your handstand your legs are bent. You're not going to get a qualifying score if every time you go into a handstand your legs are bent. Get them straight, and *please* point your toes in the handstand and for heavens sake smile. . . ."
>
> To add to this critical atmosphere, voices in a gym are by necessity . . . loud. Coaches learn to speak above all the ambient noise with raised voices.
>
> "Mary, your leg is bent."
>
> "Lyndsay, I said arms up."
>
> "Stacey, you're wobbly, tighten up." I shout.
>
> Students often complain of being "yelled at." Gym speak has evolved into a steady steam of "corrections," where the most an athlete can hope for is "That was better . . . but next time you need to. . . ."
>
> TAG Teaching changed these procedures. TAGteach lessons follow behavior analytic principles and a systematic approach to shaping behavior. What students do wrong is replaced with a specific finite goal, a TAG *point.* "Don't bend your knee" becomes "the TAG point is, *straight leg on the first step.*" With that one clear target the student executes the handstand. At the precise moment she straightens her legs she hears a clicker sound. The sharp click cuts through the ambient noise in the gym and communicates that her performance was correct. If her legs are not yet straight, nothing happens. The student does not get "yelled at" for bent legs. If necessary the TAG point is simplified, or if it is obtainable, the student tries again. The coach feels comfortable saying, " perfect!" and the students gain success on increasingly difficult targets.
>
> Due to the yes or no nature of properly stated TAG points, students as young as four years old can tag each other accurately. They thrive on this role reversal, as they become the person they so often want to please, the coach!

Needless to say, students much prefer TAG Teaching to traditional coaching. In addition, when they tag each other, they not only get more practice, they alternate between being the student and the teacher. Coaches, too, appreciate no longer needing to shout to communicate.

For more academic subjects, behavior analytic techniques hold similar advantages over traditional teaching practices.

Example: Replacing Loud Talking with Writing in Second Grade

A second-grade class in a small elementary school in West Virginia began the school day at a decibel level that was conspicuous throughout the entire neighborhood. The teacher, trying to be heard, raised her voice, the children raised theirs, and the result was the same kind of escalation one gets in a crowded restaurant or bar. Enter the behavior analyst. To start the day off quietly, she told the students they were going to so something new. When school began, no one would talk for five minutes. But they could pass a note to anyone they could reach without getting out of their seat.

"What if we don't know how to spell a word?" one asked.

"Write how you think it is spelled, and I'll see if I can figure out what you mean."

They started. No one spoke, but everyone started writing. Hands went up for help with spelling and the behavior analyst wrote the correct spelling for the students. Some of the words that students requested were put silently on the board. At the end of the five minutes, the class was quiet and the school day began at a refreshing sound level. After several days of this (during which spelling and handwriting improved), one day the principal walked into the room and started talking to the behavior analyst. She put her finger to her lips, went over to the blackboard and wrote, to the great delight of the students, "You can't talk. You have to write."

Example: Using Positive Procedures Instead of Paddling to Reduce Disruptive Behavior

The insistence on using only positive contingencies to improve behavior has been especially important with students who are often punished in school. All behavior, including "misbehavior," is being *supported* or it wouldn't continue. Think of it. How unfair is that—to punish the very behavior the school environment, though unintentionally, is maintaining? The answer is "very unfair." To locate the relevant contingencies over the "problem" behavior, behavior analysts do a **functional assessment.** With questionnaires or direct observation, the three parts of a three-term contingency are identified. Then appropriate changes are made.

> A **functional assessment** is a procedure that identifies antecedents and postcedents of specific actions to locate factors likely to be related to the occurrence of the behavior.

The following case study involves a second-grade student, called Bob, who had received spankings about every three weeks before a functional assessment was started. Seven spankings were documented in the weeks preceding the study.[9]

Bob's teacher recorded the antecedents and postcedents of Bob's disruptions. When Bob made noises so annoying that the teacher could not continue teaching, his peers laughed, the teacher talked to him (teacher attention), and he usually got removed from the classroom and did not have to continue working. Bob's appropriate behavior rarely received any notice by the teacher.

The treatment involved catching Bob working. A timer was set to remind the teacher to check on what Bob was doing every five minutes or so. If he was working, he got a sticker on a card on his desk, and the teacher gave verbal approval. Cards with 80% of the blanks filled could be exchanged at the end of the day for trinkets like pencils, erasers, and stamps. If Bob was successful, his peers got five minutes of free time. That encouraged them not to laugh at Bob's antics.

After a few days, checking on Bob's behavior was extended from five minutes to 10. In cases like this, procedures are usually fazed out slowly until they are no longer needed. By gradually extending timings while maintaining positive attention for working, eventually no trinkets would be needed.

After the positive procedures were started, Bob did not get one spanking for the remaining weeks of the study. Punishment did not improve Bob's behavior. Positive methods did.

Example: Increasing High School Attendance

Students who skip school usually receive some kind of punishment. At the secondary level, three assistant principals enrolled in a graduate research class were concerned about a dozen seniors in their buildings who had missed so many days of school that they were in danger of being permanently suspended. (The logic of removing students from school because they have missed too much school escapes me, but that was the district's policy.) The students were in danger of failing to graduate, with all the disadvantages of not getting a high school degree. These were "normal" kids, though several came from broken homes. Instead of individual conferences with the students, threatening them with the dire financial consequences of failing to graduate, the three assistant principals took a positive approach. Every day they walked around their buildings, looking for their target students and saying things like, "Glad to see you here today, Rick," using each student's name. That was it. To the amazement of the assistant principals, most of their students' attendance improved. Not only that, but in one of the schools, a couple of the students began arriving early enough to pop into central office, waving at the assistant principal and saying, "Hey Mr. Jones. Look. I'm here today."

Example: Improving Note-Taking in a Large College Lecture Class

Although lectures are common in education, not all students always pay attention. My first college teaching assignment was the same class where 500 students "taught" their five-minute lessons by lecturing non-stop. In addition to their section meetings, students attended lectures by me. Like all new instructors, I wanted to do a good job. My first week I designed what I thought was a good presentation complete with practical examples, nice visuals, and a clear structure. Excited, I went to the large lecture hall. I began my carefully designed presentation, speaking clearly, varying my speed and tone for examples, presenting my visuals, some even with humor in them. It didn't take long before I saw that I was losing a good part of my class. In the back, several males were rather conspicuously reading the student newspaper. I could hear the rustle as they turned the pages. Clearly something had to be done.

The next week as students entered the lecture room, they picked up what I called a **lecture fill-in** sheet. One page long, it contained an outline of the day's lecture but with all the important parts missing. For example, Number 3 might read, "We define reinforcement as _____." I began the lecture. On my visuals I had the same items as the students had on their sheets, but with the missing parts filled in. So I'd say, for example, "So you see, you can't tell what will be reinforcement just by what you like. We define it as—this is Number 3 on your handout (and here I would reveal the definition)—any event immediately following an action that increases the strength or likelihood of that action's occurring in the future."

Eureka. Suddenly the missing words became important. Unlike the previous week, I could see students moving their heads to get a good view so they could fill in their blanks. If I moved on to the next visual too fast, students would protest. Best of all, the same students who had so blatantly been reading their newspaper the week before, now were craning their necks to get every word down. At the end of the lecture, one of them even came up to me saying, "Dr. Vargas, what was Number 4a? I'm not sure I got it all."

I won't make any claims about whether or not my lecture fill-in sheets produced more achievement. But it solved my problem of rustling newspapers and inattentive students both of which are rather distressing to a novice lecturer. My new procedure also had another salutary effect. Like most teachers, I had more to do than time to do it in. Because I had to get my fill-in sheets to the secretaries at least three days before my lectures, I completed the lectures earlier than I had before. In the intervening days, I improved my presentations with better examples, more attractive graphics, and relevant news items.

FEATURES OF BEHAVIOR ANALYSIS

Why do these examples represent behavior analysis? First of all, a problem was identified and goals were specifically stated as clearly measurable student actions. Procedures concentrated on building student skills. Instead of attributing the cause of what students were doing to something inside them such as poor concentration, lack of co-ordination, inadequate intelligence, or low motivation, the educators looked at contingencies. Their procedures did not rely on telling students about the importance of behaving appropriately, but focused on the consequences of their actions and the settings in which behavior occurred. Instead of punishing inappropriate actions, positive consequences were added for the actions desired. Although only in two cases were data kept, in all cases progress was clearly visible and, at least in the gym example, the next step depended on each student's performance on the last step. That, too, is a feature of behavior analysis—adjusting each teaching step according to the students' performance on their current task.

> **Applied Behavior Analysis (ABA)** is the engineering side of the science of contingency relations. Behavior analysts analyze and adjust contingencies to improve behavior.

No doubt one could find aspects of each of these cases that aren't perfect for an illustration of behavior analysis in action. The point is not to show the ideal, but rather the practical. Even a small amount of training can help a teacher solve classroom problems. But it can also frustrate early efforts when subtleties are missed and the procedures that the science says *should* work aren't working. There is no guarantee that reproducing the procedures described above will lead to the same outcomes. That does not mean that the science is faulty. One does not blame physics when a spacecraft fails to perform as expected. One makes a more detailed analysis to find out what was responsible for the problem.

COMBINING ART WITH SCIENCE

Along with the underlying science, there is an art to teaching. Individual and creative ideas bring variety and interest to education. What do you have that is special? Certainly your own interests and knowledge are unique. So are the interests of your students, and anything unusual about the setting of your school. Art involves taking advantage of those idiosyncrasies. Perhaps your old building has a lot of visible rust. What is rust? How does it occur? Does all metal rust? What percentage of your students' lockers have rust inside? Finding questions to ask is part of the art in teaching.

The art of teaching also includes sensitivity to subtleties in student behavior. Why is Tricia's eye twitching today? What are your students' interests? Their special talents? What are the dynamics between individuals and between groups? Can you use activities they like to do outside class to clarify critical concepts or principles or to motivate activities such as reading? All that is unique in your students and situation offers creative opportunities.

This book addresses the contingencies involved in effective teaching. With more efficiency in teaching the skills needed for mandated testing, and the reduction of "discipline" problems, you will be able to spend more time and energy doing what you entered your profession to do: helping students learn more effectively and enjoyably than they would on their own so that they can live productive and happy lives.

SUMMARY

One of the most critical professions for the long term health of a society is teaching. As a teacher you are charged with a tremendous responsibility. You are supposed to enable the next generation of youngsters to acquire whatever skills they will need for their future success in a career and in life in general, including behaviors such as "positive attitudes," "consideration for others," "creativity," "good citizenship," and so on. To do this, you must do more than present information. You are expected to design instructional procedures and activities that will improve your students' academic and social behavior and to monitor and improve your own effectiveness.

The procedures, materials, and interactions within an educational environment determine the kinds of behaviors students will engage in and what they will learn. Whatever you do or fail to do affects student behavior. Some of the changes you produce will be intentional, some unplanned. Some will benefit students, some may not. Some of what you do may even be detrimental. Everyone occasionally makes mistakes. Whether planned or unplanned, whether beneficial or not, the way student behavior changes as a result of their time with you is what you have taught them.

Behavior analysis is based upon a science of behavior that analyses the interaction between moment to moment actions and features of the environment that affect future behavior. The beauty of the science and its power come from the basic principles that underlie the incredible variety of behavior both of non-human animals and of human beings. In analyzing contingencies you can identify factors responsible for behavior, most of which can be changed. By providing positive methods for change, behavioral procedures eliminate or substantially reduce aversive techniques of control—punishment procedures—that have traditionally been associated with the profession of teaching. That, in turn, makes teaching more enjoyable both for your students and for you as a teacher.

CONCEPT CHECKS

Definition of Teaching (Objective A)

DIRECTIONS: Which three of the following are consistent with a behavioral definition of teaching?

1. Teaching is assisting another to gain skills through the design of activities and feedback.
2. Teaching is providing information, demonstrations, and explanations that clearly explain a subject matter.
3. Teaching is getting out of the way of students so they can construct their own worlds in their own way.
4. Teaching is setting up contingencies that change the way students interact within their worlds.
5. Teaching is whatever one person does that directly or indirectly affects what another person does.
6. Teaching is only the positive effects you have on your students.

Characteristics of Behavior Analysis (Objective B)

DIRECTIONS: Select the three statements below that best characterize behavior analytic procedures:

1. Immediately criticizing performance that is not the best the student can do.
2. Talking with students about their behavior as a way to get them to do something they have failed to do.
3. Finding behavior to build to replace behavior that is blocking a student's progress.
4. Changing what we ask students to do in the classroom when their skills are not improving.
5. Designing what each student is to do according to lesson plans for his or her age level.
6. Replacing "disciplining" as a consequence for misbehavior with a change in instructional procedures.

Definition of Contingencies (Objective C)

DIRECTIONS: Fill in the missing words.

1. Contingencies refer to the _____ between student actions, the events that immediately _____ those actions, and the antecedent situations in which those _____ – _____ pairs occur.

ANSWERS FOR CONCEPT CHECKS

Definition of Teaching

The three statements that are most consistent with a behavioral approach are numbers 1, 4, and 5.

Number 2 mentions what a teacher might be doing, but not whether or not any student behavior is altered as a result.

Number 3 abdicates the teacher's role altogether. If teaching is getting out of the way of students and letting them "construct their own worlds" (whatever that means!), teachers are not needed. Of course, no one really suggests we put students into schools and then leave them alone. Advocates of "constructivism" expect teachers to design activities to encourage productive behavior. Whether or not one calls what students do as "constructing one's own world" the school environment is supposed to help them learn that is to give skills that alter what they do and can do in the future.

Number 6 is wishful thinking. Teachers have an effect on student behavior in destructive ways as well as positive ones. Behavior analysis considers all of the changes brought about in student behavior by a teacher as part of what that teacher taught.

Characteristics of Behavior Analysis

The three statements that best characterize behavior analytic procedures are statements 3, 4, and 6.

Number 1 is punitive. Criticism is meant to decrease something the student is doing. Behavior analysis avoids punishment except in extreme circumstances where health or safety are involved. Criticism is not needed for the simple skill building described as "not doing the best the student can do." Behavior analysis concentrates on building, not tearing down actions.

Number 2 is a form of lecturing. It ignores the postcedent contingencies that are the heart of behavior analytic procedures.

Number 5 fails to take into account what each student can or cannot do. Behavior analytic procedures are designed for individuals, not age normed averages. No individual has all of the behaviors typical of a particular age level. Behavior analytic procedures design activities around current skill levels, not chronological ages.

Definition of Contingencies

1. Contingencies refer to the *relations* between student actions, the events that immediately *follow* those actions, and the antecedent situations in which those *action—postcedent* pairs occur.

Equivalent wording is acceptable, such as the following:

Contingencies refer to the *relationships* between student actions, the events that immediately *come after* those actions, and the situations in which those *behavior—consequence* pairs occur.

2

FINDING THE "CAUSES" OF BEHAVIOR IN FUNCTIONAL RELATIONS

"It's common for men to give pretended Reasons instead of one real one."

Benjamin Franklin[1]

OVERVIEW

As a teacher, you deal with behavior. To understand why a student is or is not behaving a particular way, it helps to avoid "pretended reasons" and to find "real" ones that can be changed. How can you tell what kinds of reasons actually make a difference? Chapter 2 introduces the concept of **functional relation** as a way to find aspects of the educational environment that can be altered to improve behavior.

OBJECTIVES

By the end of this chapter you should be able to:

A. Select statements about behavior that are in the form of an explanation.
B. Define **functional relation** and identify or give examples of functional relations.
C. Identify the **dependent** and **independent** variables in explanatory statements.
D. Distinguish between statements that are **explanatory fictions** and those in which the proposed causes can be assessed independently of the behavior to be explained.
E. Pick out explanatory statements that describe contingencies from a list of explanations of behavior.

WHAT IS A "CAUSE"?

Why does Saul complete his class exercises? Why does Janet wear six earrings? Whenever you ask "Why?" you are asking for conditions or events upon which behavior depends. The answers have a stated or implied "because": Saul completes his class exercises *because* they count towards his grade. Janet's boyfriend gave her the six earrings she wears, *which is why* she wears them. The word "because" does not necessarily appear in explanatory statements, as in the case of Janet's boyfriend. It is implied.

Wearing earrings is less likely to affect classroom achievement than assignment completion is. Thus it is the latter that you would address. When adopting strategies to improve behavior, you are essentially conducting an experiment to find out events on which behavior *depends*. Your targeted behavior is thus called your **dependent variable.** Dependent variables are stated as actions that can be counted or measured so that their values vary (see Chapter 4). For teachers, dependent variables include academic targets such as the number of problems or assignments completed, as well as social actions such as how often a student volunteers or shares.

> A **dependent variable** is a behavior to be explained, stated in a measurable way.

Once you have specified a dependent variable, you need to find what influences that behavior. Whatever you change in an orderly way, whether or not it makes a difference, is called your **independent variable**. Independent variables are called "independent" because they exist *independently* of the behavior being measured: they may or may not be present when the behavior occurs. The seating arrangement in your class, the kind of assignments or explanations you give, the way you present a topic or manage your classroom, all are independent variables when their effect on behavior is assessed.

> A **"cause"** of behavior is a condition or event on which behavior depends.

You can never change all factors that may enter into the causes of behavior. The color of your classroom walls or the sound of school bells might have an effect on what your students do, but they would not be called "independent variables" unless they were systematically varied to see their effects.

> An **independent variable** is a condition or event that is varied to see its effect on the dependent variable.

Other things being equal, if you change your independent variable and get a change in student behavior, you have identified a **functional relation**. For practical purposes, then, a "cause" of behavior is a factor on which it depends.

The question "Why?" is answered by identifying functional relations between the behavior you are interested in and factors that determine whether or not it occurs. If Saul completes only those exercises that count towards his grade, his working is (at least partly) a function of grading procedures. If you change the exercises that count towards a grade, Saul's behavior will react accordingly. Many independent variables may be involved. Saul may complete assignments only if his friend is absent, or he may work steadily only when he gets time on the computer for finishing before the end of the period. Any behavior occurs in a hodgepodge of events, any of which may be altered to determine the effect.

To "understand" behavior, you must find the variables responsible for it. Finding "causes" becomes a search for functional relations among all of the contingencies that occur in a setting.

Functional Relations

A functional relation specifies the relation between the behavior to be explained and one or more of the variables that affect that behavior. The word comes from mathematics and implies a relation between variables that can be expressed as an equation, like F = MA (force equals mass times acceleration) in physics. In the classroom, functional relations are usually not so precise that one can give the exact value of the dependent variable by knowing the value of the independent variable. Still one can at least predict the direction of change once a functional relation is found. For example, you may find that the greater the point value of an assignment, the more likely Saul is to complete it.

Any functional relation holds only within certain limits. If Saul already has an A for a grading period, he may fail to complete an assignment even if it has a high point value and "counts." All "laws" of science work within constraints. Only when certain conditions are met does a particular functional relation apply.

A functional relation can *theoretically* be put to an experimental test. In practice, such a test may not be feasible for ethical or practical reasons. If you suspect that cancer is functionally related to teenage smoking, you would not conduct experiments with human teenagers, though related research might be done with other species (as in fact was done). Manipulation would be impractical if the independent variables involved gender. You cannot randomly change a student's sex to see how that would affect

> A **functional relation** is a systematic relationship between dependent and independent variables. The functional relations that are of interest to teachers involve behavior and contingencies that reliably produce it.

his (or her) behavior. Even when testing a variable is impractical, other kinds of evidence can suggest that a functional relation exists. The first evidence for the relation between smoking and lung cancer came from hospital observations that lung cancer patients were more likely to be heavy smokers than patients admitted for other illnesses.

A functional analysis tries to find features of the instructional setting that are related to the likelihood of specific behavior occurring. You cannot see a functional relation; you see only its results. A part of an instructional setting is altered and any changes in behavior are recorded. You do this informally when you change the seating of a disruptive student, or try out a new worksheet to see whether performance improves. Although a professional researcher would be more systematic, the procedure of trying something and noting the result is basically the same.

When functional relations are shown in a graph, you can see the result of a change in procedures. Figure 2.1 shows evidence of a functional relation between aggressive behavior and activities on a playground (organized games versus free play).[2] The dependent variable is the number of aggressive incidents occurring before school on a playground where between 300 and 350 kindergarten through second-grade children played. (For those recording the data, what was counted as an "aggressive action" was clearly specified.) The dependent variable measure is plotted on the vertical axis, with

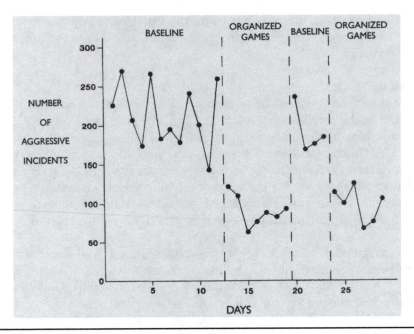

Fig. 2.1 Evidence of a functional relation between aggressive behavior and type of activity on a playground
H. Allen Murphy, J. Michael Hutchison, and Jon S. Bailey. "Behavioral School Psychology Goes Outdoors: The Effect of Organized Games on Playground Aggression." *Journal of Applied Behavior Analysis* 16 (1983): 33. Reprinted with permission of the Society for the Experimental Analysis of Behavior.

each day of school shown along the bottom of the graph. You can see that when games were organized (days 13–19 and days 24–29) aggressive incidents occurred less frequently than on the other days; that suggests a functional relation between organized games (independent variable) and aggressive actions (dependent variable). Still, aggressive actions occurred even when games were organized. There is rarely only one reason that a given kind of behavior occurs. By changing an independent variable, you see whether or not it is a relevant factor. If a functional relation exists, knowing the value of the independent variable gives you at least a rough idea of the level of the dependent variable.

Dependent and Independent Variables in Explanation
In the behavioral sciences, dependent variables are more difficult to state than in the physical or biological sciences, and the task is made more difficult still by the way in which people talk about behavior. Educators often talk in labels using words such as "intelligence," self-esteem," "attention deficit disorder," "proficiency," and so on. These labels summarize clusters of actions that often occur together, but they do not specify what a particular student does (see Chapter 4). Worse still, these summary words are often turned around and used as explanations for the very kinds of behavior they describe. Thus cause and effect become two ways of talking about the same actions that are observed. The proposed independent variable is not independent at all. It is just another way of stating the dependent problem or goal.

No one would seriously consider a statement such as "Jenny reads well because she reads well," as an explanation. But rephrase the presumed "cause" and you have a statement that *sounds* reasonable: "Jenny reads well because she has a high reading aptitude." If the evidence for her "reading aptitude" comes from the same observations as the evidence for her "reading well," your statement is no better than "Jenny reads well because she reads well." The presumed cause is not an *independent* variable. It refers to the same performances as those we wish to explain. To find causes we need *independent* variables. Otherwise we have a "circular explanation" also called an "**explanatory fiction**," which is no explanation at all.

Cause and effect in explanatory fictions are not independent. They are different ways of describing the same kinds of behavior observed.

> A **circular explanation** or **explanatory fiction** is a statement that has the form of an explanation, but in which the cause given is essentially a restatement of the behavior to be explained.

EXPLANATORY FICTIONS: EXPLANATIONS THAT DO NOT EXPLAIN

In education, many statements made to explain behavior are circular. Here is an example: during an in-service workshop an elementary school teacher brought up the following problem. She had a student, she said, who did well on weekly spelling quizzes but misspelled badly on his daily compositions—the very same words he had spelled correctly on his spelling tests! "Why," she asked, "did Peter misspell those words when he knew better?" The rest of the teachers offered explanations, some of which are listed in Table 2.1. Their explanations sound reasonable enough, but if we look at them closely we discover that *not one* is an explanation in any testable way. All they do is state the problem over again and make their restatement the "cause." Then they put that "cause" inside the learner. They are all "explanatory fictions."

Table 2.1 Examples of practicing teachers' explanations for why Peter spells correctly on Friday's test, but then misspells the same words in his compositions

1. Because he is careless about spelling on compositions
2. Because he isn't motivated to spell correctly except on tests
3. Because he doesn't proofread
4. Because he isn't interested in spelling correctly in his daily work
5. Because he doesn't apply what he has learned
6. Because he has a defeatist attitude
7. Because he doesn't associate—make a connection between a word on Friday and later
8. Because he's too intent on getting his ideas down in creative writing
9. Because he doesn't correlate the idea that spelling is the same as writing
10. Because he doesn't try
11. Because he has a perceptual problem
12. Because he doesn't hear sounds—he has a hearing problem

Let's look at these reasons. The dependent variable is "misspelling on compositions." It would normally be measured by the number of mistakes made on compositions (possibly compared with the number of correctly spelled words). Trying our test to see if the independent variables are truly independent, we look at how they would be assessed. For Number 1, what evidence would we use to judge Peter's carelessness? How do we know that Peter "isn't motivated to spell correctly except on tests (Number 2), or that he "isn't interested in spelling correctly in his daily work" (Number 4)? The evidence for each of these statements would most likely be his misspelling on compositions, the very behavior we are trying to explain! Those statements are all explanatory fictions.

The same case could be made for the other statements in Table 2.1, although it is less clear for some. Perhaps we would look at something besides spelling errors to see whether Peter proofreads (Number 3), or has a "perceptual problem" (Number 11), or "hearing problem" (Number 12), but why then Peter spells correctly on *tests* is a mystery. But remember that these statements were made about a student the teachers did not know. The only information they had was what Peter's teacher had said about his spelling. If we ask, "How do you know that Peter doesn't proofread," and hear "Well look at his awful spelling," the teacher is using misspelling to explain misspelling and we have an explanatory fiction. Not all the teachers' explanations were explanatory fictions. Many of the teachers gave good "testable" explanations. Table 2.1 shows just the circular ones.

Giving explanatory fictions to account for behavior resembles the following theologian's explanation of what holds up the world:

> A theologian was giving a class. He stroked his long beard and said to his students in a serious voice, "The world rests on the back of an elephant." A student shot up his hand. "Sir," he asked, "what does the elephant stand on?" The theologian peered over his spectacles. "Why, another elephant," he said. Another hand shot up. "Sir, what does *that* . . .?" But the theologian interrupted, "Save your breath," he said. "It's elephants all the way down."

Explanatory fictions can be generated ad infinitum. "The student doesn't work because *he doesn't feel like working.*" "He doesn't feel like working because *he isn't interested in the subject.*" "He isn't interested in the subject because *he isn't motivated.*" "He isn't motivated because *he has poor self-esteem.*" And so on, "all the way down."

Explanatory fictions do not help the teacher. Being told that a student doesn't work because he or she is not motivated does not tell you what to change. You get no closer to a solution if you are told "to motivate Susan" than you were when trying to get her to work harder. In practice, explanatory fictions are worse than no help. Too often they blame the student, thus discouraging you from finding classroom or social contingencies that would make a difference. If Susan doesn't work because *she* isn't motivated, isn't that Susan's problem? If only *she* would change her attitude, the problem would be solved. Many letters home to parents give explanatory fictions as reasons for poor school performance, essentially absolving the school of any responsibility. Such explanatory fictions provide no more help to parents than they do to teachers.

One more example: The college course mentioned in Chapter 1 was converted by a colleague from a lecture format to self-instructional units through which students could progress at their own pace. The course was required for education majors and had an enrollment of around 500 students. The semester started and for the first few weeks things went smoothly. True, the learning center in which the units were to be taken was nearly empty, but the few students who came seemed to be progressing nicely. Mid-semester came and went, and everyone was happy. Then, as the end of the semester drew near, disaster struck. Four hundred students who had not completed their units descended on the learning center, waiting in lines 20 and 30 deep to get one of the dozen alternate forms of the quizzes or to get the quiz they had just taken scored to see whether they could go on. Somehow, 300 students made it through by the time grades had to be sent to the registrar. The registrar called the instructors immediately. "There must be some mistake," he said. "You have 200 students marked as "incomplete." The other instructor and I had to confirm those grades: 200 students had not yet completed the course.

Why didn't the students complete the course on time? It would have been tempting to blame the students, saying things like, "These education students procrastinate too much," or "These students aren't very mature," or "They knew they had 10 units to do. They need to take more responsibility." Then the instructors could have washed their hands of any responsibility for the chaos. All of these supposed "reasons" however, are explanatory fictions. They do not identify variables functionally related to completing units.

To change the situation we needed to find out what aspects of the course design determined student progress through it. We identified three factors: (1) there weren't enough deadlines to pace performance, (2) there were no advantages for beginning earlier, and (3) students did not get clear feedback on their progress and its implications. These reasons are not just another way of describing the problem, they are independent variables that are different from "student progress." They can be changed—and were. By setting weekly deadlines with extra grade points for completing them on time and by making progress (or its lack) conspicuous, we reduced the incompletes in the semesters that followed to fewer than a dozen. Many students finished the units early and there was no more rush at the end of the semester.

TESTING OF INDEPENDENT VARIABLES

A statement may satisfy the requirement that the "cause" is different from the behavior being explained and still not be a true statement. Advertising provides many examples: if an advertisement implies that you will get a date from that special person if you switch to Brethless Toothpaste, you are likely to suspect its accuracy. "Getting a date," and "brand of toothpaste used" are clearly measured independently, so the statement is not an explanatory fiction. Unfortunately, it is also probably not true.

A proposed independent variable is just that: proposed. To determine whether or not a variable is responsible for behavior, you must test it (see Chapter 7). It is tempting to attribute the cause of a behavior to something which happens to occur at the same time, particularly when it agrees with your beliefs. Suppose, for example, you have a nursery school child who wets her pants Monday, Wednesday, and Friday. If, in talking with her mother, you discover that the child was given a large soft drink for breakfast on those days, you are likely to conclude that drinking soda caused the child to wet her pants. If, however, the mother says that on those days, and not on Tuesday or Thursday, she poured water over a voodoo model of her daughter, you are likely to dismiss the relation as coincidental. Your judgment is made, not upon the current evidence, which is equally strong in both cases, but upon your beliefs and prior knowledge about the effects of drinking on urination. To determine whether or not a functional relation exists, you could do an experimental test. For the "voodoo doll" example, you could have Mama wet the doll on randomly assigned days (without your knowledge of which days she uses),[3] and then check the child's performance. It is this ability to *test* a statement and not its apparent truthfulness that sets proposed functional relations apart from other "explanations" of behavior. Of course, if for a couple of weeks you found a relation between the voodoo wetting and the child's performance, you would still think that it was a coincidence. Causes that go against established scientific principles are always suspect until further evidence becomes convincing. To add a new scientific principle requires exceptional testing by a variety of investigators. Still, by realizing that opinion enters into scientific interpretation, you can set up procedures to counteract pre-conceptions (see Chapter 7).

Functional Assessment

In 1997 the US Congress passed a law called the Individuals with Disabilities Education Act (IDEA). The act included a section on discipline that required a functional assessment of behavior for which a student had been removed from his or her "current educational placement."

For example, imagine a student who screams so loudly and so often that it makes it impossible for his teacher to teach. Before that "special student" can be moved to an alternative placement within the school or expelled altogether, a functional assessment must be conducted. This requirement recognizes the fact that all behavior, including screaming, is maintained by its relation to environmental variables. Although the original law has been amended several times,[4] the general intent is to find out why the troublesome behavior is occurring. What is screaming a function of? It does not seem fair to kick a student out of class for behavior that is being maintained by something in the school. If, for example, teacher attention is what is maintaining screaming, then by changing the timing of attention, alternative behavior can be built. Once the student no longer screams, he or she can stay in the regular classroom with his or her peers. IDEA recognizes that problem behavior is functionally related to the student's interactions within the school environment.

"CAUSAL" VARIABLES THAT ARE NOT HELPFUL IN EXPLAINING BEHAVIOR

Many "explanations" of behavior that have no practical value circulate in schools. One involves internal "agencies." Because there is no empirical evidence for the existence of internal agencies, they are also called **hypothetical constructs**. These hypothesized "agencies" are said to reside inside the brain. Thus they are also called **mentalistic constructs**.

The Problem with Mentalistic Constructs

You will hear educators appeal to many hypothetical constructs as explanations of behavior. Two familiar constructs are "long-term memory" and "short-term memory." These are both mentalistic constructs. No one has ever seen them. They are intended to explain the very behaviors for which they are the evidence, making them classic cases of explanatory fictions. How would you feel if a student told you, "I'm sorry I did so badly on your test, but

> A **mentalistic construct** is some internal structure or characteristic that is said to cause behavior. There is no evidence of its existence other than the kinds of behavior it is proposed to explain or predict.

it's because I have a poor long-term memory. You can't grade me down for that." It would be tempting to say "Thank you for your explanatory fiction. Now let's work on your long-term memory."

Why Neuroscience is Not a Useful Level of Analysis for Teachers

Some of the "internal" explanations for behavior do have independent evidence. Neuroscience gives an example. Neurologists can observe some of what is going on inside the brain when, for example, a person is solving a problem. It is not clear whether the brain activation that is observed *causes* behavior, is *part* of behaving, or is the *result* of the task given to the participants whose brain activity is studied. As people behave, the connections between nerve cells undergo change. Studying what goes on inside the brain is interesting, but it is a different science from the science of behavior. The physiological workings of the brain will never be useful in telling you whether a student will raise his or her hand to get called on or how you should change the difficulty level of a worksheet. Only an analysis of how behavior interacts within its environment will explain daily behavior.

Developmental Stages and Behavior

Developmental stages are explanatory fictions when they are used to assert that a child behaves a particular way *because* of being at a particular stage. Say a young boy argues logically about concrete events, but has difficulty with abstract concepts. That would put him into Piaget's "concrete operational stage." If you then say he has trouble with abstraction *because* he is at the concrete operational stage, you are using his difficulty to explain that same behavior. Piaget's analysis is useful in describing the kinds of intellectual activities a student should learn, as well as the ages at which aggregates of skills usually appear, but stages do *not* explain behavior. Stages describe clusters of behavior, not reasons for why those behaviors occur.

Chronological age does not cause behavior either. Our body parts mature, but the passage of time is not the reason for specific actions. A child does not walk or talk because three years have gone by, but because of the physical growth and interactions that have taken place during that time. Even height and weight are not a function of time. Without food and water, no growth would occur. What happens *during* the elapsed time produces the change, not the ticking of seconds on a clock.

The field of development contributes to teaching when it describes skills that are prerequisites for others. For example, if a child pronounces "some" as "thum" it helps to know that the child must first hear the difference between "s" and "th" sounds. Without being able to tell the difference between sounds, a child cannot tell whether or not his or her own pronunciation is correct. In that case, distinguishing between sounds needs to be taught first.

The importance of addressing prerequisites rather than waiting for maturation was demonstrated in a special preschool for children with **autism** and other developmental disabilities. Eight students were not progressing in their curriculum. One skill these children lacked was following spoken directions. Instead of continuing with the regular program and waiting for these children to mature, the children were given a few weeks of instruction. They were taught "listening skills" until they readily followed simple requests like "stand up" or "touch your nose." To make sure they were not just imitating, the teachers did not model the actions, and they interspersed directions like "trash the graph" to make sure the children did not respond to nonsense. After the children were returned to the regular curriculum, they quickly mastered the troublesome objectives and took from half to less than a tenth of the trials to master succeeding objectives.[5] They needed additional instruction to "mature."

When the field of development identifies skills that are needed for more complex skills, it contributes to instruction. It is when developmental stages are used to explain the behaviors that define those stages that behavior analysts raise objections.

Why Future Goals and Expectations are Not Useful as Causes

In daily speech we often attribute actions to some future occurrence, as in the statement, "Sheri is taking driving lessons *in order to* pass the driver's test." An event in the future cannot have an effect on an event in the present. If our "cause" does not occur (Sheri fails), how do we then explain her behavior? Sheri's taking driving lessons could not have been caused by passing the test she didn't pass.

Since a future occurrence can't cause behavior now, we might be tempted to say that Sheri takes driving lessons, not because she *will* pass the test, but because she *expects* to pass the test. In naming an expectation, however, we have generated another question: how did the expectancy come about? Perhaps Sheri in the past has passed tests by taking lessons. We then have a three-step analysis: *Passing tests in the past by taking lessons* leads to *expectancy of passing a test by taking lessons* leads to *taking lessons now*.

Since our expectations are determined entirely by past experience, it adds nothing to include expectancy. Wielding **Occam's razor** (the simplest explanation is best), we can eliminate the middle term. *Taking lessons* is a function of *having passed tests by taking lessons in the past*. In addition to simplicity, there is a second reason for eliminating the middle step in explanation. It is possible to directly manipulate taking lessons to see if it helps students pass tests, as has been done in research on the results of tutoring on Graduate Record Exam test scores. But there is no way to directly manipulate expectancies. Behavior analysts therefore reject expectancies as independent variables.

Genetic Endowment and Its Role in Behavior

Heredity plays an important role in our behavior. The short person will not be likely to play on a high school basketball team. His joining a soccer team rather than basketball will be partly a function of his inborn physiology. Differences in overall activity level, sensitivity to physical stimuli, tastes, and even some skill clusters summarized by the term "intelligence" are no doubt present at birth. But genetic endowment is overworked as a cause for specific actions.

Say you have a student who is constantly changing activities and is diagnosed with **attention deficit hyperactivity disorder (ADHD)**. If you say he gets up and down at least once a minute *because* of his ADHD, you are back in explanatory-fiction-land. If you say he gets up and down often because he was born with a DNA disorder, you step away from using the same evidence for cause and effect. Genetic makeup is shown by different evidence (DNA extracted from blood) than the behavior of popping up and down. So far, so good.

If you follow your "hyperactive" student outside school, however, you may discover him sitting still for many minutes while playing a computer game. The behavior of standing up and sitting down, then, cannot be primarily a function of his genes. He doesn't switch DNA when he steps out of school! Something in the different environments produces the different actions. Yes, some of us move about more than others, and genetics may account for at least part of those differences. But genetics cannot explain specific actions that vary from situation to situation. Everyone behaves differently in different environments. While genetic makeup partly determines tendencies, it cannot account for specifics of what we do and when we do it.

Most people attribute far too much to genetic endowment. A study of 90,000 twins statistically estimated the relative importance of heritable and environmental factors in getting cancer at specific sites of the body. If one identical twin had stomach cancer, what do you think was the probability that the other twin would get stomach cancer before age 75? Most people guess a very high percentage. In fact, for stomach cancer, the likelihood was only 8%. For some cancer sites, such as breast cancer the probability hit a high of 42%, still less than half. The researchers concluded that "the environment has the principal role in causing sporadic cancer."[6] A genetic marker for cancer may influence the way your body reacts to substances such as cigarette smoke, but your environment determines whether you encounter smoke or other carcinogenic substances, the kinds of foods you eat, your exercise levels and other factors that affect your overall health. Recent research shows that even which inherited genes are turned on and which are switched off is influenced by your environment.[7]

Behavior is even more susceptible than human physiology to environmental influences. It is a product of our genetic endowment and all of the moment to moment interactions we have had since birth. Even such basics as the language we speak comes from our environment not from our genetic endowment. As a teacher you could not wish for a better situation. You cannot change the genes your students inherit, but you can alter aspects of your classroom interactions. Behavior is always in flux, always adapting to the contingencies encountered including those in the school environment.

WHICH ENVIRONMENT AS CAUSE?

We live in many different physical and social environments, each of which shapes different behavior. Teachers act differently in school than they do at parties, students behave differently at home from the way they behave at school. When explaining behavior in one setting, it is tempting to look for its explanation in something going on in another setting. The other setting most used by teachers is a student's home environment. In spite of the fact that student behavior varies in school—students work harder in one class than in another—teachers often appeal to home environment to explain behavior. In any school you can hear talk of broken homes, overindulgent parents, lack of supervision at home, and many other comments about home environments—all given as reasons for how the student behaves at school. This ignores the fact that every student's behavior alters according to the contingencies encountered. Students who usually take several minutes to start an assignment will rush to start a timed quiz or test, regardless of their home environment.

Of course, home environment does affect behavior. A student who has already learned at home much of what is expected at school has an easier time than one from a family that does not teach social or academic skills. All students come into class with patterns of behavior that have been established by a lifetime of past experiences, including experiences at home. Students who already understand standard English, read and write well, work steadily, and try to please, are more likely to succeed than those who come to class with fewer skills. But what any student continues to do or begins to do differently in the classroom depends upon the contingencies set up within that environment. You cannot blame Corey's note-passing day after day in your biology class on her Uncle George's drinking habits at home. You must look at the contingencies in your classroom to determine what maintains that behavior.

SUMMARY

All sciences look for relationships between variables. Behavior analysts look for relations between specific actions and variables in the environment that might be responsible for them. These "causal" variables differ from the behavior to be explained. They can, at least in principle, be altered to see the resulting effect on behavior. When you can reliably change how often a behavior occurs by altering a classroom procedure, you have provided evidence of a functional relation between the behavior and your procedure. Behavior analysts do not give "explanations" that attribute behavior to defects within the student. Such statements are circular when the action to be explained and the proposed "cause" refer to the same behavioral evidence. Such circular explanations are called "explanatory fictions" because the "cause" has no documented existence apart from the effect.

Other common explanations are also of little or no use to the classroom teacher. Characteristics of individuals, such as inherited traits, hypothesized cognitive structures, or developmental stages do not point to variables you can directly change. Most of these explanations are explanatory fictions because the "causes" are inferred from the very behavior that is being "explained."

Some variables residing inside the student are valid independent variables: a stomach ache perhaps, or positive statements said routinely only to oneself. While these are not explanatory fictions, such variables still need some kind of independent evidence if they are to help improve behavior. It is far better to shed common explanations for what students do or don't do, and to look for explanation in the contingencies operating in the classroom environment. Most contingencies, fortunately, can be changed when change is needed.

CONCEPT CHECKS

Explanatory Statements (Objective A)

DIRECTIONS: Pick out the three statements that are in the form of an explanation, that is, they mention both a behavior and a proposed cause for it.

1. Perry rarely has breakfast before he comes to school in the morning.
2. Patty skips school due to her mother's insistence that she help with the family store.
3. Peter wants to go to college so that's the reason he studies hard.
4. Pauline does not like spinach or other green foods offered in the cafeteria.
5. Patrick never was taught fractions which is why he doesn't work on his fraction seat work.

Functional Relations (Objective B)

DIRECTIONS: Write the numbers of the *three* statements below that describe functional relations between the *italicized* variables.

1. *Distance* equals the *rate* times the *time*.
2. When the *clock shows 10 to the hour* students start *snapping their notebooks*.
3. Tom *boasts and tells bragging stories* at least *10 times each hour*.
4. Joan *passes notes* only when *near Judy*.
5. Jan *finishes her assignments early* so her teacher should *let her help other students*.

Dependent and Independent Variables (Objective C)

DIRECTIONS: For each statement or article title, tell whether the *italicized* variable is a dependent variable (DV) or an independent variable (IV).

1. Peter *completes assignments on time* because the teacher gives extra points for promptness.
2. Does *test performance* increase when teachers let students select their own learning styles?
3. When the school started *sending home positive notes to parents*, student attitudes towards school improved.
4. *Racial match between counselor and client* improved attendance at counseling sessions.
5. *Academic achievement* improved by study skills course.
6. Effects of *rhythmic music* on endurance in physical performance.

Explanations of Behavior I (Objective D)

DIRECTIONS: For each item below, mark the statement in which the proposed "cause" would be assessed by different kinds of evidence than the behavior being explained (that is, mark the statement that is **not** an explanatory fiction).

1. Jackie hesitates to read aloud because she:

    1a. got laughed at by others when reading aloud
    1b. is shy about reading aloud when with peers

2. The boy shoots baskets well because he is:

   2a. very tall
   2b. talented

3. The student kept changing what he did all the time because he:

   3a. ate foods with additives
   3b. had attention deficit hyperactivity disorder (ADHD)

4. Mr. Clark's students avoided his classes because they were:

   4a. alienated from him
   4b. unsuccessful there

5. Peter arrives on time every day at school because:

   5a. his favorite subject is scheduled first
   5b. of his punctuality and responsibility

6. Tom works fast on his worksheets because:

   6a. he is a speedy worker
   6b. they are timed

7. Karen speaks up readily in class because she has:

   7a. had her contributions accepted
   7b. little communication anxiety

8. The rise in school violence is due to increased:

   8a. violence portrayed on TV
   8b. fights by school children

9. Music students sometimes don't complete their work for Thursday morning because they:

   9a. don't feel like working on Wednesday nights
   9b. have band practice on Wednesday nights

10. Student scores went down because of:

    10a. insufficient motivation to do well
    10b. overcrowding in the schools

Explanations of Behavior II (Objective E)

DIRECTIONS: Mark the three statements that most clearly describe contingencies to explain behavior.

1. Tom remembers details well because of the strong patterns of connection of dendrites in his brain.
2. Dick's mental maps enable him to find his way around easily.
3. Harry works rapidly on his spelling exercises because he gets to use the computer if there is still time left in the period.
4. Getting out of calisthenics is the likely reason for Sue's complaining of cramps at the beginning of gym class.
5. Ruth doesn't copy the homework from the board because she can't see it.
6. Didi can complete math exercises that use numbers because she is at the concrete operations stage.

ANALYSIS PROBLEMS

Kinds of Variables and Explanatory Fictions (Objectives C & D)

Listen to the reasons people give for why someone does something. Write down three of these explanations, identifying dependent and independent variables. Then, for each explanation, describe the kind of evidence used for a) the behavior to be explained and b) the "cause" given. Finally, tell whether the statement is an explanatory fiction or a testable explanation.

ANSWERS FOR CONCEPT CHECKS

Explanatory Statements

The statements that have a proposed reason are statements numbers 2, 3, and 5. Put into a sentence with the **dependent variable** first and the "cause" after the word "because," they would read as follows: (Whether or not they are good reasons is not at issue here).

2. Patty **skips school** because *her mother insists that she help with the family store*.
3. Peter **studies** hard because *he wants to go to college*.
5. Patrick doesn't **work on his fraction seat work** because *he never was taught fractions*.

Functional Relations

The three statements that describe functional relations are numbers 1, 2, and 4. Comments follow:

1. **Distance** equals the **rate** times the **time**. All formulas describe functional relations.
2. When the clock shows **10 to the hour** students start **snapping their notebooks**. The functional relation can be stated "Snapping notebooks is (at least partly) a function of the time the clock shows."

3. How often Tom boasts and brags does not provide an independent variable. You would not say "Tom's boasting and bragging is *a function of* 10 times each hour." It merely occurs 10 times.
4. Passing notes is a function of Judy's presence.
5. "Letting her help other students" suggests a procedure that has not been done, so there cannot be a functional relation.

Dependent and Independent Variables

1. Dependent Variable
2. Dependent Variable
3. Independent Variable
4. Independent Variable
5. Dependent Variable
6. Independent Variable

Explanations of Behavior I

1. a
2. a
3. a
4. b
5. a
6. b
7. a
8. a
9. b
10. b

Explanations of Behavior II

The three most behavioral explanations are 3, 4, and 5. Statement 2 is an explanatory fiction because the only evidence for "mental maps" is Dick's ease at finding his way around. Statement 6 attributes completing numerical math exercises to a "stage." If her math performance is why she is classified in the "concrete operations" stage, the statement is also an explanatory fiction. If she was classified by other behaviors, this statement still fails to identify factors in the environment that were responsible for her math performance.

3

HOW WE LEARN

"Give a man a fish and you feed him for a day. Teach a man to fish and you feed him for life."

Chinese Proverb

OVERVIEW

If you are a teacher, you work with behavior. In order to understand why students act the way they do and to help them improve, you need to know the basic processes involved in what is called "learning." This chapter presents the ways in which behavior changes. Understanding the principles involved will help you with classroom management and teaching.

OBJECTIVES

By the end of this chapter you should be able to:

A. Tell whether descriptions of behavior change illustrate operant or respondent conditioning and use "emitted" and "elicited" appropriately.
B. Define or identify examples of the following:

   an operant
   a two-term contingency
   a three-term contingency
   reinforcement, continuous reinforcement and intermittent reinforcement
   punishment
   extinction.

C. Give your own example of the Criticism Trap.
D. Explain how reinforcement differs from rewards and why the difference is important.

E. Explain the difference between extinction and forgetting.
F. Describe how you could change the two-term contingency to improve behavior in a given classroom example, including:

naming the postcedent most likely to be maintaining the current behavior
changing the timing of the reinforcing event to make it contingent on a better behavior
what outcome you would expect.

WHAT WE MEAN BY "LEARNING"

Learning is a change in behavior as a result of interacting within one's immediate environment. Learning involves changes in thinking and other internal behavior as well as in overt actions such as writing an essay. Acquired behavior differs from inherited tendencies and the results of maturation, but inherited characteristics and environment constantly interact. In fact, the most critical tendency people inherit is to adapt to the changing contingencies in their lives.

Teaching is designed to bring about changes that serve both individual students in the long run and the society in which they live. Yet few teacher-education programs equip teachers with the relevant science. Most teachers say they learn how to teach on the job. Most teachers use some behavioral procedures. But without understanding the science on which they are based, it is difficult to adjust when a procedure does not work as expected. You will be far more effective as a teacher when you have gained a clear understanding of the contingencies that determine what people do and why they behave the way they do.

Two Kinds of Learning: Respondent and Operant Conditioning

The term *learning* encompasses two very different processes, **respondent conditioning** and **operant conditioning**. Respondent conditioning was discovered first. It was described by Pavlov in the book *Conditioned Reflexes,* which appeared in an English translation in the United States in 1927.[1]

RESPONDENT CONDITIONING

Chapter 1 mentioned Pavlov's dogs and how they learned to salivate to the sound of a bell. The principles Pavlov discovered involve respondent behavior. Respondent behavior always occurs *in response to* a specific stimulus as part of a reflex. Reflexes consist of a specific physiological reaction to an antecedent stimulus. Most are inborn. Like Pavlov's dogs, you will salivate if sour lemon juice is placed in your mouth. To explain that salivation, you need only point to the stimulus that *preceded* the response. Your salivating occurs "in response" to lemon juice. Lemon juice **elicits** salivation. Reflexes are part of the functioning of your nervous system.

Pavlov showed how a new stimulus that has no initial effect on a reflex response can be made to elicit that response. His work began in the 1890s in Russia with research on the digestive system. As part of his research he needed to collect saliva. Dog owners know how copiously dogs can drool. Pavlov found dogs ideal for his digestive research.

He operated on the dogs so that their saliva would flow into a tube instead of into their stomachs, and then he put food into his dogs' mouths to get them to salivate.[2] Pavlov was a careful researcher and a good observer: He noticed something surprising: His dogs were salivating *before* the food was put into their mouths! This was interesting. Pavlov began investigating how this unexplained "psychic secretion" was generated.

Suspecting that the dogs could hear sounds accompanying the delivery of food, Pavlov set up experiments involving sound. He used a bell so he could present a sound clearly and with exact timing. To see whether a dog would salivate to the sound of the bell without training, he rang the bell to see if it elicited salivation. It did not. Pavlov called this stimulus that has no initial effect on the reflex response a **neutral stimulus**.

Next Pavlov paired the bell sound with the *unconditioned stimulus (UCS)* of the food that produced the *unconditioned response (UCR)* of salivating. He sounded the bell just before putting food powder into his dog's mouth. After a few pairings, he checked to see whether the previously neutral stimulus would now elicit salivation all by itself. He rang the bell and the dog salivated to the sound alone. A new reflex had been created that was conditional on the training (see Figure 3.1). The "neutral" stimulus was no longer neutral. The bell was now a **conditional stimulus** (CS) that elicited the **conditional response** of salivation.[3]

Respondent conditioning is often described as "stimulus substitution." No new response is created. A new stimulus produces the old kind of response.

People sometimes inaccurately say that Pavlov's dog associated the bell with the food. It was not the dog that paired the stimuli; it was Pavlov. In humans, by putting the pairing inside a person, you create an impression that the person is *aware* of the

> **Respondent conditioning** is the process of pairing a stimulus that does *not* elicit a particular response with one that already *does* until the previously neutral stimulus by itself elicits the response. The previously neutral stimulus then becomes a "**conditional stimulus**" and the response a "**conditional response**."[4]

connection. But that may not be the case. People often react in ways they do not understand. Until understanding is reached, it is tempting to call behavior as Pavlov did— "psychic."

Respondents in the Classroom

Since respondents involve only automatic physiological reactions, why would teachers care about respondent behavior? Everyone knows that students salivate to lemon juice or blink when something hits their eye. What does that have to do with learning? As a teacher, you cannot change inherited reflexes but you still have to deal with respondents that are learned. In any classroom you can find fear, anxiety, hostility, or anger, along with their operant correlates of withdrawal or aggression. These respondents come about through pairing: a formerly neutral feature of a situation comes to elicit the same emotions produced by the paired punishing or frightening events (see Chapter 11). Avoiding the eliciting stimulus keeps those emotions from occurring until other ways of handling triggering events can be established.

Not all emotions are bad, of course. Positive emotions result from pairing as well. Photographs of a person you adore often bring forth some of the affectionate feelings you hold for the person shown. A piece of music strongly paired with a lover will elicit

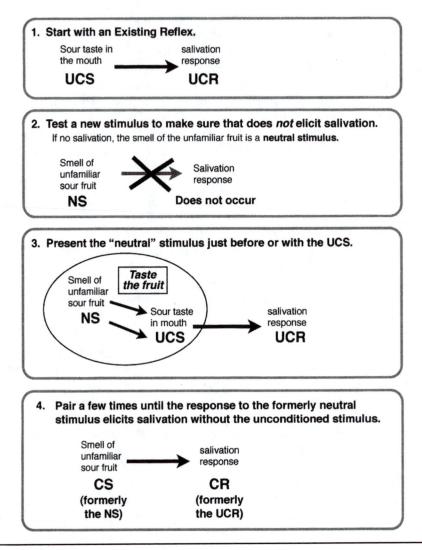

Fig. 3.1 Steps in respondent conditioning

some of the same feelings later when you hear it, especially if it has not been paired with other people too. Even a taste of an unusual food eaten during a joyous vacation may elicit some of the same pleasurable respondents on a later occasion. All emotions are part of behavior and must be considered along with operant behavior in order to understand why people behave the way they do.

Pavlov's Discovery

Fig. 3.2 Ivan Petrovich Pavlov 1849–1936
Photograph taken by a photographer at the 1929 International Congress of Physiology, with Pavlov's signature attached. Author's collection.

Although known today mainly for his work on conditioning, Pavlov worked most of his life as a physiologist in medicine. In 1904, the year that B. F. Skinner was born, Pavlov received the Nobel Prize for his work on digestion. For this work he had diverted saliva from the mouth of dogs through tubes to a collection tube, enabling him to measure both its amount and the rate of the dogs' salivating. Noticing that saliva started *before* food was inserted into the dogs' mouths, Pavlov began investigating how this unexplained "psychic secretion" came about. He found that it was the result of a specific kind of pairing procedure that we know today as **Pavlovian, classical**, or **respondent conditioning**. Although most books talk of his work with a bell, Pavlov used a variety of antecedent stimuli including sounds from whistles, tuning forks, and a metronome that allowed varying the speed of the ticking sound. He also used visual stimuli. In addition to producing new "conditional reflexes," Pavlov investigated extinction—how long it took a **conditional stimulus** to stop producing the **conditional response** when food no longer followed the sound.

OPERANT CONDITIONING

Important as respondents are, respondent conditioning does not address the kinds of academic behaviors that schools are designed to teach. Skills from talking to reading to math or science or art are acquired through operant conditioning. Operant conditioning, as mentioned in Chapter 1, was discovered by Skinner to be a process separate from respondent conditioning (see Discovery of Operant Conditioning below).

Comparison with Thorndike's Work

What was so revolutionary about Skinner's research? Everyone knows that people work for rewards. As early as 1898, Edward L. Thorndike had put cats in "puzzle boxes" with food outside, and demonstrated that by clawing at a string that opened a door most of them got out faster and faster on succeeding trials (although some of the cats never did get out). After publishing one monograph, Thorndike discontinued this line of investigation. Skinner probably had heard of Thorndike's puzzle box experiments, but that work was more than 20 years old by the time Skinner entered graduate school. In any case, his discovery of operant conditioning came out of his own experiments following, he thought, in Pavlov's footsteps.

The Discovery of Operant Conditioning

The story of the discovery of operant conditioning is the story of an ambitious student, anxious to prove himself after having failed to become a writer while living in his parents' home. Although his parents were supportive, their concern about their only son's lack of productivity must have been painfully clear to Skinner. In 1928, at the age of 24, he escaped to Greenwich Village in New York City and got a job in a bookstore. It was there he read Pavlov's work just out in English,[5] John B. Watson's *Behaviorism*,[6] and Bertrand Russell's *Philosophy*.[7] Skinner became excited by what he read. He would go to graduate school to study **behaviorism**.

Armed with his three books, he arrived at Harvard to study stimulus-response relations like Pavlov and Watson. The department at Harvard, however, could not have been less suitable for a budding behaviorist. Its chair, Edwin Boring, promoted what Watson called, in the book that excited Skinner, "the false psychological god *Introspection*."[8] Like Watson, Skinner wanted to study *behavior*, not what people said about perceptions as in introspective psychology. Fortunately Boring was out of town when Skinner arrived. The only course Skinner could find that discussed Pavlov was in the physiology department, so he signed up. Through this course Skinner met William Crozier, the caustic young chairman of the physiology department. Crozier, who had nothing but distain for Boring and his psychology department, encouraged Skinner to follow his own behavioral inclinations. Skinner's behavioristic leanings were also supported by a fellow psychology student, Fred Keller, and by a professor, Walter Hunter, who came weekly from Clark University to lecture at Harvard.

Skinner's course requirements consisted mostly of research courses. Some were in psychology, some in physiology. No one knew who was supervising the young student so he ended up doing, as he put it, "exactly as I pleased."[9] What he "pleased" was to build equipment to extend Pavlov and Watson's ideas about stimulus and response, using rats that had been given to him by another of Crozier's students.

Following Crozier's encouragement to go his own direction in research, Skinner made and tore apart a dozen pieces of equipment. He began with "trials" where an animal is put into a runway and taken out at the end. Slowly, Skinner shifted from looking at the response to a stimulus to less restricted behavior. He designed a rectangular runway so his animals could run around without interruption. They did not have to be taken out at the end of each run to return them to the beginning for a new trial.

To get the animals to go around, Skinner put a tiny food dish at one end of the rectangle. When the rat had eaten his pellet of food, it could start another run around for another piece of food. What Skinner's rats did, however, was to sit and sniff their newly emptied food dish. They took *forever* to start a new run. Skinner got tired of sitting and waiting. He designed a new apparatus to have the rats record their own behavior. He made a runway that tipped as a rat moved around (see Figure 3.3).

The scraps that Skinner used to make his tipping runway had a cylindrical drum called a "kymograph" attached. Smoke-blackened paper was wrapped around the drum which slowly turned as a "stylus" scratched a horizontal line. Events produced a short up-tick in the line, followed by the stylus's return to the horizontal. Records on the original version had the shape of square teeth cut into a Halloween pumpkin. Skinner made an important change. He connected the stylus to a weight so that each time food was dispensed, the pen moved down a tiny step and did not go back up.[10] Every run around the track then moved the line down. The faster the animals ran around the runway, the steeper the slope of the line. Skinner soon flipped his graph so the line went up instead of down. He called it a **cumulative record.** It showed the cumulative rate of actions with the angle revealing the speed with which behavior occurred.

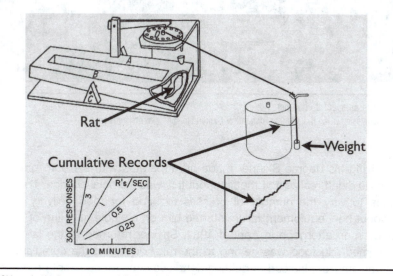

Fig. 3.3 Skinner's tipping runway and first cumulative records
Adapted from B. F. Skinner, "A Case History in Scientific Method." *American Psychologist* 11 (1956): 221–233.

The cumulative record showed minute to minute changes in rate or speed of behavior as it occurred over real time. Soon Skinner got more interested in the rat's eating than in its running around a track. He tore up his tipping runway and built a box with a door for the rat to push to get a piece of food. But now, where was the preceding stimulus?

Still looking at antecedents, Skinner recorded how long the rat had gone without being fed. To his great delight, he found clear evidence of a functional relation between eating and time without food. He wrote his parents that he had ". . .demonstrated that the rate with which a rat eats food, over a period of two hours, is a square function of the time."[11] How fast the rat ate pellets, in other words, could be predicted. It started rapidly when the rat was put into the apparatus, and decreased as time went on. The data sufficed for a thesis, and Skinner got his doctorate.

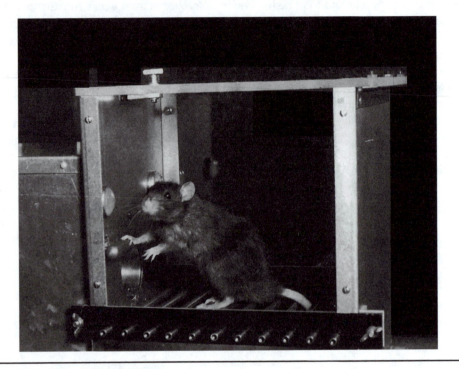

Fig. 3.4 A rat in an operant chamber
Reprinted by permission of the B. F. Skinner Foundation: Cambridge, MA: www.bfskinner.org.

After receiving his degree Skinner made an apparatus with a bar to press instead of a door. He didn't realize it at the time, but this was a crucial change. The bar made it possible to vary the number of presses required for food delivery. Skinner is candid about how equipment failure started him on a whole new line of research. It happened on an afternoon in April of 1931. Skinner returned to the lab to find his feeder jammed. No food was getting to the rat. Looking at the cumulative record, Skinner was amazed. Instead of quitting right away, the rat had kept on pressing the lever, first in rapid bursts and then in shorter bursts until it had stopped altogether. As Skinner described it:

> I can easily recall the excitement of that first complete extinction curve. I had made contact with Pavlov at last: here was a curve uncorrupted by the physiological process of ingestion. It was an orderly change due to nothing more than a special contingency of reinforcement. It was pure behavior.[12]

> It was a Friday afternoon and there was no one in the laboratory whom I could tell. All that weekend I crossed the streets with particular care and avoided all unnecessary risks to protect my discovery from loss through my death.[13]
>
> Skinner was right to be excited, but wrong about Pavlov. His rat's actions were not reflex responses to prior stimuli. Skinner soon realized that bar presses were controlled by the food that *followed* each press. He began altering contingencies and was surprise when he discovered that by reinforcing only some bar presses, the rat pressed faster. He wrote his best friend Fred Keller that he had developed "a brand new theory of learning."[14] He had discovered operant conditioning.

The Behavior of Organisms, Skinner's 1938 book about contingencies of reinforcement, documented five years of research with his "operant chamber."[15] Skinner varied everything he could think of to see the effect on the rate of bar presses. He looked at conditioning and extinction. He varied the number of bar presses required and how hard the bar had to be pressed for reinforcement. He also looked at how antecedent situations affected responding, for example, what happened when the presses were reinforced only when a light was shining. He even investigated how a few drugs affected the rate of bar pressing.

The Study of Relationships, Not Rats

The research in *The Behavior of Organisms* was done mostly on the behavior of rats. Skinner was not studying rats any more than geneticists study fruit flies. He was studying behavioral relations. Just as genetic principles drawn from fruit flies have contributed to our understanding of human genetics, principles drawn from rat behavior have contributed to our understanding of why people behave the way they do. In fact, the principles of operant conditioning, like those of genetics, operate throughout the animal kingdom. The form of responding and what reinforces a particular animal differs from individual to individual and from species to species. But the same functional relations between the likelihood or rate of responding and the contingencies in effect operate the same way in animals from alligators to zebras, from one-celled organisms to human beings.

THE ANALYTIC FRAMEWORK OF BEHAVIOR ANALYSIS

What people do depends on the moment-to-moment interactions between actions and environment that have determined the likelihood of a particular operant. No one repeats everything he or she has ever done. The kinds of behavior that survive in your repertoire out of the thousands of things you have done once in your life are those that have been *selected* by their effects. From scratching an itch to composing a poem, your daily behavior reflects this history of **selection by consequences**. Of course we are talking about operant behavior, not respondent. Inborn reflexes stay with us our whole lives and even some conditioned responses can be markedly persistent. But operant behavior is constantly open to change.

Operant Behavior

The skills that teachers are expected to teach are operant. Social behavior is operant. Even the language you speak is operant behavior. Most of what you and your students do each day is operant behavior. Walking, talking, writing, and thinking are all operants. In contrast to **elicited** respondent behavior, operant behavior is said to be **emitted** ("sent out") because the actions do not come automatically from antecedent stimuli.

> To **emit** is to send forth.
> **Emitted behavior** is controlled by its relation to postcedents, in contrast to **elicited behavior** which is controlled (and explained) as a reaction to a prior stimulus.

In Chapter 1, operant behavior was defined as behavior that depends on its immediate effects within its environment. The term "behavior" consists of a *class* of actions that produce similar effects. Moving one's legs is not walking unless the actions produce movement across a surface (the effect). "Talking" must produce audible sounds. If you have severe laryngitis, you may "try to talk," but if no sound is forthcoming you might indicate that you "can't talk." "Writing" produces visible shapes or marks. The consequences of reading and thinking are less obvious, but you wouldn't consider it "reading" if your eyes merely moved over words on a page. If you don't speak Chinese and your eyes carefully travel over Chinese characters, you are not "reading." Some change, some reaction to what is said, must occur. A similar argument can be made for "thinking."

> An **operant** is a class of actions with similar effects on the immediate environment. Operants are defined **functionally**, that is by how they affect the immediate environment of the person behaving.

The form of operants, that is, what they look like, may differ considerably from one action to another. "Writing" may be done with a foot in the sand, with a pen on paper, or with spray paint on a wall, and you would still call the action "writing." "Shoving" includes the "hip chuck," the "two-handed-push" and the "foot-thrust." All are part of the operant "pushing others" if they move the person. When you talk of an operant, then, you are referring to a group of actions with similar effects on the immediate environment.

The Two-Term Contingency

At its most basic, operant conditioning consists of a two-term contingency—an operant and the immediate consequences that control the likelihood of its occurrence. In a sense, an operant already includes the consequences that define it. In daily life, however, there are usually many results of behavior and the defining effect may not be the postcedent maintaining the operant. A push, for example, is defined by producing movement, but pushing may be *maintained* by an additional consequence, such as getting closer to the front of a line.

The consequence or postcedent of a specific action follows that action. It cannot affect the action that already occurred. Getting closer to the front of the line does not change anything about the push that just happened. What is strengthened is the *operant* of pushing, that is, the likelihood of pushing again in similar situations. The consequence affects the *class* of actions called "pushing."

The role of postcedents over behavior is not intuitive. People still tend to look at what happens *before* an action to explain why it occurred. Take crying. If you ask a person to

Fig. 3.5 First panel of a Calvin and Hobbes cartoon

explain why Calvin in the cartoon in Figure 3.5 is crying, most will say, "Because he skinned his knee," or "Because his knee hurts." Both the skinned knee and the pain are stimuli that precede the behavior to be explained. But is that why Calvin is crying? No. We must look at the consequences of crying.

If a sympathetic teacher is around, crying will probably produce attention and sympathy. Now suppose that Calvin is playing baseball after school with the "big boys." The chances are that, instead of sympathy, crying will be ignored or perhaps ridiculed. It won't take long before Calvin "takes" a skinned knee without crying when consequences for crying are not likely to be favorable. Calvin does not cry *because* he skinned his knee. His crying is controlled by the likelihood of a reinforcing consequence in each situation he has encountered, as the complete cartoon shows (see Figure 3.6).

Of course, the situation (sympathetic teacher versus big boys) is important, but only because of its relationship to the kinds of consequences an action brings in that situation. If the action–consequence relationship changes, so will operant behavior. If a sympathetic teacher decides one day that Calvin is too old to be crying over skinned knees, crying in that teacher's presence will soon stop. If the big boys start to baby younger children, Calvin will cry in their presence. The situation is important only in so far as it relates to the kinds of consequences an action brings within it.

KINDS OF CONSEQUENCES

If you have looked at the complete Calvin and Hobbes cartoon in Figure 3.6, you may have noticed the mother's reaction and thought, "That doesn't look like a positive consequence!" You are quite right. It doesn't look that way. But how something *looks*

Fig. 3.6 Complete Calvin and Hobbes cartoon

reflects only opinion. How it *works* determines the kind of consequence it is. What kinds of effects can postcedent events have?

Possible Effects of Behavior

Suppose you have a student who, during 20 minutes of quiet seat work, raises her hand about once every five minutes. For three weeks she continues at the same rate. Then, one Wednesday, you decide to try something to see its effect. Every time she raises her hand you immediately move towards her desk. What might be the result? There are three main possibilities. The vertical line in each graph in Figure 3.7 shows where your procedure started. The behavior can increase, in which case your approach is **reinforcing** hand-raising (Graph A). The behavior can show no change, in which case your approach is not functionally related to hand-raising (Graph B). Your approach can cause an immediate drop in the behavior in which case your approach is **punishing** hand-raising (Graph C). When I was in sixth grade, I had a teacher who had very bad breath. His approaching was punishing: I would do anything to keep him from getting too close to my desk!

REINFORCEMENT

> **Reinforcement** is a change in the environment that strengthens the operant that produces the change.

The only environmental change that strengthens behavior is reinforcement (Graph A in Figure 3.7). An action can change the environment by adding stimulation or by reducing it. Take, for example, adjusting the volume of music. If the music is too soft, you turn it up, thus *adding* sound. If it is too loud, you turn it down, *reducing* sound. Assuming these consequences strengthen your knob-turning, the first has been called **positive reinforcement** and the second **negative reinforcement**. The word "negative" causes problems because people confuse negative reinforcement with punishment. They are not the same: they have opposite effects on behavior.[16]

A second problem with classifying kinds of reinforcement as positive or negative is that many consequences are difficult to classify into an "add" or "remove" format.

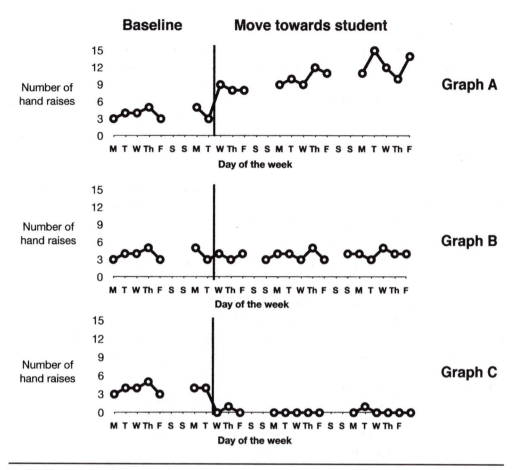

Fig. 3.7 Three possible outcomes of a postcedent procedure

When you walk, for example, each step changes your visual field and position. Are you adding more sights you can see in front of you, or decreasing the distance to your destination? When you turn on an air conditioner, are you adding cool air or removing heat? The answer to those questions is "Both." All postcedents alter your immediate environment. If they strengthen your behavior, they are called reinforcement.

Reinforcement may result from an action itself, like movement from the action of walking, or it may be provided by others, like getting information when you ask a question. Both kinds of postcedents are defined by how they affect behavior. If what you do strengthens the operant on which you make it contingent, your procedure is, by definition, reinforcement. For most practical purposes you need not worry about classifying reinforcement as positive or negative if you have a consequence that works well.

Can Reinforcement Fail to Work?
Because reinforcement is defined by its effect, there is no such thing as reinforcement that doesn't work. What you think should strengthen behavior may or may not do so. Most teachers think praise is reinforcing. It usually is, but there are cases where praise

may work differently. "Peter, that is *really good*" said in a fourth-grade class may strengthen whatever Peter was doing. When effusive praise is reserved for poor performers, however, it may punish rather than reinforce behavior. A comment that is aversive in the presence of peers, on the other hand, might function differently when said alone to Peter in a tutoring session.

The precision of contingencies is critical. If a contingency is imprecise, reinforcement may strengthen all right, but what it strengthens may differ from the behavior you expected to influence. If some consequence you have added does not improve behavior, the science hasn't suddenly stopped working. Something in your procedure needs to be changed.

Education is about building behavior. Only reinforcement builds, and only reinforcement engenders positive feelings. Thus in addition to being the most effective postcedent process for teaching, reinforcement helps create interest in the subjects you are teaching.

The interactions in any classroom are extraordinarily complex. Reinforcement is going on all the time, whether planned or unplanned. Every second, every minute, the behavior of each of your students is being affected by its interactions. A sight, a sound, an odor, a touch, hundreds of almost imperceptible events may increase a particular aspect of behavior such as the loudness of talking, the point on which eyes are focused, or the firmness of pressure on a pen. The precise relationships between properties of actions and their effects determine all aspects of how students behave.

The Difference between Reinforcement and Rewards
Reinforcement is contingent on the ebb and flow of behavior. **Rewards** are *things*: tangible items or privileges. In some circumstances, especially when working in special education, tangible items are used to build behavior. They should be used with care. They can create a dependency that may be hard to break (see Chapter 12), and their delivery is controlled by a person other than the behaving individual. In a regular classroom most tangible items and privileges that teachers use do not have clear connections to moment-to-moment behavior. Whether, for example, your student pushes firmly or lightly on her pen as she works on problem six, or whether she is thinking of recess at exactly 10:35, are actions affected by immediate contingencies, not by a distant reward. It would be nice if distant payoffs controlled behavior effectively. Then none of us would be overweight or drink too much or procrastinate.

The target of rewards also differs from that of reinforcement: you reward people; you reinforce actions. Becoming sensitive to the relationship between actions and their immediate results gives you an understanding of behavior that thinking of rewards cannot provide. Many things that reinforce behavior would never be considered rewards. Take, for example, a reminder to sit down.

Example: Unplanned Reinforcement in a First-Grade Class: The "Criticism Trap"
Telling a student to sit down would never be called a reward, but a study showed that it was a reinforcement procedure. The study was done in a first grade of 48 children. A movable divider partly separated the room into two sections, each of which had one teacher. During the study, the teachers in each section of the room worked on reading with small groups, while the rest of the children were assigned seat work.

For 20 minutes each day, two observers came into each part of the room and recorded the children's behavior. Every 10 seconds each observer counted how many children were out of their seats. They also recorded whether or not the teacher had told them to get back to their seats during that 10-second period.

During the first six days, roughly three children were standing during each 10-second observation period. Over the 20 minutes, their teachers told them to sit down about seven times. Then "some very strange events began to occur."[17] The teachers were instructed to tell the children to sit down *more* often. They did so for 12 days—telling their students to sit down almost four times as often as before. The result was an *increase* in the number of children standing: 50% more children stood up than before the teachers had increased saying, "sit down."

The sequence was tried again. For the next eight days, the teachers went back to saying "sit down" only seven times in 20 minutes. Out-of-seat behavior declined to an average of three times every ten seconds. Again the teachers were asked to tell the children to sit down more often (28 times in 20 minutes). Again the children stood up more—four times every ten seconds.

What can be going on? How do we explain such happenings? There is one further perplexing piece of information. The children actually did sit down when asked by the teacher to do so, so the result wasn't just due to a few children standing a lot.

A beautiful trap! Imagine, the teacher thought that telling the children to sit down worked, because they did sit down, but that was only the immediate effect. The effect on standing was not seen until later and might have been missed altogether by the teacher if careful observations had not been made. Her words were in fact having exactly the opposite effect on standing from what she desired.[18]

Telling students to sit down *follows* standing so it is a postcedent procedure. Telling students to sit down more often produced standing up more often; the postcedent was positive reinforcement. The authors called it the **Criticism Trap**.

There was one more part of this study. The teachers were asked to stop telling the children to sit down altogether. Instead they were asked to comment approvingly to students who were sitting and working. That produced the lowest levels of standing in the whole study.

> The **Criticism Trap** is a situation where criticizing a behavior you wish to decrease seems to work because it temporarily halts the behavior, but your criticizing actually strengthens the operant so that it occurs more frequently in the future.

Reinforcing the very behavior you wished to eliminate is a common occurrence in classrooms.[19] Whenever you criticize sloppy writing, doodling, talking out, looking out the window, or any inappropriate behavior, there is a chance you may be reinforcing just what you want to weaken. If so, you are caught in the Criticism Trap. This kind of interaction is why it is so important to understand contingencies. Many of the problems that teachers encounter in their classrooms are maintained by their own actions. If so, changing the timing of those actions will improve behavior. This was illustrated in a college lecture.

Example: Timing the End of a College Lecture to Improve Behavior

As a young professor I was assigned a lecture course to several hundred students (see Chapters 1 and 2). As I wrapped up my first 50-minute lectures, many students snapped notebooks, put on their coats, and otherwise got ready to leave. The noise and commotion bothered me and I began escaping the commotion by ending class a minute or two early. By becoming noisy, the students were setting up a situation where excusing them was reinforcing for *me*. The *students'* behavior also appeared to be strengthened by the announcement of the end of class. If this analysis was correct, I could change the students' actions by changing the timing of my dismissal.

The next session, I listened carefully as the minute hand approached the end of the lecture hour, talking all the while. Just as there was a tiny lull in the commotion, I quickly said, "See you next week." I followed this procedure for a few more sessions. The effect was dramatic. Without looking at the clock, I could tell when the hour was almost up because the class got especially quiet! For the students, going on to their next activity was reinforcing. When ending class was contingent on staying especially quiet, that behavior was strengthened. Note that I did not admonish the students by saying something like, "I'll let you go when you are quiet." The procedure worked with only the timing of reinforcement.

In high schools, you will often notice increased noise near the end of classes. Even if your school uses bells for class change, there are a few seconds just before the bell rings when you can excuse class a tiny bit early. If you consistently do so at the exact moment you detect a tiny drop in your students' commotion, you will soon notice less noise at the end of the period.

PUNISHMENT

To punish is to decelerate behavior. Like reinforcement, punishment is defined by its effect, in this case an immediate drop in frequency or strength of the behavior on which it is made contingent.[20] A young child may reach for a candle flame. If the result of putting a finger into the flame produces an immediate reduction in the tendency to put fingers into flames, we call the consequence **punishment**.

> **Punishment** is any consequence that decreases or weakens behavior upon which it is made contingent.

Because punishment also creates respondents such as fear or hostility, it cannot be recommended as the way to reduce behavior (see Chapter 11). Nevertheless it is a common method of control. It is used for many reasons. For one thing, punishing is easy. But that is not the main reason.

To understand why people punish, look at the contingencies over that behavior. No one punishes when students are behaving well. Punishment occurs when a person has lost control over what someone else is doing. Imagine a class that is so noisy that Mr. Smith cannot stand it any longer. Mr. Smith shouts, "Shut up." What is the immediate result? Probably shocked silence. Mr. Smith's classroom has suddenly changed from noisy to quiet—reinforcing his shouting. The next time his class is noisy, the likelihood increases that Mr. Smith will again shout. Worse still, if Mr. Smith shouts often, students will get used to his shouting and they will react less and less. To get the same effect, Mr. Smith's behavior has to escalate. You can see this kind of escalation in many arenas of life. Forms of punishment that are initially accepted by the public as methods of control can drift into extreme forms. That has a bad effect on the punisher as well as on the recipients of the treatment.[21]

From this brief description of Mr. Smith's shouting, you can't be sure how it affected the future behavior of his students. It is possible that his shouting could have increased or had no effect on student behavior. Whether or not it quieted students in the future, however, is different from the immediate effect on Mr. Smith's methods of control. The example was given to show how actions that stop an annoying situation can reinforce the tendency to punish in the future.

The effects of punishment are complex, but most subvert the goals of education. Punishment cannot build behavior and it produces undesirable **emotional side effects** through the respondent conditioning described above. Behavioral procedures based on reinforcement offer better methods of control.

NO CHANGE IN THE PATTERN OF BEHAVIOR

We have looked at consequences that directly increase and decrease the frequency with which an operant subsequently occurs. What about the third case? Graph B in Figure 3.7 shows an example in which the treatment did not produce any discernible change in behavior. Since operant behavior does not continue if *never* reinforced, something in the classroom must be maintaining the behavior. Whatever the teacher did, however, made no change in the relevant contingencies. Whatever was maintaining the student's behavior continued to maintain it at the same rate.

EXTINCTION AND INTERMITTENT REINFORCEMENT

Will behavior change in frequency if the maintaining reinforcement is no longer forthcoming? The answer is "Yes, but. . . ." The "but" refers to what is called **intermittent reinforcement**, reinforcement that occurs only sometimes. Most social behavior is reinforced intermittently. Raising a hand during a discussion does not guarantee getting called upon. Hand-raising is usually reinforced only occasionally. Now, suppose your teacher stops calling on your hand-raising altogether. Not every hand-raise got reinforced anyhow, so there would be no discernible difference initially. When an action is only intermittently reinforced, there is little contrast between the beginning of a period of withholding reinforcement and the usual contingencies where many responses go unreinforced. Suddenly withholding reinforcement works better when every action or nearly every instance has been reinforced in the past.

> **Intermittent reinforcement** is reinforcement that follows only some actions, in contrast to **continuous reinforcement** where every instance of the behavior is reinforced.

Reinforcing every action is called **continuous reinforcement**. In spite of its name, continuous reinforcement does *not* mean that reinforcement is continuous! Rather it means that every *instance* of behavior is reinforced. Some behavior is reinforced quite consistently in classrooms. In that case, extinction is often a major part of a procedure for change (see Chapter 11).

In **extinction**, the reinforcement that has maintained a particular action is no longer forthcoming.

Extinction is a process of no longer providing the reinforcement that has been maintaining behavior. In everyday language you could say that under extinction there is no longer any payoff for responding. Suppose Patricia brings in interesting rocks to show you before school. We will assume that showing you her rocks has been maintained for many days by the interest you have shown every time (continuous reinforcement). If one day, you ignore her behavior, perhaps attending to the starting of class, and the same thing happens the next few days, eventually her showing you rocks will stop. First, however, you can expect an **extinction burst**.

Extinction Bursts

Behavior during extinction following a long period of continuous reinforcement does not decrease smoothly or gradually. The first result is an increase in the force or frequency of the action. This reaction must have been useful for the survival of our species. If every time our distant ancestors had given up immediately when encountering an obstacle, for example a tree blocking the only route to water, humankind probably would have died out. Instead, trying harder had survival value. In any case, not getting the usual consequence results in an initial burst in effort. For Patricia, our rock enthusiast, you would expect an increase in trying to get your attention by strategies such as raising her voice, holding her rocks where you cannot fail to see them, touching or pulling at your clothes, or even throwing the rocks on your desk in exasperation.

Extinction bursts occur with inappropriate behavior too. Let's assume that you have a student we'll call Jason, who calls out answers when you have asked a question, and that this behavior is maintained by your routinely acknowledging what he says. If, one day, you decide to ignore Jason's calling-out, you must be prepared for Jason to call out louder and more often at first. If you can withstand this extinction burst, and ignore *all* his calling-out, eventually that behavior will stop. In practice, this can be tough to do. If you slip, and respond to even one comment now and then, instead of extinction you have begun intermittent reinforcement. You have just made calling-out more persistent, not less.

Because of the extinction burst, and the difficulty of being consistent in withholding reinforcement while trying to teach, extinction is rarely used alone. An alternative behavior is also reinforced (see Chapter 11). With Jason, in addition to extinguishing his calling-out, you would reinforce some alternative like hand-raising. But let's say you use only extinction and never attend to Jason's calling-out. Eventually, the bursts will become fewer, less vigorous, and further apart until calling-out stops all together. A typical pattern is shown in Figure 3.8.

Example: Extinction Burst in a Fifth-Grader

The student involved in the study shown in Figure 3.8 often whined "I can't do it" when given an assignment. The teacher had unintentionally reinforced this behavior with statements like, "Yes you can Jason. You've done this before," or other encouraging comments. At the line on the graph, the teacher ignored every "I can't do it" response by becoming preoccupied with another student. The extinction burst is clearly visible. This extinction took a very long time. This suggests that the student's protesting might have

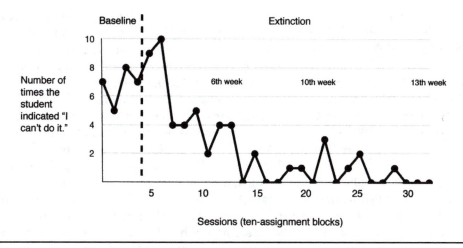

Fig. 3.8 Extinction burst in a fifth-grader
Robert Dietiker. "Decreasing a Fifth Grade Boy's 'I Can't Do It' Responses to Written Assignments." *School Applications of Learning Theory* 3 (1970): 30.

been intermittently reinforced which would have made it persistent prior to the beginning of the ignoring phase.[22] In addition to ignoring Jason's "I can't do it" teachers today would comment upon Jason's working. That would build appropriate behavior more rapidly.

The Difference between Extinction and Forgetting
In extinction the response repeatedly occurs but without its usual reinforcement. Extinction is not the same thing as **forgetting**, in which the passage of time with *no* responding results in the deterioration of performance. A Spanish-speaking student might stop speaking Spanish in school if Spanish went unreinforced (no one responded to his or her Spanish), but the student would still *remember* how to speak it. The arrival of another Spanish-speaking student would bring out the response in full strength. In contrast, a student could forget Spanish by not using it over a long period of time. A later opportunity to speak Spanish would then fail to bring forth the words and phrases that the student had formerly emitted.

> **Extinction** differs from **forgetting** in that the latter refers to a decrease in the strength of a behavior over time when it has *not* been emitted.

TWO-TERM CONTINGENCIES IN FUNCTIONAL ASSESSMENT AND ANALYSIS
Any operant action that occurs day after day is being maintained by some kind of consequence. Persistent misbehavior,[23] like appropriate behavior, is maintained by something occurring within the classroom environment. Functional assessment and functional analysis are ways of identifying this action-reinforcement relation in the contexts in which it occurs. The word "functional" refers to the relation between the specific "challenging behavior," and its surrounding contingencies, especially post-

> A **functional assessment** of a behavior uses questionnaires and interviews to identify the variables responsible for its occurrence. A **functional analysis** alters contingencies to see which ones are responsible for the behavior.

cedents. **Functional assessment** tries to identify factors responsible for the behavior through questionnaires and interviews. **Functional analysis** goes further by altering some aspect of the existing contingencies and recording the effect.

Two common postcedents of challenging behavior are teacher attention and avoidance. Think of the Criticism Trap study. Walking around was a "problem" or "challenging" behavior because it interfered with the students' learning. When consequences were altered, the frequency of wandering changed, showing that wandering was at least partially maintained by teacher attention. Then, too, in wandering around, the students avoided doing whatever assignments lay on their desks. We all tend to avoid activities we do not enjoy. In schools, the stomach aches that appear only when the day's gym activity is running laps may be maintained by avoidance, especially if cramps miraculously disappear when the second part of gym is playing basketball. While you may guess that avoidance is maintaining a specific "problem" behavior, only by checking the effects of particular postcedents can one be sure. Such a check is what functional analysis is all about.

Part of the changes in contingencies done in a functional analysis may involve temporarily failing to provide the usual reinforcement for the troublesome behavior, and that procedure is extinction. Remember the first effect of extinction? You do *not* want to witness an extinction burst in a student who is injuring him or herself, or destroying property, or attacking others! For destructive "problem behavior" a specialist is needed.

Every student with a disability who qualifies for special education is required to have an **individualized education plan (IEP)**. These plans address general social and academic skills as well as challenging behavior where functional assessments or analyses are particularly useful. A student's teacher is always part of the IEP team that diagnoses, establishes procedures, and monitors progress. Teachers are asked to observe, report, and even to collect data on students with individualized educational plans. Thus it is beneficial to understand the reasoning behind the procedures.

Every teacher encounters challenging behavior at least occasionally, and we all reinforce misbehavior by mistake. Tracking postcedents can help you identify relevant postcedents to change. When you see behavior that persistently threatens student progress or your own "sanity," you may need to call in specialists. Of course aggressive acts that could cause physical harm require immediate attention (see Chapter 11).

THE THREE-TERM CONTINGENCY—THE ROLE OF ANTECEDENTS OR CONTEXT

The two-term contingency analysis starts with behavior. Of course, no behavior takes place in a vacuum. All behavior occurs in a setting and antecedents gain control over all operants. Imagine a stranger of the opposite sex asking you to undress. Would you do it? Not if you were in a bar. Now suppose that stranger is a physician giving you an important examination. In that context almost everyone would readily comply.

When the consequences of actions differ in different situations, people learn to respond appropriately. Babies are famous for calling any male "Daddy." But soon the consequences for saying "Daddy" differ according to which male is around. The response "Daddy" then becomes restricted to the presence of the designated male, whether or not he is genetically related.

Much of any curriculum involves not only responding in new ways, but also responding appropriately. For example, a Spanish teacher introduces not only new words, but also *when* to say them. Perfectly pronouncing "muy bien" ("fine") when asked "Como se llama usted?" ("What is your name?") does not show appropriate responding. In math, the response "4" is reinforced in the presence of "2+2," but not in the presence of "2+3." In addition to building new responses, teaching involves bringing responding under appropriate antecedent control (see Chapter 9).

Differences between Antecedent Control in Respondent and Operant Conditioning

The control of antecedents over operant behavior differs from the control of antecedents in respondent behavior. Respondents involve reflexes where the responses are explained solely by identifying the antecedent stimulus. If "jumping" is a reflexive response to a loud sound, you can explain the behavior by identifying the preceding noise. The jump is elicited. Jumping when *told* to jump, on the other hand, cannot be explained by the prior stimulus alone. It is an operant, controlled by the consequences for jumping when told to do so. A student may or may *not* jump.

The relationships between an operant, the consequences that maintain it and relevant antecedents in the situations in which it occurs constitute the **three-term contingency** introduced in Chapter 1. You will hear the term **contingencies of reinforcement** to stand for these relations, although some contingencies involve punishment. Contingencies always involve antecedents as well as postcedents. In later chapters we will look more at three-term contingencies, and at four-term contingencies involved in verbal behavior.

IMPLICATIONS FOR TEACHING

Teaching involves managing the contingencies that determine student actions. Operant conditioning requires *students* to be the ones behaving. You cannot reinforce a behavior that never occurs. Since you can reinforce only behavior that already exists at least partially or in weak form you must know the current level of each student's performance. Students must also be given enough practice to become fluent in the basics needed for more complex behavior and for competent performance to last.

Student Activity

Since operant conditioning works with existing behavior, it cannot occur without the learner behaving. At the very least, the learner must be "paying attention." If, during a biology demonstration, Simon is daydreaming, he cannot be learning biology, no matter what the teacher is doing. He may be learning some other behavior, such as "how to look attentive when you are dreaming about motorcycles," but he is not learning biology.

A quick look at a classroom can reveal a lot about the learning taking place. What are the students doing? Are they performing actions they are supposed to learn, or are they sitting while the *teacher* talks, demonstrates, or works out problems? While students may learn how behavior looks from a demonstration, they must at some point perform tasks. No one would dream of teaching swimming or speaking Spanish or driving a car solely by videos or demonstrations. But educators still expect presentations to do the job where success or failure is less obvious. Demonstrations are not bad. They communicate well what is expected. But they are only a first step in teaching. Students must do more than sit and watch to become competent in a field. Thus behavioral educators put student activity at the *center* of teaching procedures.

Selection of Best Performance

Student responding is not enough. Students do not "learn by doing," alone. If they did, teachers would not be needed. Teaching requires the selection of effective actions. Some reinforcing consequences occur naturally. When Ricardo focuses a microscope, for example, the sharpness of an image that resembles the cell he's looking for lets him know he has performed correctly. For many paper and pencil exercises students also know when they are correct, for example, when an answer "comes out right," or a problem is easy for them. If you answer the problem, "$2 + 2 = $ ____ " you wouldn't need anyone to tell you that your answer is correct.

When you are learning something new you don't necessarily know which actions are best. Then the better of your actions needs to be selected—and that requires reinforcement. Providing the contingencies that select the best of what students do is an essential part of operant conditioning. The more immediate the consequences, the better. It is not immediate feedback to return papers the next day—or even to correct a worksheet as soon as a student completes it. To be considered immediate, the student must receive a consequence for one problem before beginning the next. Only then are contingencies timed for optimal progress.

Next Step Determined by Student Performance

Operant conditioning selects among existing responses. But what if the actions your students need to learn don't ever occur for you to select? Then you have to **shape** the new action from the behavior you have. Demonstrating, explaining, or guiding helps produce initial student steps which can then be strengthened. As you reinforce new tentative actions, you shift the pattern of responding towards increasingly better performance (see Chapter 8 for a full discussion of shaping). What you ask of each student therefore must depend on what he or she can and can't do *already*. When tutoring one student alone you would never work on factoring polynomials because it was October 16 and that was October 16's lesson. You would find out what your student already could do, and base the first step on that level of performance.

In most classrooms what is asked of each student rarely depends upon individual performance levels. Materials are designed for a mythical average student. Those for whom the lesson is too easy are bored, while those for whom it is too advanced squirm and flounder. The latter students may learn in remedial sessions or after class by themselves, or they may never achieve mastery.

The Need for Fluent Performance

Complex behavior builds on underlying **repertoires**, the current behavior of students. Reading a sentence aloud requires being able to pronounce individual words. Solving word problems requires both reading and computation. Doing a handstand on a balance beam requires skills mastered on the floor. The competent performer behaves **fluently**—accurately, smoothly, and without hesitation (see Chapter 4). A competent reader can not only read more accurately than a beginner, but also more rapidly, effortlessly, and without having to concentrate on each word pronounced.

> **Fluency** is the combination of accuracy, smoothness, and lack of hesitation in performance. Often measured in actions per unit time.

To successfully move to more complex performance you must have both *prerequisites* and *component* skills. Prerequisites are general conditions needed for a performance, but are not necessarily *part* of the performance. Being able to see shapes and to speak English are prerequisites for reading English. *Sounding out* words in a passage is a component skill. Even when prerequisites are met, a lack of fluency on component skills hampers progress. By helping your students master a component until they can perform accurately and without hesitation, you make it possible for them to progress on to more advanced skills. In one case, a student's multiplying of double-digit times double-digit multiplication was stuck at a low level. Instead of continuing to work on that level of problem, her teacher went back to the component skill of single-digit times single-digit multiplications. Once the student had reached a very high rate on single-digit problems (100 digits correct per minute), she immediately made progress when returned to the double-digit problems.[24]

SUMMARY

Learning consists of two processes, respondent conditioning and operant conditioning. Respondent conditioning explains how new reflexes are created. Through pairing with an eliciting stimulus, a new stimulus gains power to elicit the same kind of response. No new behavior is created. Little academic behavior involves respondents, although emotional responding can intrude into classroom activities. Academic and social behavior is almost entirely operant, controlled by the surrounding contingencies in the classroom.

Contingencies involve relationships between specific actions, immediate postcedents, and the contexts in which those relationships occur. This chapter concentrated on the relations between actions and their immediate postcedents, including reinforcement, extinction, and punishment.

In the ebb and flow of interactions between people's actions and their physical and social environments, operant conditioning is always going on. You and your students may or may not be aware of how behavior is being affected or even of what changes are being produced. Becoming sensitive to the basic processes described in this chapter enables you to teach more effectively and to prevent problems or solve those that occur. As an added benefit, increasing control by reinforcement rather than punishment produces a positive, productive classroom climate both for you and for your students.

It seems incredible that the basic processes described in this chapter could be responsible for the impressive diversity of human behavior. Science always looks for basic relationships underlying the complexity of the world. Just as a few physical laws underpin everything from hurricanes to the path of a paper airplane, a few basic behavioral laws underlie all operant behavior from creating a stage play to writing "4" when asked to write the sum of "2+2." The basic laws include the postcedent controls described in this chapter, and the antecedents to be discussed in Chapters 8, 9, and 10. Like physical principles, operant principles deal with relationships. For behavior, the relationships occur between individual actions and the swirl of events surrounding everything we do. Just as physics abandoned flogiston and other inner properties of objects to explain motion and fire, behaviorology explains behavior without appealing to inner agencies. Your students do not remember something because of their "intelligence" or "memory." If they remember at all, it is because of the kinds of contingencies they experienced while you taught. Your students' behavior, and your own, is always malleable, always in flux, always susceptible to change through the contingencies that are encountered.

CONCEPT CHECKS

Operant and Respondent Conditioning (Objective A)

DIRECTIONS: For each of the following, write O if it describes operant conditioning or R if it describes respondent conditioning.

1. Often called "stimulus substitution"
2. Often called " selection by consequences"
3. Explained by looking at preceding stimuli
4. Involves emotional responding
5. Discovered by Pavlov
6. Discovered by Skinner
7. The process by which social behavior is learned
8. The process by which academic behavior is learned
9. The process by which new reflexes are learned
10. Controlled primarily by postcedent stimuli
11. Controlled primarily by antecedent stimuli
12. The process involved in learning to talk
13. Explains anxiety when having to give a talk
14. Is "elicited"
15. Is "emitted"

Terms (Objective B)

DIRECTIONS: Check *each* correct ending.
An operant is defined by . . . (check *all* that apply)

a. what an action looks like
b. the form of the behavior
c. the effect of an action
d. how it affects the behaver's environment
e. results of a class of actions
f. the person doing the action

Terms (Objective B)

DIRECTIONS: For each of the following, write the letter of the process best illustrated, using

R for Reinforcement
P for Punishment
E for Extinction
N for none of the above (you can't tell from the information given)

1. you say "good job" to a student's oral answer
2. graphing increases the number of words written
3. the result is an immediate increase, then decrease
4. shouting increases a student's running away from you in the future
5. shouting decreases the tendency to volunteer to be captain
6. when a student starts to run off the playground you shout at him to come back
7. greeting a student by name improves his attendance
8. you write an A grade on a student's paper as he stands at your desk watching
9. you call on students who are not paying attention during discussions
10. a click on a webpage that has always worked, suddenly fails to work and you click on it several times before giving up

---

ANALYSIS PROBLEMS

1. Give Your Own Example of the Criticism Trap (Objective C)

2. Tell How Extinction Differs from Forgetting, Using Your Own Example (Objective E)

3. The Case of the Disappearing Pencils (Objective F)

The following is a true story: Before the start of the school year, a new teacher was given 10 boxes of pencils for her fourth-grade class. She passed them out on the first day. By the next day some students didn't have their pencils when they were assigned seat work. When they asked for a pencil, the teacher gave new pencils from her supply. Needless to say, the pencils were disappearing fast. So the teacher spent an hour after school taping student names to each pencil. Still students lost their pencils, so she kept giving out new ones to those who didn't have any.

a. What was the consequence of asking for a pencil to do seat work?
b. How could you make getting a new pencil contingent on bringing a pencil to class?
c. What could you give students so they could do their work without using the new pencils?
d. What do you think would happen with this change in contingencies?

ANSWERS FOR CONCEPT CHECKS
Operant and Respondent Conditioning

1. R
2. O
3. R
4. R
5. R
6. O
7. O
8. O
9. R
10. O
11. R
12. O
13. R
14. R
15. O

Terms

An operant is defined by c, d, and e.

Terms

1. N—no effect on behavior is mentioned
2. R
3. E
4. R
5. P
6. N
7. R
8. N
9. N
10. E

FEEDBACK FOR ANALYSIS PROBLEMS
3. The Case of the Disappearing Pencils: One Solution

The teacher realized that when not having a pencil and asking for one, students were getting brand new pencils. So she announced one Monday: "I'm going to pass out new pencils in exchange for your old ones." Everyone who had a pencil got a new one. She mentioned she would do this again. The old ones she put into a jar. Anyone who didn't have a pencil could take one of the pencils that had been turned in. Not only did the students start bringing pencils from home to turn in, they became proud of hanging on to their pencils. Some kept their labeled pencils the whole term, showing the shortening stub occasionally to the teacher with a comment like, "See, I've still got it!"

Part II
Planning for Improvement

4

SETTING GOALS TO IMPROVE ACHIEVEMENT

"If we could first know where we are, and whither we are tending, we could then better judge what to do, and how to do it."

Abraham Lincoln, 1858

OVERVIEW

Why care about objectives? They are your goals. What you concentrate on and how you conceptualize your objectives affects all other aspects of teaching. Setting important goals and stating them clearly helps both you and your students to "better judge what to do, and how to do it."

OBJECTIVES

By the end of this chapter you should be able to:

A. Identify definitions or examples of the following terms:

event-governed behavior   verbally-governed behavior
convergent behavior   divergent behavior

B. Mark the most behaviorally stated objective in a list (20 a minute).
C. Write or edit objectives so they meet the criteria for behaviorally stated objectives.
D. Explain the advantages of recording student accomplishments rather than "paying attention" or "time on task."
E. Give your own example of how fluency in one or more underlying skills for something you teach would enable students to problem-solve or create more effectively.
F. Write objectives for a subject you teach or might teach that include at least one

---

objective in each cell of the matrix for creating worthwhile objectives shown in
Table 4.5.

G. For a given classroom situation, describe the ethical procedures that need to be
followed.

A PROBLEM-SOLVING APPROACH

Any teaching assignment poses challenges. In practice, "challenge" can be translated
into behavior that needs to be acquired or improved. You would not consider teaching
a challenge if every assignment you gave was completed enthusiastically by all your
students and they aced every test they took. But that rarely happens. A challenge is a
problem to be solved—how to teach skills your students need to master or social
behavior they need to learn. Problem-solving usually involves steps:

1. Clearly specify the goal.
2. Assess the current state of affairs and your resources.
3. Try a procedure.
4. Evaluate and change as necessary.

For *teaching* the steps look like this:

Step 1: Pinpoint what will most benefit each student, along with the skill levels
needed.

Step 2: Assess each student's current repertoire and your resources, including other
personnel.

Step 3: Design or change relevant contingencies. (This includes designing
instructional steps.)

Step 4: Evaluate and adapt procedures according to student progress.

This chapter focuses on Step 1. While it is not necessary to specify objectives for
everything you teach, thinking about what students need to be *doing* helps with all other
steps.

Step 1 looks easy. That is misleading. Often how you specify a problem is critical for
its solution. For example, in the early space program of the United States, the problem
of re-entry into Earth's atmosphere was solved only after changing the statement of
the problem. Initially solutions were sought for a material that could withstand the
incredible heat from air friction at re-entry speeds. By changing the problem to mini-
mizing friction rather than seeking new heat resistant materials, scientists came up with
a solution: They designed the capsule with a blunt shape to slow it down as soon as it hit
the thin edges of the Earth's atmosphere. Like the original spaceship designers, teachers
sometimes concentrate on the wrong problem as we shall see.

TEACHERS' CONCERNS

In workshops over a period of 20 years, practicing teachers were asked what they would
most like to see their students do more often and less often. A few replies, like "include

music as a regular daily activity," or "practice more effective health behavior" mentioned specific subject matter. Most replies were more general. Whether teaching first grade or high school, special education classes or regular education, in urban or rural schools, teachers had the same concerns. Here are the ones most frequently mentioned (see Table 4.1). Phrasing differed over the years, so that instead of writing "feel like failures" a teacher might write "poor self-esteem." But the general concerns were remarkably consistent from year to year. Although all are desirable in a classroom, some, such as "pay attention," target the wrong goal.

STATING OBJECTIVES IN TERMS OF STUDENT ACTIONS

Why would you want students to pay attention? Presumably because there is something you are saying or showing that will help them behave more effectively. The objective is *not* to pay attention. The objective is the behavior they will achieve by doing so.

> An **action** has a clear beginning and end. Behavior is active if it has an immediate effect on the environment of the person behaving.

Table 4.1 Most common teacher answers to "What would you like your students to do more often or less often?" (Items paired were not necessarily given by the same teacher.)

More Often	Less Often
pay attention	daydream
follow directions	not listen
study harder	waste time
establish self-discipline	disrupt the class
begin work sooner	procrastinate
finish their work	talk out in class
willing to learn	do minimum just for the grade
respond more in class	sit and not speak
do their own work	copy from others or word for word from books
enjoy school	dislike school
question more	depend on adults
be creative	memorize irrelevant facts
prepare for class	miss class
think for themselves	rely on others rather than selves
adopt acceptable social behavior	fight, curse
be kinder to each other	be cruel and unkind to each other
take responsibility for own behavior	blame others
reach out to other people when in need	take drugs
feel confident	feel like failures
cooperate	argue and complain
tell the truth	lie

Improving on Attention as a Goal

Attention is not an action. An action has a clear beginning and end. You cannot observe either the beginning or the end of "paying attention." You can tell where your students are looking, but that is not "paying attention." When you think a student is paying attention you are interpreting actions you see or hear. Just because Justin is facing you and nodding does not mean he is listening to what you are saying. He may be figuring out how to keep you from noticing the hamster he has hidden in his t-shirt. Or maybe he hasn't done his homework and figures that you will call on someone else if he looks attentive. Paying attention is not your educational goal. Your goal is the behavior your students are to master.

Of course watching and listening to a teacher are helpful. These actions are not the goal, however. They are a byproduct of good instructional contingencies. Students pay attention when what you say or do is important. Think of the last time your class was listening intently. Students pay attention when they don't want to miss what you are saying, like information on upcoming events or the punch-line to a joke, or directions that are needed immediately, especially if they will not be repeated.

Even when tutoring one-on-one, attention may not be guaranteed. In special education it is common for tutees to avoid eye contact with tutors. Many sessions begin by the tutor repeating "Look at me." If, instead, the tutor makes it important to the *student* to gain *the tutor's* eye contact, you do not have to say "Look at me." For example, suppose you are tutoring a non-verbal preschool boy who likes to put rings on a stack and you are handing him rings to reinforce behavior. You could start by handing a ring when the boy looks you in the eye. Once that occurs readily, ask him to perform a simple task you are sure he can do, giving the task only when he is looking into your eyes. Soon, the *child* will seek *your* eye contact for an opportunity to respond. You don't need to tell him to look at you. The child has learned to seek your eye contact to get an opportunity to perform.

In a regular classroom setting, by making it important for students to hear and see what you are doing, you create the behavior called "paying attention." Chapter 1 gave an example of how lecture fill-in sheets gave students immediate reasons for listening and looking during a lecture. No one had to exhort the 200-plus students in the lecture hall to "pay attention." No one said, "now listen carefully—this will be on the exam," to get their attention. The students made sure they could hear the definitions and see the graphics so their sheets would be complete. Using blanks in the lecture fill-in sheet was a critical design feature. Had the outlines been filled in already, there would have been no incentive for capturing the critical words.

Changing from paying attention as a goal to the skills that students need to master moves student behavior from passively sitting to actively participating. That is a first step towards more effective teaching.

Why Tasks Completed is a Better Goal than Time on Task

A sister goal to paying attention is **time on task**. Wouldn't students perform better if they work longer or were "on task" for more of their "seat work" time? Not necessarily. In fact, encouraging more time on task may actually be counterproductive.

When you hear that Corey was on task 90% of her work time, you probably visualize her working diligently on an assignment. You imagine active responding. But activity itself is rarely a goal. When it does not further competence it is called busy work. What students are supposed to accomplish *while* being on task is the real objective.

Working Smarter, Not Longer

Concentrating on the wrong goal may actually hinder learning. If you reward "time on-task," students quickly learn to appear busy. Their productivity, however, may decrease. I observed this effect when I was visiting my daughter's fifth-grade class. I noticed her working away, seemingly busy for a whole spelling period. After the class I asked her, "Why did it take you 20 minutes to finish your spelling assignment? You do it in 10 minutes at home."

"Mom," she said in a voice that implied I was being extremely dense, "if I finished in 10 minutes, Mrs. Maxine would just give me *more* work to do."

One last problem with both attention and time on task involves what people now call *ownership* or *empowerment.* Both ownership and empowerment occur when the person behaving controls the outcome of his or her actions. That requires not only active behavior, but also being the judge of success—achievement does not depend on someone else's opinion or whether or not anyone even noticed. Judgment of paying attention or the amount of time on task is based on the opinion of observers, not by the student involved. In contrast, with goals stated as specific behavior, student success or failure depends entirely on what *they* do. Their performance does not depend on whether or not their teacher likes or dislikes them or is having a good or bad day. Students can tell whether or not they solved a geometry problem that they could not have solved the week before, or whether they beat their own record on some other kind of performance measure. Their accomplishment rides entirely on what they have done—the essence of "ownership" and "empowerment."

From Labels to Behavioral Targets

Students often gain labels. Some, like "attention deficit hyperactivity disorder" (ADHD), are useful for gaining additional resources for a student. Unfortunately labels fail to communicate what an individual does or does not do that prevents him or her from being successful. Worse, labels have a dark side. They imply that the "problem" lies inside the labeled person, encouraging a medical solution, as with the overuse of Ritalin in children diagnosed with ADHD.

Labels are not reserved for special students. If Paul rarely completes his homework, he may be called "unmotivated," "lazy," or "undisciplined." These labels place blame inside Paul. *He's* not motivated. Something is wrong with *him.* (As we saw in Chapter 2, the label is often given as a cause of Paul's behavior, creating an explanatory fiction.) In contrast, by stating Paul's problem as "failure to complete homework," you are more likely to ask helpful questions such as whether he knows what to do, whether the work is at his level of skill, whether he takes assignments home, whether he has a place to work after school, whether the homework counts towards a grade, is just graded and returned, or disappears after being handed in. For college students, a very small number of points added to homework assignments that were turned in, and revised if needed, produced 100% submission rates. When assignments were graded but didn't "count," the submission percent averaged less than 20% even though students were told that the homework would help them with chapter quizzes.[1] By talking of behavior rather than labels or internal states like "aptitudes," "self-concept," or "responsibility," we shift our attention to factors in a student's life that we can work to change.

Of course, students also must take responsibility for their behavior. Taking responsibility for one's actions, however, is no more innate than motivation. Like academic tasks, "taking responsibility" must be restated like any other goal, perhaps as "turning in homework on time." For Paul, once he reliably hands in homework, if there are other "responsibilities" he lacks, we can specify what actions are involved and tackle them just the way we would any other behavior.

In addition to hindering solutions, labels have one more disadvantage: they make problems sound eternal. Teacher and parents too often see a "diagnosis" as a permanent characteristic of a child. That implies that little or no change will ever be possible. When problems are stated as **behavioral deficits**, that is, actions or skills a student lacks, it is clear that improvement is possible.

Response to Intervention/Response to Instruction (RtI)

The federal government continually amends the **Individuals with Disabilities Education Act** (**IDEA**).[2] The government's website is extensive and helpful, but it provides more combinations of capital letters than a child's block set. Part of the law signed in 2006 permits using a child's response to scientific research-based intervention as a factor in determining whether or not a specific learning disability exists. **Response to Intervention (RtI)** requires specifying particular skill or performance deficits in "struggling" students and assessing their progress once changes are implemented (the **intervention**). The recommendation is designed to provide help to *any* struggling student, not just those labeled "special." RtI is also part of the **Individualized Educational Program (IEP)** required for students who qualify for special services. The regulations include "a statement of measurable annual goals" and a description of "how the child's progress towards meeting the annual goals . . . will be measured."[3] To determine skills any students lack, or progress on them, goals must be formulated as measurable behavior. Those goals are called behavioral objectives.

Behavioral goals are not just for students having difficulty and they are not just for academic subjects. All areas, including social behavior, require clear goals if they are to be unambiguously assessed so that progress can be seen.

BEHAVIORAL OBJECTIVES FOR ACADEMIC GOALS

Teaching consists of building new repertoires. By pinpointing critical skills at the beginning of instruction you are in a better position to make sure they are accomplished than if you wait until grading time or, worse, never specify to yourself what your goals for students are. Stating objectives behaviorally focuses attention on what students are doing. This not only lets them know what is expected, but it lets you see progress along the way, so you can help in case of problems.

> A **behavioral objective** is a statement of what one or more students should be able to do by the end of a unit of instruction. Behavioral objectives are also called **performance objectives**.

Behavioral objectives are statements of what students need to be able to do—what active behaviors they are to perform. They fulfill three functions:

1. They communicate to students what performance is expected of them
2. They suggest relevant instructional activities to you, the teacher, and
3. They provide a standard for evaluating student progress both during instruction and at the end.

You may feel that stating goals in terms of specific actions trivializes objectives. Saying that your teaching objective is "providing an understanding of musical styles" sounds more worthy than a collection of specific actions such as "students should be able to name the period of a piece of classical music after hearing it played." Without clarifying what constitutes understanding, however, you only put off the task of deciding what students should be able to *do* until you have to grade their performance. Of course, you will write more than one behavioral objective for any general goal such as "understanding." Behavioral objectives do not have to be simple: you could ask students to write a piece of music in a given style.

What you evaluate reveals your objectives. In the crush at the end of a grading period, it is tempting to fall back on the easiest kinds of performances to grade, and these rarely evaluate any kind of sophisticated "understanding." In any case, the end of a grading period is too late to help students who are "struggling," and much too late to let them know what is expected of them. In contrast, by starting out with a clear idea of what students with "understanding" can do that those without "understanding" cannot do, you are more likely to communicate well, to design activities that help them reach the specified skills, and to see progress during the term. Behavioral objectives also help you design appropriate performance measures.

PLANNING AHEAD: SETTING GOALS BEFORE SCHOOL BEGINS

Before you even meet a class, you will have academic goals to consider. If you teach in a public school, your state will have objectives for the subjects or grades you teach. These objectives are posted on the internet.

State-Mandated Instructional Goals and Standards

State goals are usually presented in layers with general objectives followed by more behaviorally stated objectives with names like "content standards", "learning standards," "performance indicators," or "student learning expectations." It is a good idea to print out a copy of the content standards for your grade or subjects if your school district does not give them to you. As you read the goals you will see that achieving the entire list of objectives for every student is an ambitious goal. Few classes reach all the goals for their grade level, so remediation turns up in state standards: Massachusetts, for example, recognizes that not all students typically master the "parts of speech" that have supposedly been taught. Note the "standards" for "Beyond Grade 6" in Table 4.2.

It is unrealistic to expect that all your students will have mastered all of the goals set for classes they have taken before coming to you. I'll never forget a student teacher's near panic coming back from her first day of teaching in an elementary math class.

"They're supposed to be able to add single digits " she wailed. "But they can't do it. I'm supposed to teach two and three digits with *regrouping*. How can I do that when they can't even add 2 plus 2. My whole lesson was ruined. What am I supposed to do?"

Table 4.2 Massachusetts curriculum framework: structure and origins of modern English (from Standard 5)

Grade 3:	Identify three basic parts of speech: *adjective, noun, verb.*
Grades 3–4:	Identify four basic parts of speech: *adjective, noun, verb, adverb.*
Grade 5:	Identify seven basic parts of speech: *noun, pronoun, verb, adverb, adjective, preposition, conjunction.*
Grades 5–6:	Identify eight basic parts of speech: *noun, pronoun, verb, adverb, adjective, preposition, conjunction, interjection.*
Beyond Grade 6:	Continue to address earlier standards as needed.

Even before you meet your class, you must consider what prerequisites are needed as well as the skills you are assigned to teach. Most critical are skills that underpin entire subject areas or that will enable students to become more independent.

Setting Priorities

If you are new to a school, you may wish to consult other teachers about local objectives and what you can expect of incoming students. Experienced teachers may also tell you about local concerns and resources that will give you ideas for objectives. A rural school may provide more "nature" for biology classes, an urban school more opportunities for visiting museums. There may be classes that students take before yours, that run concurrently with yours, or that follow yours and build upon what you will be teaching. A short talk with the teachers of related courses can help avoid duplication and insure that prerequisites are addressed.

Deciding what to teach is thus more complex than meets the eye. As a teacher, you are in the best position to set priorities because you are in closest contact with both your content and your students' daily behavior. You are also in the best position to set priorities.

Among the objectives of a course, some skills are always more important than others. Some, like the terms for new concepts, are critical for mastery of a subject. Other skills may not officially be part of curricula, but are required for problem-solving or creating. In general, it is better to teach a few skills well than to "cover" a lot. Education is supposed to be preparation for life. Thus you must consider which competencies will best serve your students not only now but in the future. Taking the time to make sure your students master those critical skills will save you and your students much frustration down the line.

Picking Goals That Will Serve Students Outside of the Classroom

Some skills **generalize**, that is, they are applicable both inside and outside the classroom. Basic reading and math skills, for example, will be of use to students in almost any circumstance. Other skills are rarely needed outside of a particular class.

Textbooks and materials provide many exercises that students are supposed to be able to solve. But just because a textbook includes a topic does not mean that the skill involved is important. When I taught fourth grade, my textbook had several exercises on separating words into syllables. Students had a hard time with them, so I designed additional worksheets and spent extra class periods teaching the skill. Reflecting later, I realized that there are very few circumstances where syllabification is needed. If the exercises were supposed to help with pronunciation of multisyllabic words, it would have been far better for the students to practice pronouncing such words. In any case, the time spent on syllabification robbed time from teaching skills with a broader benefit.

Remediating Missing Component Skills

If you have students who seem to have reached an impasse, there may be prerequisites that are lacking. For example, a speech therapist might have a child who, in spite of trying again and again, just cannot seem to pronounce the sound "r" correctly. An underpinning competency for good pronunciation of "r" is *hearing* the difference between a pronounced "w" and a pronounced "r" sound. If the reason for Terry's incorrect pronunciation is that he cannot distinguish between sounds, there is no way he can tell whether his own pronunciation is correct. In that case, a therapist might have him work on exercises to teach hearing differences. For example the therapist might pronounce "rabbit" as a sample, and then ask the child which word, "wabbit" or "rabbit," was the same. Learning to hear the difference might solve his pronunciation problem with little or no more practice saying the words. The importance of this kind of skill was demonstrated in a school for handicapped children. The teachers taught children who had never vocalized to match a spoken word with one of two spoken choices. They also taught them to tell whether a spoken sound was a word or a nonsense syllable. Once these skills were mastered (and fluent), the children were able to echo a teacher's sounds and repeat simple words. They vocalized for the first time.[4]

At all levels, basic repertoires are essential. Students who have not mastered pre-requisites will have a tough time with any skill that depends on them. Mastery, in turn, involves a dimension missing from many state goals and from most educational exercises. Interestingly, this aspect of performance is not missing from major tests. Assessments used for the No Child Left Behind Act, for example, measure fluency.

FLUENCY: THE MISSING CRITERION

Chapter 4 mentioned fluency as a critical component of mastery. If you visualize the differences between a proficient and a beginning reader, or basketball player, or clarinet player, you will include smoothness, effortlessness, and speed of performance. The skilled reader no longer thinks about how to pronounce individual words or wonders whether the main verb is in the present or past tense. The skilled basketball player automatically adjusts to the movements of his teammates. The skilled musician concentrates on expression, not on what fingerings to use. Mastery combines accuracy with rapid, smooth, and seemingly effortless behavior in what is called **fluency** or **automaticity**. Since it is difficult to assess how "automatically" an action occurs, mastery is best judged by fluency.

Fluency measures *always* include time. How fluently a person reads includes words read correctly *per minute,* a measure of **rate** or **frequency**.[5] These two terms are generally used interchangeably. Both are calculated by dividing the number of actions observed by the time period over which the count was taken: 60 pages read in an hour gives a rate of 60 pages per hour, or one page per minute. For academic subjects, short one-minute timings are often used. The resulting

> **Rate** or **frequency** of behavior is a count of actions divided by the time period over which the count was taken.

count is then already a count per minute: If a student correctly solves 20 problems during the one-minute timing, his or her rate is 20 correct problems divided by one minute or 20 correct *per minute.*

In academic subjects, teachers often record both number correct and number incorrect per minute. This shows the two major components of fluency, *speed* and *accuracy.* Often just recording rate correct is good enough, since when students have very high rates, they cannot be making many mistakes.

Benefits of Fluency

Fluent behavior is relatively effortless and thus more enjoyable than halting, slow, and faulty performance. If you have ever taken a year or two of a foreign language you know how frustrating it is to try to read a book in that language. You start reading, only to find a word you have to look up. Ah, so *that's* what "morado" means: "purple." But now you have forgotten the beginning of the sentence, so you have to back up and start over. Even when you know all the words in a sentence, concentrating on grammar or other aspects of the language makes reading laborious. Few people who have taken a foreign language read for pleasure in that language either during instruction or afterwards unless their fluency approximates that of reading in their native tongue. Students encounter similar frustration when reading text with unfamiliar terms or words they have to sound out. In mathematics, solving word problems or basic algebra problems is hampered by slow computation even if the students understand the processes involved.[6] Just seeing a few large numbers creates enough distraction to intrude on the thinking process. In the classroom, you can check on whether large numbers are hindering performance by substituting single digit numbers in complex word problems. If students then perform better, you know the difficulty lies in lack of fluency in computation, not in figuring out what process to use. To make any skill enjoyable for students, you must teach it to fluency.

> **Fluency** is a combination of speed, smoothness, and accuracy of performance, usually recorded as a **rate (frequency)** of correctly performed actions.

Traditionally, educators record only percentage correct and ignore speed. Say that Margaret scores 100% on a sheet of basic multiplication facts on Monday. If she scores 100% on Tuesday, on Wednesday, and for the rest of the week, no improvement is recorded. Add the time dimension, and daily change will become visible. Margaret may not be getting a higher *percentage* correct each day, but her *rate* correct will improve with practice. Without measuring fluency, high achievers cannot see improvements they are making, and they have little to challenge them. That may be one reason so many top students are turned off by school.

It is not only high achievers who suffer under the blinders of percentage correct. Every time students at the bottom of the class see their scores, they are reminded of their inferior performance. You might think that they would be even more disadvantaged when time is added. For a single timing, that would be true, but with the procedures of **Precision Teaching** (described in detail in Chapter 5) *improvement* is what counts. The student who goes from naming five chemical elements a minute to 10 a minute shows the same percentage of *improvement* as one who starts at 20 a minute and goes to 40. Looking at percentage of change over time evens the playing field. Anyone can improve, no matter where he or she starts. Among the consequences that strengthen student behavior in a classroom, progress is probably the most powerful. Because rate reveals change that percentage correct hides, students can see and thus experience success more often when you include rate in at least some of your goals.

Not everything should be timed. But the skills that underpin any subject area must be fluent if students are to perform easily and to move on to more complex topics. For most skills, one-minute timings can replace the tedious pages of practice problems usually given as seat work or homework. That leaves more time for problem-solving and creative activities during class. Best of all, including fluency in objectives enables you to get precise measures of progress on the student competencies needed to succeed in a field. It is thus one of the best measures to document the Response to Intervention that schools are being asked to provide for students having difficulty. Whether required or not, only records that let you see each student's progress from day to day or week to week let you know what that student should do next.

Fluency and Creativity

Some teachers worry that working on fluency will kill creativity. Quite the opposite occurs. Fluency not only does not kill creativity, it facilitates **creative behavior**. Jazz musicians who improvise know the value of having rapid scales and arpeggios "in their fingers." To create, you need something to create *with*. How easy would it be for you to write original music on a standard music staff if you didn't know where to put notes or what the notes would sound like? Or take writing poetry. Wouldn't building a more fluent vocabulary help students be more creative? The answer is yes.

Example: Fluency Practice Helps Writing Creative Haiku

A study of elementary students demonstrated how short daily fluency exercises helped their creativity. Two groups were involved. Students in both groups wrote a poem that was put aside as a baseline or pre-study product. One group continued activities the way they had in previous years. The second group had short, daily timed Precision Teaching exercises. Before they got to class, their teacher hid an object under her desk. At the beginning of class, students got out paper and pencil. Their task was to write as many words describing the to-be-revealed object as possible in one minute. At a "go" signal the teacher started a timer and put the day's object on top of her desk. When the time was up, students counted how many descriptive words they wrote and discussed and shared their results. At first, most of the students could think only of a few adjectives, but as the days passed they increased their rate of writing descriptive words. Since this was a Precision Teaching project, the students also graphed their daily rates (see Chapter 6). After several weeks, both groups wrote a haiku poem. To make sure that the results would be evaluated fairly, all poems were graded by teachers who did not know which class the writers came from. The results were clear: at the beginning, neither class had written poems that the teachers judged as creative. By the end of the project, the class with the timed practice wrote haiku that was judged as more creative that that from the other class.

If you think again of a language you speak only hesitantly, how easy would it be for you to write a poem in that language? Gaining fluency in basic vocabulary, computing, or any other relevant skill makes both problem-solving *and* creating easier—and also more fun.

WRITING CLEAR BEHAVIORAL OBJECTIVES

Statements of goals lie along a continuum. Some are more behaviorally stated than others. You may not be able to specify the skills involved in all general goals. The point is not to write perfect objectives for every aspect of "understanding," or "quality of compositions," or "creativity," or "appreciation," but to move in the direction of identifying critical components. If you teach the same unit more than once, you have the opportunity to reflect on what your students can do and what skills they lack. Over the course of teaching you will discover what would make their performance better, and you can refine your objectives accordingly.

A well-stated objective meets the following criteria:

1. It is stated in terms of student behavior to build.
2. It specifies actions that have a clear beginning and end (and thus can be counted).
3. It indicates the general level of difficulty of problems or materials used.
4. It indicates standards (or a standard) for acceptable performance including fluency where appropriate.

Stating Objectives in Terms of Student Behavior to Build

Goals in education are often stated as what will be covered. Behavioral objects specify what students will be able to *do*. The only caveat when stating goals as behavior is to be careful to distinguish between means and ends. Activities are sometimes confused with behavioral objectives. **Activities** describe what students will do *during* instruction, but not what they should be able to do as a *result* of their experiences. A statement such as "The students will read Jane Austen's *Pride and Prejudice*," for example, tells what the students will do, but it is not an objective. An objective must state what the students should get out of their reading, such as "to describe the plight of women in the seventeenth century using illustrations from Jane Austen's *Pride and Prejudice*." The objective is the final behavior, not what one does to get there.

In writing behavioral objectives, you might find it helpful to write a lead-in phrase first, such as "By the end of this unit (course), the student will be able to . . ." In completing that sentence, grammatical structure leads you to stating actions. To avoid repetition, write the lead-in phrase once at the top. Each objective then completes the sentence.

Specifying Actions You Can Count

To state student behavior in concrete terms is more difficult. Words like "understand," "know," and "appreciate" creep in. Thinking of what you would count to evaluate achievement helps you visualize the behaviors that are involved. How would you know if a student "understood" hydraulics? When you visualize what a student must do to show understanding, you imagine concrete actions such as "describe," "give examples," "put together a model," "solve," "write," "state in the student's own words," and so on. You can count how many times these actions occur during an observation period. You could even give your statement of actions to other teachers and be pretty sure they would get the same counts you would if watching the same student. What students do is the only evidence you have of their "understanding," "knowing," or of achieving any other goal.

Including the General Difficulty Level of Problems or Materials Used
What is missing from an objective like, "By the end of the course, the student will be able to circle the nouns in a given sentence at a rate of 35 a minute"? The objective is stated in terms of student behavior, and circling is a concrete and countable action. The problem is that the objective does not specify any difficulty level of the sentences used. Circling the nouns in sentences like "The cat ran" is a very different skill than circling the nouns in sentences like "After spotting the dead hawk, the vulture swooped down upon his prey." You need to give an idea of the general difficulty level of the task you expect students to perform. This can most easily be done by adding a reference ("like those in Chapter 7 of the text"), or general difficulty level ("at the sixth-grade reading level"). Better still, state the difficulty level once, at the top of all your objectives.

Setting Standards for Mastery
How would you grade the following essay by a sixth-grader?

> "The Civel War was caused by the South the South had slaves and the North didn't. So the North wanted to free the slaves the South didn't want to free the slaves. THE END :)"

If your objective reads only, "By the end of this unit the student should be able to write an essay on the causes of the Civil War," the writer could justly claim that he or she has met the objective. You didn't specify any standards for what the essay should contain, how long it should be, or how detailed.

Setting standards for acceptable performance is the most difficult part of writing objectives for any kind of creative behavior. It is easy to say that students should be able to write a story, or create a work of art. But how will you and your students tell whether what they have produced is, as they will put it, "good enough"? The more you can specify what an excellent product will contain, the better performance you will get from your students. Standards specify what to look for in performance.

For an essay on the Civil War, you might state points to be covered. To encourage the free flow of ideas, it is best to teach and grade spelling and punctuation separately from the ideas expressed in an essay. Worrying about sentence structure and grammar chokes thinking and produces "writer's block" (see Chapter 10). Mechanics of writing are better taught with fluency exercises apart from the content of essays, or by providing time for a revision before handing in a product. To specify content for the Civil War essay, you could ask students to include "A. how the economies of the North and South differed in terms of goods produced, B. the kind of labor required for factories versus plantations," and C. or D. or E. for whatever other points your students should cover.

If you have a **scoring key** for grading, give it to students as a part of an assignment. That helps them produce quality work. If you don't have a set of criteria you could consider developing one with student input. Whatever method you use, your evaluation criteria, or what educators call a **rubric**, both guide students as they work and give you standards for evaluation. The Association for Supervision and Curriculum Development (ASCD) defines rubric as a "specific description of performance of a given task at several different levels of quality."[7] A sample that ASCD gives as a rubric is shown in Table 4.3.[8]

Table 4.3 Sample rubric for oral performance

Level 4—The main idea is well developed, using important details and anecdotes. The information is accurate and impressive. The topic is thoroughly developed within time constraints.

Level 3—The main idea is reasonably clear and supporting details are adequate and relevant. The information is accurate. The topic is adequately developed within time constraints but is not complete.

Level 2—The main idea is not clearly indicated. Some information is inaccurate. The topic is supported with few details and is sketchy and incomplete.

Level 1—A main idea is not evident. The information has many inaccuracies. The topic is not supported with details.

Table 4.4 Sample scoring key for the first section of a research report

INTRODUCTION & LITERATURE REVIEW SECTION—Evaluation (Numbers in parentheses indicate point values. This section has a total of 20 possible points):

(5) Opening sets the stage so that the general reader has some idea what you are talking about and why it is of interest or important. Assertions are backed up with studies or authorities including references.

(9) Three relevant research studies (primary sources only) are described so that the reader has an idea of what the researchers did and what they found **including numbers** to indicate the degree of the effect. Includes a summary citing agreements and/or disagreements among studies cited. Conclusions you make are warranted from the data.

(1) References at the end agree with those cited in the text (i.e. same dates, authors, etc.).

(5) Overall: Argument and points flow logically. Sentences are complete and make sense (i.e. proofread your paper before turning in). Spelling and grammar are correct. The word data is plural, i.e. say "data are" not "data is." Pages are numbered.

Instead of a scoring with only four options, a point system gives students more guidance. Table 4.4 shows a 20-point scoring key for the first section of a research report that could have been scored by a rubric like that in Table 4.3. In a way, this 20-point evaluation was written by students themselves. The criteria reflect the differences between the best reports and the poorest reports over a number of years. One semester an excellent report gave numbers to indicate the degree of the results described in the research that was reviewed. Other reports said only that the treatment "made a substantial difference." You would be surprised at what researchers call a substantial difference—everything from a 100% improvement down to 1% or less! As a result of the student report that included numbers, the bolded "including numbers" was added to the scoring key. Succeeding semesters' students wrote noticeably better reports than students who were not given the new scoring key.

It is obviously impossible to determine all the standards relevant for judging a complex product. However, each time you grade papers, if you note what would make the poorer papers better (or what the best papers contained) you can refine your evaluation methods and your objectives.

Setting Fluency Standards

For the skills that underpin the basic skills in a field, you need to set fluency standards. How fast should students be able to pronounce words, or identify nouns, or multiply to 100, or come up with descriptive words for writing haiku? One way to set a standard is to take your quizzes yourself using your speed as a benchmark for fluency. If, in class, you also take quizzes along with your students, your top scorers will love beating your score.

Precision Teachers work for high levels of fluency. For a simple skill like multiplying single digit numbers, rates would be set in the 80–100 digits written per minute range. For pronouncing grade-level words, rates as fast as flashcards can be turned over might be used. For circling nouns in a paragraph similarly high rates would be set. The fluency levels you set can be stated along with your objectives.

With high rates of corrects per minute, several advantages have been documented. First, performance does not deteriorate over time. Multiplication facts are not lost over the summer break. Second, distractions do not hinder performance. Students can circle nouns even with a radio on, or with other background commotion. Third, high rates encourage persistence when working. Students do not give up easily or stop working after completing only a few problems when their fluency is high. And lastly, skills that have reached high fluency levels generalize better to novel situations. Students with fluent skills are more likely to use them outside of class.[9] As an added benefit, students working at high rates cannot cheat. There simply isn't time to look at what someone else is doing if you must complete 50 problems a minute correctly.

Avoiding Redundancy in Lists of Objectives

It is boring to read or write the same phrases over and over. Whenever you find yourself repeating the same words in each objective, group objectives to remove the redundant words. Putting "By the end of this unit, the student will be able to . . ." once at the top of a list has already been suggested. Similarly, if your goal is for students to master several skills at a rate of 60 a minute correct, state that criterion once. Redundancies creep into objectives in other ways. Instead of writing the following:

1. Define and give an original example of "metaphor."
2. Define and give an original example of "onomatopoeia."
3. Define and give an original example of "sibilance."
4. Define and give an original example of (more terms follow).

group the terms as follows:

1. Define and give original examples of the following terms:

   metaphor
   onomatopoeia

sibilance
(rest of terms)

"Covering" Content Versus Teaching
Teachers are usually encouraged to "cover" a lot of material. Cover is another word for "present" and it does not tell what students gain from your presentations. It takes much more time to make sure that students master a skill than to "cover" it, so keep essential objectives to master to a minimum. As a rough rule-of-thumb, one or two objectives per hour of instruction is plenty. Of course, there are cases where this "rule," like any other, should be ignored. In any case, you must make sure that the most critical skills are achieved and fluent rather than "covering" a lot of things that students will forget as soon as they walk out of your classroom—or even sooner.

WORTHWHILE OBJECTIVES AND PERFORMANCE DOMAINS

Writing good behavioral objectives for important goals such as "critical thinking," "creating," or "showing ingenuity" is more difficult than writing objectives for simple skills like "defining terms." Educators have proposed "domains" to encourage teachers to include more complex behaviors in what they teach. You may have heard of Bloom's *Taxonomy of Educational Objectives* or Gagné's *Domain Hierarchy*. Here we will use three levels:

1. *Knowing* (fluency in basic facts, principles, terminology needed in any field): knowing is a **convergent** goal because students are to respond in similar ways.
2. *Problem-solving* (skills needed to solve novel problems): problem-solving involves both **convergent** goals (reaching common solutions), but also **divergent** goals that encourage unique methods.
3. *Creating* (producing unique products): creating is primarily a **divergent** goal. Uniqueness is required.

Knowledge objectives aim for behavior that is similar in all students. All students using this text, for example, should give the same or very similar definitions of "behavioral objective." As you go up the hierarchy, however, the goals require behavior that increasingly differs between students. A product is not judged as creative if it is the same as what other students produce. To succeed in and contribute to society, students need both to know facts and principles and to come up with their own ideas. The three levels lie along the continuum shown in Figure 4.1.[10]

Objectives for Verbally-Governed and Event-Governed Behavior
Most teachers try to bring features of the world into their classrooms. Intuitively they realize the difference between responding to events themselves (**event-governed behavior**) and responding to descriptions about events (**verbally-governed behavior**, also known as **rule-governed behavior**).[11] Working with real materials differs from using even the most sophisticated simulation, as anyone who has tried to shape a real rat rather than a simulated rat knows. This is not to disparage simulations. They are good intermediate steps in moving from verbally-governed to event-governed behavior. Where direct experience is dangerous or impractical, they are as close as you can get.

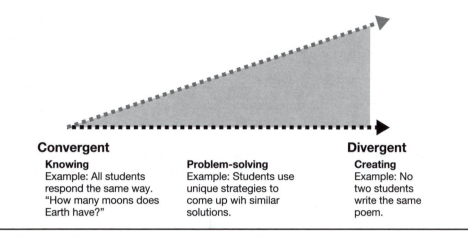

Convergent

Knowing
Example: All students
respond the same way.
"How many moons does
Earth have?"

Problem-solving
Example: Students use
unique strategies to
come up wih similar
solutions.

Divergent

Creating
Example: No
two students
write the same
poem.

Fig. 4.1 Domains and the convergent and divergent goals of education
Designed after E. A. Vargas. "The Triad Model of Education (II) and Instructional Engineering." *The Spanish Journal of Psychology*
10 (2007): 314–327. Used by permission.

Pilots, for example, work in simulators that pose crisis situations for them to handle. Emergencies such as an engine fire would never be used for training in a real airplane. The objective, however, is the event-governed performance that would be needed in a real emergency. When writing objectives it helps to visualize where students would use what you are teaching in their daily life or jobs. The closer you can get instruction to approximating event-governed behavior the better.

If you try writing objectives in all six squares of the matrix in Table 4.5, you may find that the challenge gives you new ideas for how to bring the world into your classroom and for insuring that both convergent and divergent skills are included.

Writing Objectives from Evaluation Procedures or Test Items

One of the easiest ways to formulate objectives is to first think about how you will evaluate performance. Write a sample performance task or test item. What is the student doing when completing it? That is your objective. If a test item asks for a student to "pick out the word or words that mean the same as the following terms . . . effete,

Table 4.5 Matrix for creating worthwhile objectives

	Knowledge	Problem-Solving	Creating
Verbally-governed			
Event-governed			

spurious, indisposed. . . ." the objective should specify that the student will "select among alternatives." The directions for behavioral objectives are often identical to the wording required for performance or for a test item.

Test Item One: In each row, *circle the word or words that have the same meaning* as the bold first word:

effete	affected	weak	worn out	torn down
spurious	rapid	impure	false	unkind

Objective One: (The student should...) *Circle the word or words that have the same meaning* as the following terms: effete, spurious, (rest of list).

Test Item Two: *Describe the system of "triangle trade" in the American colonies during the early seventeenth century, giving an original example to illustrate how it worked, including:*

a) countries participating
b) products they produced for export
c) products for which there was a market in each country.

Objective Two: (The student should be able to . . .) *describe the system of triangle trade in the American colonies during the early seventeenth century, giving an original example to illustrate how it worked, including:*

a) countries participating
b) products they produced for export
c) products for which there was a market in each country.

Curriculum Alignment and Action Words

In writing objectives from test items, it is easy to unintentionally switch the behavior involved. The objective might say "explain," but the test item might ask the student to pick out the best explanation. That is a different behavior. Objectives and test items should match in terms of the actions involved. Instructional activities, too, should involve the same activities. When all three parts—objectives, learning activities, and evaluation methods—involve the same behavior, they are said to be *aligned*.

To match the components of instruction, use the same active verb form for each. Table 4.6 gives examples of verbs for the three domains.

Objectives for Social Behavior

The best laid plans often must be changed once you meet your students. Some students may need to be taught prerequisites, like the students who were supposed to learn adding two- and three-digit numbers with regrouping (carrying)—without being able to add single digits. Other students may fail to interact well with their peers. At this

Table 4.6 A few action words for objectives

	Knowing	Problem-solving	Creating
add	✓		
analyze (give criteria)		✓	✓
arrange (in order)	✓	✓	
calculate	✓		
choose (correct option)	✓	✓	
circle (best option)	✓	✓	
compare (orally or in writing)	✓	✓	✓
compose		✓	✓
compute	✓	✓	
conduct (experiment, etc.)	✓	✓	✓
contrast (orally or in writing)	✓	✓	✓
create (a unique product)			✓
define	✓		
demonstrate (a movement)	✓		
demonstrate (a procedure)	✓		
design		✓	✓
draw	✓	✓	✓
draw (original, not copy)		✓	✓
explain	✓	✓	✓
give examples	✓	✓	✓
illustrate (by examples)	✓	✓	
list	✓		
outline	✓	✓	✓
place (in order, etc.)	✓	✓	
play (as in music)	✓	✓	✓
play (improvisation)		✓	✓
point to	✓		
put (into categories)	✓	✓	
put together	✓	✓	✓
recite	✓		
relate (in writing)	✓	✓	✓
repeat	✓		
say	✓		
show how to	✓		
sing (from music or by heart)	✓	✓	
sing (own composition)		✓	✓
sketch	✓	✓	✓
solve (on paper)	✓	✓	✓
state	✓		
write (a copy of....)	✓		
write (unique product)		✓	✓

point, you may want to work on social behavior as well as on academics. The extra time this requires is most easily taken in the younger grades or for older students during playground duty.

Behavioral objectives for social behavior have the same requirements as those for academics. Some are easy to specify. Inviting others to join in activities, saying "thank you" or "please," or physically offering materials to others can be counted fairly reliably no matter who is watching interactions. Other parts of social behavior are more subtle. They require the same attention to differences between behavior of the more socially successful students and those shunned by others. Like refinements in academic objectives, critical components come from your observations of student behavior.

In addition to social behavior to increase, most teachers encounter behavior that needs to be decreased.

OBJECTIVES FOR BEHAVIOR TO DECREASE

Behavior that interrupts the planned activities of a school is called **challenging** or **problem behavior** if it occurs frequently or is severe.[12] Frequency matters here as well as in academics. Talking out in a class once every nine weeks is very different from talking out once a minute. Even cutting class is not much of a problem if it occurs only once a year. Of course, extreme actions, like physical attacks on peers (or on you!) are serious even if done only once, and they require immediate attention.

Challenging or **problem behavior** is any kind of action that endangers the student or others, or behavior that interrupts ongoing activities frequently enough to hinder student progress.

Even before you meet your students, it is a good idea to find out what kinds of incidents require assistance and what kinds you are expected to handle yourself. Help is usually provided if you have students who have been classified as disabled, or those who for other reasons have Individualized Educational Plans.

Building Alternative Actions to Replace Challenging Behavior

Thus far, this chapter has addressed academics and not disruptive behavior. There are several reasons. First, if you get students working enthusiastically, behavior problems decrease. Second, it is easier to build behavior than to eliminate it. Third, when you concentrate on what you want students to do, you pay attention to their best behavior. (If you concentrate on actions to decrease, you are likely to *attend* to those actions and may inadvertently be reinforcing them.) Fourth, procedures to build are positive: Procedures to reduce behavior are too often punitive.

Students who exhibit challenging behavior usually have a history of punishment. They do not need more. That is not to say that they can do whatever they like. But they will respond better when academic improvement pays off than when punishment is used to keep them in line. The energy you expend on building skills helps students succeed academically. Delivering positive consequences also converts you, the teacher, into a "reinforcing agent" whose approval is sought, rather than as a policing agent whose attention is avoided or feared.

Undesirable Effects of Punishment

Skinner argued consistently against punishment because of its harmful effects on the behavior of the individual punished, on the behavior of the person punishing, and on social groups that observe it being used. People seldom consider the effects of punitive procedures on the person doing the punishing. Chapter 3 mentioned how shouting to quiet a class strengthens the tendency to shout when a class gets noisy. Teachers who do not know how to control classroom behavior with positive methods tend to drift into more punitive modes. We will look at the harmful effects of punishment in more detail in Chapter 11.

Because of the escalation that punitive techniques often produce in both frequency of use and of severity, most behavior analysts advocate eliminating punishment altogether. Certainly in the public schools, there is never any need for *corporal* punishment. Eliminating all other punishment is difficult if not impossible, but it is still a good goal. Whenever you find yourself shouting or employing harsh words to stop an action, a red flag should go up. Stop and think how you could have handled the situation better. Of course, you have to follow your school's procedures, including punishing infractions of rules, but you can do so calmly. In any case, contingent punishment should not be part of a *planned* program for a student.

Positive Behavior Support (PBS)

Behavior analysts help students with challenging behavior by building alternative actions. Thus objectives must be specified to "replace" behavior that is inappropriate in a classroom setting. Goals that improve a student's overall independence and "quality of life" help a student fit in with the procedures and expectations of school. Within the field of education, the label **Positive Behavior Support (PBS)** is used to indicate an emphasis on reinforcement-only procedures. Positive Behavior Support follows behavior analytic procedures of forming a team including everyone who interacts with the student, conducting a functional assessment of the most challenging behavior, changing relevant contingencies to strengthen alternative behavior, tracking progress, and adapting as necessary until success is achieved. PBS differs in practice in that its practitioners more often extend procedures outside the classroom to the home, after school programs, and to entire schools. **School-Wide Positive Behavior Support (SW-PBS)** sets up procedures to help *all* struggling students, not just those recommended for special services: a constructive trend. Training for school personnel emphasizes tracking individual progress and, of course, reinforcement rather than punishment to bring about change.

As a teacher you will be part of any team that sets objectives and implements change. You do not have to sit idly by while an assessment is being done. Right away you can concentrate on building **incompatible** behavior, that is behavior that cannot be performed at the same time as a challenging behavior. You cannot write and clap at the same time so writing and clapping are incompatible behaviors. However, you can write and smile at the same time. Those actions are not incompatible.

> Two actions are said to be **incompatible** when you cannot do them both at the same time.

Example: Reducing Swearing in a Ninth-Grade Student by Building Academics
Even when strengthening behavior that is not incompatible, challenging behavior usually decreases. A ninth-grade teacher worked in a residential school that took students expelled from regular placements. She had a student with an impressive frequency of extremely vulgar swearing. He was constantly grounded. He wanted to go home for Spring Break, but that seemed an unachievable goal. Instead of tackling his swearing directly, his teacher worked on building academic behavior in class. She introduced timed Precision Teaching exercises designed at his level, complete with graphing and goals for each week. To the teacher's amazement, when the student began seeing progress on his daily graph, his swearing began to disappear. Within a matter of weeks, he stopped swearing in her class altogether, and the effect must have carried over to other classes, because he earned his visit home.[13]

Student swearing is often maintained by the discomfort it causes in teachers. The teacher above might have concentrated so hard on the timings and graphing that she failed to react to her student's swearing, a classic case of extinction if her discomfort was the maintaining consequence. Not every problem behavior disappears so easily when academics are improved, but building academic skills is a good place to start.

Procedures for specifying an incompatible or alternative behavior parallel those for formulating regular academic objectives. You set priorities rather than trying to solve everything at once, you directly target student behavior, and you count actions, adding the time dimension for fluency. Once you have your objectives stated, you are ready to begin collecting data. But before sharpening your pencil, there is one more step. It involves the ethics of research.

ETHICAL STANDARDS

One would hope that good ethical conduct is so self-evident that it does not need to be discussed. Unfortunately, abuses exist. Most institutions now have committees that check the appropriateness of research conducted with human participants. These regulations arose in response to abuses, mostly in the medical field where drugs were being tested on patients who were unaware that they were participants in studies. Like most rules, the human subjects review requirements can become ridiculous in the extreme. At universities, professors are not supposed to do research on students in their classes. This could be interpreted as meaning that professors can try out whatever instructional procedures they like, so long as they do not scientifically evaluate the results! Still, you can see why such a regulation is needed: students are a captive audience. A professor could require participation in any kind of activity for a grade, whether or not that activity was in the students' best interests. Tedious as human subjects reviews can become, they do make sure that prospective studies pose no harm to the participants and that researchers, including teachers, follow the guidelines of confidentiality and informed consent.

Confidentiality

The United States guarantees certain civil liberties, among which is the right to privacy with regard to personal information. Teachers have an obligation to respect confidentiality of private information about students.[14] The Behavior Analysis Certification Board website, http://www.bacb.com, gives many resources including ethical guidelines that include confidentiality.[15]

Even for non-sensitive areas, whenever presenting data to anyone outside of those working with a particular student, confidentiality must be maintained. Most people prefer to call participants by name rather than number. Fine. Make up a fictitious name for any presentation of information. Sometimes particular aspects of data still make it clear who particular data are about. By inventing fictitious schools or institution names, identity can still be protected. Then you will need informed consent. When taking photographs or videos it is, of course, impossible to preserve anonymity. In that case you *must* get informed consent.

Informed Consent

Informed consent is a process to insure that a participant understands what is involved in a research project and agrees to participate "willingly," that is, that there are no penalties for not participating. Usually you write a document that explains, in language the participant can understand, the following:

> **Informed consent** is a set of procedures established to insure that anyone participating in a research study understands what will be involved and participates without coercion.

1. What will happen.
2. Benefits and any possible risks a participant can expect.
3. What the alternatives are if the participant does not participate.
4. What data will be collected, who will have access to them, and how they will be used.
5. Assurance that a participant can withdraw at any time.
6. Contact information for a person or persons who can answer questions about the project.

This document is signed by each participant (or a person legally authorized to represent the participant) saying that the signer understands the above points and grants permission for the participant to be included in the project. Most institutions have standard consent forms that you can edit for your project (see Table 4.7 for an example). The United States Health and Human Services website (http://www.hhs.gov) can also be a good resource.

When is Informed Consent Needed?

Within your own classes, so long as all you are doing is evaluating the effect of normal educational procedures, there is no need for written informed consent. If you plan to share data with people not involved in a project, for example to fellow students in a graduate class or at a convention, you must follow the guidelines for confidentiality. To show pictures of students or to put videos onto the web, you need the permission of everyone shown. In general, it is best to consult your school rules if you have any question about whether informed consent is needed.

If you can't easily get informed consent, there are alternatives. One graduate student wanted to present the results of a study she had conducted in her music class. Instead of photographing her students, she took a photograph of their empty chairs. One could easily imagine what her classroom was like full of active seventh-graders.

Table 4.7 A sample consent form

PARENTAL or GUARDIAN CONSENT and INFORMATION FORM
The Effects of Group Feedback on Individual Math Performance

I, (parent or guardian) have been asked to allow my child (name of child) to participate in this study of the effects of group feedback on individual math performance. (Name of researcher) is conducting this research to fulfill the requirements for a masters thesis in (name of discipline) at (name of university), and has explained the study to me.

Purposes of the Study: The purpose is to see the effect of group feedback on the number of math problems completed during normal math time.

Description of Procedures: This study will be performed at (name of school). My child will be asked to complete his or her regular math assignment in the normal math time given by the teacher. After several days, the total percentage of problems completed by the entire class will be graphed on a chart, and displayed prominently in the classroom. In addition goals will be set for the entire class as a whole.

Risks and Discomforts: There are no known or expected risks from participating in this study, except for mild frustration sometime associated with failure to complete assignments.

Benefits: This study hopes to directly benefit my child by providing motivation for completing math assignments. In addition the knowledge gained may help others.

Contact Persons: For more information about this research I can contact (name and phone number of contact persons).

For information regarding my child's rights as a research participant, I may contact the Executive Secretary of the Institutional Review Board at (phone number).

Confidentiality: I understand that any information obtained as a result of my child's participation in this research will be kept as confidential as legally possible. I understand that these research records, just like hospital records, may be subpoenaed by court order or may be inspected by federal regulatory authorities. My name or that of my child or any information from which we might be identified may not be published without my consent.

Voluntary Participation: Participation in this study is voluntary. I understand that I may withdraw my child from this study at any time. Refusal to participate or withdrawal will involve no penalty or loss of benefits for me or my child. I have been given the opportunity to ask questions about the research, and I have received answers concerning areas I did not understand. Upon signing this form, I will receive a copy.

I willingly consent to my child's participation in this research.

_____	_____	_____
Signature of Parent or Guardian	Date	Time
_____	_____	_____
Signature of Investigator	Date	Time

SUMMARY

Conceptualizing goals in terms of what students should be able to *do* is a big departure from traditional curricula that describe content to cover. Objectives stated in terms of student behavior shift the focus of teaching from presentation to active student participation. Behavioral objectives help you see individual student progress, the only true test of what works and what does not with your students. It is not good enough to adopt an "evidence-based-program" that has been shown to "work" somewhere else. You are a professional. You are expected to make evidence-based decisions about how your students respond to the materials and procedures you use. A clear conception of behavioral goals lets you make those judgments, so you can continually improve your own performance as well as that of your students.

Aside from the way in which they are stated, some objectives serve students better than others. The quality of objectives depends on how critical they are, not only for performance in class but also for later life. **Performance domains** include complex skills and divergent behavior as well as basic skills for a curriculum. In writing objectives for problem-solving and creativity, you are addressing basic questions about what, in your subject, is important for students, and what they will do with it after they graduate. Similarly, moving from verbally-governed actions to event-governed performance creates teaching situations that are likely to transfer well to daily life. Table 4.8 summarizes the recommendations in this chapter.

Table 4.8 A checklist for writing behavioral objectives

DO ...

Pinpoint skills most needed for progress.

State objectives as student actions you can count, or their immediate products, rather than delayed effects or someone else's reaction to, or evaluation of, the behavior.

Add a fluency criterion for skills that underpin more complex activities.

State objectives in small enough units to show daily variation. Including rate helps here.

Include a level of difficulty of materials to be used and a criterion for acceptable performance.

Specify skills that students will get out of activities, rather than only what they will be doing.

Write objectives without redundancy and make sure you include problem-solving and creative behavior as well as both verbally-governed and event-governed skills.

If problem behavior most needs attention, pinpoint a positive behavior to replace the actions to decelerate and check your institution's ethical guidelines for procedures.

Change your pinpoints whenever you or your students see a better behavior to work on.

Both for academic skills and for social behavior, how you formulate goals affects every other aspect of teaching. Beginning with your students' entering skills, to communicating expectations, to the kinds of activities you plan or how and when you assess performance, concentrating on each individual's behavior increases your sensitivity to what really matters: each student's progress from day to day and from week to week.

You may not write down objectives for everything you teach. Few teachers do. But writing down even a few objectives in behavioral terms focuses your thinking and helps you notice more about what your students are doing and should be doing. If you teach the same course more than once, your students' performance will tell you what actions constitute competence, letting you refine objectives further. Being clear about priorities and the behaviors required lets you make the best use of your time and that of your students.

CONCEPT CHECKS

Terms (Objective A)

DIRECTIONS: Fill in the terms that correctly complete each sentence, using the following terms:

event-governed   **verbally-governed**
convergent   **divergent**

1. Driving lessons consist of having a student operate a car because the goal is to produce behavior that is _____ -governed.
2. In putting together a swing set, a father began without the instructions, relying on _____-governed behavior, but resorted to _____-governed behavior when he could not figure out what to do.
3. In writing an essay, high school students need both to use 1) their own ideas and experiences, but also 2) standard English. The first requires unique, or _____ behavior. The second requires _____ behavior.
4. Objectives that require every student to prepare modeling clay the same way are called _____ objectives in contrast to _____ objectives that encourage students to make unique sculptures.

Behavioral Objectives (Objective B)

DIRECTIONS: Mark the one *most* behaviorally stated objective in each set. (Mastery = 20 a minute correct with no errors.) (Assume all have the lead-in "By the end of training the student will.. . .")

1. Grasp the point of existentialism at the 90% correct level.
   Tell which authors in a given list are existentialist, which not.
   Comprehend the implications of the existentialist position.
   Enjoy the ideas expressed by existentialist authors.

2. Realize the importance of good safety habits.
   Apply safety habits in the school shop.

Understand the importance of good safety habits.
Wear ear protection when using the band saw.

3. See the value of an experiment on fruit flies.
Predict the eye color of the crossing of given fruit flies.
Observe the outcome of given fruit fly crossings.
Recognize that male and female fruit flies differ.

4. Be shown the rules of volley ball and when they apply.
Co-operate with team mates in volley ball games.
Hit four out of every five serves within court bounds.
Gain accuracy in serving in the game of volley ball.

5. List three differences between the philosophies of Locke and Hume.
Have a grasp of the three main differences between Locke and Hume.
Gain insight into the three basic tenets of Locke and Hume.
Exercise judgment about the three main aspects of Locke's and Hume's ideas.

6. Complete a worksheet on adding two digits plus two digits with carrying.
Add two digits plus two digits with carrying at a rate of 20 a minute correct.
Correctly solve addition problems involving adding with carrying.
Become proficient in basic addition of two digits plus two digits with carrying.

7. Participate co-operatively in class discussions.
Pay attention to what others say during class discussions.
Be responsive to the opinions of others in class discussions.
Refer to what others have said when contributing to class discussions.

8. Be exposed to the calculation of the volume of a cylinder.
Watch how to calculate the volume of a cylinder.
Have the formula for calculating the volume of a cylinder.
Calculate the volume of a cylinder given a diagram.

9. Play Chopin correctly on the piano with expression.
Play Chopin's *Minute Waltz* correctly in a minute.
Learn to play well the *Minute Waltz* by Chopin.
Master the correct fingering in Chopin's *Minute Waltz*.

10. Label cafeteria foods according to their main food group.
Comprehend the four food group classification system.
Gain exposure to good eating habits via the four food groups.
Apply the four food groups in maintaining a healthy lifestyle.

11. Think critically when reading an unfamiliar selection.
Evaluate the writer's intention in writing a paragraph.
Demonstrate critical reading skills with an unfamiliar passage.
State whether a given conclusion is a fact or opinion.

12. Understand what a vanishing point is.
Feel the effect of vanishing points in pictures with perspective.
Appreciate the use of vanishing points in drawings.
Sketch three dimensional objects using a vanishing point.

13. Gain insight into computer viruses.
Protect school computers from viruses.

Trash emails from unknown sources.
Think before opening unknown attachments.

14. Show creativity in problem-solving in fifth-grade math.
    Develop problem-solving skills in multiplication and division.
    Exercise critical thinking about mathematical processes.
    Write a word problem which requires multiplication to solve.

15. Describe four main differences between the roles of men and women in World War II.
    Locate original sources on the Web about the role of men and women in World War II.
    Stay on task when studying the roles of men and women in World War II.
    Become proficient in the economic issues involving men and women in World War II.

16. Be exposed to the concept of moles.
    Understand why moles are central in chemistry.
    Write a concise definition of mole.
    Gain experience with moles in chemistry.

17. Graph 20 data points on a given chart in one minute.
    Know how to graph 20 data points on a given chart.
    Internalize the importance of charting on a given chart.
    Practice charting given data on a given chart using one-minute timings.

18. Give examples of two differences between a territory and country.
    Grasp the concept of the difference between a territory and country.
    Understand the difference between a territory and a country.
    Pay attention to discussions of the difference between a territory and country.

19. Understand spoken conversational Spanish at a first year level.
    Spend at least four hours a week in the first year Spanish language lab.
    Feel comfortable speaking first year level conversational Spanish.
    Transcribe spoken Spanish at the first year conversational level.

20. Appreciate why the sky looks blue from the Earth's surface.
    Diagram the scattering of light as it hits our atmosphere.
    Understand why the sky looks blue from the Earth's surface.
    Watch a film showing how light scatters when hitting air.

Editing Objectives (Objective C)

DIRECTIONS: For each objective below, first write the letter of the one or two improvements *most* needed. Then edit the objective to make it a better behavioral objective.

A Describe student, rather than teacher, performance.
B Change unobservable goals to measurable, countable actions.
C Add the general level of difficulty of problems or materials used.
D Give criteria for the acceptable performance.
E Eliminate unnecessary words.

1. Students will know Webster's definition of "constitution."
2. Students will understand the principle of using no more than three colors when designing advertisements.

3. Students will be shown how to multiply single digits times single digits at a rate of 30 a minute correct.
4. Students will write the Spanish equivalent of English sentences.
5. Student tutors will show empathy towards tutees by saying "good try" instead of "wrong" for incorrect responses.
6. Students will decide whether to use "good" or "well" by circling "good" or "well" in given fourth-grade level sentences.
7. Students will write a report on the science experiments in their textbooks.
8. Students will follow school procedures in an emergency by lining up silently during fire drills.

Don't forget to edit the items.

ANALYSIS PROBLEMS

1. Accomplishment Versus Paying Attention (Objective D)

Think back on your own experiences as a student when you tried to look like you were paying attention or staying on task, but found your thoughts wandering. Describe what the teacher was trying to "cover" or teach and what you were doing instead of paying attention. Finally, write a behavioral objective for the lesson to specify one or two skills you were supposed to master.

2. Fluency (Objective D)

Give an example from your own experience, as a student or teacher, of where fluency in one or more underlying skills would enable students to problem-solve or create more effectively. Specify (a) the specific underlying skill, (b) what you would consider a fluent level, and (c) how the skill relates to the more complex performance.

Better still, if you are currently teaching, bring your students' performance in some missing underlying skill up to fluency levels, and then check how much difference it makes in the more complex skill.

3. Informed Consent (Objective F)

You plan to post the best essays from your ninth-grade class on your public website. What must you do first? (use either the BCBA requirements, or those of your school)

ANSWERS FOR CONCEPT CHECKS

Terms

event-governed	**verbally-governed (or rule-governed)**
convergent	**divergent**

1. Driving lessons consist of having a student operate a car because the goal is to produce behavior that is ***event***-governed.

2. In putting together a swing set, a father began without the instructions, relying on **event**-governed behavior, but resorted to **verbally**-governed (or **rule**-governed) behavior when he could not figure out what to do.
3. In writing an essay, high school students need to use (a) their own ideas and experiences, but also (b) standard English. The first requires **divergent** behavior. The second requires unique, or **convergent** behavior.
4. Objectives that require every student to prepare modeling clay the same way are called **convergent** objectives in contrast to **divergent** objectives that encourage students to make unique sculptures.

Behavioral Objectives

The best objectives in each group follow:

1. Tell which authors in a given list are existentialist, which not.
2. Wear ear protection when using the band saw.
3. Predict the eye color of the crossing of given fruit flies.
4. Hit four out of every five serves within court bounds.
5. List three differences between the philosophies of Locke and Hume.
6. Add two digits plus two digits with carrying at a rate of 20 a minute correct (completing a worksheet is an activity not an objective).
7. Refer to what others have said when contributing to class discussions.
8. Calculate the volume of a cylinder given a diagram.
9. Play Chopin's *Minute Waltz* in a minute on the piano.
10. Label cafeteria foods according to their main food group.
11. State whether a given conclusion is a fact or opinion.
12. Sketch three-dimensional objects using a vanishing point.
13. Trash emails from unknown sources.
14. Write a word problem which requires multiplication to solve.
15. Describe four main differences between the roles of men and women in World War II.
16. Write a concise definition of mole.
17. Graph 20 data points on a given chart in one minute.
18. Give examples of two differences between a territory and country.
19. Transcribe spoken Spanish at the first year conversational level.
20. Diagram the scattering of light as it hits our atmosphere.

Editing Objectives

The letter of the one or two improvements most needed is followed by a sample editing. Use your judgment about how well your own editing solves the same problems.

                    write

1. **B.**   Students will ~~know~~ Webster's definition of "constitution."

                    use

2. **E & B.**   Students will ~~understand the principle of using~~ no more than three colors when designing advertisements.

3. **A & E.** Students will ~~be shown how to~~ multiply single digits times single digits at a rate of 30 a minute correct.

4. **C.** Students will write the Spanish equivalence of English sentences. *(Add some level of difficulty of the English sentences to be given, such as "like those in Chapter 5 of the text.")*

use (or *say*)

5. **E & B.** Tutors will ~~show empathy towards tutees by saying~~ "good try" instead of "wrong" for incorrect responses.

circle

6. **E & B.** Students will ~~decide whether to use good or well by circling~~ good or well in given fourth-grade level sentences.

7. **D.** Students will write a report on the science experiments in their textbooks. *(Add some criteria for acceptable performance, such as "including a statement of the problem, methods used," etc.)*

line

8. **E.** Students will ~~follow school procedures in an emergency by lining~~ up silently during fire drills.

IMPROVING SENSITIVITY TO PROGRESS: RECORDING METHODS

"You see, but you do not observe,"
    said by Sherlock Holmes to Watson in Conan Doyle's *A Scandal in Bohemia*

OVERVIEW

Can you describe the progress that each of your students made in the last week in each subject you teach? Few teachers can. The purpose of measuring is to increase your sensitivity to changes in your students' performance that otherwise would remain hidden. How you record and monitor progress determines what you can see. This chapter looks at various measures used in education, and recommends recording methods that best reveal individual progress.

OBJECTIVES

By the end of this chapter you should be able to...

A. Name the recording method defined, exemplified, or best used for a given purpose, using the following:

time on task	percentage correct	rate (frequency)
duration	latency	percentage of occurrence
interval recording		

B. Calculate rates for given data.
C. Classify measures as direct or indirect measures of behavior.
D. For a given Discrete Trial procedure, describe an alternative that would provide a fluency measure, including the following:

the entering (or entry) behavior of the student for which the exercise is designed

---

the setting and materials needed
the behavior the student will engage in and
directions for conducting the exercise.

E. Calculate the counting period ceiling for given scenarios.
F. Design a Precision Teaching worksheet or exercise to teach and evaluate fluency in an important skill for a course you are teaching or might someday teach.

WHY RECORD?

Imagine that you have found a new job teaching in a high school. You are assigned beginning algebra. By the end of the first class session you discover that many of your students lack basic math skills. They are having problems with solving equations, not because they don't understand what to do, but because they can't readily multiply and divide. You need to find out the **entering behavior** (also called **entry behavior**) for each student, and to help remedy lack of fluency in those whose lack of skill is preventing their progress in solving equations. Entering behavior includes all relevant skills, including the *prerequisites* and *component* skills mentioned in the last chapter. Prerequisites are skills required for learning something new: components are a part of the new behavior. In many cases, the same skills (multiplying and dividing in this case) are both prerequisites for, and components of, the new performance.

> **Entering behavior** consists of what a student does or can do prior to instruction, especially that part of his or her repertoire relevant to the skills to be taught.

While most teachers record behavior on assignments and tests, few record in a way that shows progress from day to day. Yet that is exactly what you need in order to see what change is occurring. To evaluate change, you must measure behavior.

> **Measurement** is the process of determining rate or other properties of an action or event by assigning numbers for units that are equivalent.

Example: Misjudging the Effect of a Treatment for a Kindergarten Student's Pinching

Mere opinions about what is getting better or worse are often incorrect, as the following describes:

A boy in the laboratory preschool frequently pinched adults. Attempts by the teachers to ignore the behavior proved ineffective, since the pinches were hard enough to produce at least an involuntary startle. Teachers next decided to try to develop a substitute behavior. They selected patting as a logical substitute. Whenever the child reached toward a teacher, she attempted to forestall a pinch by saying, "Pat, Davey," sometimes adding, "Not pinch," and then strongly approving his patting, when it occurred. Patting behavior increased rapidly to a high level. The teachers agreed that they had indeed succeeded in reducing the pinching behavior through substituting patting. Then they were shown the recorded data. It showed clearly that although patting behavior was indeed high, pinching behavior continued at the previous level. Apparently, the teachers were so focused on the rise in patting behavior that, without the objective data, they would have erroneously concluded that development of a substitute behavior was in this case a successful technique.[1]

Only by measuring behavior could the reality of what was happening be seen.

Judgments about Progress in Academics

Teacher judgments about individual changes in academic behavior are rarely better. In a classroom, how can you remember exactly what words each student has learned to spell on Thursday that he or she could not spell on Tuesday, or what improvement each student made in solving quadratic equations from one Friday to the next? These precise bits of information are the only way you can tell where progress has been made and what still needs work.

In addition to enabling you to determine where to start your students and to make progress visible, recording performance serves an additional function. It gives *you* feedback on the effectiveness of the procedures you are using. Feedback is the key to improvement for you as well as for your students. In monitoring progress, you may see something you could improve midstream. Getting that feedback lets you change. If you can't change in the middle of a term, fine. You will probably teach the same subject again in the future, and can make changes the next time around. Feedback on effectiveness of changes in procedures shows the student **Response to Intervention (RtI)** that is often requested by supervisors.

WHAT TO RECORD: PROPERTIES OF BEHAVIOR

As we saw in the last chapter, to assess mastery of objectives underpinning any subject, like multiplication and division for algebra, you need to look at how fluently students can perform. In spite of the importance of rate, the conventional grade book ignores rate altogether in favor of numbers without a time dimension.

Simple Counts and Percentage Correct

Typically, teachers record the number of points an assignment or test is worth with each student's score, perhaps converting the numbers into percentages. Table 5.1 shows a portion of a detailed grade book showing counts of items correct on assignments each of which is worth 20 points. If converted into percent correct scores, the measures would indicate accuracy, but not the speed part of fluency.

Table 5.1 A portion of a typical grade book showing scores on 20-point assignments

Name	Monday	Wednesday	Friday	Monday	Wednesday
Carter, Joe	18	16	19	15	Absent
Garcia, Jane	20	20	20	20	20
Wong, Wen	18	19	18	17	20

Jane is obviously a "good" student, but is she improving? You cannot tell from what is recorded here. Nor can she.

Rate or Frequency of Behavior (Count Per Unit of Time)[2]

By adding frequency (rate) to accuracy, daily variation will appear as shown in Table 5.2. Rate is a very sensitive measure. These scores are not real, but the progress shown is realistic. In five working days, Jane has nearly doubled the speed at which she completes these problems. Doubling performance in one or two weeks is often set as a target for improvement by Precision Teachers.

Table 5.2 The same portion of a grade book as in Table 5.1, but showing problems correct *per minute*

Name	Monday	Wednesday	Friday	Monday	Wednesday
Carter, Joe	8	7	11	10	Absent
Garcia, Jane	13	13	20	18	25
Wong, Wen	9	6	8	10	13

Calculating Rate (or Frequency) of Behavior

To record rate you need two numbers: 1) the number of actions completed (correctly or incorrectly or both) and 2) the number of minutes, hours, or other time period over which the actions were counted. By dividing the number of actions by the units of time you get rate: 44 problems correct per minute, 28 laps run per hour, three compliments per day.

$$\text{Rate or frequency} = \frac{\text{Count of occurrences}}{\text{Number of minutes, hours, or other time period}}$$

Rate can be expressed as count per minute, count per hour, or count per any other unit of time. Schools look at dropout *rates per year!* If you take 15 or 20 minutes each period for answering questions at the ends of chapters, you already have your timings. To get an equivalent *rate per hour*, multiply the counts by four in the first case (15 minutes times 4 = 1 hour), or three in the second (20 minutes times 3 = 1 hour). Or, if you don't mind decimals, you can divide each count by the number of minutes and get problems completed per minute. 10 problems correct in 20 minutes = .5 a minute.

As mentioned in Chapter 4, one-minute timings work well for practice on basic skills. They do not take up too much class time, and the resulting number does not require division. It *is* the rate per minute. If Wen completes 26 problems during a one-minute timing, his rate per minute is 26 divided by 1, or 26 problems per minute. With one-minute timings, even students in the primary grades can "calculate" their rates, simply by counting the number of problems they completed correctly and incorrectly. Typically, with Precision Teaching, students grade their own papers. When calling time you will hear students make comments like, "Yes!!! I got two more than Monday," or "Ooh, Not time already. I didn't even get to the third row!"

Will students count accurately? That depends on the consequences for getting high numbers. You will usually get an accurate count if no grade depends upon the number achieved, especially if students have a part in setting their own goals. Usually it takes a few days before all students settle down to recording accurately from day to day. They soon learn that if they inflate Wednesday's figure too much, they ruin the chance of improving the next class session. That does not mean that students should grade everything. If you plan to use a particular timing for a grade, collect the papers and grade them yourself.

To see how rapidly a student can respond, you must remove instructional restrictions so that whatever behavior you are counting is free to occur at any time during the timing period. This **free operant behavior** is not really free, but it is not restricted by a limited number of opportunities to respond.

Removing Restrictions Over Frequency or Rates: Counting Period Ceilings

To get a good measure of frequency, you must remove restrictions over how rapidly a student can respond. A **counting period ceiling** is the maximum rate possible because of the way a task is designed. For example, suppose you want to see how rapidly Justin can pronounce words written on index cards. As he pronounces each one, he turns over the card. Is his speed of handling cards a limiting factor? If he can turn over *blank* cards only at a frequency of 40 a minute, that imposes a counting period ceiling for his performance. Give him a page of 100 words printed in rows and he may be able to pronounce them correctly at 100 a minute.

> A **counting period ceiling** is the maximum rate it is possible to obtain, usually because of the way an instructional task is designed.

Counting period ceilings may slow responding in computer drills. If a rocket takes off following each correct answer and takes two seconds, the program has a counting period ceiling of 30 a minute: At two seconds per answer, no one can get more than 30 a minute correct. Ever.

When designing worksheets for one-minute timings, make sure they contain enough problems so that there are more than any student can complete. A worksheet with 20 problems on it with a one-minute timing has a counting period ceiling of 20 a minute. Saul, who could have correctly completed 40 problems in that minute, can't do more than the 20 he is given. To get an accurate picture of an unrestricted rate of performance, you must always include more tasks than any student can complete in the time given. Once a timing begins, students should be able to go as fast as they can without running out of problems.

When you introduce your first Precision Teaching exercise, students who have always been told to finish worksheets may be alarmed by the number of problems on a page. The first time you do a timing, you must emphasize that no one should be able to finish them all. For some students this announcement will come as a challenge. Students love to complete all the available tasks before the time limit after being told that they are not supposed to be able to do so. Some teachers make a game of this. They groan, "Oh no. Don't tell me you finished them *all*! I thought there were more problems than anyone could *possibly* do. Now I'll have to go and add more." Making the teacher add more problems becomes a challenge. Even college students seem to take pleasure in outdoing the expectations of instructors.

Duration

Duration is the time it takes to complete one action —the time from start to finish of a behavioral episode. While rarely the best measure for academic achievement, it is appropriate to measure length for

> **Duration** is the length in time from the start to the end of an action.

some kinds of behavior. For crying or arguing or fighting, you might want to know not only how many times the action occurred, but also how long each episode lasted. If you were recording crying during a 20-minute snack time, and a four-year-old cried only once, it would be useful to know whether that cry lasted the full 20 minutes or not! You would want to measure duration.

Duration is also used for positive actions. If you are working on speaking extemporaneously, you might want to note the duration of talking without a two-second pause. Duration figures in physical training, for example increasing how long you can hold your breath underwater, or how long you can stand on one foot without falling over. Stamina is largely a matter of duration: how long can you run without stopping?

Duration is the measure typically used for paying attention. While progress on specific skills is better measured by rate, there are many activities that do not have easily counted units. It would be tough to get a rate for activities such as putting together a web page, working on a science project, or making a sculpture out of clay. Paying attention in these cases would be judged by duration of activity. Informally teachers also use duration as an indication of "interest" or "motivation," noting, for example, how long students play at one activity rather than another during recess. In the classroom, when students continually work without prompting or threats, and don't want to quit when the time is up, they are called motivated. However, many other factors must also be considered. A student may hesitate to complete one activity not because of its appeal, but because of avoiding what comes next. Duration is also related to skill level: students with higher rates of performance persist longer than those with slower rates, even on work they would call boring.[3]

Disadvantages of Duration Measures

If you have ever taken lessons on a musical instrument, you can probably remember practicing. If you recorded anything about your practice sessions, it was probably duration. However, not all practice sessions are equal. Going over the parts you play well is not the same as practicing the parts that need work. To conquer difficult sections you must work on them, and do so until they are mastered. One way is to take several minute timings each day and record the number of times you correctly played each short section of a difficult passage in the minute. Not only does this provide more repetitions, it encourages slowing down to get the notes right. Teachers are always telling students to play slowly enough not to make mistakes so that fingers get used to correct sequences. Because pieces don't sound good when played slowly, it is hard to slow down when practicing. But you *do* slow down when counting the number of times you play a section correctly in a minute. Of course, as you improve, you can speed up. For mastering the mechanics of playing, rate records are better than duration of practice sessions.

The same problem occurs with counting minutes spent exercising or doing homework. Everyone knows how easy it is to occupy time without really accomplishing anything. The exerciser goes through the motions without concentrating or with little energy. The student starting a paper discovers that the printer needs a new cartridge, or that books could be rearranged, or that coffee is needed to help alleviate the "sleepies." Even when reading, you have probably reached the end of a page and realized that even though your eyes have moved over every word, you have no idea of what those words said. If you record time spent working, you cannot see differences between productive and non-productive sessions. Counting problems completed, notes taken, words written, or other products gives a better picture of behavior. That said, where accomplishment can't be easily measured in numbers, as when editing something you have already written, recording duration is better than not recording anything at all.

In general, use duration when the *length* of actions is important, rather than what students need to accomplish during the time available.

Latency

Latency is the time it takes to start an action once a "go" signal is given. Where speed of reacting is important, such as the time taken to reach the brake of a car in an emergency, you are looking at latency. In the classroom, teachers often reserve some class time for working on assignments. Not all students begin to work as soon as they are told they may begin. A group of teachers in West Virginia wanted to reduce the latency of starting to work in their classrooms. They measured the minutes from the time they told students to begin their assignments to the time that all students had started to write. The latencies ran from around 30 seconds for a sixth-grade math class to around 500 seconds for a "learning disabled" math class. A first "treatment" of reminding the students to begin brought the latencies down a bit, but when the teachers also wrote instructions to begin on the board, the latencies approached zero in four of the classes. Even in the "learning disabled" class, latencies between giving directions and the time everyone was working decreased to under a half a minute.[4]

> **Latency** is the time period between the presentation of a task or start signal and the beginning of the specified response.

Latencies of actions are usually very short when you are timing performance. Competitive runners do not stop to readjust shoelaces after a "go" signal. Nor do many students hesitate to begin when being timed on quizzes or tests.

Rate, duration, and latency all involve counts of behavior and time measures.[5] Of course, there are other aspects of behavior besides speed. An advanced biologist can not only work faster than a beginner, he or she can do things a beginner cannot do at all. In music, a competent performer must be able to do more than run off notes at the right tempos. Tone quality, phrasing, subtleties of style and color are equally important. Think of hitting a baseball, of handwriting, or dance, or social interactions, or sketching. In each case frequency is only one property to consider. Two others are force (**magnitude**) and quality.

Force or Magnitude

While frequency is one measure of the strength of behavior, you might also be interested in the force or magnitude of individual actions. Perhaps a student speaks up readily, but too softly to be heard. Another student may speak too loudly. Force is a property of concern mainly in physical actions. Bowlers may work on rolling balls harder, rather than how many balls they can roll per minute. In baseball, force can make a difference between an out and a home run.

Magnitude is of concern where size is critical. Perhaps a student writes correctly formed letters, but makes them so large that only three words fit on a standard line. In this case, you would work on reducing the size of handwriting.

Quality: Form or Topography of Behavior or of Behavioral Products

The quality of behavior consists of look, feel, taste, or sound in comparison to some standard. More than the previous properties of behavior, quality requires judgment. The need for scoring keys or rubrics reflects the difficulty of evaluating quality. Even for simple products, such as letters written, form determines whether handwriting is legible or not, and whether it is considered "beautiful." Form is also called **topography** to distinguish the physical form of an action from its functional characteristics. Two shoves might have the same topography in the placement of the hands and the force used, but you would interpret the actions very differently if one moved the shover ahead in line and the other saved a peer from stepping on a pile of spilled spaghetti.

> **Topography** of behavior refers to its physical properties—its form or physical dimensions. Topography or form is contrasted with **function** which takes into consideration the contingencies that control the behavior.

Rate and form are related. As an action becomes more fluent through repeated practice, the form becomes smoother and more stable. For example, students who write with such force that they engrave grooves into their papers usually apply less force when timed. Similarly, in shooting baskets, increasing speed of practice increases accuracy. A study of shooting baskets from the foul line surprised the coach who thought that shooting faster would result in sloppier throws. The coach provided over a dozen balls. During practice, one student at a time shot fouls as fast as he or she could for one minute. The rest of the class ran around retrieving the balls, so the student practicing always had balls available. The percentage of balls that went in the hoop did not decrease when the students shot faster, it *increased*.[6]

Using Rate for Improving Quality

When working on improving quality, you may wish to set a minimum acceptable criterion and then count the rate of actions that meet or exceed that standard. In a half-minute handwriting timing, first-graders may count the number of letters that stay within guide lines on their papers. In the TAG Teaching sessions for sports, like that described in Chapter 1, a gym coach may "tag" legitimate basketball dribbles with a clicker as a student moves across the floor, or students may tag each other's performance. If both time and count are recorded, you have a rate. For some physical performances, quality may show only as a performance unfolds, rather than in the end result of an action. In teaching figure skating or a gymnastic dismount, form itself is critical. An audible click at the split second a student enters the correct position strengthens the muscle movements involved at that exact moment. Although not part of the TAG Teaching procedures, students often count the number of TAGS they received in a class session, thus getting a kind of daily record of performance. Since what is "tagged" changes as one movement after another is mastered, comparisons can't easily be made from one day to the next. Nevertheless the counts indicate how many times a student correctly executed the actions he or she worked on, thus giving a sense of achievement.

USING PERMANENT PRODUCTS TO EVALUATE BEHAVIOR

Rather than observing each action as it occurs, much of a student's academic behavior produces a durable product. In drawing a graph, or writing an essay, student behavior leaves tangible records. Rather than watching every action as it occurs, it is easier to evaluate these **permanent products**. If there is a one-to-one relationship between each action and its end result, permanent products are considered equivalent to counts of actions as they occur—where, when you think of it, you are recording some kind of product too, such as the sound of a word said.

A **permanent product** is a tangible record of an action or set of actions where there is a one-to-one correspondence between each action and its durable result.

Of course, in using permanent products to evaluate performance, you must make sure that the work was completed by the student whose behavior is of interest. Products created as homework may be suspect. Some science projects reflect more a parent's performance than the student's! Even when in class, students may not do their own work. Rather than calling copying "cheating," behavior analysts look for reasons why a student didn't perform on his or her own. Copying others' work reveals faulty instructional contingencies, not moral ineptitude. For timed exercises such as those in Precision Teaching you will want to watch that students don't continue after time is called. During the timings, students rarely look at a peers' papers. There simply isn't time.

GATHERING DATA: WHAT TO RECORD AND WHO SHOULD RECORD

Obviously you can't record everything that goes on in your classroom, no matter how useful it would be to have those data.[7] Part of the effort can be shared by having your students record data on their own behavior. They may already be grading homework or other assignments. Add recording those scores in a systematic way, and you have help with some of the clerical tasks needed for good records of progress. Recording (and graphing) data also brings your students more closely in touch with their own performance (see Chapter 6).

With short Precision Teaching exercises, your data collection may be restricted to the first few minutes of a class. But even if looking at behavior that could occur over an entire period, you do not need to gather data the whole time. If you are recording the rate of writing words on compositions, for example, you could ask for counts at the end of the first five minutes. You can always increase the timing period later if you feel you are missing too much. The point is to gather data without making it so burdensome that it interferes with other aspects of teaching or doesn't get done at all.

The Problem of Units

Behavior is a fluid and ongoing process. That makes it more difficult to measure than, say, the length of an object that stays still from moment to moment and place to place.

To date, there is no universal unit for behavior.[8] A "response" or "action" is defined differently for each project. For academic or social goals in the classroom you need to see daily variation. Any specific behavior you pinpoint becomes your unit. For Johnny who rarely talks to others during recess, you may count "one" for each word spoken, for a more verbal Sarah your unit may be sentences. Over the course of recording data you will refine your criteria for what counts and does not count. Like "perfect" objectives, perfect units in a classroom setting are only ideals. With experience, however, you will move towards more precision to better serve the purpose for which you are gathering data.

In order to compare performance from day to day, units must stay equivalent over the course of observing. If you are still refining your criteria, wait until your measures are consistent enough so that different numbers reflect changes in behavior, not in observation methods. For many academic actions, judgment enters in. If you are counting tasks, such as "assignments completed," you would check that assignments do not differ markedly in length or difficulty. Alternatively you can count problems assigned and problems completed for each assignment.

DIRECT MEASURES OF BEHAVIOR

Numbers that indicate how many times or how rapidly a particular action occurred, or its latency or duration, are called **direct measures**. The numbers are obtained by "directly" observing behavior *as it occurs* or the permanent products of those actions. To tell whether a measure is direct, it helps to look at the words following the number, that is, the measurement *units*. If the units consist of *actions* or their permanent products or how fast the actions occurred, you have a direct measure. In 15 *problems completed*, 10 *sit-ups* or 60 *steps* per minute, the unit of the count is actions or accomplishments with nothing in between the number and the behavior. You, or someone else, saw the problems or sit-ups or steps that occurred. Measures of the time it took for a response to occur (latency) or the duration of an action are also direct measures. The behavior is still directly observed, as in the number of seconds a student takes to *begin writing*, or how long it takes a student to *run a mile*. With direct measures your numbers are identical with the number of actions that occurred, the number of actions per unit of time (rate or frequency), or the time until an action began or how long it lasted.

You might have noticed that in recording rate, a conversion is used: 60 steps *per minute* does not necessarily mean that a student took 60 steps. Perhaps he or she only took 30 steps in a 30-second timing or took 600 steps in 10 minutes. Rate is still considered a direct measure because the number indicates a **property of behavior**: its speed. Note that the word following the number is still an action. Direct measures put you in closer touch with what is going on than indirect measures.[9]

INDIRECT MEASURES OF BEHAVIOR

Indirect measures have units that do not name the actions that were counted. For example, in "*60% correct*" the 60 is not 60 actions. Even if stated as 60% *of problems completed*, the unit is still *percent* ("per hundred") not the actions the student took. Percentage requires a conversion of direct counts. Reporting that a student completed six problems correctly and four incorrectly gives a direct measure. Converting those numbers to 60% makes the measure indirect. All percentages are indirect measures. Percentage of occurrence, percentage of intervals in which an action occurred, and percentage of trials all require conversion of counts of actions to a scale of 100. One last indirect measure is *trials to criterion*. This number refers to the number of times tasks were presented to a student before the student successfully performed at the level set as a criterion.

Many indirect measures, such as standardized test scores, have an even more distant relation to countable actions than percentages or trials to criterion. A standardized test score does not refer to behavior. A SAT Reasoning Test score of 450 is not 450 of anything a student did. The number indicates relative standing and has no units at all! Relative standing is a useful measure for comparisons between students or between classrooms or schools. The numbers given are less useful for specifying what a student can and cannot do. Nothing in a standardized test score tells you how *competently* a learner performs. A state test could be made easier and scores would go up even if no improvement in actual skills occurred.

Although direct measures indicate better what numbers mean than indirect measures, many indirect measures are used by behavior analysts, probably because of the **Discrete Trial** format of instruction common in one-on-one tutoring.

Discrete Trial Training Versus Alternative Behavior Analytic Procedures

Discrete Trial Training, or DTT (also called Discrete Trial *Therapy*), is only *one* form of Applied Behavior Analysis. DTT is based upon a three-term contingency format, but it has the disadvantage of using repetitive *trials* that prevent measuring rates of student actions. Trials also permit students to make errors repeatedly, unacceptable in shaping where the next action to be reinforced depends on the last response so that the student continually succeeds.[10] Formats like Precision Teaching, TAG Teaching, and shaping in a natural environment are behavior analytic procedures that, in my opinion, are better than DTT for teaching most skills. Exceptions are discussed below.

> **Discrete Trial Training (DTT)** is a teaching format usually used with one teacher and one student in which the teacher asks a question, the student responds, and the teacher gives feedback. Usually the sequence of tasks is set beforehand and records are made of each student's response.

Discrete Trial Training (DTT) breaks down skills into small parts. Each subskill is addressed repeatedly in a session with one teacher and one student. They usually sit side by side or across a table from each other. A session typically has 10 or 20 "trials," each of which consists of three parts:

1. a question or task given to a student,
2. a student response, and
3. consequences that differ depending on whether or not a correct response is made.

Correct responses are followed by reinforcement.[11] Verbal approval such as "good job" may be used, or for low-functioning individuals, some kind of treat or brief activity that has been shown to be a reinforcer. When a child makes an incorrect response or fails to respond within a specified time, additional help may be given until the student answers correctly,[12] or materials may be gathered and the student given the next trial.

Example: Discrete Trial Training

Imagine a student in a special education preschool class. Perhaps the day's lesson is on identifying shapes. Three shapes are placed on a table between teacher and student: a triangle, a circle, and a square. The student is asked, "Give me the *circle*," or "Give me the *square*." For each trial the three shapes are rearranged on the table to prevent the student from selecting on the basis of location (always picking the one on the right, for example). Only "circles" may be requested, or sometime one shape then another in random order. Each trial begins with the teacher's request. A session may have 10 or 20 trials. Each of the student's responses is recorded. While the resulting numbers could be reported directly, they are usually converted to percentages. As mentioned above, percentages hide how many responses a student completed, making 18 out of 20 the same as 9 out of 10. When DTT projects are published, actual numbers are reported somewhere in the reports, but most graphs use a scale of 100. Since graphs are what leave an impression on the reader (as we will see in the next chapter), percentage graphs give an impression one step away from the behavior that occurred.

Example: A Better Format Than Discrete Trial

In DTT procedures, the student cannot respond until a task is given. Why not change to a format where the student is free to respond at any time during a timing? Here is an example. Suppose you had a table full of triangles, circles, and squares and three buckets each with one shape drawn on it. You would pick one shape and hide the other two buckets. Say you start with triangles: you say to your student, "Put in all . . . . . . *triangles.*" As you say "triangles," you place the triangle bucket within reach of the student and start a timer, perhaps for 30 seconds or a minute. The student begins to pick up shapes and put them into the bucket. Each time the student drops a triangle into the bucket, you indicate that the action is correct, perhaps with a click sound. Wrong items (putting a circle into the bucket) are ignored. When the timer rings, you count the correct (and incorrect) items in the bucket, getting the student's rate correct and rate incorrect.

A next step might be giving the student all three buckets to teach matching to the sample shapes on the sides of the buckets. To prevent students from selecting a favorite shape first, you could put the shapes into a bag where they are hidden but easily reached. That way the shapes the student would take out would be in random order. Adding clicks for putting a correct shape into a bucket would teach the different shapes effectively during the timings. At the end of the timing, all shapes in the correct buckets and those in wrong buckets would be counted. In contrast to the often slow response to Discrete Trials, timings without the restriction of trials provide a lot of practice in the time available. Where 20 Discrete Trials might take four minutes or more, you could easily have 200 unrestricted selections in the same time. That's *10 times* as much practice. Rate also reveals areas where a student isn't so sure of his selections even when they are all correct. Very slow responding indicates lack of confidence. Further, during initial learning, no "correction" is used, thus eliminating the emotional effects of being wrong. As a teacher, you tag (click) only correct selections. The one disadvantage to timing selection of shapes in this format is that it requires a great many objects for each shape.

However, to teach students to identify all triangles and not just one or two examples of triangles, you would include triangles of different sizes, colors, orientations, and kinds anyway (see Chapter 9).

Where Discrete Trial Formats are Appropriate

There are some kinds of skills for which a Discrete Trial format is needed. Some skills cannot be taught without a question or direction preceding each response. In teaching conversation skills or imitation, for example, you must give an antecedent for each student response. A student saying "Fine, how are you?" is only appropriate when it follows a specific question such as "How are you?" It would make no sense to follow a student around counting the number of times he or she says "Fine, how are you?" "Fine, how are you?" "Fine, how are you?" without a suitable question having been asked. You need a question each time. You cannot get a rate of the student's behavior because how often the student responds depends on how often questions are asked.

Another kind of behavior requiring trials is imitation. You cannot get a rate of imitating, because a student must wait for someone to demonstrate an action before imitating it. For these skills, you have to follow a restricted format, although the "trials" can be interspersed into activities such as recess or lunch time rather than presented one after another while sitting at a table (see Chapter 8).

In addition to percentage of trials correct, Discrete Trial Training often records trials to criterion.

Trials to Criterion and Its Weakness

As mentioned above, trials to criterion is the number of times a student responds to a task or question until successfully meeting a set performance standard. The problem with this measure is that, unless the number of "trials" is very small, you do not have good teaching. Any number more than one or two trials to criterion means that the student is mostly *failing* (always a sign to change procedures): 24 trials to criterion for tying shoe laces means that 23 times the student did not succeed. That is poor instruction. Chapter 8 discusses ways to break down complex behavior into achievable steps that let students nearly always succeed as they progress.

A second disadvantage of trials to criterion is that the criterion rarely involves the fluency needed for performance to last. If a particular rate is targeted, you should measure rate to begin with. Then you will see day-to-day improvement, not one failure after another. You can still set a final criterion. With graphing, you can even predict when that target will be met (see Chapter 6).

A "trial" does not name a specific student action. If you were counting the number of "trials to criterion" for basketball, you would have to explain what actions you call "trials," and what performance level is set as the criterion. Perhaps you were counting the number of throws that fail to go in before a student makes a basket. Why not say so? The direct measure does just that. For teaching a beginner, instead of number of throws until the first ball goes into a standard hoop, you could insure higher rates of success by starting with a lighter or smaller ball or a lower hoop or both.

Percent of Intervals

Some behavior occurs now and then with different durations. For example, a child may suck her thumb, sometimes for a long period, sometimes for a short time. Instead of recording the beginning and end of each episode of her behavior, you might spot check her thumb sucking. That is the rational behind *interval recording*. All interval recording methods divide observation time into intervals often as short as 10 or 15 seconds. At the end of each interval a mark is made indicating whether or not the behavior:

1. occurred at all during the time observed for *partial-interval* recording
2. occurred during the entire interval for *whole-interval* recording or
3. was occurring at the end of the interval for *momentary interval* recording, also called *momentary time sampling*.

Interval records are converted to percentage of intervals in which the behavior occurred, with all of the disadvantages of percentage. Since interval recording methods are labor intensive, they are used more by researchers than by teachers. You might, however, be asked to check whether thumb-sucking in a child is occurring every 10 minutes when a cell phone vibrates in your pocket. You would then be doing momentary interval recording or momentary **time sampling**.

Interval recording is often used for problem behavior like thumb-sucking. As an alternative, *positive* behavior like writing might be recorded. Whenever possible, recording (and thus attending to) only the positive actions of students is better than recording behavior that needs to be decreased. Concentrating on behavior to build shifts treatment methods to reinforcement. Even with interval recording, the targeted behavior can be a positive one. A summary of recording methods is shown in Table 5.3.

Table 5.3 Recording methods

Name and description	Example	Comments
Count: The number of discrete actions.	Luciana completed 5 problems.	Direct measure, but lacks precision that a time dimension would give.
Duration: The length of time from start to finish of an action.	Maria held a high A for 30 seconds.	Direct measure: Useful in physical performance. Often used for inappropriate behavior such as tantrums.
Latency: The time from the presentation of a task or question to the response.	Sandra took 4 seconds to answer the question after she was called on. The latency was 4 seconds.	Direct measure: Slow latencies, like the one in the example, usually indicate weak behavior.
Percent correct: The number of correct divided by the total completed multiplied by 100.	David scored 4 out of 5 for 80% correct.	Indirect measure: The most common measure of academic performance, but less sensitive than rate.

(Continued)

Name and description	Example	Comments
Percent of occurrence or percent of opportunity: The number of actions taken divided by the opportunities to respond multiplied by 100.	Joe raised his hand to answer 4 of the 5 questions the teacher asked, taking 80% of the opportunities available.	Indirect measure: Appropriate when opportunities to respond are limited as in recording conversational skills or performance in a class discussion.
Rate/Frequency: The number of times an action occurred divided by the number of minutes, hours, or other unit of time during which they were counted.	Alan answered 40 problems correctly in two minutes, for a rate of 20 per minute correct.	Direct measure: The most accurate and sensitive measure of academic performance.
Time on task: The number of minutes a student is judged to be "working or paying attention." Usually converted to percent.	Joey was busy writing from 10:15 to 10:20 and from 10:45 to 11:00 or 20 minutes out of the 30-minute period, or 67% "on task."	Indirect measure: Requires the judgment of an observer. May encourage slowing down to fill time.
Interval Recording/Time Sampling: At specified times or during specified intervals, the behavior of the student is recorded as: 1) having occurred during the **whole interval**. 2) at any time during the interval (**partial-interval recording**). 3) at the moment the time period ends (**momentary time sampling**). All interval recording methods are usually converted into percentage of intervals.	Pam's behavior is checked every five seconds. The observer checks "writing" if Pam was writing: 1) throughout each whole interval. 2) at any time during each interval. 3) at the moment each time ends (when a timer rings). With whatever method is used, if *writing* gets 35 checks and *not writing* occurs 15 times out of the total of 50 intervals, 70% of intervals would be recorded for the percentage of "writing."	Indirect measure: Not practical for a teacher to do while teaching. The proportion of time a behavior actually occurred is underestimated by **whole interval** recording methods and overestimated by **partial-interval** recording methods. **Momentary time sampling** has been effective when students record their own positive behavior each time a timer goes off.

PRECISION TEACHING FOR QUICK SNAPSHOTS OF FLUENCY AND CELERATION

With all of these alternatives, you might like to visualize how the recommended daily monitoring of rate works in a classroom. For this example, we return to the teacher of the high school algebra class and how she solved her students' lack of fluency in basic multiplication and division.

Example: Precision Teaching in a High School Algebra Class

Here again is the scenario: the high school algebra class is in a mid-sized public school in a mid-sized town.[13] There are upwards of 20 students in the class, and it is scheduled right after gym. The teacher, whom we will call Ms. Jones, notices that her students are having trouble with the multiplication and division they were supposed to already know cold. Time for Precision Teaching.

Ms. Jones makes up (or downloads copies of) five paper quizzes, each with the 100 single-digit times single-digit combinations in random order. She begins the next class by handing out the first quiz, telling the students to keep it face down.

"We're going to do a short timed quiz," she tells her students. "There are more problems here than you can possibly do in the minute you will have. You are not supposed to be able to finish them all. Now write your name on the back." She notices Patrick searching in his backpack.

"Patrick, do you have a pencil?"

She makes sure everyone has a pencil ready.

"When I say go, turn the paper over and do as many problems as you can until I say stop."

The class is quiet!

"Ready (pause), set (pause), GO."

There is a flurry of papers turning over, then only the sound of pencils scribbling away. The minute seems like a long time to Ms. Jones because this is the first time she has done this kind of timing.

"Stop." There is a smattering of "Oh nos" and other comments.

"OK. Now compare answers with the person next to you." Ms. Jones starts walking among the desks.

"Ms. Jones," a student asks, "Isn't seven times eight 58?"

A nearby student answers, "No, you dummy. It's 56."

Before Ms. Jones can respond, the first student says, "Oh, yeah."

An answer key is given to one student who has completed more problems than anyone else so he can check his last answers.

When the students have checked their answers, Ms. Jones asks them to count how many they got *correct*, and to write it on the corner of the quiz. She checks that students have done so. Then she has them count the number they multiplied incorrectly, and to write that down, too. Several students begin counting the problems they have not done as incorrect, so Ms. Jones tells them to count only the ones they *completed*, not any of the ones they have not reached.

"We'll do this again on Friday," Ms. Jones says. It is 20 past the hour. Ms. Jones thinks, "That is about how long it usually takes to settle down this class after gym."

On Friday, the procedure takes only 10 minutes. On Monday, the students grab a quiz as soon as they come in and sit down looking at Ms. Jones for the start signal. After the quiz, Ms. Jones explains the special charts on which they will graph their progress (see Chapter 6). Her students graph their first three scores. Most have shown improvement. Some have reached enough fluency to "graduate" to the division sheet. Ms. Jones worries about what to do when these students master division. Could she give them free time? The Precision Teaching procedure takes only a few minutes. Or should she let them make up a series of algebra sheets for themselves? The rest of the class could eventually use algebra practice too. She decides to have students make up practice worksheets on algebra that gradually increase in difficulty.

If you give a one-minute timing on practically any skill your students are supposed to know, you may be surprised at the results. Many teachers are amazed at how poorly some students do and at how well others perform. Student attitudes towards the timings also sometimes surprise teachers. Often, once a routine is established, including the charting discussed in the next chapter, students often ask for their Precision Teaching timings if you forget, or if a substitute is teaching your class. If, however, your students seem to be resistant, the first thing to check is the design of your Precision Teaching worksheets. Precision Teaching exercises should be readily accepted, if not actually fun.

Designing Worksheets for Precision Teaching
While more details about the design of worksheets are in Chapter 9, a few suggestions are presented here. The requirement for more problems than anyone can complete has already been mentioned. The examples so far all have answers that are either correct or incorrect. You can also have students select the best example from a list like the first Concept Check in Chapter 4. When students check their responses to this kind of worksheet, they often discuss disagreements, leading to clarifications that are needed.

The main problem in design is picking the right level of skill. Are students working slowly? Do some stop working before the time is up? Your worksheet is too hard if so. Change to an intermediate step or to a different format. If you have a sequence of sheets, you can have each student working at his or her own level. Still, you must make sure that whatever sheet each student gets permits working rapidly.

Are students improving overall from class to class? If not, changing the design of worksheets can help. One high school teacher gave his social studies class blank maps of the United States. The task was to write in all the names of the states and their capitals. After filling in two or three states many students stopped, way before the time was up. By the third day, they were in open revolt. Another teacher recommended a different format. He suggested putting state names in rows with four city names beneath each and asking students to circle the city that was the capital of the state at the top. With that format students began improving immediately and enjoyed their new timed worksheets.

SUMMARY

There should be a measurement parallel to Occam's razor. Occam's razor says, "the simplest explanation is best." The measurement parallel would say, "the most direct measure is best." Behavior moves through time, and thus requires a time element for accurate portrayal. The closer a number is to representing the flow of actions over time, the more clearly numbers reveal changes that are occurring.

Not everything must be recorded. However, there are always some skills for which student progress is critical. They may be prerequisites or component skills on which progress in a field depends. Although prerequisites are supposed to have been taught in a prior class, you may have to teach missing skills. Beyond prerequisites, there are always concepts, manipulative skills, computations, problem-solving skills, or other basics needed to become competent in the subjects you teach. It is your job to move students towards mastery. To avoid wasting time in activities that are not improving performance, you must assess the effectiveness of activities you use. Monitoring student behavior frequently is the only way to track progress and to do so in time to make adjustments in instruction if they are needed.

Gathering data does not detract from teaching; it is an essential *part* of teaching. This chapter has recommended ways to assess rate of performance over time as an unobtrusive part of the daily activities of a class. Not only will this benefit your students, it will let you find out what you do that is most effective and what strategies you should change. Good measurement lets you see individual changes in fluency of performance over time, and that is the most sensitive and precise measure we have of learning.

CONCEPT CHECKS
Identifying Recording Methods (Objective A)

DIRECTIONS: Name the main kind of recording illustrated in each description below, using:

TT for Time on Task
PC for Percentage Correct
D for Duration
L for Latency
R for Rate or frequency
OT for Opportunities Taken (out of a number given)
I for Interval based measures

1. A driving simulator records .5 seconds between the time a pedestrian is flashed on the screen and the driver takes his foot off the accelerator.
2. A student can read 30 words a minute.
3. During art class, a student worked here and there on his sculpture, for a total of 15 minutes in all.
4. A student answered 15 questions (some correctly, some not) out of the 20 times he was called upon.
5. You spot-check a student every 20 seconds and record whether you saw him writing during that interval.
6. Roger Bannister broke the four-minute mile in 1954.
7. A score of four right answers out of five answers is converted to 80.
8. A student answers a question, but it takes him 20 seconds to respond.
9. Each five minutes, you record a + if a student is singing along with the others, or 0 if he is not.
10. The teenager sat on a flagpole for 14 hours before coming down.

Calculating Rate (Objective B)

DIRECTIONS: Using the data collected by a seventh-grader below, write the rate per minute of Mr. Talker's saying each of the following. Include "per minute" or "a minute" with each number to show that it is a frequency (or rate). Calculating to 2 significant digits is fine.

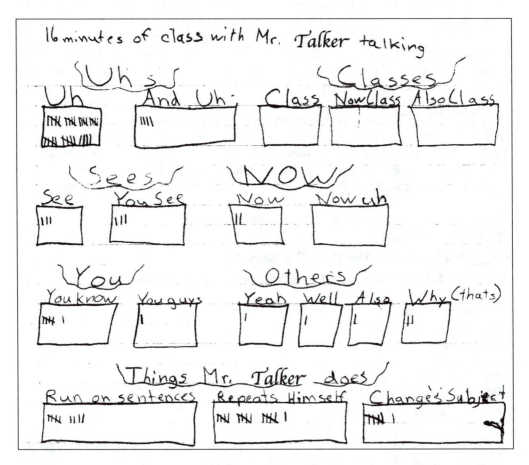

1. Uh
2. And Uh
3. See
4. You see
5. Now
6. Now uh
7. You know
8. You guys
9. Run on sentences
10. Repeats himself

Direct and Indirect Measures (Objective C)

DIRECTIONS: Write **D** for Direct or **I** for Indirect to indicate which kind of measure each item exemplifies.

1. A score of 18 on an opinion checklist
2. 19 steps taken
3. An IQ of 114
4. 120 words pronounced correctly of the 220 works on the Dolch list of common words
5. Three offers of help
6. 16 cherries eaten
7. Three homework problems done
8. An SAT score of 620
9. 80% correct on a paper
10. An English Language Proficiency score of 950.

Counting Period Ceilings (Objective E)

DIRECTIONS: For each of the following, calculate the counting period ceilings or write "none" if there is no ceiling imposed by the task.

1. The number of steps taken around a circular track in a one-minute timing.
2. The number of items out of 20 items that are completed in a one-minute timing.
3. The number of items completed on a computer program that has five seconds of entertainment between each problem.
4. It takes a student 10 seconds to get a ball for her next tennis serve during a one-minute timing of number of serves per minute.
5. The number of original uses of wood written in a one-minute timing.

ANALYSIS PROBLEMS

1. Changing Discrete Trial Procedures Into Learning Activities That Permit Rate Measures (Objective D)

A teacher is tutoring an individual student to name colors in a "trial" format. The student is presented with three blocks, one of each color of red, blue, and yellow. The student is asked, "Hand me the **red** block." If correct, the teacher says, "Good job." If incorrect, the teacher prompts by repeating "the **red** one" and by replacing the incorrect block a bit behind the other two until the correct one is handed to her. The blocks are rearranged and the student is again asked "Hand me the red block."

Describe how you would redesign the color-naming lesson so that you could get a rate measure of the student's performance, including:

the entering behavior of the student for which the exercise is designed
the setting and materials needed
the behavior the student will engage in and
directions for conducting the exercise.

2. Designing Precision Teaching Worksheets (Objective F)

Design a Precision Teaching worksheet or exercise to teach and evaluate fluency in an important skill for a course you are teaching or might someday teach. Make sure that there are sufficient items so that there is no problem with a record ceiling.

ANSWERS FOR CONCEPT CHECKS

Identifying Recording Methods

1. **L**—Latency.
2. **R**—Rate (or frequency).
3. **TT**—Time on Task.
4. **OT**—Opportunities Taken. (This is not percentage correct, since the number included answers that were not correct. They were still opportunities taken.)
5. **I**—I for Interval based. (This is partial interval recording.)
6. **R**—Rate.
7. **PC**—Percentage Correct.
8. **L**—Latency.
9. **I**—Interval based. (This is momentary interval recording, also called time sampling.)
10. **D**—Duration.

Calculating Rate

1. Uh: 34/16 = 2.125 a minute (or 2.1 per minute) Rates with whole numbers are usually rounded to no more than one decimal point or none, since differences that small are insignificant.
2. And Uh: .25 per minute or .3 a minute. (Precision Teachers usually round to the first significant digit.)
3. See: .1875 per minute or .2 per minute.
4. You see: .1875 a minute or .2 per minute. (When you have calculated one, you have the rate for other counts that are identical.)
5. Now: .125 per minute or .1 per minute. (A rate of .1 is one tenth of an action per minute, or one every 10 minutes, not a very high rate.)
6. Now uh: 0 per minute. (Zero divided by any number is zero.)
7. You know: .375 a minute or .4 a minute
8. You guys: .0625 per minute or .06 per minute
9. Run on sentences: .5625 a minute or .6 a minute (.5 is once every two minutes.)
10. Repeats himself: one per minute or once a minute. (16/16 is an easy one. Mr. Talker repeats himself on the average of once a minute: an indication that students aren't listening the first time.)

Direct and Indirect Measures

1. **I**—Indirect
2. **D**—Direct
3. **I**—Indirect
4. **D**—Direct
5. **D**—Direct
6. **D**—Direct

7. **D**—Direct
8. **I**—Indirect
9. **I**—Indirect
10. **I**—Indirect

Counting Period Ceilings

1. None—The task poses no limit on how many steps the individual could take.
2. 20 per minute is the counting period ceiling. No one can do more than the 20 problems given.
3. 12 per minute is the ceiling. Even with instantaneous responding, with five seconds between each problem, a student cannot do more than 12 a minute (since there are 12 five-second intervals in one minute).
4. Six per minute is the counting period ceiling. The student has only six 10-seconds in a minute so he or she cannot perform faster than that.
5. None—While a student might eventually reach a physical limit to his or her speed of writing, the task does not restrict how many uses a student can write in a minute.

MAKING PROGRESS VISIBLE: CHARTING METHODS

"The farther back you can look, the farther forward you are likely to see."

Winston Churchill

OVERVIEW

As a teacher, you need to monitor individual student progress. Through the pictorial representations that charts and graphs provide, you can not only see how rapidly each student is improving, but also project into the future. This chapter looks at various graphic data displays and which purposes each best serve.

OBJECTIVES

By the end of this chapter you should be able to:

A. Name the most appropriate kind of display for a given purpose, using:

"Gee Whiz" graph
Percentage graph
Cumulative graph or cumulative record
Equal interval bar graph
Equal interval line graph
Standard Celeration Chart.

B. Use example graphs of the types above to fill in information about what they do and do not show.
C. Fill in words that describe general characteristics of the graphs above.
D. Plot data on the Standard Celeration Chart at a speed of 20 per minute with no errors.
E. Identify which learning pictures show changes in speed and/or accuracy and/or 100% correct.

WHY GRAPH?

With many students or many classes or even many skills to teach to one student, how can you remember where each student's performance is, where it is progressing satisfactorily, and where change in instruction is required? You can pull information out of a string of numbers, but that takes up valuable time. Graphing permits you to assess progress instantaneously and to estimate where performance will go in the future.

Revealing Details of Progress

Take, for example, the following data for Darsi's multiplication (Table 6.1):[1]

Table 6.1 Problems correct per minute for Darsi

11/17	42
11/18	49
11/19	48
11/30	36
12/1	45
12/3	46

On which days did Darsi's rate increase most? Where did his performance dip? Even with so few numbers, you will find it much easier to answer those questions (and many others) with the following graph (Figure 6.1 top half).

The "Gee Whiz" Graph

Graphs give a picture of performance change over time. Whether that picture corresponds to the *amount* of change, however, depends upon how it is drawn. Compare Darsi's progress with that of Karen in Figure 6.1. Whose performance was more stable? It certainly looks as though Darsi's data bounced around much less than Karen's. If you check the axes and data points, however, you will see that both graphs display the same data. Only the range of values on the y axis differs.

In the middle of the last century, a writer named Darrell Huff wrote a book called *How to Lie with Statistics.*[2] In spite of the title, this was not a manual for swindlers. It was a warning about misuses of statistics. One chapter was on graphs. Huff called graphs that exaggerate effects, like Karen's in Figure 6.1, "Gee Whiz" graphs. He showed how, by cutting off parts of the vertical axis (0 to 36 in Figure 6.1) data will be stretched to fill the available space, leading to misinterpretation. Gee Whiz graphs are popular where people want more to influence than to inform. Your eye sees relative distances and most people interpret lines accordingly. A line that goes from the bottom of a graph to the top looks like a change of 100%. Karen's increase from 11/17 to 11/18 fills more than half the distance from bottom to top, so it *looks* as though her performance more than doubled though it went only from 42 to 49. If someone wanted to promote a particular teaching technique used with Darsi, chopping off the bottom of the graph would sell it better than showing the whole axis. The way a graph appears may or may not accurately represent the degree of change that is taking place.

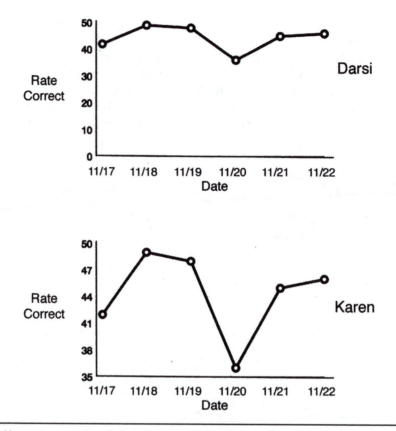

Fig. 6.1. Problems correct per minute for Darsi (above) and for Karen (below)

In order for lines or columns to fill most of the space of a graph, today's computer graphing programs generally default to "Gee Whiz" formats. They take the highest number to be graphed and make the top of the vertical axis (also called the y axis) at or just above that value. The lowest number on the axis is set near the lowest data point. With one graph showing values on the vertical axis from 0 to 3, another with values of 0 to 25, a change of 3 on the first graph looks the same as 25 on the second. You can, of course, set the y axis to include all values down to zero and to make the axes the same on graphs you wish to compare. But in looking at graphs drawn by others, standardization may not have been done. In interpreting any graph, therefore, you must first check the y axis to determine the degree of change shown.

Occasionally you may wish to exaggerate change for motivational purposes. Preschoolers respond well to coloring in blocks that make adding one block look impressive. In charting homework turned in, a graph that magnifies change may encourage improvement more than a modest representation.

Although Gee Whiz graphs suit motivational purposes, other graphs give a more realistic view of what is really happening. By designing instruction so that students make few errors, any kind of graph will reveal success, with all of its motivating effects. For students as well as for teachers, graphs track progress better than a series of numbers. They often encourage students to work harder or more co-operatively.

Example: Using Graphs for Motivating Composition in a Second Grade
A study done in a second grade demonstrates the motivating effect of a graph. Ms. Miller wanted to encourage writing. Each day she gave five minutes for writing, with students grouped into pods of four to five desks each. Many of her students stopped writing well before the time was up. To get them to write more (without initially worrying about quality), she posted the day's productivity as follows. At the end of the five minutes, students counted the number of words they produced. Ms. Miller added the numbers on a calculator and divided the result by the number of students present. That gave an average of the words written per student. This number was posted in a chart on the board at the front of the class.

The numbers improved for a few days, but then leveled off. For days 11 through 15, no number reached as high as on day five or day 10. Something had to be done. On day 16 Ms. Miller started a new procedure. She posted a graph of the students' data. Figure 6.2 shows the result. Since the numbers depended on everyone's writing, students started helping each other. If someone stopped writing, another student would say something like, "Did you say what it looked like?" or "Tell how you felt." In addition to producing more words, the quality of the students' compositions improved with the short daily practice.

The relation between performance and the line on a graph is best referred to as "feedback" rather than "reinforcement." For a graph to influence effort, the connection between performance and the display must be established. At the least students must realize that a "corrects" line going up is good.

No graph should show only inappropriate behavior. Plotting any event focuses attention on it. Being constantly reminded of undesirable behavior is punishing for students. It also continually pairs negative actions with those students, rather than drawing attention to the positive things they do. Instead of graphing targets to decrease, pick a behavior to build and graph that.

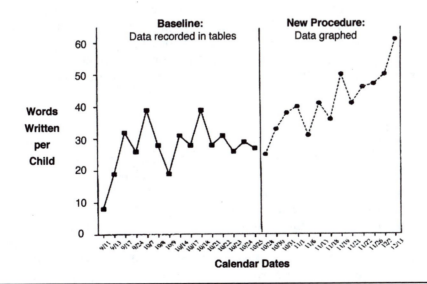

Fig. 6.2 Result of graphing second-graders' writing productivity
Class project by Ms. Miller for Dr. Roy Moxley. West Virginia University.

Feedback on Effectiveness for Improving Instruction
No teacher can graph everything of interest in a class. As with objectives, you must set priorities. What you graph depends on what most needs work. Students can take a role in setting their own goals especially when they see where their performance is headed. Ten data points usually give a good projection into the future, giving realistic targets to achieve or to beat. Graphs also help you spot something that is going on with a particular student or to assess how well a new instructional procedure is working.

The second-grade teacher who did the project shown in Figure 6.1 wanted to encourage writing and used one graph for the whole class. More often individual graphs are used. In a large class of students you don't have time personally to graph everyone's scores. In any case, it is better for students to do their own graphing so that they attend to their own accomplishment. With preprinted charts and short timings, only a small time out of each period is required for students to plot daily progress. That progress is useful to you too. You need to see the results of your efforts. Instead of waiting for a supervisor's comments or your students' standardized test results at the end of the year, graphs of student progress put you in charge of assessing your own teaching practices.

GRAPHING FORMATS

The two most common graphs are bar graphs and line graphs. Bar graphs are usually used to show contrast rather than progress over time. There is an exception: very young children are often given bar graphs so they can color in boxes, with one box for each task completed. The changing heights of each day's stack of boxes shows progress.

Bar Graphs for Contrast or Category Comparisons
In a **bar graph** that compares two or more populations, dates, or summaries of conditions, the vertical axis shows a straight count of the numbers involved. Each category is labeled under its respective bar along the x axis. These bars, appearing next to each other, emphasize comparisons. Figure 6.3 shows a bar graph designed to compare various postcedents of what the researchers called "problem behavior."[3] You can see that for 100% of the children, attention followed one or more of the actions defined as "problem behavior," more than the percentage received for materials or getting out of an activity (escape).

Line Graphs for Progress
Of more interest to teachers than overall comparisons is student progress from day to day. While bar graphs can be used to show progress, lines show trends better. For showing change over time, line graphs are preferable to bar graphs. If data are entered into a computer, line graphs also take less ink to print.

To track progress over time, the measure of student actions goes up the y axis. Along the bottom, time is represented. Except for the Standard Celeration Chart (discussed below), traditional behavioral journals show only days on which data were gathered. That misrepresents what actually happened. When dates are labeled only as "sessions," a graph does not show weekly patterns, nor how long it took to go from one dot to the next. Going from five to 10 in one day will look the same as going from five to 10 with a week or more in between. This problem is not totally ignored by behavioral journals.

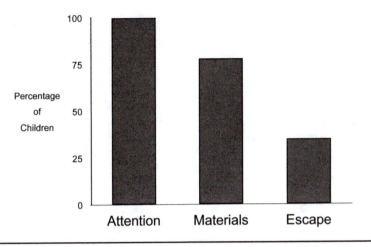

Fig. 6.3 Use of a bar graph for comparison

Paige M. McKerchar and Rachel H. Thompson. "A Descriptive Analysis of Potential Reinforcement Contingencies in the Preschool Classroom." *Journal of Applied Behavior Analysis* 37 (2004): 436. Reprinted with permission of the Society for the Experimental Analysis of Behavior.

When an unusually long time period occurs, for example "follow-up" data from weeks after a project has ended, two hatch marks are placed along the axis to show the break in time. But shorter breaks are ignored. If continuous time is *not* shown along the bottom of a graph, equally steep progress lines do not show the same rate of change, even within the same graph. You cannot compare angles of line segments when only sessions are shown.

Darsi's data in Figure 6.1 were reported with actual days so they can be re-plotted with actual time along the bottom as in Figure 6.4. The dip on November 30 in the top graph looks different when plotted next to the dot for November 19 than it does following 10 days of Thanksgiving Break. As Darsi's teacher, you might have checked to see what happened when Darsi's performance dipped. Following a vacation, you interpret the drop differently. In this case, the original graph at least *showed* actual dates. Had it shown only sessions, you would not have been able to re-graph with actual time along the bottom.

Cumulative Records

The graphs that first showed the effect of postcedents on rate of behavior were cumulative records designed by Skinner. They showed *every action* where it occurred in real time. Each action moved a pen held against a moving strip of paper as shown in Figure 6.5. When the strips of paper were turned sideways, the line went up. The angle showed behavior. The steeper the slope or the line, the faster responding was occurring. This kind of detail would be possible to get with computer-assisted instruction. Each action taken could be graphed in real time, letting you see where each student paused or responded especially rapidly. Although this level of detail would be beneficial for instructional designers, it is rarely recorded.

An early educational cumulative graph is shown in Figure 6.6.[4] This was a classic study showing how social behavior adapted when contingent attention changed. The graph shows continuous time across sessions. The solid line moves steadily to the right

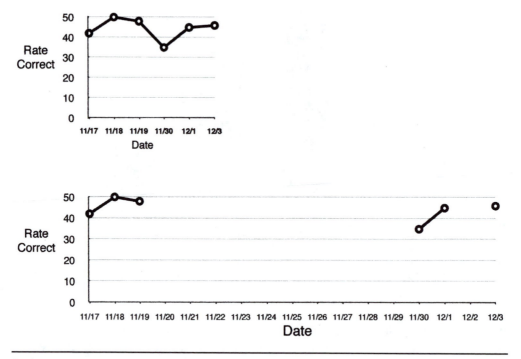

Fig. 6.4 Darsi's graph ignoring missed days (top) and with all days shown (bottom)

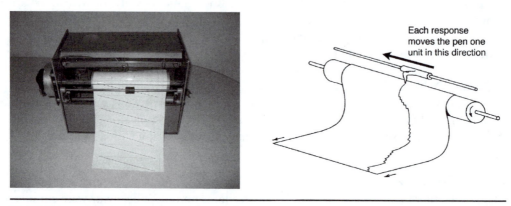

Fig. 6.5 The cumulative recorder and cumulative record
Diagram taken from Charles B. Ferster and B. F. Skinner. *Schedules of Reinforcement*. Cambridge, MA: B. F. Skinner Foundation, 1997, 24–25. (Originally published in 1957 by Appleton-Century-Crofts, New York.)

as each 20 minutes proceed. The line goes up one unit on the y axis each time Danny commands his mother to do something. The dotted line moves up one unit each time Danny asks questions or makes a comment (judged a "co-operative" action). If Danny does not speak at all, the line will run parallel to the horizontal x axis because no additional responses are added. The angle of each line thus shows the rate of behavior. The key to those rates is shown in responses per hour (R's/Hour) in the box at the side.

Before starting this project, that is, during baseline, commands ran consistently at a

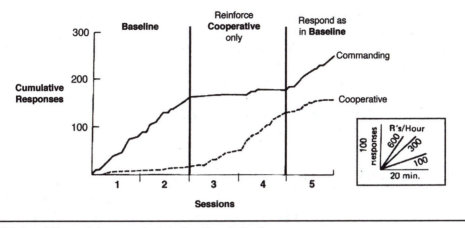

Fig. 6.6 Cumulative graph from an early study of contingent attention
Reprinted from *Behaviour Research and Therapy* 3, Robert G. Wahler, Gary H. Winkel, Robert F. Peterson, and Delmont C. Morrison. "Mothers as Behavior Therapists for their Own Children." 113–124 (1965). Used with permission from Elsevier.

rate of 300 per hour or around five commands a minute (You can see why this mother sought help!) During baseline the mother complied with Danny's commands as usual. When, at the treatment line, she started responding to all talking *except* commands and ignored commands, Danny's co-operative talking increased and his rate of commanding practically stopped as shown by the flat sections of the line where no commands were added. Note that lines in a cumulative graph cannot go down. When, in Session 5, the mother went back to complying with Danny's commands as she had during baseline, his commanding returned to baseline rates. By 10 minutes into Session 5 (Respond as in Baseline), co-operative responding too went back to baseline levels. The cumulative graph shows not only how contingencies changed the frequencies of kinds of statements, but how they changed minute by minute.

Because progress is best shown with line graphs, the remainder of this chapter addresses line graphs, though most of the same points about graphing could apply to a bar graph of the same data.

PERCENTAGE GRAPHS: THEIR USES AND LIMITATIONS

Any time you convert data to percentage, you change the numbers involved. "Percent" means "per hundred." By converting to a percentage you change the number obtained to an equivalent score out of 100 items. Three out of every four is equivalent to 75 out of 100. Three hundred thousand out of four hundred thousand would also be 75 for each 100. Percentages standardize to amounts compared against a scale of 100.

Percentages are easily understood. Grades are often based on percentage of points possible, and students are familiar with these numbers. That goes for teachers, too. If you hear that Josh got 27 correct out of 30, you don't react to the quality of performance as quickly as if you hear, "Josh scored 90%." If goals are set in percentages, converting daily scores to an equivalent scale of 100 tells you how close you are to meeting those goals. In schools, assignments often differ in total possible points. Converting to a percentage makes it easy to compare improvement in the *proportion* of points achieved. Percentages thus standardize different totals from day to day or from student to student.

Because of their standardization and ease of reading, graphs with percentage up the y axis are common in education.

Where students work one to one with a tutor in the Discrete Trial format described in Chapter 5, results are often graphed as percentages. As with problems on classroom assignments, the number of tasks a tutor gives may differ from day to day. Converting all numbers to a scale of 100 makes the proportion of correct items comparable from one set of tasks to another. Graphing in percentages is an improvement over not graphing, but there are more informative kinds of graphs.

NUMBER GRAPHS (COUNT WITHOUT TIME)

Because percentages change all numbers to a scale of 100, a percentage is one step away from the numbers that were originally taken.[5] The original numbers can be plotted directly. A count of actions (your dependent variable) goes up the y axis and time goes along the bottom. If assignments differ in length, you can plot the total possible along with the number correctly completed. Plotting both the number of problems assigned and the number completed (see Figure 6.7 top) gives two lines and looks messier than percentages (Fig. 6.7 middle) but it includes information you might want to know as a teacher. The top graph in Figure 6.7 shows that this student completed fewer problems when the number assigned was larger. He never completed all of the problems when more than 14 items were assigned (circled points). In the percentage graph in the middle, you cannot tell that those same days (also circled) were days on which more problems were assigned. All you can tell is that the scores on those days were low.

Percentage does not show in number graphs, but you can deduce percent from the heights of dots shown in graphs like the top one in Figure 6.7. On the days when open and black dots overlap, the student completed 100% of the problems assigned. If the open dot (completed problems) comes halfway up to the solid black dot, half or 50% of the problems were done. Percentages are, of course, easier to read from a percentage graph than from line graphs that show numbers.

If you want to show proportions and you also want to indicate numbers, a shaded bar format makes proportions conspicuous (Figure 6.7 bottom). Each day, an outline is drawn for the total assigned, and the number completed is colored in. Percentage correct can also be shown by shading the number correct in a bar whose height shows the total completed. The white section then indicates the problems incorrect. When students do the shading, they see both the goal and how much of it they achieved. Even very young students quickly learn what darkened proportions of bar graphs mean.

All graphs that show total numbers of problems, tasks, or events that were involved and those that were completed or done correctly give more information than percentage graphs. The one critical property they do not include is the time over which actions occurred. Chapters 4 and 5 discussed how important rate is in developing competence. To see improvement in fluency, you need a graph that shows count per unit of time up the side.

RATE GRAPHS

A rate graph shows the speed of responding, and thus includes a time dimension for your dependent variable. The y axis is thus labeled with labels like "research notes

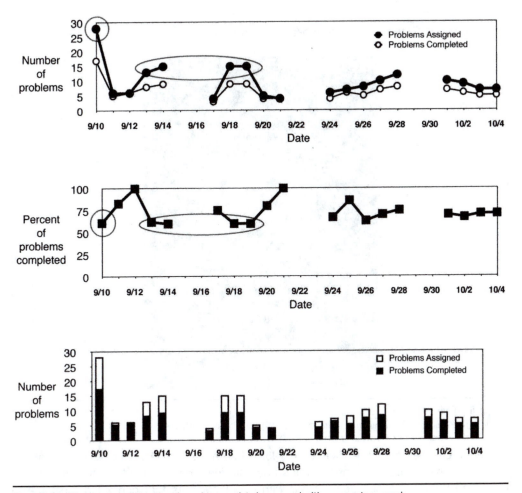

Fig. 6.7 Graphing number assigned and number completed compared with a percentage graph.
All three graphs show the same data from a ninth-grader in a learning disabled class (from a teacher's project completed in 2003).

written *per day*," "Problems correct *per minute*," or other actions per unit of time. Rate graphs give a good idea of behavior in action. If a graph shows that Sandra volunteered twice, you need the time period to get a feeling for her behavior. Twice a week is very different from twice a day.

Rate graphs are often used with functional analyses to show how often different actions occur under differing contingencies. In a classroom, challenging behavior can occur at any time and does not depend on a particular question being asked or task being assigned. As mentioned in Chapter 4, except for actions that endanger others or the student him or herself, frequency defines behavior that presents a "challenge" or "problem." Most students at some time or other throw something, make loud noises, or shove others. Actions like these become problems when they occur at high rates.

With all of these differing methods of graphing, the same data can be shown in many different ways. Not having a standard graphing method makes comparisons between graphs and between procedures difficult, if not impossible. That was why Ogden Lindsley designed the Standard Celeration Chart.

From Basic Science to Behavioral Engineering

Fig. 6.8 Ogden R. Lindsley 1922–2004
Photograph from early 1970s. Photographer unknown. Used by permission of Nancy Hughes.

Ogden Lindsley met B. F. Skinner in 1950 when he went to Harvard as a graduate student. As an assistant for Skinner's undergraduate course, Lindsley trained a rat named Samson to pull down a bar with counterweights that controlled the force needed. By gradually increasing the weights, Lindsley taught Samson to lift over two and a half times his own body weight. The rat had to brace his rear paws to accomplish this feat. The speed and precision with which Samson learned turned Lindsley into a "free operant conditioner."

In 1953, Lindsley received a grant to study the behavior of acute chronic psychotic patients in a back ward of Metropolitan State Hospital. Lindsley named the work **behavior therapy**. Patients came to rooms equipped with a specially designed round handle to pull for reinforcers like a penny, a slice of apple, or a cigarette. Lindsley recorded vocalizations and movements over the floor of the room as well as the rate of the patients' pulls on the handle. In addition to improving the patients' lives, the project yielded a wealth of information about behavior. Over 10 years, more than 900 professionals visited the lab, including medical and psychological researchers and nearly all of the behavior analysts of the time. Funding became difficult, and in 1965 Lindsley moved to the University of Kansas, ending up as a professor of education. It was there he developed Precision Teaching to promote rate of response and charting of progress within the field of educational practice.

THE STANDARD CELERATION CHART

The Standard Celeration Chart was born from a need. Lindsley was teaching an off-campus course for practicing teachers. Like a good behavior analyst, he had his students doing projects back in their schools. Each week the students shared the progress on their students' performances. Lindsley noted that in presenting their graphs, most of the time was taken up describing the method of graphing, not with what the graphs revealed about behavior. Teachers needed a standard graph.

There was an additional problem. The teachers used traditional graphs that showed gains in terms of the *numbers* of actions gained or lost per week. If Saul was working rapidly, say at a rate of 20 a minute correct, and his rate increased in one week to 22 problems correct per minute, his progress looked the same as that of Peter who went from two problems correct per minute to four (left side of Figure 6.9). Comparisons between the two performances would come across as unfair. Peter's performance *doubled* while Saul's improved only 10%. Saul would have to go to 40 per minute correct to show the same proportion of improvement as Peter (right side of Figure 6.9). But then Saul's improvement looks much better than Peter's. Only the fastest students look good when the distances up and down on a graph show the number added or subtracted.

From his engineering background, Lindsley was familiar with different kinds of graphs. In thinking about a standard graph, he realized that to see the *proportion* or *percentage of improvement* teachers needed a graph where ratio of change was a standard distance up or down. Improving the same percentage, like doubling performance, should look the same over time. That required a logarithmic or ratio scale up the side. The chart he designed utilized a *semi*-logarithmic format. The days along the bottom are not logarithmic; only the y axis shows a ratio scale.

To understand graphs that show ratio of change, think of the stock market. Say you put $400 into each of two stocks on September 15, 2009. Stock A costs you $20 a share,

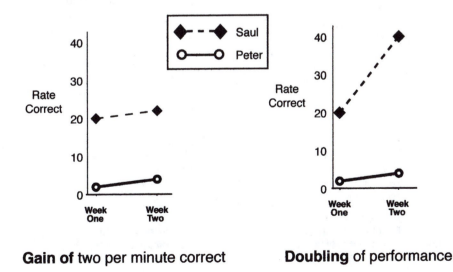

Gain of two per minute correct   **Doubling** of performance

Fig. 6.9 Graphing gain in *number (plus 2)* versus graphing gain in *doubling of performance (times 2)*

so you would buy 20 shares. (We will assume, for this illustration, that there are no commissions or other costs.) Stock B costs you $2 a share so you would buy 200 shares. If, in one year, both prices went up $2, a graph of gain in *number* of dollars would look like the graph at the left of Figure 6.10. But that makes the gains you made with each investment look the same. They were *not* the same. Two shares at $202 each comes to $404, a growth of 1%. Two hundred shares at $4 each would double your money ($800)! If you graph your investments, you do not want these two stock price changes to look the same. You want to see the proportion or *ratio* of change in the stock price (shown in the left part of Figure 6.10).[6] The ratio of change with the $20 stock was 1%, that of the $2 stock 100% or doubling. In the classroom you need to see growth, too, regardless of where a student starts, and that means graphing ratios or percentage of change.

Unlike interval graphs where vertical distance shows amounts added or subtracted, on ratio graphs, vertical distances show *proportions* of change. If you multiply or divide by the same number on a ratio scale, you will go up or down the same distance. Even on the abbreviated graph at the right in Figure 6.10, you can see from the hatch marks on the axis that the vertical distance from one to 10 (times 10) is the same as the distance as 10 to 100 (times 10). Anywhere on this graph, if you multiply or divide by the same number, the vertical distance will look the same. For this reason ratio graphs are often called "multiply-divide charts" because equal distances up or down show multiplication or division by the same amount. Multiply-divide graphs differ from "add–subtract" graphs where equal distances up or down reflect equal amounts *added* or *subtracted*.

With the vertical axis settled, Lindsley asked, "What about the horizontal axis?" It, too, should be standard. Lindsley designed his chart to show every day over a standard public school half year. Saturdays and Sundays are included too. Leaving gaps in time

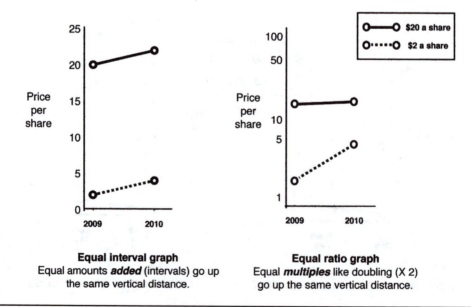

Equal interval graph
Equal amounts **added** (intervals) go up the same vertical distance.

Equal ratio graph
Equal **multiples** like doubling (X 2) go up the same vertical distance.

Fig. 6.10 How interval and ratio graphs show gains

makes as much sense as leaving out parts of a scale up the side of a graph. Time does not leap from Friday to Monday or stop dead just because a student happens to be absent. As a teacher you know that Mondays and Fridays differ from the days in between. You also need to see the effect of absences or vacations or special events. By including all days for everyone, you can see the effects of events across all students. The Halloween party that came just before Avi's spelling improved will be at the same place on his graph as the Halloween party is on Darlene's chart.

Figure 6.11 shows two weeks of performance of 21 students in Ms. Meier's class. For clarity, the day lines are shown only at the bottom of the chart, but you can see the weekly five-day groupings without them. The charts show the students' speed of pronouncing "energy terms." In this class there were four students labeled "gifted." There were also three "special education students." Can you tell which are which?[7] Most people cannot. The graphs Lindsley designed do not make "gifted" students' gains look better than those of the "slower" learners, unless, of course, they make better *ratios or percentages* of improvement.

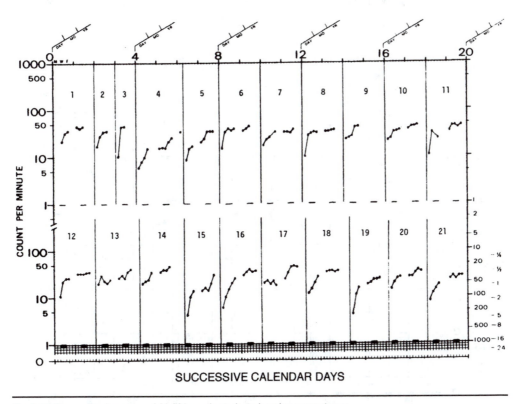

Fig. 6.11 Two weeks of progress of 21 fifth-grade students learning energy terms

Because the graph shows rate of improvement on a Standard Celeration Chart it is difficult to pick out the four students labeled "gifted" and the three "resources students" that qualified for special services. Their identification can be found in footnote 7 for this chapter.

Robert Bower and Ken Meier. "Will the Real 'Slow Learner' Please Stand Up?" *Journal of Precision Teaching 2* (1981): 3–12. Used with permission from the Standard Celeration Society, www.celeration.org.

Celeration

To show progress (or its lack) graphs must show change over time. Like the change in the rate of the speed of a car, change in the rate of responding can **accelerate** or

> **Celeration** is the change in the rate (speed) of a specific behavior over time. The most common Precision Teaching celerations are changes in actions per minute per week.

decelerate. Lindsley picked the root of both words, **celeration**, for change in speed of performance over time.

Lindsley called his graph the **Standard Celeration Chart** (see Figure 6.12). The slope of a line shows celeration. Whether it goes up or down, a given angle always shows the same degree of change per week in the speed of performance. This feature, the

ratio of change in performance over weekly calendar time, is the closest a daily graph can get to showing progress.

The Standard Celeration Charts used in schools are full page size and printed in a pale blue, so that pencil marks can be easily seen. The paper is also made to take erasing without tearing![8] When introduced to this chart, most people immediately figure out that the little M, W, and F at the top stand for days of the week. All of the dark vertical lines are thus Sunday lines. They separate one school week from another over the

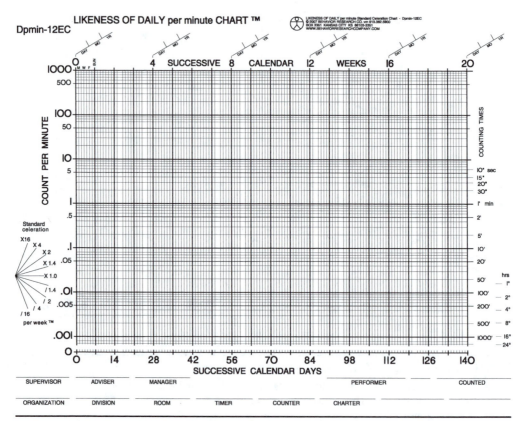

Fig. 6.12 A likeness of the Standard Celeration Chart (SCC)
Used by permission of the Behavior Research Company/The Ogden Lindsley Trust.

20 weeks of a standard half year. To co-ordinate charts, you start recording on the same date even if some students are absent. If a new student arrives after school begins, you would co-ordinate his or her chart with the rest of your class.

The scale up the left is a ratio scale like the graph to the right of Figure 6.10. The decimals are needed for timings that are longer than one minute, like 10 minutes or 200 minutes (shown on the right side). If you used a 10-minute timing and a student completed one task, the rate would be 1/10 or .1 per minute. Lindsley used the numbers from .001 to 1,000 to include all frequencies anyone would want to chart in a day. You can chart any action that occurs from once a day to a thousand times a minute! To plot action in one day, Precision Teachers use .001. One action in 1,000 minutes is close enough to one action in the 960 minutes of a 16-hour day that it makes essentially no difference (60 minutes per hour times 16 hours equals 960 minutes). If you wanted to count the number of times you had a new idea for teaching, you could count all day and you would need the entire chart down to .001. If, one day, you failed to have any new ideas, you would put your dot *under* the .001 line. The scale doesn't go all the way to zero for a technical reason. If you did not record any action in 1,000 minutes of observing, you could have had a new idea the minute you stopped counting, that is during minute number 1001. All you can show on the chart is that what you were counting happened *less than* once during the 16-hour period you were observing.

Counting Period Floors

The same principle holds for a zero count whether you are timing for one minute or 10 minutes or any other number of minutes. The smallest number you can observe during the time you are observing is one action. That minimum for the time you are recording is your **counting period floor**. It is the smallest number possible to graph in the time you used: one divided by the minutes in the timing period. You can't plot behavior that occurs at slower rates because that part is under the "floor." It is hidden from view. If Percival records a zero during a two-minute timing, it is plotted just under the counting period floor of one divided by two (or .5 a minute). This avoids the inaccurate bouncing up and down shown at the left of Figure 6.13. You can see from these data where the floor should be. The correct plotting is shown at the right.

Counting Period Ceilings

If you see data bumping *up* against an invisible barrier, you probably have a **counting period ceiling**. As mentioned in the last chapter, this can happen if you have too few problems on a worksheet so that a student finishes before the time is up, or a student has reached the top speed at which a computer program can run. By checking charts often, you or your students will catch this kind of problem. Occasionally physical limits prevent going faster, but you do not need to change your strategies for them.

> A **counting period floor** is the minimum rate possible or the number one divided by the number of minutes in your counting period. A **counting period ceiling** is the highest rate possible because of limits imposed by tasks or opportunities. To calculate the counting period ceiling, the total number of items or opportunities possible is divided by the number of minutes in the timing period.

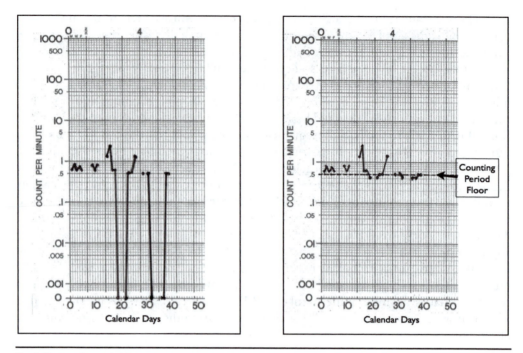

Fig. 6.13 Counting period floors

Plotting Celeration Lines

It probably will not amaze you that a Standard Celeration Chart is designed to show celerations. If you draw a line diagonally from one corner across the entire chart to the opposite corner, you have just drawn a celeration line. If your line goes up, you have drawn a celeration of times two (× 2) or doubling of performance each week. If it goes down from left to right, you have just drawn a celeration of divide by two per week (represented as "/2"). Lines drawn through dots on this chart always refer to changes in rate *per week*. The angles shown in celeration lines are standard, with corner to corner always being times two (or divide by two) per week. Like charts used in medicine or other engineering endeavors, standardized graphs represent everyone's data in the same way. They do not differ from institution to institution or from school to school.

Celeration lines show progress (or its lack). By drawing a line through as few as five to seven dots, half of the time you will accurately project where behavior will end up in a week or two.[9] You might want to predict where each student's skill level will be, for example, by the date of a major achievement test. If you draw a line from where a student is to a goal (the "aimstar" shown as a big A in Figure 6.14), you can see whether or not progress is on track. So long as no more than two dots fall below that line, Precision Teachers keep the same procedures. If three dots fall below, they do something different. Why three dots? Experience has shown that students often bounce back after two poor days, but with three dots the likelihood is slim of getting back on track without a change in procedures. As a field, Precision Teaching is full of suggestions based on the experience of teachers and on an analysis of the first 12,000 Precision Teaching projects sent to a collection center in Kansas.[10]

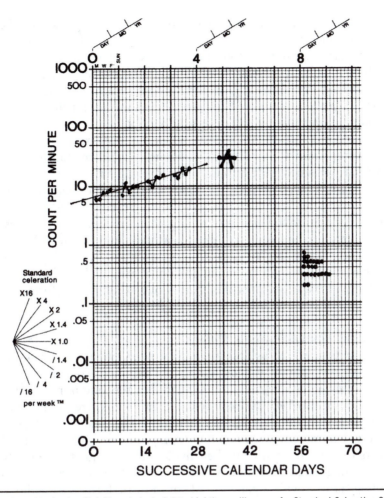

Fig. 6.14 Celeration with aimstar (A, left) and stacked dots (right) on a likeness of a Standard Celeration Chart

Drawing celeration lines through a minefield of dots is easier than it looks. While there are formulas for plotting exact celeration lines, if you just put your line in the middle of most of at least 10 dots, you will not be far away from a mathematical calculation.[11] Some dots may fall on your line, or no dots may do so. Ignore any dots that differ markedly from all of the rest (though you might want to find out what happened on that day), and use as many dots as you can—at least five to seven dots. Because most behavior bounces around from day to day, fewer dots cannot be counted on to show a trend that will persist a week or two into the future.

Advantages of the Standard Celeration Chart

It takes a while to become comfortable with the Standard Celeration Chart, but once you are, you wonder why everyone doesn't use one. You do not have to draw different graphs for different projects. You do not need to draw graphs at all. Any timing, any frequency can be plotted on the same chart. True, the lines are close together, but having a whole half year on one page lets you see an extended record. Students usually plot their own data so they, too, stay in touch with their daily progress. (See the simplified chart below for elementary students.) The actual amount of change that a line or series of dots shows is standard so you can immediately assess performance without having to figure out the axes. Weekly patterns are clear, as are the effects of vacations or absences. A steeply declining line without intervening days means a rapid decrease in daily behavior, not a dip over a vacation. Standard Celeration Charts bring you as close to the change happening over a whole school term as a graph can.

If you give more than one timing each day, which performance should you graph? Ideally you would want to see all of the timings. There are forms of the Standard Celeration Chart designed with minutes instead of days running along the bottom.[12] Even with the daily chart, however, you can show each performance manually by stacking dots as shown at the right of Figure 6.14. Of course, if you chart data every day, one day's data will bump into the next, so stacking dots is not feasible. For most classroom purposes, students don't have to chart every practice timing. Students like to chart their best performance. Doing so gives incentives for trying to beat one's own record when several timings are given on a single day. When labeling a chart that plots the best of several timings, an indication that the chart shows daily best performance should be included.

A Simplified Chart for One-Minute Timings

Although students as young as first grade have been taught to plot on the Standard Celeration Chart, a simpler version exists for timings of one minute or less (see Figure 6.15). Elementary teachers sometimes call the one-minute timings "magic minutes." After the timing, students count their own corrects and incorrects and write the numbers in the spaces to the right with corrects in the larger part of the box, incorrects below. With a one-minute timing, no computation is needed to convert numbers to rates, since any number divided by one equals that number itself. (A two-minute timing would require dividing the corrects and incorrects by two.) One-minute timings also provide a good sample of most performances without taking too much time out of a class period. They are the most popular timings used by Precision Teachers.

The simplified graph shows most of the upper half of the full graph and has space for nine weeks. While the spaces between lines is expanded, the abbreviated graph maintains the same "times 2" slope from the lower left corner to the upper right corner as the original Standard Celeration Chart. Improvement thus shows the same angle on both graphs. While most Precision Teachers prefer the original chart, elementary students find it easier to plot on the simplified version, if only because lines are farther apart. Having each day's data written next to the graph also makes it easier for you to check the accuracy of plotting.

Introducing Students to the Standard Celeration Chart

Graphing is only informative if you have progress to graph. Thus, it is best to introduce the Standard Celeration Chart after your students have some data that will show change. Five days is usually enough to show improvement over time. You might want to make sure that everyone's correct rate is going up before introducing the graph, particularly with elementary level students. That way they see improvements when they first plot their data. To take the sting out of errors, some teachers call problems done incorrectly

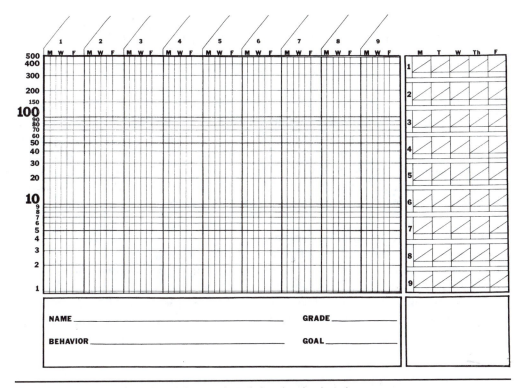

Fig. 6.15 Likeness of a simplified graph for one-minute timings (magic minutes)
Designed by Skip Berquam and used with permission. This chart is in the public domain.

"not yets," or "learning opportunities," or "problems to master." For ease of understanding, however, "incorrects" will be used here.

Teaching Students to Read Their Own "Learning Pictures"
Progress involves both speed and accuracy. As mentioned before, Precision Teaching counts as incorrect only items that students answer incorrectly, not those they do not complete. The pattern that graphed corrects and incorrects make over time is called a **learning picture**. It is most easily seen when celeration lines are drawn. For example, a sheet designed for teaching geography might have names of countries with spaces underneath for students to write the continent where each country is found. Both correct and incorrect responses per minute would then be graphed. By the time five to 10 days have been plotted, students could be shown how to draw celerations for their correct and incorrect rates. Counting period floors can also be drawn. If the full Standard Celeration Chart is used, you would have to show where the floor goes. With the abbreviated chart and one-minute timings, the bottom *is* the counting period floor.

In some Precision Teaching classrooms, students evaluate their own learning pictures once a week, and *they* inform the teacher when progress is flagging. Figure 6.16 shows a poster to help students evaluate their own progress. It shows several learning pictures with a dot for correct and an x for incorrect. The counting period floor is show by a dotted line.[13] By evaluating their own learning pictures, students take a more active role in making sure they are improving.

Clearly, some learning pictures are better than others. Number 2, for example, shows a rapid acceleration of corrects, with errors dropping quickly to under the counting period floor, a healthy picture of progress. Other learning pictures are not so good. A learning picture with only error rates accelerating (number 10) requires an immediate change in strategy. Where correct and error rates go up in parallel (number 7), speed is increasing, but not accuracy. Two of the learning pictures show errors rapidly dropping below the counting period floor (numbers 2 and 4). In general, since errors are discouraging, it is best to avoid them if possible. There are three pictures where errors are consistently below the counting period floor, indicating no errors were made. Only number 5, however, shows improvement. Deceleration of 100% correct performance (number 13) would be desirable only where a student needs to slow down as, for example, where he or she talks too fast while giving a speech.

Technical Features of the Standard Celeration Chart

In addition to a general picture of progress, Standard Celeration Charts reveal other statistics such as percentage correct: vertical distances on the chart show ratios between the two frequencies plotted. The distance between correct and error rates on the chart thus gives the ratio between the two values. Correct and incorrect dots on the *same* frequency line on the y axis means that the two rates were equivalent. When corrects

What is Your Learning Picture Telling You?

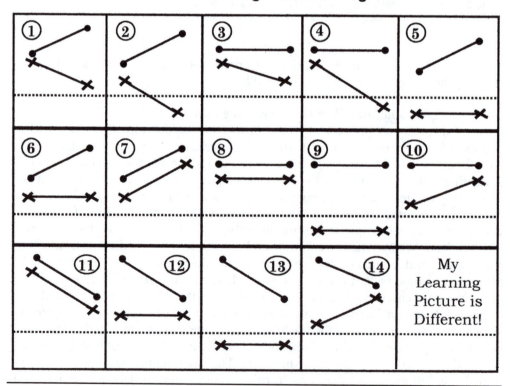

Fig. 6.16 A poster to help students judge their own learning pictures

and errors occur at the same rate, performance is at 50% correct. Whenever the rate of incorrect answers is below the counting period floor, no errors were made so the percent correct is 100. The sophisticated user of the Standard Celeration Chart can also see statistics such as standard deviation (a measure of the bounce of dots around an average value or celeration line).[14]

GRAPHING WITH COMPUTERS

Although students usually graph their own data in pencil on the Standard Celeration Chart or its simplified version, there are programs on the web that will create a printed copy.[15] Computers are also useful for regular interval (add–subtract) graphs. They make it easy to change the range on an axis, and you can easily make different graphs for the same data as when converting between line and bar formats.

To enter data in a spreadsheet for graphing, days go down the side (see Table 6.2). If you leave Saturdays and Sundays (and any other days a student missed) blank, most graphing programs will differentiate between those days and days that have a count of zero. Thus your time line along the bottom will be continuous.

Graphing programs allow you to set the y axis to whatever range of values you wish. To show all values of counts or percentages down to zero on a computer graph, set zero as the minimum y axis value. That will override the default format that will otherwise create a "Gee Whiz" graph. You can also set the top value. For percentages that value should be 100. If you would like to change the y axis from an interval scale to a ratio scale, you can use what is usually called the "log scale" or "logarithmic" option. This will probably not match the x2 from corner to corner of the Standard Celeration Chart, but it will make a graph that shows ratio of change.

Table 6.2 Entering data into spreadsheets for graphing

	A	B	C	D
1		Correct	Incorrect	
2	11/3	17	1	
3	11/4	14	0	
4	11/5	25	0	
5	11/6	28	1	
6	11/7	32	1	
7	11/8			
8	11/9			
9	11/10	29	1	
10	11/11	33	0	
11	11/12	34	0	

ADDING GRAPHING INTO A BUSY TEACHER'S LIFE

As a teacher, you lead a busy life. Even outside of the school day, you probably design activities and grade papers. How can you possibly add another task? Will the benefits of seeing the detailed progress of each student in your class outweigh the added work?

Obviously, this chapter says, "Yes." You already observe your student's behavior. Graphing is like a magnifying glass or a pilot's radar that reveals more clearly whatever you would like to see. Without a daily picture of the progress of each student, you are flying blind. You may be wasting time with an ineffective or unneeded procedure or failing to catch progress or slow-downs in student performance. Graphs give the feedback you need on the instructional strategies you use.

Every topic of study relies on a body of skill and knowledge without which problem-solving and creating are difficult, if not impossible. You are expected to help your students, *all* your students, gain competence. By picking one critical skill at a time and having your students graph their own performance (especially if you use the pre-formatted Standard Celeration Charts), you can manage the task without much additional work. True, you must create or find suitable activities or worksheets, and teach your students to graph. But that is only an upfront cost. You may find, like the algebra teacher described in Chapter 5, that you actually save class time once the procedures are in place. You will certainly better observe changes that are occurring in each student's mastery of critical skills.

SUMMARY

Behavior constantly changes from second to second, from minute to minute, hour to hour, and from day to day. Most teachers write numbers in grade books to record performance. Rarely do those numbers reveal change over time in fluency on critical skills, nor do they provide students with a picture of their daily progress. Graphs do both. When used to show changes in a skill over time, especially when showing improvements in rate of performance, graphs give your students a visual picture of their own success. They give you feedback on what works and what doesn't as well as the level at which each student is working. What better kind of feedback could you and your students have?

Human beings respond more to pictures and lines than to strings of numbers. The impression given by a graph depends upon the way in which the axes are drawn.[16] People are sensitive to proportions, thus lines that occupy most of the space of a graph look impressive, whether or not they reveal much change. For motivational purposes, especially with low-functioning students, you might want to exaggerate progress, but for most purposes graphs that accurately represent changes in a standard format better represent changes that are occurring.

Different kinds of graphs serve different purposes. This chapter has concentrated on line graphs that show progress over time. Table 6.3 summarizes information shown in those kinds of graphs.

The Standard Celeration Chart was designed specifically for showing celeration. The same *degree* of improvement in the slowest and fastest student looks equivalent on the graph. Slower students—the ones most in need of encouragement—no longer have

Table 6.3 What different kinds of graphs show
("**YES" in bold** indicates information that is readily apparent. "Yes" in lower case indicates information available but not prominent.)

	Shows *percent*	Shows *numbers*	Shows *rate*	Shows *celerations*
Percent Graph	**YES**	No	No	No
Number Graph	Yes	**YES**	No	No
Equal Interval Rate Graph	Yes	No	**YES**	No
Standard Celeration Chart	Yes	No	**YES**	**YES**

their graph lines dwarfed by the larger numbers added by more advanced students. Comparable gains show in comparable upward slopes of celeration lines. At the same time that ratio graphs do not penalize low performers, high-performing students also benefit from these special graphs. Top students in a class usually get problems they already know how to solve. Many high achievers don't see themselves learning *anything*, and they become bored and turned off by school. But with timing, a challenge is added. Anyone can improve in speed. Fluency graphs show that progress; progress that is invisible in the traditional sequence of consistent 100% correct scores. Furthermore, with timed performances, the difficulty of worksheets can be graded, so that the more advanced students receive more advanced problems than their slower peers. Thus they can see improvement that shows that their time in class is not wasted.

Lastly, what about your own activities as a teacher? You work with behavior that never stays still. Of all of the things about your students that you need to know, their daily progress is number one. Anything that brings you more closely in touch with your students' progress helps your teaching effectiveness. Graphing, especially on the Standard Celeration Chart, lets you instantly spot subtle changes in daily rates of behavior. Graphs put you in touch with each student's progress.

CONCEPT CHECKS
Appropriate Kind of Graph for a Given Purpose (Objective A)

DIRECTIONS: Two fifth-grade teachers are running a project to encourage students to bring in examples of where they used something they learned in school in daily life. They are plotting data each week. For each purpose (1 to 5 below), name the kind of graph that would *best* show that property using:

GW for "Gee Whiz"   **CG** for Cumulative graph
BAR for Bar graph   **EI** for Equal interval line graph
SCC for Standard Celeration Chart

1. the running total number of items brought in so far
2. an exaggerated picture of the data for Classroom Two
3. how close each class is to doubling performance each week
4. a clear comparison between the two classes' weekly totals for the first five weeks
5. the number of items brought in each day for Classroom One

What Different Graphs Show (Objective B)

DIRECTIONS: Using the graphs A to F below, fill in the missing information:

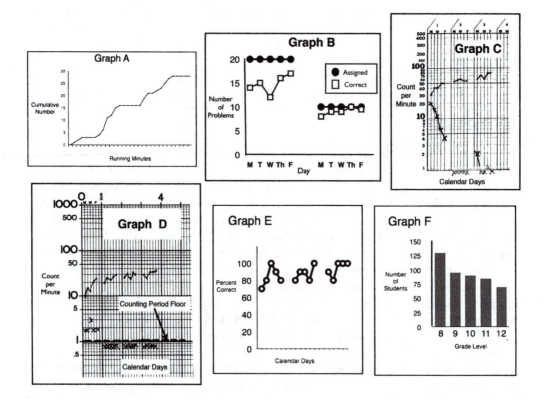

1. The graph designed to show percentage correct is graph _____, but you can also see percentage correct in graphs _____, _____, and _____.
2. The graph that shows the total number summed on any day is graph _____.
3. In graph C the student made errors in weeks _____ and _____.
4. Weekly celeration can be seen in graphs _____ and _____.
5. From the first Monday to the second Monday in graph D, the student increased from a count per minute of _____ to one of _____ for a celeration of times _____.

Characteristics of Different Graphs (Objective C)

DIRECTIONS: Fill in the missing words.

1. The best way to see whether a graph is exaggerating what is shown is to look at the y _____. A tell-tale sign of a "Gee Whiz" graph is that the numbers for counts or percentages on the y axis do not go all the way to _____.
2. Of the two purposes, comparison versus trends over time, bar graphs are best used for _____, while line graphs better show _____.
3. In a cumulative record, the height of the line shows the _____ of all values up to that point. The line in a cumulative record cannot go _____. A horizontal line on a cumulative record indicates _____ responding.

4. A number graph (count without time) has an advantage over a percentage graph because it shows the actual _____ obtained.

5. The Standard Celeration Chart (SCC) was designed specifically to show celeration, that is the _____ of change in rate per week. On the full chart you can plot a behavior that occurred up to 1,000 times a _____, and down to less than one time per _____. Unlike charts with "sessions," the x axis of the daily Standard Celeration Chart shows every _____ whether or not _____.

6. Student A on Wednesday named five vertebrates in one minute, and 10 the next Wednesday. Student B named 10 per minute the first week, and 20 per minute the second week. An equal interval graph will make Student A's progress look _____ than student B's. But both students _____ their rates. Their progress lines will look the same on a(n) equal-_____ graph.

7. The smallest number possible to score (which is one) divided by the time observing is called the counting period _____ and the highest possible is called the counting period _____. If you increase the time of recording from 10 to 20 minutes, you can see more of the graph and your counting period floor will go _____.

8. A line going from the bottom left corner to the top right corner on a daily Standard Celeration Chart shows a celeration of times _____ which means the speed of performance is doubling each _____.

Reading Standard Celeration Charts (Objective E)

DIRECTIONS: Which graph or graphs (graphs A to E following page) show(s):

1. a higher rate of errors than corrects initially? Graph ____.
2. a rapid improvement in accuracy but not in speed correct? Graph ____.
3. a rapid decrease in accuracy? Graph ____.
4. 100% correct the whole three weeks? Graph ____.
5. an increase in speed but not in accuracy? Graphs ____ and ____.

ANALYSIS PROBLEMS

1. What Graphs Show (Objective B)

What might you graph in the subject you teach or might someday teach? Sketch a graph that would best show progress in that subject, fill in values for three weeks, and describe what your graph shows.

2. Plotting Data (Objective D)

Using data you gathered from your students or the web (or even made up rates), time yourself charting it on the Standard Celeration Chart, available from http://www.behaviorresearchcompany.com.

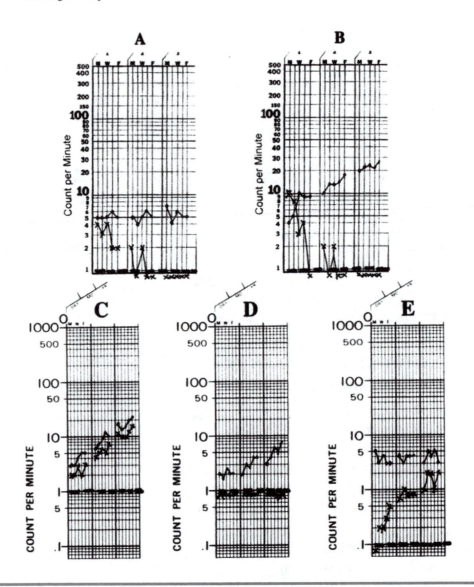

ANSWERS TO CONCEPT CHECKS

Appropriate Kind of Graph for a Given Purpose

1. **CG** (Cumulative graph)
2. **GW** (Gee Whiz)
3. **SCC** (Standard Celeration Chart)
4. **BAR** (Bar graph)
5. **EI** (Equal interval line graph)

What Different Graphs Show

1. The graph designed to show percentage correct is graph **E**, but you can also get percentage correct in graphs **B**, **C**, and **D**.
2. The graph that shows the total number summed over the whole time shown is graph **A**.

3. In graph C the student made errors in weeks **1** and **3**.
4. Weekly celerations can be seen in graphs **C** and **D**.
5. From the first Monday to the second Monday in graph D, the student increased from a count per minute of **10** to one of **20** for a celeration of times **2**.

Characteristics of Different Graphs

1. The best way to see whether a graph is exaggerating what is shown is to look at the y **axis**. A tell-tale sign of a "Gee Whiz" graph is that the numbers for counts or percentages on the y axis do not go all the way to **zero**.
2. For the two purposes, comparison versus trends over time, bar graphs are best used for **comparisons** while line graphs better show **trends**.
3. In a cumulative record, the height of the line shows the **total/sum** of all values up to that point. The line in a cumulative record cannot go **down**. A horizontal line on a cumulative record indicates **no/lack of/zero** responding.
4. A number graph (count without time) has an advantage over a percentage graph because it shows the actual **numbers/count/actions/responses (or equivalent)** obtained.
5. The Standard Celeration Chart was designed specifically to show celeration, that is the **ratio/proportion/percentage** of change in rate per week. On the full chart you can plot a behavior that occurred up to 1,000 times a **minute**, and down to less than once a **day**. Unlike charts with "sessions," the x axis of the daily Standard Celeration Chart shows every **day** whether or not **data were taken/the student was present (or equivalent)**.
6. Student A named five vertebrates in one minute on one Wednesday, and 10 the next week. Student B named 10 per minute the first week, and 20 per minute the second week. An equal interval graph will make Student A's progress look **smaller/less** than student B's. But both students **doubled** their rates. Their progress lines will look the same on a(n) equal-**ratio** graph.
7. The smallest number possible to score (which is one) divided by the time observing is called the counting period **floor** and the highest possible is called the counting period **ceiling**. If you increase the time of recording from 10 to 20 minutes, you can see more of the graph and your counting period floor will go **down**.
8. A line going from the bottom left corner to the top right corner on a daily Standard Celeration Chart shows a celeration of times **two** which means the speed of performance is doubling each **week**.

Reading Standard Celeration Charts

1. a higher rate of errors than corrects initially? Graph **B**.
2. a rapid improvement in accuracy but not in speed correct? Graph **A**. The correct rate is staying the same, while the rates are going down.
3. a rapid decrease in accuracy? Graph **E**.
4. 100% correct the whole three weeks? Graph **D**.
5. an increase in speed but not in accuracy? Graphs **C** and **D**.

7

THE TEACHER AS RESEARCHER

"For a successful technology, reality must take precedence over public relations, for Nature cannot be fooled."

Richard Feynman

OVERVIEW

Part of teaching is identifying instructional activities that work best with your class and with individual students. Ineffective activities waste your time and that of your students. How do you determine what works and what does not? Just as your students need feedback on their performance, you need ways to determine whether or not a particular strategy is working the way you hope it will. This chapter presents several research designs that let you sort out, from among all that goes on in a classroom, the effectiveness of specific procedures you use.

OBJECTIVES

By the end of this chapter you should be able to:

A. Identify characteristics of the following formats that can be used in the classroom to evaluate new procedures:

   AB design
   return to baseline (also called "withdrawal")
   reversal design
   changing criterion
   multiple baseline
   multielement (also called "alternating treatment").

B. Identify the most stable baseline from a number of examples, telling why it is the most stable.

C. Sketch a research plan using one or more of the designs in Objective A, graph given baseline data, and add lines to show what the data after the start of intervention might look like if they show a functional relationship between the given dependent and independent variables.

RESEARCH AND CURIOSITY

Why does Sandra want to stay in from recess? Which lab exercises best get across the concept of momentum? If you ask questions such as these, you have the researcher's curiosity. Many questions you can probably answer from informal observation or from asking your students. If Sandra tells you that Tommy and Paul gang up on her during recess (and that the teacher on duty tells her she has to solve her own problems), you may have your answer for why she avoids recess outside. Still you might note whether she goes out when other teachers are on duty or when Tommy and Paul are absent. You are then acting as a researcher. You are informally gathering data on a variable you think might explain Sandra's behavior.

Evaluating Instructional Procedures

Many of the questions about teaching center around instructional procedures. Teachers inherit traditional practices like "correcting" papers. How many of us really know to what extent the time we spend correcting papers helps students' writing, or what kinds of corrections are responsible for improvement? Say that you ask students to write compositions and that you spend a lot of time on each page correcting mistakes in grammar and spelling. Is the effect on their achievement worth your time and effort? Would your students improve as much (or better) if you simply read the whole paper quickly and made just one positive comment at the end? Would they improve if you had peers edit each others' papers first, saving you the time you usually spend on sentence structure or spelling? Most teachers try new strategies, but few have any real idea of how well they work. If you systematically evaluate a new procedure, you are doing research.

Example: Facilitated Communication Fails a Basic Test of Effectiveness

Sometimes procedures become popular even when they do not work. Take facilitated communication for children with autism who had never talked. This technique involves a "facilitator" teacher sitting with an individual child and guiding the child's hand over a keyboard to "help" the child select letters to type. Can you imagine the excitement that parents felt when their child, who had never communicated with them, suddenly began to type out messages? Unfortunately hand-guiding continued to be needed, and questions were asked about who was really controlling the letters that were being typed. You can probably guess how researchers answered this question. They gave the child one question to answer and the facilitator a different question. Sure enough, the child "answered" the question given to the facilitator. It was the facilitating teacher who was composing the messages all along.

Most facilitators probably had no idea that *they* were answering the questions.[1] That is because they failed to evaluate the procedure. Dozens of classrooms spent money on a useless procedure, wasting teacher time, student time, and resources that were needed for procedures that work. Even worse, some messages spelled out events that never happened. In one case the facilitator's message talked of sexual abuse and the child was taken away from his parents while the case went to court. Nothing of the sort had ever happened.[2] Had the facilitated communication been scientifically evaluated, all of the suffering of parents and child, not to mention the financial expenses of litigation, could have been avoided.

If you or your school district are devoting time and resources to some special program, you need to determine its effectiveness. It is hard to accept facts when they go counter to your wishes. On the other hand, facts may substantiate procedures you thought worked well. In both cases the techniques in this chapter clarify relations between procedures and effects.

Checking What Others Tell You

How often have you been told all about a student you are going to get next year? Comments about students, especially negative ones, abound in teachers' lounges and in hallways. It is tough not to approach such students with assumptions about what they will do or to interpret their actions through the prism of others' opinions. However, it is always better to respond to actual behavior rather than to what someone else has said about it. Collecting data helps. Many times, by counting how often a challenging behavior occurs, you realize that the "talking out" you were told was constant, actually occurred only two times in an hour's discussion. Data are also useful when talking with parents or administrators or with students themselves. Without data it is easy to get into a fruitless dispute with a student, especially about behavior that needs to be decreased.

By showing data to parents or administrators you avoid disagreements about what is happening with a particular student. Decreasing challenging behavior targeted in a student's IEP (Individualized Educational Plan) usually requires data to be collected on the behavior. By also recording constructive actions of the student, you can report on things that make everyone feel more positive about the student involved.

Modeling Curiosity and Inquiry

Educators often talk about enhancing curiosity, for example, helping students learn to ask questions rather than believing everything they see on TV or read on the internet. When you conduct research to answer classroom questions, you model good inquiry practices. Questioning is key to a successful democracy. Without inquiring about policies, citizen behavior slips into control by propaganda. In the United States, where fewer than 25% of children live in homes with both parents, and where many single parents hold two jobs to make ends meet, the public expects the educational system to teach values as well as academic content. Among those values is good judgment: acting on the basis of facts rather than irrationally against one's own best interests. What better way to teach this than by experimenting in class?

Partnering with Students

Involving students in classroom research pays off in two ways. It helps them learn scientific procedures and it provides you with help in gathering data and coming up with ideas. Like Mrs. Miller described in the last chapter who graphed the words written by her second grade (Figure 6.2), you can partner with the whole class. Or you can work with individual students. In the case of the second grade, the teacher selected the "treatment" of posting a graph of everyone's words, but the entire class gathered the data and were as excited as the teacher when the graph line went up.

When it is only one student who is causing problems, you can avoid pointing out that student by setting a positive goal and extending it to the whole class. It could have been just one student who didn't write anything in Mrs. Miller's class. If so, no one could tell, and the project helped everyone. Alternatively, you can have individual students pick their own strategies to improve skills on which the whole class is working.

Example: A Graduate Student Selects a Unique Practice Method

Many "problems" involve improving academic performance. For university level courses, fluency drills help students master new terms. A professor teaching a graduate class of about a dozen students had found that students had difficulty with the terms in Skinner's book *Verbal Behavior* (see Chapter 10). The students were asked to make flashcards. (In Precision Teaching these are called SAFMEDS—Say All Fast a Minute Each Day, Shuffled). On the front side the students wrote examples of each kind of verbal behavior. On the back they wrote the name of the term illustrated by each example.[3] Students were asked to shuffle their flashcards and then run through them once a day for exactly one minute. They graphed results on the abbreviated celeration chart shown in Figure 6.15. Each week at the beginning of class, students were paired. While one student said each term, the partner checked the backs of the cards. When there was an odd number of students, the instructor paired with the student without a partner. Needless to say, the first time a student paired with the instructor, he or she was very nervous. At the end, if performance showed a drop, the student usually made a comment such as. "I usually do much better than that." Looking at the student's chart, the instructor would reply, "Yes I can see that," adding a positive comment like "You really went up last Tuesday. What did you do that day?" This often led to information about sleep or practicing beforehand. Interestingly, some students' performances went up sharply when doing their timing with the teacher.

To make sure that the charts reflected actual data, the instructor did not criticize blank days, nor give any credit for having lots of dots. The only contingencies for practicing involved social pressure of doing well in front of peers during the weekly timings and a written timed quiz given near the middle of the semester. The quiz used different examples from the flashcards, but the technical terms the students were to fill in were the same.

One semester a student approached the instructor soon after the flashcard assignment was introduced. "Suppose," he said, "instead of doing the flashcards every day, I count the number of days from now to the midterm quiz and then the day before the quiz I do the same number of practices all in one day. I could do them for one minute each half hour throughout the day."

The instructor agreed.

The progress lines of this one-day blitz using "day-lines" for each half hour looked very much like the weekly charts of others who practiced every day. Further, the blitzing student aced the flashcard quiz. Since the terms from the flashcards were used during the remainder of the semester, there was little chance they would be forgotten.

Interestingly, the fastest flashcard callers each semester did not necessarily complete the written quiz the most rapidly. Clearly talking and writing are different behaviors. But there was another possibility. In watching the students doing their flashcards in class, the instructor had noticed some cards being completed too rapidly to have been read. It looked as though students had memorized irrelevant details of individual cards, such as a smudge in the corner, the physical length of an example, or particular words used. A student might answer "mand" (see Chapter 10) because of a coffee stain, not because the description exemplified the mand. The student's response would be called "correct," even though the student was not responding to the defining features of the mand. On the written test with different examples, the give-away cues would be missing. Students would have to think about each example. The problem of responding to irrelevant details could be solved by having students swap packs of cards in class. Or, by putting the quizzes on computer, give-away cues could be nearly eliminated by randomly presenting items from a huge flashcard "bank." A card with a particular wording would not come up very often and there would be no telltale marks.

If your students' performance isn't generally increasing on timed quizzes, you will notice a drop in their enthusiasm. It is time, then, to try something different. Often students will come up with ideas you would not have thought of, so they will be real partners in research.

BASIC AND APPLIED RESEARCH

Many writers distinguish between basic and applied research. Although they differ in their goals, procedures overlap considerably. Applied research is done to produce socially important results. Basic researchers are usually less concerned about the immediate usefulness of what they study. Applied researchers may use a "shotgun" approach, trying everything that might help all at once. That makes it difficult to identify the particular variables that are responsible for any change that occurs. Basic researchers are more careful to isolate experimental variables. Many applied researchers, however, also do carefully controlled research. Like basic researchers they may vary only one aspect of a procedure at a time until they can tell which variable is responsible for results seen. Teachers, especially those tutoring one-on-one with special students, often fall in between these two extremes.

Contributing to Knowledge about Effective Teaching

Whether called "basic" or "applied," behavioral research looks for factors that are responsible for specific operants. As a teacher, your job is first to improve behavior. Research techniques are designed to identify what works and what does not. You are in closer contact with your students' daily behavior than anyone else. Thus you are in the best position to gather data, to try new procedures, and to evaluate the results. Information you discover may also be useful to others, particularly if you follow basic research protocols. Work in applied settings has much to contribute to the understanding of behavior.

Interactions between Basic and Applied Research

Advances in understanding phenomena often come from applied fields. In the eighteenth century scientists thought that heat was a substance contained inside objects.

When heat was "activated" the mass of the object was believed to decrease, like the mass of wood when it burns. Count Rumford's practical work with boring the insides of cannon challenged that misconception. By rotating a borer in a section of a cannon submersed in water, Rumford found that the water got hot, but no decrease in mass occurred. In two hours the water boiled! After a series of experiments he wrote:

> By meditating on the results of all these experiments we are naturally brought to that great question which has so often been the subject of speculation among philosophers; namely: what is heat?[4]

His conclusion was that heat came from *motion*, not from a material essence inside objects. This knowledge substantially advanced the physics of his day.

In the behavioral sciences, the understanding of the process of induction (responding to dissimilar stimuli in similar ways) was furthered by a practical problem.

Example: The Beginning of Equivalence Relations in a Boy with Developmental Disabilities

Murray Sidman, a professor at Northeastern University was working on a project at a state school for students with developmental diabilities. He and his colleagues were looking for a faster way to teach reading to a boy diagnosed with "severe retardation." It would take too long to teach the child all combinations of printed text, sounds of words, and pictures for each word. The student had been taught the names of 20 pictures. He could point to the correct picture when told its name using the format in Figure 7.1, top left. If the teacher said "cat," he would touch the picture of the cat. He could also name all 20 pictures when each one was presented alone (top right of Figure 7.1). But he could not respond to printed words. Over four weeks his teachers taught the child to pick out the word that was pronounced (Figure 7.1 middle row left) using the same 20 words. He was also taught to pronounce each of the 20 printed words (Figure 7.1 middle row right side). The training involved only text and pronunciation. No pictures were used. Then the researchers scheduled the critical session on comprehension. Would the boy be able to match the printed words he had learned with their pictures (Figure 7.1 bottom), when that had *never been taught*? On the test day, the child was given each of the 20 printed words with eight pictures as choices (Figure 7.1 bottom.). If he touched the correct picture, it would show that he understood the meaning of the word in the middle. Here is Sidman's description of that day.

> During the final session, the excitement in the laboratory was palpable. We were all outside the experimental cubicle, jumping up and down with glee as we watched correct choice after correct choice registering on the recorder. My son, who was helping in the lab that summer, said to me, "Dad, I never saw you lose your cool like that before." Looking inside the cubicle through a one-way window, we could see Os Cresson, good lab technician that he was, sitting quietly behind the subject, hands folded in his lap, not moving—hardly breathing, saying nothing, only his eyes, wide open and unblinking, betraying his tension. But when the boy had completed the tests, Os could contain himself no longer. He grabbed the retarded boy in a bear hug and cried out "Goddammit, Kent, you can read!"[5]

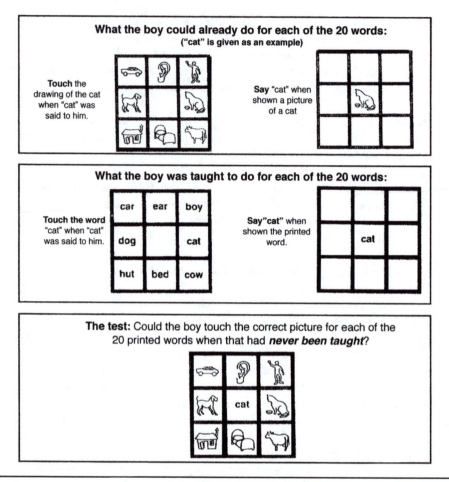

Fig. 7.1 The sequences from Sidman's original formulation of equivalence relations

Murray Sidman, *Equivalence Relations and Behavior: A Research Story* (Boston, MA: Authors Cooperative Inc., 1994). Used by permission.

Thus began the entire field of **equivalence relations** (see Chapter 9). It was born out of a practical need and practitioners' curiosity.

In the classroom, you do not have the luxury of selecting your participants or of presenting just the activities that will answer a particular question. But even within an ongoing class, you can find functional relations that would be useful to you, to other teachers, and to educators in general.

COMPARISONS IN APPLIED RESEARCH

Experimental research consists of comparisons. Asking "What will happen if . . ." compares a new procedure with what would have occurred under the current conditions. In education, many research studies use **group designs** that compare a new procedure given to one group with an established technique used with another group. Behavioral research rarely uses group designs. They will be described only briefly, as a contrast to the single-subject research designs in which measures are obtained repeatedly on the performance of the same individual or individuals.

Comparisons between Groups Receiving and Not Receiving Treatment

In group designs, the *experimental* group gets the new procedure, the *control group*, stays with the way things were usually done. Procedures are not changed during the course of the experiment. Usually the only measures of performance are taken at the end of the experiment in a *posttest*, although sometimes initial measures are used to equate groups with a *pretest*. In the simplest case, posttest performances are compared using statistics to see whether the differences found are big enough to attribute them to the treatment rather than to the usual variation between two groups of a similar size. Most evidence-based practices are based on group designs.

Because the probability of two group averages differing decreases as size increases, statistical studies use large groups whenever possible. Think of average heights: would the average height differ between two groups of students randomly selected from your school roster? That would depend on how many students were in each group. If you took two groups with only three students in each, you would expect the average heights of the two groups to differ more than if you had a hundred students in each group. Any unusually tall individual, such as a very tall basketball player, would increase the average of three measured heights more than if it occurred in a hundred measures. Very tall individuals are more likely to be distributed between *both* groups when you randomly select many individuals. Statistics rely on large numbers to wash out the effects of extreme cases. Of course, in many random selections of 100 students, at some point you might get most of the tall people in only one of the two groups. Statistical tests compare that likelihood with whatever differences are found. That is where probability levels come in. Probability tables give the likelihood of numerical differences occurring by randomly assigning individuals into groups. A difference that would occur by chance less than one time in a hundred random selections of a specific sized group is said to be statistically significant at the .01 level (p<.01). Roughly translated this says, "The likelihood of getting such big difference by chance is less than one time in a hundred."

Drawbacks of Group Designs

Even if a study finds a difference that would occur by chance only one time in 100 or even one time in 1,000, you cannot be *sure* that the difference was due to the procedure used. Any other difference between groups could be responsible. Perhaps the teacher of the experimental group was more encouraging than the teacher of the control group. Her students might have done better even if they had been in the control group. Or maybe a school, in addition to adopting the new "experimental" curriculum, might also have started an effective parents' group that the control school did not have. Randomly assigning groups to experimental and control conditions decreases the likelihood of this kind of problem, but any two groups differ in many characteristics. Any difference between groups could be responsible for results even if they are extremely unlikely to have occurred by chance.

Statistical significance also differs from practical significance. Small numerical differences in large groups can be statistically significant but unimportant. A program that is found to improve SAT scores by one point could be statistically significant if large groups were used, but for practical purposes the difference between an average score of 523 and 524 may be too small to be worth adopting a whole new program. Such a small difference is unlikely to change the number of students getting into the colleges of their choice.

Group designs work with data that are averaged. One of the greatest disadvantages of group designs is that the effect on individual students is hidden. For an SAT study, Sarah could have gained 50 points and John lost the same amount. Assuming the test preparation program was responsible for both changes, the gains by Sarah would be offset by John's losses when calculating an average. Even when everyone improves, averages hide individual data.

For classroom teachers, group designs are also impractical. If you teach, you rarely have two roughly equivalent groups to treat differently. If you think a new procedure is better than the old, wouldn't you want *all* your students to benefit? Suppose you have a new idea to try. Changing procedures midstream is not permitted in group designs. In repeated measures work described below, you have the flexibility to change to a new procedure if you see something that will work better—so long as you keep careful records of what you did. Finally, if only statistics will tell whether a new procedure made a difference, the improvement is probably too small to bother with anyway. There are better ways to do research in the classroom.

Comparisons between Conditions: Single-Subject (Repeated Measures) Designs

Fortunately, behavioral research rarely uses group designs. Instead comparisons are made between experimental and control *conditions* with the same individuals experiencing both. Differences you find with repeated measures cannot be attributed to differences between participants receiving and those not receiving your procedures. They are the same people. Your participants "serve as their own controls." The only difficulty against which you must guard is that something besides your independent variable happened to occur at the same time you changed from one procedure to another. That possibility is handled in different ways by the different experimental designs.

Repeated measures research is usually called "single-subject" research. The name came from the original work by Skinner that was done on single animals. The name for these procedures should be changed to "repeated measures." Neither "single" nor "subject" is appropriate any longer. Often groups are used, and participants are no longer called "subjects." All of this kind of research, however, takes repeated measures of behavior over time. Where group designs take vertical data (lots of scores on different individuals at the same time), repeated measures designs have horizontal data (lots of scores on the same individuals taken over time). For both designs the more data points you gather, the better.

It is risky to give names for various designs because static models restrict imagination. Nevertheless, general procedures have been given names and they offer a number of options to consider. But when reading about these research designs, remember you can alter features of them or combine them to suit your situation. Just because you start with one design does not mean you cannot switch to another, so long as you continue to record the same behavior, and note when you made the change.

Whenever you are interested in how something works, you are entering into the realm of research. With very little additional planning, informal opinion about effectiveness can be tested without interfering with daily activities. You may never have considered conducting a research project, or contributing an article to a journal. When you spend time developing a unit or working with a particular student, if you evaluate your results you have something to contribute to the field. Information can be shared in many ways including over the internet. By following one or more of the research designs below, you increase your confidence that your procedures are responsible for the changes you note.

REPEATED MEASURES DESIGNS BASED UPON SEQUENCES OF PHASES

Several of the basic formats for repeated measures research rely on comparisons between phases. A **phase** is a period of time with consistent conditions. Phases relate to your procedures. Major changes that are not part of your study, for example two new students joining your class, should be noted on graphs, but events that are not part of your planned procedures do not constitute a new phase of your study. The naming of phases is, however, flexible. While you keep recording the same behavior of your students, you can start a new phase if you change what you have your students do.

> A **phase** is a period of time during which similar conditions are in effect. A **baseline phase** consists of a period of time during which data are taken before a procedure is implemented.

Data that exist before you try an experimental procedure are called **baseline** data. The time during which the baseline data were recorded is called the **baseline phase**.

AB Designs

In **AB designs** a baseline is compared with behavior during a subsequent experimental phase. The fourth-grade teacher who was recording her class's total words written during her five-minute writing time had a 15-day baseline before she tried posting a class graph.[6] Her project used an AB design (see Figure 7.2). In this graph you can see that initially the baseline went up rapidly. It wasn't until day 11 that the baseline became **stable**. For a convincing comparison, you need a stable baseline before changing strategies.

Stability

Stability refers to behavior that is not likely to change. Unfortunately you cannot accurately judge stability by looking at the bouncing around of a line in a graph unless you are using a Standard Celeration Chart and even then you have to know

> **Stability** means consistency of performance or lack of change over time.

what normal variation is. As we saw in the last chapter, how much space a line fills in a graph is determined as much by how the axes are drawn than by the actual values plotted. To determine stability, therefore, the sharpness of angles and space filled does not tell you how much values are differing numerically. You need some kind of rule of thumb.

The more data points you have, the more certain you can be that performance will continue unchanged if you do not alter procedures. But even with as few as five data

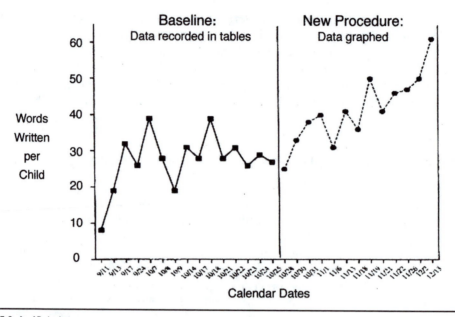

Fig. 7.2 An AB design
Class project by Ms. Miller for Dr. Roy Moxley. West Virginia University.

points that hover around the same values, you can get a rough idea of stability. What is the difference between the top and bottom numbers? If your top value is not more than twice the value of the lowest of your five dots, you are probably safe in predicting that behavior will stay in the same general range. On the Standard Celeration Chart, that distance of "times two" is about the width of a pencil. If a pencil laid on top of a chart covers up all of your dots, you have pretty stable data. The data in Figure 7.2 are not plotted on a ratio scale, but you can see that for the last seven dots, the top value of about 40 is not more than twice the lowest value of about 25.

This guideline isn't infallible. For Kit's exam scores that rarely fall below 50%, you might not consider scores to be stable just because his top one of 100 was less than twice his bottom one of 55. You need to know what a general pattern looks like. If you are unsure of whether you have stability, collect more data points. When data show consistent patterns over many days you can feel confident that without changing procedures behavior will continue as usual.

Some performances are cyclical. Mondays and Fridays in a school often differ from the days in between. With several weeks of data, you can see weekly patterns against which to judge how a change in procedures affected behavior. The need for several days of data is shown in Figure 7.2. Had the teacher used only a five-day baseline, the change produced by graphing would have looked very different than it did after the words written became stable.

When performance is consistently moving upwards or downwards, researchers do not consider the data stable. In a classroom steady improvement is common. So long as you are not approaching a ceiling or floor (see Chapter 6), you may have to make do with baselines that are going up or down. Of course, here too, the more data points you have, the better you can project what future performance would have been like without a change in contingencies.

Because the number of words written started increasing and kept on going up just after Ms. Miller started graphing, most people would be satisfied that it was the graphing that made the difference. Of course, something else might have been responsible. Maybe the topics for writing improved at the same time the graphing was started and it was the change in assigned topics that produced the increase in words written. Or perhaps students in a different grade boasted about how many words their class could write and it was that challenge, not the graphing, that improved performance. Such coincidences are unlikely, especially when changes are dramatic and the phases are long, but they do happen. Stronger research designs make a better case that an observed change is due to your procedures only. Two of those stronger designs are called return to baseline and reversal designs.

Return to Baseline Designs (also called Withdrawal Designs)
If your results depend upon ongoing contingencies, then if you remove or withdraw those contingencies, behavior should go back to baseline levels. The fourth-grade teacher could have stopped graphing to see whether words written then leveled off again. Her design would then have been a **return to baseline design** (also called **withdrawal** or **ABA design** [A = baseline phase, B = first "treatment," A = back to baseline]). If she tried a second procedure, such as introducing competition between pods of four desks, that phase would be given the letter C in a shorthand description of the procedure (an ABC design). In a graph it is better for each phase to have a descriptive title.

For most classroom projects you do not want to go back to baseline, at least not for long. If a treatment is working well, you want to keep it until it is no longer needed. If you do return to baseline, it would be for a very short time before ending with the effective procedure in an ABAB design.

More than One Initial Baseline
Sometimes you start taking data and then realize that you want to change what you are doing even before entering your experimental phase. Perhaps you decide to count for a different number of minutes, or you change the kind of worksheet you are using, or you refine the criteria for your **target behavior**. If you fine tune your procedures, either note that on your graph with an arrow, or call it a second baseline. In a project in an elementary school, data appeared to change when the researcher sat in the classroom and counted problems completed, compared with the data collected by the classroom teacher. The researcher called the time when she was taking data a second baseline.

If your student or students progress sufficiently to increase criteria to a new level, you would indicate that new level as a separate phase. A sequence of gradually increasing levels is called a changing criterion design. Since it is always best to adapt instruction to progress, it is not a good idea to preset mastery levels unless students themselves pick levels to try to beat. Using predetermined criteria, such as an increase of 10% a week, ignores sensitivity to ongoing behavior. Whether setting increasing criteria or not, whenever you change procedures, a line goes on your graph to show a phase change.

Comparing Two or More Treatments without Any Baseline
Some studies alternate two experimental phases without any baseline phase. The first phase is still given the letter A. Figure 7.3 shows an example.[7]

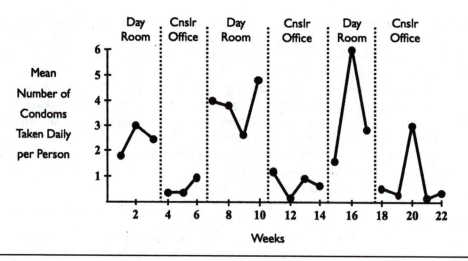

Fig. 7.3 An ABABAB design alternating two locations

D. R. Carrigan, K. C. Kirby, and D. B. Marlowe. "Effect of Dispenser Location on Taking Free Condoms in an Outpatient Cocaine Abuse Treatment Clinic." *Journal of Applied Behavior Analysis* 28 (1995): 466. Reprinted with permission of the Society for the Experimental Analysis of Behavior.

Example: Two Treatments in an Outpatient Clinic

The study shown in Figure 7.3 took place at an outpatient clinic for cocaine users. Since cocaine use increases risky sexual behavior, patients were encouraged to take free condoms. The consistently higher number of condoms taken when they were made available in the day room as opposed to the counselor's office shows a clear effect of location. This study could have started with the condoms located in the counselor's office just as well as in the day room. Two treatments were compared rather than a baseline versus one treatment condition. This design is essentially an ABABAB design because one condition was in effect for a number of days (in this case weeks) before conditions were changed back to a former condition. Note that conducting this study was a simple matter of noting the number of condoms taken and where the box was located. Many research studies do not require a lot of additional work.

Reversal Designs

Another way to show the effect of a treatment is to reverse it. Instead of returning to a baseline condition, you implement contingencies that are *opposite* to those first implemented. That usually means changing the behavior upon which reinforcement is contingent.

Example: A Reversal Design in a Preschool

Children attending a preschool at the University of Kansas were given time each day to play with blocks. The teachers noticed that several children built the same forms day after day. Part of the reason for blockbuilding was to encourage the children to be creative. Clearly, building the same thing over and over was not creative. The teachers decided to count the number of different forms in each construction the children made as a measure of creativity. If the child placed two blocks side by side, they called that "fence." Placing one block on top of another was called "story." If a block was placed on top of two other blocks that were not touching each other, the researchers called that an "arch." They gave other names to all the different forms they could think of. Altogether, 20 forms were named. The researchers took baseline data on the number of different forms three girls were making when no teacher attention was given (the *n* data points in Figure 7.4).[8]

During the first treatment phase, teachers commented approvingly on each new form created that day (Letter D in Figure 7.4). All three girls started making more new forms than they had before. Were the new contingencies responsible for the change? Perhaps. But it is also possible that the children learned better building skills or started copying new forms from each other. With baseline and treatment only, you could not tell whether the teachers' comments were responsible for the change or whether the variety of constructions improved for other reasons.

The teachers wanted to find out whether there was a relation between building novel forms and their contingent attention. Rather than just stopping treatment (which would have been a return to baseline) they used a **reversal design**. For three days, the teachers paid attention to each form that *repeated* one a child had already used (the S data points in Figure 7.4). The results were immediate. A few days were sufficient for the researchers to conclude that it was teacher attention that was responsible for the variety of forms and the reversal phase was ended. The teachers went back to attending

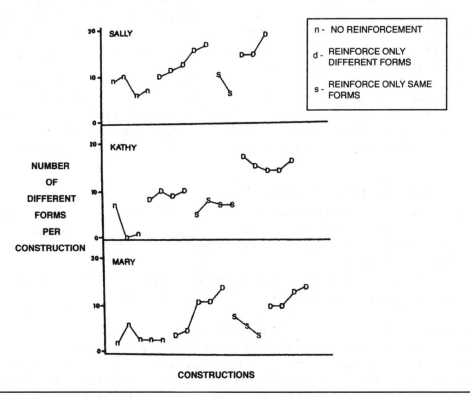

Fig. 7.4 A true reversal design
Elizabeth M. Goetz and Donald M. Baer. "Social Control of Form Diversity and the Emergence of New Forms in Children's Blockbuilding." *Journal of Applied Behavior Analysis* 6 (1973): 213. Reprinted with permission of the Society for the Experimental Analysis of Behavior.

to novel forms one more time and, of course, kept encouraging novel block building from then on.

Limitations of Return to Baseline and Reversal Designs

For many, perhaps even most, educational projects you *cannot* remove a treatment or it would be unethical to reverse it. Say that you are graphing your students' performances on timed quizzes. The quizzes have the names of the 50 states printed in random order, and the students are to write the state capital under its name. Let's assume that over a week or two you don't see much improvement. Then one day, you ask your students to come up with mnemonics to help them remember state capitals. They come up with things like "What happens to a horse that loses the Kentucky Derby? It becomes a Frankfort." For the state of Kentucky this helps them remember that the capital is Frankfort. For Maine they say "Maine has lots of sailors who always want Augusta wind." Suddenly their scores start improving. Once mnemonics are known, you cannot go back to baseline. There is no way for all your students suddenly to forget their mnemonics. Nor would it be ethical to do a reversal to teach *wrong* answers, for example, changing your mnemonics to things such as, for Kentucky "It is turned into a hamburger."

Even if you can withdraw procedures, you may find that behavior during the second baseline does not return to the original levels. For example, if the teacher who graphed her students' words written had returned to noting numbers and *not* graphing, students might have continued to increase the number of words written anyway. That is not bad. After all, for most projects you hope that contingencies used to bring about new patterns of behavior are no longer required after the behavior is established. You hope that other contingencies will take over.

When you cannot or do not want to undo contingencies, you end up essentially with an AB design. That gives only one clear comparison. Since each comparison between procedures strengthens the evidence of a functional relation, several comparisons are better than just one. A design called the **multiple baseline** solves the problem of too few comparisons without requiring returning to baseline or requiring a reversal phase.

MULTIPLE BASELINE DESIGNS

The standard multiple baseline design consists of two or more treatment-only procedures started at different times. The power comes from the number of comparisons possible. Instead of comparing one baseline with one treatment, "multiple" baselines make many comparisons possible.

As with any comparison, treatments effects are compared with how baseline data would have continued without treatment. Figure 7.5 gives an example.[9]

Example: A Multiple Baseline Study in an Internet Writers' Group

The project shown in Figure 7.5 involved members of an international fiction-writers' group. The writers wanted to produce more words each day. Ten writers were selected from those answering an email solicitation. Here was a case where no one would want to go back to writing fewer words, so a multiple baseline was done. The 10 writers were split into two groups and baseline data were taken for each. At the end of the first week, one group was given a "shot-gun" procedure: goal setting, web-based graphic feedback, email praise for goal completion, and online editing of manuscripts. The other group continued as before. After two weeks, the second group started the same treatment.

The solid lines in each graph show projections from each baseline. Taking just the top group of six writers, the evidence is weak that the procedure made a change in the cumulative words written. There does seem to be an increase at the dotted line. Had this been the only group, the evidence of the effect of the treatment would have been weak. That change could have been due to something else that happened on the first intervention day. Perhaps that day was the end of a holiday week, when family and travel keep productivity low for most people. However, with the multiple baseline, you can see that Group Two did *not* start improving at that time. Their improvement did not increase until after *they* started the treatment program. Three comparisons between baseline and treatment are thus shown: each group's baseline versus their treatment phase, and also days 8–14 for Group One (treatment) versus those same days for Group Two (no treatment).

With each change from baseline to treatment, the number of comparisons increases. When data improve only when those changes are made, you have a very compelling case for your contingencies being responsible for the changes that occurred. Sometimes

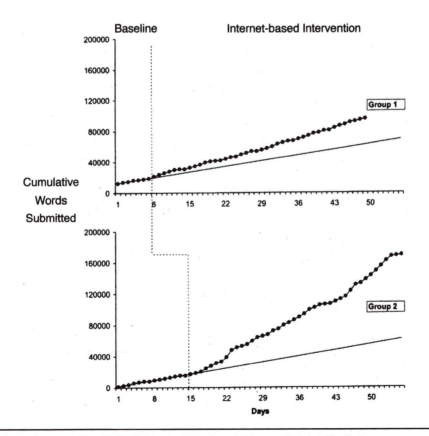

Fig. 7.5 Comparisons possible with the first treatment implemented in a multiple-baseline design
Matthew Porritt, Andrew Burt, and Alan Poling. "Increasing Fiction Writers' Productivity Through an Internet-based Intervention." *Journal of Applied Behavior Analysis* 39 (2006): 396. Reprinted with permission of the Society for the Experimental Analysis of Behavior.

those changes are dramatic. Figure 7.6 shows the number of minutes it took to teach two fourth-grade boys (diagnosed as "learning disabled") to spell four new words when the words were taught with letters equally spaced (like "provincial") or broken into syllables (like "pro vin cial"). You can see that as soon as the technique using "broken" words was started, the time the boys took to learn dropped immediately and stayed low.[10]

In a single classroom, multiple baselines can be taken across students, across subject matters, or across any other category you can think of. The word "across" refers to whatever differs between the graphs where the change was first initiated and those where the change was implemented later. The teacher who was working on state capitals could have divided the states into four zones and done a multiple baseline *across map zones* such as "the Northeast," "the Southeast" and so on. That would involve using mnemonics for the states in only one of the zones at a time, while continuing with a quiz that covered all the states. If performance improved markedly only when

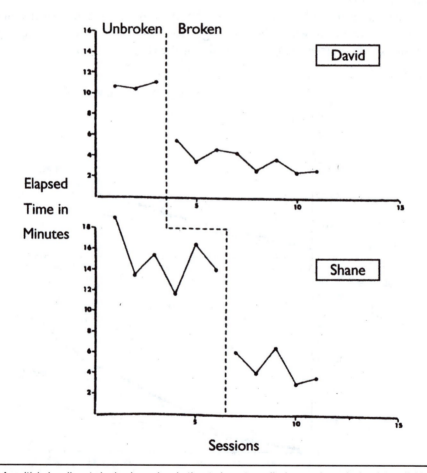

Fig. 7.6 A multiple-baseline study showing a drop in time to learn to spell when words are broken into syllables during teaching

With kind permissions from Springer Science+Business Media: *Journal of Behavioral Education,*"The Effects of Breaking New Spelling Words into Small Segments on the Spelling Performance of Students with Learning Disabilities," 1 (1991) 399–411, Ron Van Houten and Joy Van Houten. Figure 2 © 1991 Human Sciences Press.

mnemonics were introduced for a particular area, the case for a functional relation between mnemonics and writing state capitals would be convincing.

Determining When to Change Treatments: The Role of Stability

All of the designs that compare phases to judge the effect of an independent variable require judgment about when to change from one phase to another. Phases are not predetermined. Instead of saying to yourself, "I will try such and such a treatment for two weeks," your data will tell you when to change. The power of the multiple baseline helps mitigate the requirement of long baselines. Still, if possible, pick the most stable baseline for the participant or group that gets your treatment first. If, for the mnemonics idea, student performance on the Northeast was bouncing around, but that for the Southwest was stable, you would start with the Southwest states for your first mnemonic sessions. Even with the multiple baseline you must project into the future to predict what behavior would be like had you not implemented your procedures.

There is one exception to the general principle of changing phases according to what your data tell you. Multiple baseline studies occasionally stagger treatments at regular intervals when schedules require it. For example, a school district might have a training session scheduled at equal intervals across schools. The school with the first scheduled training is thus the first school to receive "treatment," regardless of the stability of each school's baseline.

The research designs described so far all require phases where procedures are consistent for several days or sessions in a row. But what if you do not want to wait before doing something to improve behavior. You need to change *now*. The **multielement design** is then appropriate.

MULTIELEMENT DESIGNS (ALSO CALLED "ALTERNATING TREATMENTS")

Phases are periods of time over which many data points are taken. Instead of comparing relatively long periods of time under each condition, you can switch rapidly from one treatment "element" to another.[11] An elementary school may have reading taught both in the morning and in the afternoon. A multielement design would try one procedure (randomly picked) in the morning, the other procedure on the same day in the afternoon. Comparisons are then made between behavior under each of those conditions. Sometimes adjacent days are alternated. You can even change treatments every few seconds so long as rates are high enough to show differences.

Example: Multielement Research to Help a Competitive Rower Improve Her Rowing Performance

A female rower was practicing daily. She wanted to qualify to represent her country in an upcoming international event. She worked on a rowing machine that recorded the number of revolutions of a wheel as a measure of her speed and distance traveled. Her performance record was periodically sent to the sport governing board. Instead of her performance increasing from day to day, it was decelerating (see Figure 7.7 baseline). The deadline for team selection was approaching fast. The rower didn't have time to try different procedures for five to 10 days, so a multielement design was used. The

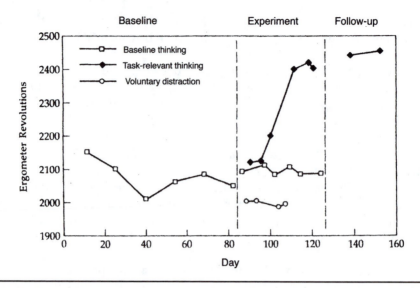

Fig. 7.7 A multielement design comparing rowing performance while thinking different thoughts
Brent Rushall, "The Restoration of Performance Capacity by Cognitive Restructuring and Covert Positive Reinforcement in an Elite Athlete," From Cautela/Kearney *The Covert Conditioning Casebook*, 1E. ©1993 Wadsworth, a part of Cengage Learning, Inc. Reproduced by permission. www.cengage.com/permissions.

"elements" were her thoughts while rowing. Each day, while rowing, she concentrated on the topic assigned randomly for that day. The rower was not told the results until the study was over, though she felt that some days were better than others. The researchers, however, saw the poor performance during the "voluntary distraction" and dropped that procedure after four days. Task relevant thinking continued to be superior to the rower's usual thoughts, and when only that kind of thinking was continued, her performance continued high. Six months after the study was completed, the rower made the team, and she subsequently won a bronze medal.[12]

Note that lines connecting dots are drawn between data points under the same conditions, so they run the length of the multielement phase of a study. If there is a functional relation between the kind of treatment and behavior, it can appear right away as it did in Figure 7.7.

When behavior analysts conduct functional analyses of challenging behavior, they usually use multielement designs. Certainly if a child is disrupting class or harming him or herself or others, you want to find out as rapidly as possible what is maintaining that behavior. In a functional analysis, the dependent variable is the challenging behavior. The different contingencies that might be maintaining the behavior are the different elements that are alternated. Several different actions might be part of what is called "challenging" or "problem" behavior. An IEP might include a number of specific actions as "problems relating to peers," counting each instance of shoving, hitting, or shouting obscenities at peers as one "problem behavior." While combining actions reduces specificity, if they all disrupt ongoing activities, lumping them together is simpler than counting each action alone.

Example: Using a Multielement Design to Determine Which Kinds of Attention Maintained Problem Behavior in a Nine-Year-Old Boy

A multielement study was done with Johnny, a nine-year-old boy diagnosed with "pervasive developmental disorder not otherwise specified" (PDD-NOS).[13] His "problem behavior" consisted of "hitting, kicking, pinching, hair pulling, ripping or throwing materials, screaming, cursing, and saying "no." In one part of the study, four procedures were alternated, each lasting five minutes (see Figure 7.8). Each procedure was held in a room where a therapist sat reading a magazine while Johnny played with toys. In the "reprimands" condition (open diamonds), when Johnny hit the therapist, she would say something like, "I don't like it when you hit me." In the "unrelated comments" condition, statements like "Today is Monday," immediately followed problem behavior. Looking at the graph in Figure 7.8, you can see that Johnny's challenging behavior differed depending on which kind of attention was contingent on it. His rate of problem behavior was highest (between nine and 10 times per minute or about once every six seconds) when problem behavior was followed by verbal comments whether they were reprimands or unrelated comments. Johnny's rate was considerably lower when the consequences of problem behavior were 20 seconds of tickling (black triangles), 20 seconds of eye contact (black diamonds), or 20 seconds of holding his hands down to his side (open triangles). As a result of this analysis, verbal statements were determined to be reinforcers. They were then selected as the consequences for *appropriate* behavior.

Multielement designs can be used only when treatments can be alternated fairly quickly and you do not expect their effects to be long lasting. Suppose, for example, that researchers are examining the effects of a drug on behavior. If the drug stays in the body for several days, there is no way to give the drug in the morning and then remove it for the afternoon's multielement session. The researchers could, however, alternate weeks. Then the way they connect their datapoints will show their interpretation of their design. Connecting all days with the drug with one line and those without the drug with another would show a multielement design. Drawing phase lines between weeks would show a repeated return to baseline design. Repeated measures designs are very flexible!

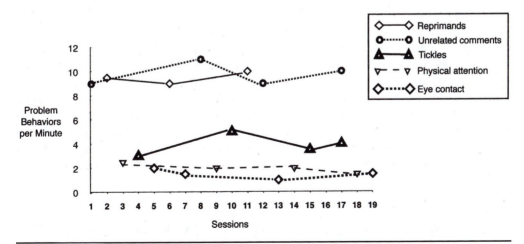

Fig. 7.8 A multielement study of the effect of differing kinds of contingent attention on problem behavior

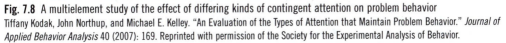

Tiffany Kodak, John Northup, and Michael E. Kelley. "An Evaluation of the Types of Attention that Maintain Problem Behavior." *Journal of Applied Behavior Analysis* 40 (2007): 169. Reprinted with permission of the Society for the Experimental Analysis of Behavior.

All of these experimental designs help isolate relations between a dependent variable and specified independent variables. Sometime, however, you may be called upon to help evaluate an entire intervention program involving not only a "shotgun" of independent variables, but also a number of dependent variables.

EVALUATING A TREATMENT/INTERVENTION PROGRAM

A treatment program may consist of a single change in contingencies designed to alter a single operant or it may consist of many parts designed to change a whole range of behavior. In evaluating the result of any procedure, it helps to have a clear idea of the importance of behavior to a student's overall life.

The Importance of Social Validity

Not every graph shows something worthwhile. You could graph the number of quarters students bring to school, or the rate at which each individual can pick out four-leaf clovers on a lawn. Graphing does not make something more worthwhile, it just makes it easier to see the effect of a change. **Social validity** is a term for the usefulness of a behavior to the student involved. Behavior that enables a student to function more effectively both in and out of school is said to have high social validity. Picking out four-leaf clovers has low social validity. Even though finding four-leaf clovers might bring some peer approval, it is not a skill that is highly valued or useful for overall success in American society. Skill in picking out four-leaf clovers has less social validity than skill in interacting with peers or reading.

Interpreting Changes Shown in Graphs

The graphs in this chapter show clear differences between procedures. Not all results of changes are so clear. Making sense of graphs requires interpretation of the changes shown; training and experience help.[14] Does a graph show a difference? A decision is helped by a large number of data points, by many condition changes and by big differences in level, trend, or variability.

Number of Data Points

The more data points you have, the more you can assume that behavior would continue the same way if you made no changes. Although a treatment-only design affords only one comparison, the number of data points in Figure 7.2 makes a good case that something happened after October 25. Whether or not that something was the graphing procedure or some other event you cannot tell for sure, but most teachers would attribute the change to graphing data, since that was so directly related to the children's words written. Had the number of data points been fewer, very little interpretation could have been made from the graph. Figure 7.5, too, gains credibility from the large number of days charted.

Number of Comparisons

The more comparisons you have, the stronger the case is that differences result from implementing a procedure and not from something else. In Figure 7.3, even with the few data points in each phase, the number of comparisons makes a convincing case that changing location led to a difference in behavior. Figure 7.4 showing blockbuilding has three comparisons, from each baseline (n) to D (reinforcing different forms) to S (reversal) to D again. The fact that opposite contingencies in the reversal phase produced opposite effects makes the case especially strong.

Level, Trend, and Variability

The effects of one or more treatment conditions is revealed by differences in the level, trend, or variability of behavior under each condition. **Level** refers to where the values of the dependent variable lie on the y-axis; how high or low they are. **Trend** refers to the direction behavior is heading. **Variability** describes the up-and-down bounce of behavior. It is the opposite of stability or consistency of performance. Actions that jump from 2 to 30, to 5, to 27 show more variability than data with values of 14, 16, 18, and 16. Both sets of numbers have the same level (an average of 16).

Change Primarily in Level

Figure 7.3 shows a change in the **level** of behavior when location of condoms was changed. There is only one day where a value for the counselor's office falls above any of the values for the day room phases. The graph for Kathy in Figure 7.4 also shows differences in levels between her behavior under the D (reinforcing different forms) and the S (reinforcing "same") conditions. Finally, the conspicuous drop shown in Figure 7.6 in the time David and Shane took to spell new words shows a difference mostly in level.

Change Primarily in Trend

In Figure 7.2 there is no jump in level when the fourth-graders' performance was graphed, but the data line starts to go up again—a change in the trend of words written. A change in trend can also be seen in Figure 7.4, especially between the D phase and the S phases for Sally and Mary. In Figure 7.5, the change following the treatment package shows entirely in slope. Any time you have a change in trend, the values that are increasing or decreasing over time will change the average level. It is *how* behavior changes, whether gradually and steadily or abruptly, that determines whether the change is described primarily as a change in trend or in level.

Changes in Variability

None of the figures in this chapter show much change just in **variability**—the up-and-down bounce of values in behavior across time. Figure 7.7 shows a small change in variability in the open squares during baseline compared with the open squares during the experimental phase. During baseline the values jump around between 2,000 and 2,150 revolutions, but in the experimental phase they vary only between 2,100 and 2,125. The most conspicuous difference in this graph, however, is the change in the trend when the rower thought about her rowing technique rather than about other things.

The result of procedures often shows in a combination of changes in level, trend, and variability, as the figures show. For practical purposes, you look for differences that make a change worthwhile. Would you conclude that graphing is worthwhile for the second-graders in Figure 7.2? Most teachers would say, "Yes." (Chapters 8 and 12 mention ways to fade out a procedure without losing progress.) Sometimes you might hope for no change in student performance. If correcting grammar in your students' papers costs you much time (and sleep!), you would be happy if your students' performance showed no change when you tried peer correcting instead. Whatever change is or is not occurring, judging its effect is critical for improving your students' performance, and your own.

Assessing Difficult-to-Graph Change in Behavior

Some improvements are clear to see, but difficult to measure or graph. For example when a teacher shifts from giving tasks where students are often wrong to steps where they see themselves improve, changes occur besides improvements in academic skills. Where a youth formerly looked mostly down or slouched in his seat or shuffled from room to room listlessly, success may change his behavior so he makes eye contact, sits up straight, and walks energetically. While not part of a project's dependent variables, such changes are important and well worth writing down.

Educators often urge building self-esteem to improve academic performance. One's opinion of oneself comes from successful performance and peer reaction more than from teacher praise.[15] Self-concept improves with improved performance. The rower who sought help reported a lack of confidence in her ability prior to the multielement sessions. After the third week of the experimental phase, she started making more positive reports. Even though she was not given the data on the number of revolutions, she felt her smoothness and length of pull was improving, and she mentioned that the whine of the ergonometer sounded higher in pitch. That indicated a faster rowing speed. No amount of assurance that she was a good rower or that she would surely make the team had helped her self-confidence. It took improvement in performance to change her attitude.

SUMMARY

Teachers are always looking for ways to help their students be more successful. If you are a teacher, whenever you try a new strategy to see whether it works better than what has been done before, you are doing research. Your research may be informal and your conclusions tentative. But the desire to find out what causes behavior is a scientist's curiosity.

Like other scientists, as a teacher, you make predictions about the future and about the effect on student behavior of everything you try, from a new worksheet to a new arrangement of desks, to a whole new curriculum. You need evidence to tell what works and what does not with *your* students and in *your* environment. It is not good enough to rely on what others say. As Skinner put it, "Science is first of all a set of attitudes. It is a disposition to deal with the facts rather than with what someone has said about them."[16] To get a clear idea about changes that are occurring you must relate them to what is going on in your classroom and school. The research designs presented in this chapter do not tell you what to do next if a procedure is not successful (see Chapter 8). But at least they move you from informal observation to a more clear evaluation of classroom procedures.

You can't tackle every behavior that should be improved. As suggested in Chapter 4, you might start by picking the one problem you would most like to solve. If you pick a behavior to reduce (often what bugs teachers most), target positive behavior that should take its place. Usually all your students will benefit from increasing that action, and they all can gather data and participate in procedures. Research is thus changed from an added task on top of all your other duties to an integral part of classroom activities. Everyone benefits from learning problem-solving procedures and interpreting what data show.

If you are using Standard Celeration Charts for timed exercises, your dependent variable is already pinpointed and your data are already being graphed. Individual students can design and evaluate their own strategies for improving their performance. Everyone loves to share success stories when graphs show improvement.

The experimental designs described in this chapter are classic designs. Increasingly behavior analysts are combining features of different formats or switching from one to another as data suggest a change. You can follow any of the basic designs or their combinations while teaching. Keeping track of procedures and their results lets you see the relations between changes in behavior and specific procedures—exactly the information you need to improve your own performance as a teacher.

CONCEPT CHECKS
Identifying Experimental Designs (Objective A)

DIRECTIONS: Next to each description below write the name of the experimental design that it characterizes using the following abbreviations (10 correct answers a minute):

AB design (Baseline followed by one treatment)
RB for **R**eturn to **B**aseline (but not a true reversal)
V for Reversal design
MB for **M**ultiple **B**aseline
ME for **M**ultielement
G for **G**roup designs

1. Requires taking several baselines and then starting treatment with one individual or group at a time.
2. Best when you wish to start treatment with a disruptive student right away.
3. Goes back and forth daily between treatment and baseline conditions.
4. Requires a period of several sessions of recording behavior prior to treatment and then again for several days after treatment is over.
5. After the treatment has shown an effect for several days, the researchers do the opposite of what they did for the treatment to see its effect on behavior.
6. Best when your baseline is going up or down and has a lot of variability.
7. Can be done with only one measure on one day of each participant's behavior.
8. Gives treatment to one individual or group, then after a period of time to the next individual or group, then to the next individual or group.
9. Permits the most rapid determination of whether or not the independent variable is improving behavior because differences show right away.
10. An example would be measuring pronunciation of "r" for several therapy sessions, next letting the child put a marble in a jar for each correctly pronounced "r," then

after several days of that, having him put a marble in a jar for each incorrectly pronounced "r."

11. An example would be measuring pronunciation of "r" for several therapy sessions, then
letting the child put a marble in a jar for each correctly pronounced "r" and then going
back to the original procedure.

12. Changing once from a phase of the usual conditions to one experimental phase.

13. There may be no phase lines in this repeated measures design.

14. Does not show when a treatment affects different people differently, for example helping
one improve but making a second person worse.

15. Best design to use when your treatment involves skills that, once learned, stay with the
participants and you want to track individual progress over a long time period.

16. Requires a lot of participants.

17. Changes from treatment to baseline and back to treatment more times than the other
methods.

18. Includes individuals who never get the treatment during the course of the research.

19. Repeated measures with only two phases: before the new curriculum and after its
implementation.

20. Instead of a second baseline, you change contingencies to see whether you can
increase the opposite behavior.

Stability (Objective B)

DIRECTIONS: Use graphs A to D to answer the two questions below.

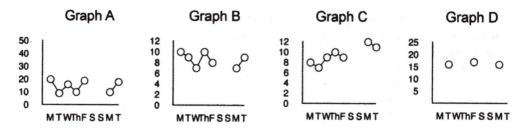

1. Which graph has the most stable baseline? (Hint: note values on each y axis.)
2. What is the problem with each of the others?

ANALYSIS PROBLEMS

DIRECTIONS: For problems 1 through 5, use the following scenario:

Ms. Kurios, a tenth-grade teacher, used a Powerpoint presentation at the beginning of each
unit for each of her two science classes. Students were handed out copies of each slide so
they could follow along and make notes. At the end of each lecture, she gave a 10-minute
quiz on the lecture content. One day she wondered whether her lowest scorers on the
10-point quiz would improve if she put blanks for the key words on the student copies
instead of giving them the material with all the words filled in. She decided to find out. She
used Mike for class A and Tabitha for class B.

1. Sketching Research Designs (Objective C)

DIRECTIONS: Fill in the missing words.

For this study, what would your dependent variable be? _____. Your y-axis would be labeled _____.

Your independent variable would be _____.

DIRECTIONS: For all designs below, assume that you have five weeks of baseline data for each student as follows:

	Week 1	Week 2	Week 3	Week 4	Week 5
Mike	5	3	3	7	2
Tabitha	5	4	5	6	5

2. Sketching a Return to Baseline (ABA) Design (Versus True Reversal) (Objective C)

2a. How would you address this question using an ABA design? Use *only* Mike and fill in the table showing what you would do for each phase of the study. Do not use the word "treatment"—instead specify what the treatment involves.

Student	Baseline	Phase Two	Phase Three

2b. On a separate piece of paper, draw a graph of results that show that the treatment worked. Use the data given above for your baseline. Label both axes.

3. Sketching a Multielement Design (Objective C)

3a. Fill in the table below to show how would you address this question using a multielement design. Again use *only* Mike.

Week 6	Week 7	Week 9	Week 10	Week 11	Week 12	Week 13	Week 14	Week 15	Week 16

3b. On a separate piece of paper, plot Mike's data for a baseline phase and then go to the multielement phase you outlined. Show that the treatment produced an increase. Label both axes.

4. Sketching a Multiple Baseline Design (Objective C)

4a. How would you address this question using a multiple baseline design? Use data from both students and sketch the sequence of treatments (taking into account that the student that gets the independent variable first should depend on stability).

Student	Baseline	Next Few Weeks	Next Few Weeks	Next Few Weeks	Treatment

4b. Graph results showing that the treatment "worked." Use the data from above for the first five days of each baseline. Label axes and treatment phases.

ANSWERS FOR CONCEPT CHECKS

Identifying Experimental Designs

1. MB
2. ME
3. ME
4. RB
5. V
6. ME
7. G
8. MB
9. ME
10. V
11. RB
12. AB
13. ME
14. G
15. MB
16. G
17. ME
18. G
19. AB
20. V

Stability

1a. The most stable baseline is in Graph B.

1b. Why not Graph A? If you look at the y axis, you can see that the top value in Graph A is more than twice that of the smallest value (20 versus less than 10). In Graph B the ratio of the top value of 10 is not twice the lowest of 7. The ratio of top to bottom values is smaller (10/7 = 1.4 versus 20/9 = 2.2).

Why not Graph C? The data show a trend upwards. Data with no trend are considered more stable than those with a trend.

Why not Graph D? There aren't enough data points to assess stability.

Part III
The Design of Instruction

8

SHAPING BEHAVIOR: THE ROLE OF POSTCEDENTS

"When we tug on a single thing in nature, we find it attached to everything else."

John Muir

OVERVIEW

All behavior is *fluid*, shifting from moment to moment according to the contingencies encountered. Shaping is the process of altering the form, direction, or intensity of properties of behavior by strengthening only those that come closer and closer to a specified goal. All teachers seek to produce new behavior, but the principles of shaping are rarely taught in education classes. This chapter discusses shaping principles and how they improve instruction and classroom management.

OBJECTIVES

By the end of this chapter you should be able to do the following:

A. Fill in terms to describe shaping and conditioned reinforcers, and describe how to use them in teaching.
B. Identify critical characteristics of the following:

active responding	backward chaining
Direct Instruction (DI)	Discrete Trial instruction
fading and vanishing	immediate feedback
Programmed Instruction (PI)	prompting methods
successive approximation	

C. Suggest how to improve one or more of the following in a given teaching scenario:

1. active responding *per student*
2. timing of feedback

> 3. probability of correct responding (via successive approximation techniques)
>
> D. For a lesson you might one day teach, describe how you could incorporate one or more of the following:
>   1. increasing rate of responding for everyone
>   2. successive approximation techniques
>   a. asking for selecting before producing
>   b. starting with high contrast before moving to subtle differences
>   c. backward chaining
>   d. fading and/or vanishing prompts
>   e. delayed prompting

Many critics of education have pointed out that while physicians of a century ago would be lost if they were transported to the twenty-first century, teachers would be right at home. While it is true that lecturers from the early 1900s would be right at home on a podium today (except, of course, they would not show computer presentations), teachers from the early twentieth century would *not* be "right at home" in a behavioral classroom. They would not know specific techniques of shaping behavior and they would rely on punishment for control.

ORIGINS OF SHAPING

The procedures that came to be known as shaping were born out of a practical problem during the era of World War II. The United States was not yet involved in the conflict, but Americans watched the developments in Europe with a good deal of alarm. The US military had begun preparations for war, just in case. In those days, weaponry was still primitive. Radar had not been invented and there were no missiles that could seek targets. Planes had a hard time hitting ships at sea. Pilots would swoop down as close as they dared before letting bombs go, but accuracy was abysmal.

One day B. F. Skinner, then teaching at the University of Minnesota, was riding on a train looking out the window thinking about the war. A pigeon was flying alongside the train, happily keeping up with its speed. All of a sudden Skinner got an idea: why not train birds to guide missiles?

To guide missiles, pigeons would have to be taught behavior no pigeon had ever exhibited before. For Skinner's first try, he built equipment that held a pigeon but let it move its body up or down or from side to side. He put this on a rolling office chair that he could push across the floor. He must have looked like a sitcom scientist as he tried out his contraption:

> "I would put a bulls's-eye on a far wall of the room, with a few grains of food in a small cup in the center, and push the apparatus toward it. By moving itself up and down and from side to side the pigeon could reach the wall in position to take the grain. My pigeons became quite adept at this, and I pushed them faster and faster across the room."[1]

After the Japanese attacked Pearl Harbor, Skinner's idea was funded, and he and a team of coworkers constructed complicated apparatus to shape complex behavior in the birds.[2] One day, bored with awaiting notification from Washington about the next steps, he and two graduate students decided to teach pigeons to bowl. He describes the incident as follows:

> "The pigeon was to send a wooden ball down a miniature alley toward a set of toy pins by swiping the ball with a sharp sideward movement of the beak. To condition the response, we put the ball on the floor of an experimental box and prepared to operate the food-magazine as soon as the first swipe occurred. But nothing happened. Though we had all the time in the world, we grew tired of waiting. We decided to reinforce any response which had the slightest resemblance to a swipe— perhaps, at first, merely the behavior of looking at the ball—and then to select responses which more closely approximated the final form. The result amazed us. In few minutes the ball was caroming off the walls of the box, as if the pigeon had been a champion squash player."[3]

Why did the result amaze Skinner? He had been talking about methods of **successive approximation** for six years?[4] In all of his previous work, however, reinforcement had been delivered by equipment when a final action (like a peck) occurred. He had never before *gradually produced new forms of behavior by hand*. If you could start with incomplete actions and gradually build complex performance and do it out in the open, you would not need apparatus. You could shape behavior in classrooms, in the home, in a business setting—anywhere at all.

Skinner named this process of reinforcing successive approximations **shaping**. Shaping differs from plain operant conditioning in that shaping involves *continual shifting* of the form of actions that are reinforced.

Skinner's elaborate training of pigeons showed how to shape new behavior without constructing elaborate apparatus.[5] As he later put it, the project "had given rise to a technology."[6] That technology was immediately put to work with animals and with children, and later by Skinner himself in higher education.

> **Shaping** is the process of reinforcing the form, direction, intensity or other properties of existing actions that most closely approximate or lead to new behavior. The student actions that come closer and closer to the goal are called **successive approximations**.

SELECTION BY CONSEQUENCES: TWO-TERM "FREE OPERANT" SHAPING

What is often called "free operant shaping," like teaching the pigeons to bowl, involves only two terms, actions and postcedents. Of course, the behavior is not really "free," but it does not have any initiating stimulus before each action. It would better be called **two-term** or **unrestricted shaping**. It stands in contrast to the **Discrete Trial** format where the student (or animal) can't respond until given each task to do.

In the classroom, two-term shaping goes on all the time concurrently with planned activities. Chapter 3 described how saying "sit down" to standing first-graders increased their wandering about, and how timing "See you next week" shaped sitting still at the end of a lecture. Two-term shaping is most easily seen in situations where you cannot just explain or demonstrate what you want your learner to do. How would you teach a whale to swim onto a weighing platform and hold still while being lifted out of the water? The only way is by shaping that behavior.

In the same year that Skinner taught pigeons to bowl (1943), a reporter from a popular magazine called *Look* called his office. If shaping worked so well, could Skinner teach a dog to jump two feet off the ground while the magazine took photos? Skinner had no hesitation. Of course he could teach a dog to jump! All he would need, he said, was food the dog particularly liked and a scheduled time before the dog was usually fed. He would do the rest.

For Skinner, the goal was for the dog to jump high in the air. Food would work as a reinforcer. But he had to get food to the dog at the precise moment that a particular height was reached. There was no way he could deliver food when the dog was in the middle of a leap. He needed a **conditioned reinforcer**, a brief stimulus that would reinforce behavior through its relation to an existing reinforcer.

> **A conditioned reinforcer** is a stimulus that has been presented just before an existing reinforcer until it becomes a reinforcer itself. The original reinforcer is then called a **backup reinforcer**.

For the training session, a flash would be needed for the photographs. The flash of light would work as a conditioned reinforcer. To begin the training, Skinner flashed the light, then immediately put a bit of food in a dish. Within one or two flashes, the dog checked the dish as soon as a flash occurred. Then Skinner was ready to begin shaping. To accurately judge how high the dog jumped, lines were drawn on the wall.

Shaping and Variability

Shaping works on variability, selecting successive approximations towards a goal. That sounds as though behavior comes in nice even steps along one dimension. It doesn't work that way. Behavior has many properties of form, direction, and intensity that vary continuously. A single reinforcement strengthens many characteristics that are occurring, shifting entire *distributions* of actions. Skinner began with movements towards the wall. Once he got the dog near the wall it was time to flash his light at a slight raise of the head. But when strengthening a head lift, the dog might also have his front left paw raised as in the one-minute picture in Figure 8.1, or perhaps his tail is wagging to the left, his tongue hanging out, or he might be exhaling or swallowing. Which of these would be affected by the flash of light? Most likely all would be strengthened.

What is Strengthened During Shaping?

Reinforcement acts primarily on the direction of change.[7] If a change in head position is greater than other positional changes, reinforcement is most likely to affect the new direction of head movement more than other properties of behavior, though they will also be strengthened. Just as a genetic trait that has no role in survival may accompany one that does, operant selection strengthens properties that just happen to occur along with the one on which reinforcement is made contingent. The ending photo of the dog

Fig. 8.1 Shaping jumping in a dog
Douglas Jones, photographer, Look Magazine Collection, Library of Congress, Prints & Photographs Division [reproduction number e.g., LC-L9–60–8812, frame 8]. Photograph taken March 10, 1952. Photograph of Skinner used by permission of B. F. Skinner Foundation.

jumping in Figure 8.1 ("Harvard Trained Dog") shows a marked curve of the body towards the left.[8] That was never part of the criteria upon which reinforcement was based. It was strengthened inadvertently.

When you want to reinforce movement towards a goal, you need to be careful to catch *movement* rather than a particular static position. Had Skinner been working on raising the head, but operated the flash a tiny bit late, he would have caught the head coming back down, creating a bobbing head instead of a higher jump. In order to shape well, you have to anticipate actions. Anticipation is also critical when working with people.

Is Lack of Success an Error on the Part of the Student?
Even with a skilled shaper, occasionally distributions of behavior shift away from the goal. It is disappointing when an action you have just reinforced isn't repeated, or a prior behavior reappears. Such events do happen.

It is tempting to blame the learner. Whether dog or student, it is tempting to think "You did it yesterday. Why can't you do it now?" Your learners are doing exactly what they *should* do under their current circumstances and history. The learner's actions are always "right" in that they are always a result of the behavioral interactions that individual has experienced.

The concepts of "right" and "wrong" only exist when you define one behavior as correct and another as incorrect. The only real "errors" then are in the contingencies that failed to produce what you call "correct." In any case, when your student's progress deteriorates or comes to a standstill you have three options. You can reinforce the best of what you now have (at a "lower" level), you can end the session for the day, or you can shift to a different behavior. What you do *not* do in shaping is to punish or "correct" the behavior you call "incorrect."

The Lack of Punishment or "Correction" in Two-Term Shaping

Since behavior is always "right" in the sense of resulting from the contingencies in operation, there is no role for punishment in shaping. Worse than not being fair to the learner who is, after all, doing what circumstances produced, punishment disrupts further progress. The harmful effects of punishment can be hard to eliminate (see Chapter 11). Pairing even a mild jerk, or a "no" with behavior during a training session makes a learner hesitant, anxious, or confused. In a dog, the tail droops. In human beings, signs of distress include squirming, crying, aggression, or escape. Punished individuals also become wary, shifting their attention from the task at hand to the person who is punishing. That distracts from learning. As a procedure, punishment can *never* build behavior, and there are better ways to eliminate actions. Chapter 11 goes into punishment, and alternative procedures for decelerating behavior, in more detail.

Disadvantages of Lures

The shaping described here has involved just the two terms of actions and consequences. For human beings, antecedents like explaining or demonstrating are helpful for most skill development. Another kind of antecedent is *not* helpful. If you produce behavior with promises of rewards or by **luring** with some desired object, you are likely to create dependency on those antecedents. If Skinner wanted the dog to jump, he could have tied a piece of tempting meat high on the wall where the dog would have to jump to reach it. Why, if he then reinforced the jump, wouldn't that work better than shaping? The answer is that the dog's jump would be under the antecedent control of the lure. He would not jump unless the meat was there. It is often more difficult to eliminate lures than to shape behavior from scratch, especially with people.

> A **lure** is a reward offered *just before* a behavior in order to get it to occur. It differs from a **contract** in that, while both specify contingencies, a contract is established well before a problem or opportunity to respond occurs.

Many parents or teachers who use lures have complained about the results. After offering a few rewards like a cookie, or money, or a coveted CD to get their son or student to do something that he won't otherwise do, they complain, "Now whenever I ask him to do *anything*, he says, 'What'll you give me if I do?'" Bad contingencies produced this behavior. The timing of the promise of a reward *before* a desired action made behavior dependent on that promise. Further, if the offer is given during signs of reluctance or after outright refusal, the offer has just strengthened reluctance or refusal. That is the opposite of what you want. Exchanging rewards for specific actions can be helpful, but only if the arrangement or contract is offered at a calm time, not when a problem is brewing.

TWO-TERM SHAPING IN DAILY LIFE

Shaping goes on all of the time. In addition to planned shaping, people shape behavior in each other without realizing it. If you are standing at a checkout counter at a grocery store, you may witness an almost perfect example of shaping whining in a child. Watch how more pleasant requests by the child are ignored. More and more annoying tones or actions like grabbing candy or pulling on a parent's clothes are made to get the adult's attention. Even if the adult says only "no" or "not now," *any* response will usually reinforce whatever attention-seeking behavior the child engages in. Sometimes you can see behavior escalate until it is so embarrassing the adult finally gives in: "Oh, all right, but just one." You can imagine what this is teaching!

On the positive side, nearly everybody does a fine job of shaping verbal behavior out of the nonsense sounds of an infant's babbling.

Shaping Beginning Talking in a Baby

Infants the world around babble with similar sounds. Syllables you cannot pronounce as an adult, you pronounced just fine as an infant. Those sounds disappeared when your social community failed to reinforce them. In other communities where they were selected, they became part of normal oral behavior.

Some people are surprised at the variations of spoken English found in the United States when everyone hears standard pronunciation on television and radio. When you realize that behavior comes through selection of particular properties, that is not surprising. What people say and their pronunciation is shaped by their local community. The role of reinforcement in the development of speech-like sounds was shown in a study with mothers and their eight-month-old infants.

Example: The Importance of Timing of Attention in the Development of Talking

The mothers involved were told they were participating in a study of infant play, so they were unaware that the study involved verbal behavior. Each mother and infant interacted alone in a room equipped with toys that might be found in a home. Cameras were placed in three corners of each room so the experimenters could see and hear the mother–infant interactions. Each mother was instructed via headphones to briefly move closer, smile, or touch their infant only when asked to do so, and not to talk during the sessions. (Attending was assumed to be reinforcing and turned out to be so.) The mothers were paired. The directions to move closer, smile or touch were given to one mother each time the infant babbled. In a second room the paired mother was given the same instructions to attend to *her* baby, but the timing was linked to the timing for the first mother. Thus the second baby received the same amount of attention but it was not contingent on babbling, though it might have coincided with babbling occasionally. Not surprisingly, the infants whose babbling received contingent attention babbled more than those children with the paired mothers. Not only did they babble more while receiving contingent attention, but also later in a period of free play following the experiment. The researchers also checked the *quality* of babbled sounds. Those babies whose babbling had received contingent attention emitted more resonant vowels and more consonant-vowel combinations than the infants receiving the same amount of non-contingent attention. The authors point out that "changes in babbling were not a result of maternal modeling: the social feedback [used in the experiment] was not similar in form or even modality to infants' changes in vocalizations."[9] The results were due to the contingent timing of attention.

As babbling improves in clarity of sounds that resemble those in the caregiver's language, contingencies shift. In English-speaking countries, a babbled syllable that approximates "Ma" initially gets special attention the first few times it appears. As soon as a baby often says "Ma," adults stop responding much to that syllable. But now "Ma*ma*," gets selected by the caregiver's response. Note that you don't call the other babbled syllables "errors" any more than you call movements of a dog that don't approximate a jump "errors." They are just actions that are not at the moment selected. Eventually, of course, antecedents become important too, so that saying "Mama" is restricted to the mother (see Chapter 9), but here we are dealing with two terms: actions and their consequences.

SHAPING IN THE CLASSROOM

Whether you are working with a dog, a baby, a classroom full of students, or even your spouse or partner,[10] the features of shaping are similar. Shaping works on variability. To catch the best of existing behavior, you have to know what each student is likely to do in the classroom situation as well as what behavior is needed. Reinforcement must be delivered quickly and often as successive approximations are strengthened. Features interact. A hesitation or a sudden gain on the part of a learner may shift a goal or change the reinforcement given. In any shaping situation control goes both ways: learners and teachers each determine what the other does next.

Clarity: Setting One Behavioral Goal at a Time
Shaping strengthens particular properties of an action. You will improve a particular property most effectively if you do not wait until other properties also improve. Suppose a gymnast is dismounting from a balance beam with her left leg bent and her arms too low. It is not likely that better leg positions *and* arm positions will occur at the same time. The best moment to reinforce leg position will almost never be the exact moment for her arm position. In a school if you are shaping complying with requests, ignore posture or tone of voice. In shaping, you pick *one* action until it meets criterion, and then move on to the next.

Academic skills are more complex than physical actions, but the same principles apply. When students are having difficulty, steps can be broken down into components to teach one at a time. There are many behavioral programs that provide detailed sequences of component skills, providing both diagnostic tools and curricula.[11]

What to Use as Reinforcement in the Classroom
Shaping is a process of building new behavior. It requires nearly constant selection of the best of a student's actions. The selection is done, of course, with reinforcement. While you can't be sure that something strengthens behavior without trying it out, you can make pretty good guesses about what will work. Such a small thing as greeting a student by name has been shown to improve class performance, at least for a short time.[12] For shaping, of course, you need something that can occur repeatedly. Signs of progress or clear signs of success are nearly infallible. Recognition or approval also usually strengthens whatever behavior is in process at the time you give it. Like food,

however, approval is best given in small bits. Exaggerated enthusiasm may reinforce actions of young children, but with older students it can **satiate** or cause ribbing from peers. Real praise is best saved for the end of a sequence of behavior, or for exceptional performance, and it may be best given privately.

Like praise, other "large" reinforcers can be broken down into parts where students earn points, or checks on a card, or marbles in a jar towards a pizza party or a field trip or a grade. However, in regular public and private schools, you rarely need consequences of high value to strengthen behavior. This came home to me in my first teaching job: teaching third grade in a private girls' school smack in the middle of New York City.

Example: Two-Term Shaping of Going to Desks in a Third Grade:
"She's Timing Us"
Classes in Spense School were small. I had fewer than 20 third-graders. The first day of school, I anxiously awaited their entry. In they came, *full* of energy and talking non-stop. "How was your summer?" "You've got to hear *this*!" Some actually chased others around the room, shoving aside my carefully arranged desks. At 8:15, I hit the bell the principal had given us to start school. Nothing happened. Absolutely nothing! My students continued to slam their locker doors, talk non-stop, and run back and forth. With no response to my ringing the bell, I demonstrated a beautiful extinction burst: I hit the bell again, only harder. Bang, bang (pause) bang, bang, BANG. Still no response. I added "OK, let's get ready," and finally went around asking individual girls to please get to their desks.

"There has to be a better way," I thought to myself.

The next morning I rang the bell once and stood silently in the front of the room. My students behaved like the day before, running all over and talking energetically. Soon I could hear other classrooms beginning the Pledge of Allegiance. *My* students were still banging their locker doors, dropping books, running around, and talking. Finally, and it seemed like *ages*, they all sat down. I went to the board and wrote a number. I remember it as somewhere around 243.

"What's that?" my students asked.

I began the Pledge of Allegiance. The next day, I did the same thing. This time my students got to their desks a bit sooner, and the number was lower. After three or four days, someone figured out that the number had to do with timing. Within a week as soon as I hit the bell, my students dashed for their desks.

Then I thought, "Why should I have to ring the bell? They can read the clock."

So the next day I sat at my desk. Of course, without the bell, the number was quite large. But my students caught on quickly and in a few days suddenly the room would get quiet. Checking the clock I would see that it was time to begin school. We got to zero!

Then one day my students got quiet. I checked the clock and they were ready several minutes *before* the 8:15 beginning of school! They were all sitting quietly in their desks with their hands folded (folded hands was never part of my criteria). That day we had to go into *negative* numbers.

In addition to solving the beginning-of-school problem, I found that I could glance at the clock as a way to get order any time during the day. That freed me to permit boisterous activities, like a shucking corn contest during the study of pilgrims. I knew I could always get instant quiet if the principal appeared. To make sure that my glance at the clock didn't wear out, I didn't use it more than a couple of times a week.

The power of that simple number on the board came home to me one day far into the school year. The school had several floors with elevators between them. My students had gone down three floors for their dance class. I went down to pick them up a wee bit late. Oh, Oh. They had already taken the elevator back to our floor. Panic! All of my nine-year-olds were completely unsupervised. I could only imagine the chaos. I grabbed the next elevator. It seemed to take forever to reach our floor. I rushed out and turned the corner of our hall where I saw a face peering out of my classroom. It disappeared immediately and I heard a hushed, "She's coming." By the time I reached the door, my students were all sitting quietly at their desks, hands folded and smiling.

I was very pleased. "Wow, look at you all. That is so nice . . ." I stopped. Their faces had fallen.

"What's the matter?" I asked.

One of the students answered, "Aren't you going to put the number on the board?"

Feeling just a little bit confused, I said, "of course," and wrote a zero. Then they were happy and I began the next period.

Analyzing my reactions later, I realized that I had been disappointed that my students hadn't behaved in order to please *me*. Pleasing the teacher is rewarding for the *teacher*, but it is better for students to be under control of their *own* achievement. My students' performance showed in the number on the board, not in my pleasure. That number had become the significant reinforcer for getting ready for class. It showed me how something one would normally call worthless and insignificant can serve as a powerful reinforcer when it reflects successful performance.

Pure two-term (non-restricted) shaping begins with actions by the learner. No directions or explanations or demonstrations precede the selection process once shaping begins. Most teaching does not use pure shaping. Most of what you teach requires explanations, demonstrations or directions, all of which are antecedents. Even with these antecedents, you can come very close to "two-term" shaping in your timing of conditioned reinforcement, applying successive approximation techniques, and eliminating correction or punishment altogether. An example of the combination of antecedents with shaping principles is the TAG Teaching mentioned in Chapters 1 and 5.

SHAPING SIMPLE SKILLS WITH TAG TEACHING

If shaping with clickers is so effective with non-human animals, why not use auditory stimuli to shape human movement? It's amazing that it took until the turn of the twenty-first century for someone to use a specialized conditioned reinforcer for gymnastics, speech therapy, and for simple academic skills. TAG Teaching, officially founded in 2004, ported over shaping procedures lock, stock, and barrel. As mentioned before, TAG stands for Teaching with Acoustical Guidance. The "acoustical guidance" is, of course, the click or other auditory conditioned reinforcer. The "teaching" part consists of reinforcing successive approximations. When TAG Teaching is used with students who can understand directions, goals for each step are stated. Teachers may also demonstrate or explain before the student's turn. What distinguishes TAG Teaching from other methodologies is the reinforcing of single properties of student actions and the prohibition of any punishment or correction procedures (see Table 8.1.)

Table 8.1 Steps in TAG Teaching

Step One:	Observe your students to see their current level of performance and what behavioral properties you can build upon.
Step Two:	Establish the click as a conditioned reinforcer.
Step Three:	Set the "TAG point," the *one* pinpointed action or property of an action that will most improve performance of each individual.
Step Four:	Arrange for high rates of tagged behavior in every student, using peers as taggers if desired.
Step Five:	Continually adjust TAG points to make sure that each student almost always succeeds and progresses.

Making the Click a Conditioned Reinforcer

TAG Teaching uses a clicker as a conditioned reinforcer. Why do you need a clicking sound? Why not just say "good" or "good for you" or "awesome"? First of all, words don't have the sharp precision of a click. By the time you finish the word "awesome" the student dismounting from a balance beam has left the position you wanted to strengthen or a student pronouncing the French "r" is already onto the next syllable. Second, words of praise have been paired with many different things so their meaning is not clear. **Meaning** lies in the circumstances under which a statement is made. Praise may have been paired with "Good, *but...*" or given where it was not seen as genuine. The sound of the clicker has none of this history.[13]

To make the sound of a click a reinforcer, all you usually do is to tell your students that a click means "correct." If that isn't sufficient, you can pair the sound with some kind of backup reinforcer. If you are working individually with a child with special needs, you click and immediately give a bit of banana, blow a few bubbles, give a tickle or whatever else has been shown to be reinforcing. At first you pair each click with the treat, then two clicks, then three, then five, until you can click several times for each treat. Then, for repetitive actions, like taking steps towards a particular door, you would click each step at first, then click each second step, and so on, gradually requiring more steps until the behavior occurs without any more clicks. You want the student's behavior to become independent of your reinforcement.

For a regular class if you need more than "clicks mean you did it right," clicks can earn points that can later be exchanged for a preferred activity: grade points, certificates, trinkets, or other rewards. For all students, keeping clicker sessions short helps to maintain the power of the sound. Like any reinforcer, the sound of a click satiates if overused.

Some teachers who use clickers with young children have encountered objections that using a clicker is treating children like dogs. The clicker is not operating on either a child or a dog. It is operating on properties of behavior. Still, as a teacher you must consider others' concerns, particularly if they come from parents. Instead of a clicker, try a different kind of sound-maker (see Figure 8.2). Attendance counters make a loud enough noise to work as conditioned reinforcers, and they have the added advantage of keeping a tally of actions completed. If you have a large budget, you could even use headphones to deliver a sound. Most students think wearing earphones is "cool." Whatever sound-maker is used, students prefer learning with clickers to traditional teaching.

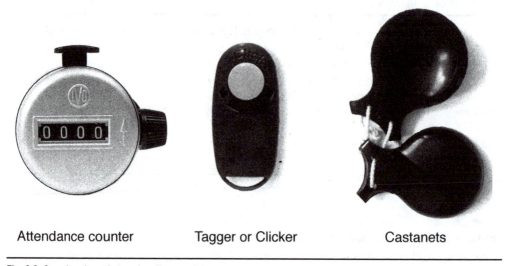

| Attendance counter | Tagger or Clicker | Castanets |

Fig. 8.2 Sound-makers that work well as conditioned reinforcers

As one fourth-grader gymnast put it, "Coaches tell you what you have done wrong. The clicker tells you what you have done right."[14]

Setting Initial Goals: TAG Points

At the beginning of a TAG Teaching session the *one* action to work on is set. TAG teachers call this the *TAG point.* As a teacher, *you* may pick that action, or it may be part of a student's IEP, or you may suggest several targets and let individual students select which one they would like to work on first. Or, for fun, don't tell the students what you will click and see if they can figure it out.[15] Whatever you do, pick only one target at a time.

If you are working with a child with limited verbal ability, you may not state a goal, but rather do straight shaping. In that case, what you click will constantly shift. For example, in shaping movement across a floor, the first click might not even be contingent on foot movement. You might tag looking in the right direction. The next click might be for shifting weight, or foot placement, or arm movement. The action clicked will shift from click to click.

For advanced performance, a specialist may be needed. While a peer can see whether or not a leg is straight, it may take a coach to note the tensing of particular muscles that lead to a correct position. A language teacher or speech therapist may be the only one to differentiate correctly between sounds so that the best pronunciation can be clicked.

Goals for each step must be readily achievable. If in five repetitions, at least four performances have not met a criteria, your goal is too high. An intermediate step is needed. Or if a student is just having a bad day, you can change to an activity where he or she will be successful. Extra practice on an already mastered skill never hurts, but failure does.

Pacing and Its Effects

Shaping requires a sensitivity to pacing. In two-term shaping if you wait too long before reinforcing the next "good" action, behavior will deteriorate. Too much behavior intervenes between one reinforced action and the next, making the direction of change unclear. Rapid pacing and high rates of success generally result in energy and continued effort. If you note a student losing interest or failing to improve, try picking up the rate at which you deliver reinforcement. Of course, that means dropping back a bit in the steps towards your goal until you get the behavior occurring easily and rapidly.

Since each time you reinforce an action you strengthen it, high rates of reinforcement also produce more rapid change than lower rates. If you have a reinforcer, like a special event that cannot be given frequently, let students earn points towards that event. Points can be given instantly and frequently.

Arranging for High Rates of Performance in a Classroom Full of Students

How can you use shaping if you have more than one or two students to work with? You don't want most of your students waiting for their turn. Teachers using TAG with a whole class pair students so they can tag each other's performance. First they have students practice clicking. Clickers are given to all the students. The teacher rapidly demonstrates actions that meet and do not meet a criterion. One format is like a speeded up version of "Simon Says." The teacher says, "The TAG point is three fingers showing." The teacher rapidly lifts and drops her fingers, alternating three with two, four, and one finger. At first students will have a hard time. Even when they click for the correct number of fingers, their clicks are scattered across the room like a drum roll. They will also click when the wrong number of fingers is shown. As students practice, their accuracy and timing improve until almost all clicks sound together and only for "three fingers showing."

Students as young as four can tag reasonably accurately if given practice and clear TAG points. Most students enjoy "being the teacher." The careful observation required to tag correctly also draws students' attention to important features of performance, something often hard to get them to attend to otherwise. When you have students working in twos, or in other combinations, you are free to move about, helping out where there are problems, and checking on individual progress.

Like Precision Teaching, or other instructional contingencies that produce intense concentration on a repeated skill over short time periods, TAG Teaching is usually reserved for only a small part of a class session, leaving time for more leisurely problem-solving or creative activities. If you plan more than one TAG session for a class period, you would do well to vary the formats. In Spanish you might pair students first in a flashcard format for verbs, then later read a story to them while they click every subjunctive verb form they hear. In basketball, you could pair students to tag each other's correct hand position while dribbling, then later ask students to line up for individual goals for shooting baskets.

Adjusting According to Moment to Moment Progress

TAG points are ephemeral because shaping keeps moving to new levels. If one TAG point is not mastered in a few minutes to be replaced by a new TAG point, you need to find out why. Are the steps too large? Is the click still a conditioned reinforcer? Has a particular student overworked particular muscles or reached a physiological limit? No one should be stuck at a fixed level. If performance does not improve at least in rate, change the TAG point and work on a different behavior or a different property of the same behavior. You can come back to a former TAG point later.

Keeping Teaching Individualized and Flexible

Because in shaping you specify a goal, it might be tempting to write a sequence of steps for all students to follow in the same order. While a fixed curriculum can guide general areas to work on, shaping requires adjusting your actions according to the moment to moment performance of each of your students. Shaping relies on sensitivity to subtleties in the behavior of individuals and to their progress. As with other behavioral procedures, going through the motions without attending to the resulting behavior will not be effective.

TAG Teaching focuses on the action and consequence parts of shaping. Most academic content, however, requires not only responding, but responding appropriately to antecedents. Imagine that you wanted to learn to translate Chinese. (I am assuming you do not know Chinese.) Here are the first characters for you to translate: 睡衣.[16] No one would shape your behavior using only postcedents. Even if you kept saying all the words you could think of, shaping successive approximations might never work. Anyone teaching Chinese would first *tell* you what these symbols meant. Shaping such basics as reading or math or responding to aspects of one's world from "ant" to "zabaglione" utilizes antecedents as well as consequences.

SHAPING OF COMPLEX ACADEMIC PERFORMANCE WITH PROGRAMMED INSTRUCTION

Complex behavior is taught with antecedent directions and explanations. In the 1960s a method of shaping complex skills was developed under the term Programmed Instruction. Again, it was Skinner who began the work. This time, his interest came from a visit to his daughter's fourth-grade classroom on her school's "Father's Day." Like the other fathers, he sat in one of the little chairs, watching what was going on in the class. The teacher explained the computation procedure for the day, worked examples on the board, and then passed out worksheets for the students to do. As Skinner watched the various students doing their seat work, he got increasingly uncomfortable. As he later put it, "through no fault of her own the teacher was violating almost everything we knew about the learning process." What was wrong? Shaping required adapting each step to each individual's current performance level. But in that math class, a few students clearly had no idea of how to solve the problems, others wrote but erased frequently, and still others looked bored as they completed one problem after another or finished and sat with nothing to do. In shaping, you *immediately* reinforce every best response. But in that math class, the children did not find out whether they correctly solved one problem before encountering the next. Whatever feedback they got occurred much too late to be of much use. But how could one teacher with 20 or 30 students reinforce each correct response? No one could possibly do what was required. Teachers needed help. Skinner designed a progression of problems and feedback that could be delivered by machine to shape individual behavior.

Linear Programming

In 1954 there were no microcomputers, so Skinner made his first teaching machines out of metal and wood. The first models gave practice on math problems, but did not teach anything new.[17] That changed. By 1956 when he was finishing his book *Verbal Behavior*, Skinner was writing about **prompting**, **probing**, **vanishing**, and **fading** as ways to teach *new* material, and **Programmed Instruction** was born. Skinner insisted that students write answers instead of selecting from multiple-choice alternatives. This form of Programmed Instruction was called *linear programming*.

> **Programmed Instruction** is a series of increasingly difficult sequential steps that students take until they have mastered skills they could not perform at the outset.

The heart of Programmed Instruction consists of shaping: a high rate of responding by individual students to increasingly complex material that insures success at each step. Each student goes through the sequences at his or her own rate. Being correct is assumed to be reinforcing, but to avoid assuming its function, programmers talk instead about **immediate feedback** for each response. Material is presented in *frames*. Each frame has a small amount of text and areas for responding to the material (see Figure 8.3). The first responses are prompted, that is, extra help is given. No one would have trouble copying the word "manufacture" in the first frame of Figure 8.3. As each sequence progresses, prompts are withdrawn by fading (literally making less visible), or vanishing (removed parts of the help as in numbers 2 through 5 in Figure 8.3.) The

1. Manufacture means to make or build. Chair factories **manufacture** chairs.
   Copy the word here: ☐☐☐☐☐☐☐☐☐☐☐

2. Part of the word is like part of the word **factory.** Both parts come from an old word meaning *make* or *build.*
   manu☐☐☐☐ure

3. Part of the word is like part of the word **manual.** Both parts come from an old word for *hand.*
   ☐☐☐☐ facture

4. The same letter goes in both spaces: m ☐nuf☐cture

5. The same letter goes in both spaces: man☐ fact☐re

6. Chair factories ☐☐☐☐☐☐☐☐☐☐ chairs.

Fig. 8.3 A few frames of a Programmed Instruction text

B. F. Skinner, "Teaching Machines," in *Science*, October 24, 1958, 128, pp. 969–977. Reprinted with permission from AAAS. Also reprinted in B. F. Skinner, *The Technology of Teaching.* Cambridge, MA: B. F. Skinner Foundation, 2003, 40.

sequencing of material resembles what a good tutor would do one-on-one. Because the first machines were mechanical rather than electronic, the only adjustment they could make for incorrect responses was to bring the missed "frames" back until the student completed them correctly.

Programmed Instruction (PI) boomed in the 1960s, but for lack of a standard machine most programs were produced in paper format. Hundreds of booklets appeared in education, business, and the military. The material looked easy to write and many authors produced books by adding a few blanks to text here and there. Others included so much material before asking for a response that the books were hardly programmed at all. The paper format also lacked contingencies. Students could look at answers *before* making a response. No doubt because of the poor quality of many programs, paper versions of Programmed Instruction lasted only a short time in schools. Paper formats are still used, but more Programmed Instruction is now written for computers or instruction over the internet.

With microcomputers and the internet, quality Programmed Instruction is possible. The teaching of new skills can be so individualized that the steps students are given depend not only on whether they answer correctly, but how rapidly they do so. Unfortunately many "tutorials" do not follow good shaping principles. Pressing an arrow to see more material does not qualify as responding to content. A student can press arrows without understanding anything that is on the screen.

Shaping Principles in Instructional Design
The central features of Programmed Instruction follow shaping as closely as possible:

1. Active responding by the student: Students respond to the content of each small frame or step of instruction.
2. Immediate feedback: Each student response is evaluated before the next question, task, or problem appears. In sophisticated programs what the student next receives depends on performance at each step.
3. Successive approximation: The student encounters tasks that build, beginning with responses that are prompted. Less and less help is given within each sequence until students preform the new skill on their own. With successive approximation there are few, if any, "errors."
4. Progression depends upon mastery: Successive approximation requires that students master each skill before being given more difficult sequences.

All of these characteristics are similar to good tutoring sessions: when working with one student at a time, you can continually adjust what you do to make sure the student is always successful while tackling more and more difficult material. Even with a whole classroom, incorporating these characteristics of shaping improves student performance.

INCREASING ACTIVE RESPONDING IN THE CLASSROOM

How active is active responding? The more students respond, the better. If you were tutoring one student, how many times would that student respond in a 20-minute period? You would expect at *least* a couple of responses each minute.

When we look at the number of responses each student makes in a typical class, some techniques that appear full of active responding come up short. Take class discussions. I once was talking to a teacher when she looked over my shoulder into her classroom with obvious pride. I turned and looked, too. It was a tenth-grade English class. A student teacher was leading a discussion. She sat on a desk with her feet on a chair. The students sat in two rows of chairs facing her. The teacher was leaning forward, listening intently while two of the students in the front row argued vehemently. Three or four others jumped into the conversation and the volume picked up as emotions increased.

> **Active responding** requires students to answer questions or respond in other ways that reveal understanding of content in each step of instruction. Moving to different pages by clicking on arrows in a computer program is not active responding because anyone could do that without understanding the content presented.

The teacher beside me was getting excited too. "Look at that," she said. "Look at that involvement. What a discussion!"

It was true. It was an excellent discussion. Seven or eight students were talking at a great rate. But what about the others? There were six or seven students in the back row who were not talking. How profitable was the discussion for them? Only one student in the back row was contributing. The others were quiet. As you moved away from the teacher, the students sat farther and farther back in their seats, like a wave falling back from its crest. At the far end of the back row, a couple of students sat slouched in their chairs, feet outstretched, only half listening.

I did a rough calculation: 22 students in the class, seven I had seen talk, three of whom talked at a great rate. That meant that two-thirds of the class hadn't said one word, although I guessed that half of them were at least listening. And this was a *good* discussion as discussions go!

If you had 22 of your friends standing around at a cocktail party and only seven did any talking, would you be happy with the "active involvement"? No. You would hustle around trying to get *everyone* involved. You might start by splitting up the large group into smaller ones. It is nearly impossible to have everyone talking in a circle of 10 or more people. A classroom is no different. If you really want discussion, you must make as much effort for everyone to participate as you would in hosting a party. You can start by breaking a large group into smaller ones. Of course, you must make sure that each group keeps to the topic. Asking for some written product or a group report helps.

How about class participation when presenting new material like adjectives? Usually the teacher does the most talking.

Low Rates of Responding in Typical Lessons

The teacher, Mr. Temple, is introducing the concept of adjectives to his class.

Teacher: "Today we're going to talk about adjectives. I'm going to project three sentences on the screen. All the adjectives are in bold. See if you can tell what adjectives *do*."

The teacher shows the following sentences:
   The boy hit the *red* ball.
   The *old* shirt hung on the nail.
   I ate my *first* egg.
   "Can you figure out what an adjective does? (pause) Suzi."
   Suzi: "It describes something."
   Teacher: "Good. An adjective describes something. What does "red" describe? Frank."
   Frank: "Ball."
   Teacher. "That's right. 'Red' describes 'ball'." The teacher points to the words as he says them. "*Old* describes *shirt, first* describes *egg.* So we can say that an adjective is a word that describes something. What kind of a word does an adjective describe? Sam?"
   There is a pause. Sam looks uncomfortable.
   "Joe."
   Joe: "It describes a noun."
   Teacher: "Right. An adjective describes a noun. We say it *modifies* a noun. Sometimes it tells which one we're talking about. The boy didn't hit any old ball; he hit the *red* one. Now see if you can pick out the adjectives in these sentences."
   He shows three new sentences.
   "Jo Ellen, you try the first."

This kind of question and answer session goes on in most schools. In perhaps a minute and a half, Mr. Temple asked for four answers. Not a bad rate. But how many questions did *each* student answer? Except for Suzi, Frank, Joe and Jo Ellen (who each responded once), he can't be sure that other students were thinking of the answers or whether they could have answered correctly if called upon. Two ways to increase participation from everyone are with writing and choral responding.

Increasing Responding with Lecture Fill-In Sheets and Guided Notes
One way to insure that every student is responding is to have *each one* write the answers to your questions. Mr. Temple could have asked students to take out a piece of paper, number it from 1 to 10, and write the answers to each question he asked. By looking quickly around the class, he could have seen Joe's difficulty, and given him some help (perhaps using a student who was answering quickly). With a bit of advance planning, he could have made a fill-in sheet like the worksheet in Table 8.2.

   While fill-in sheets improve active responding in a presentation, they do not exemplify successive approximation. Yes, feedback is given for one response before the next question is asked, but students cannot progress until the *instructor* goes on. With all of your students responding, however, you at least become more aware of what each can do. You can spot the Sams without embarrassing them, and provide additional help where needed.

Table 8.2 A fill-in sheet for a lesson on adjectives to allow for active responding by all students

1. An adjective _____ something.
2. In the sentence on the screen, "red" describes _____ .
3. An adjective describes a _____ .
4. Write the adjectives in the sentences on the screen:
Sentence #1 _____ Sentence #2 _____ Sentence #3 _____

For large lectures, fill-in sheets often consist of lecture notes with critical terms left out. This kind of fill-in sheet, sometimes called **guided notes**, does not ask students to answer questions or solve problems. Students only write down what the lecturer says or presents on a screen. Yet even with this drawback, leaving out critical terms in lecture notes improves problem-solving skills.[18] Students at least pay enough attention to have their blanks filled in. Guided notes can be improved by throwing in an occasional quiz item that requires thinking about what has been presented. How readily students respond without looking at what others are writing gives you a pretty good idea of whether they are understanding what you have been presenting.

Increasing Oral Responding with Groups: Direct Instruction
Another form of instruction that demands a high rate from every student is **Direct Instruction (DI)**.[19] It was developed initially in the early 1960s by Siegfried Engelmann, around the same time as Programmed Instruction. Engelmann, who was working for an advertising agency, started doing research on what was required for children to learn a slogan. Soon he switched to academic content. He came up with instruction in small groups with a high rate of choral responding. Finding it hard to train teachers to give effective sequences of steps, he wrote scripts for exactly what they should say for each question. He and his colleagues, particularly Carl Bereiter and Wesley Becker, continually edited the sequences to make them more effective. The early sequence was called DISTAR (Direct Instruction System for Teaching And Remediation).[20]

The most common format for Direct Instruction today involves students responding aloud to each question asked (see Figure 8.4). The sequences are graded, but like fill-in sheets DI lacks two features of successive approximation: students must wait for the teacher's questions before each response, and their progress does not depend on individual mastery. The whole group moves through the sequences together, though DI teachers have the flexibility to adjust what the group does next depending on the choral response of the majority of students. Nevertheless, DI gets a high rate of response from every student and it has been shown to be an effective practice in **Project Follow Through**, the largest educational research program ever conducted by the federal government.

Project Follow Through provided disadvantaged children with special programs designed to help them succeed in school. The project lasted over 20 years in all. Over 75,000 low-income children in 170 different communities participated in the special programs. Parents from each school district selected one of nine different models of early intervention. The district then trained its teachers and implemented that model (with added funding of $750 per student). Students from schools in equivalent socio-economic communities were also followed as comparisons.

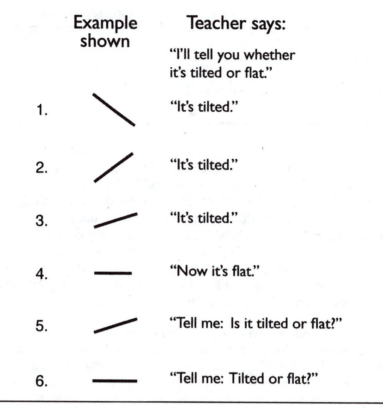

Fig. 8.4 A sample Direct Instruction script
The teacher holds a yardstick at the angles shown for the examples.
Siegfried Engelmann and Douglas Carnine. *Theory of Instruction: Principles and Applications*. New York: Irvington Publishers, Inc., 1982.

The federal government evaluated the various models to see which were most effective. It was an enormous undertaking. Thousands of children receiving each program were followed as well as those from the comparison schools. Student performance after the programs ended was used as the measure of success.

The nine models evaluated fell into three categories (see Figure 8.5). The *Basic Skills* models were called "behavioral." They directly taught reading, arithmetic and language skills that disadvantaged students lacked. The *Cognitive Skills* models gave disadvantaged children age-appropriate materials for problem-solving and language development with teachers assisting development rather than directly teaching basic skills. The *Affective Models* provided learning centers and placed responsibility for learning on the children: basic skills were not directly taught at all. Teachers were to create environments "in which children can move toward the goal of self-actualization through making their own free choices."[21]

Figure 8.5 shows the standing of students from each model at the end of third grade. There were many differences between individual schools, with *some* of the non-behavioral schools doing better than *some* of the behavioral ones, but the overall results were clear. Figure 8.5 groups all similar models together. The zero dividing line is the average level of achievement of students from similar backgrounds who were not in any

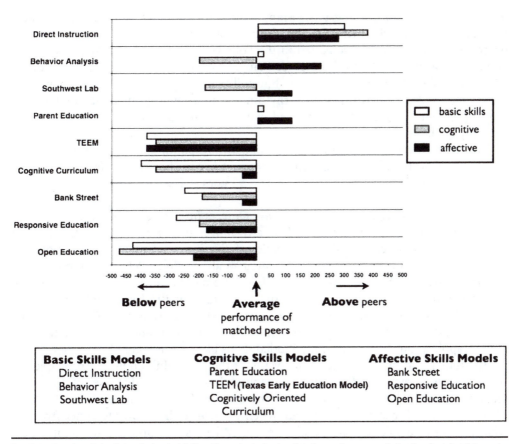

Fig. 8.5 Results of the federally funded Follow Through study showing the performance of disadvantaged children who had been in each model of Follow Through compared to national averages of peers from similar disadvantaged neighborhoods

Based on L. B. Stebbins, R. G. St. Pierre, and E. C. Proper. *Education as Experimentation: A Planned Variation Model Effects of Follow Through Models.* Vol. IV-A and B (Cambridge, MA: Abt Associates, 1977). Used by permission.

of the programs. This level is the 20th percentile of all students nationwide. As you can see, the only models that improved performance over standard educational practices were the behavioral models and the Parent Education mode, with DI leading the pack. The students in the DI schools gained enough to perform at an average of the 50th percentile on nationwide achievement tests (the white bar represents a gain of 30 percentile points). Not only did students from the DI program have better academic skills (on the Metropolitan Achievement Test), they also tested higher on measures of problem-solving and self-esteem than the programs that were designed to favor those areas. Students from all but one of the non-behavioral programs scored *lower* than students from in the comparison schools who had received no special instruction. A long-term study that followed the DI students showed statistically significant higher high school graduation rates than students from similar background who had not participated in DI programs.

In spite of its demonstrated effectiveness, DI has not become the predominant teaching method for youngsters. Many educators support models like "whole language," and "developmentally appropriate practices" that follow the educational practices similar to those discredited in the Follow-through study. Many kindergarten and elementary school teachers have been taught to consider repetition as a way to kill motivation. Rapid pacing is repetitive, but children enjoy repetition when sequences like 5, 10, 15, 20 are performed in a rhythmic fashion by a group. The emphasis on "No Child Left Behind" has encouraged evidence-based practices. Direct Instruction certainly qualifies.

Whether written or choral, the amount of active responding increases up and down the whole educational age range whenever practices are based on effectiveness. One such case arose with a teacher of introductory physics at Harvard University.

Increasing Responding with Multiple-Choice Quizzes Interspersed into Lectures

The teacher of a physics course at Harvard University, Eric Mazur, changed from lectures to what he called **Peer Instruction** following a rude awakening about his students' performance. Dr. Mazur's students had always done well on textbook exams and they gave him high ratings as a teacher. One day he read an article about how students have "common sense" beliefs that contradict physical laws and that physics courses don't change these false beliefs. Mazur reported on his reaction: "When reading this, my first reaction was 'Not *my* students!'"[22] But he went ahead and gave the suggested "application" test anyway. It included items like that in Figure 8.6.

His students' answers stunned him. Many of them couldn't apply the principles he thought he was teaching. How could so many of these bright students select the wrong answers when they had correctly solved the more difficult problems about the same phenomena on his tests? Mazur shifted the entire focus of his course to concentrate on what physics principles mean in daily life. He broke his 50-minute lectures into short

A bowling ball accidentally falls out of the cargo bay of an airliner as it flies along in a horizontal direction.

As observed by a person standing on the ground and viewing the plane as in the figure below, which of the paths 1-5 would the bowling ball most closely follow after leaving the airplane?

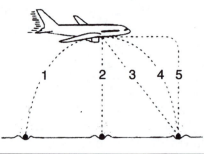

Fig. 8.6 An item testing a practical application of principles of Newtonian mechanics. The correct answer is path 4. Exercise 14, p. 51 from PEER INSTRUCTION; A User's Manual by Eric Mazur. Copyright © 1997 by Eric Mazur, Reprinted by permission of Pearson Education, Inc.

sections. Following a seven to 10-minute presentation of a principle, he gave a quiz item like the one in Figure 8.3 that used the principle just presented. Every student in the class selected the answer he or she thought was correct, without discussing it with anyone else. All the student choices were sent via electronics to a screen that Mazur could see, so he knew how many students had picked each answer. (Mazur pointed out that similar feedback could be obtained with students holding up index cards showing letters or colors to indicate answers, a simpler procedure that behavior analysts have successfully used.[23]) After sending in their first electronic answers, Mazur's students were given a couple of minutes to convince peers sitting close to them of the correctness of their individual answers. During this peer instruction time, Mazur came down off the lecture platform and listened to what his students were saying. He was impressed at some of the reasoning and examples students used, and spotted misconceptions he still needed to correct. After the peer discussion, the students were asked to answer again individually. If, this time, most of them got the item correct, Mazur quickly summarized the reasons for the correct answer and went on to the next concept. If fewer than 90% of students selected the correct alternative, he gave more explanation and another "concept test" on the same principle. The whole class period proceeded this way.

Mazur's procedure incorporated a very high rate of responding for a lecture. There were six to 10 quiz items in each 50-minute class (counting the repeats), and the peer clusters of three to five gave a lot of opportunity for discussion. Of course, group format could not permit individual progression. A student who could answer all the questions before going to class got the same activities as everyone else. But at least the more advanced students could benefit by helping their peers.

While allowing only for group progress, lecture fill-ins, DI, and interspersed quizzes incorporate high rates and rapid pacing of student responding. You can even ask for raising hands as a method of getting students to take a stand on the answer to a question.[24] All of these strategies incorporate notonly active responding but also feedback following each response. Knowing whether one answer is correct before getting the next problem or question is called **immediate feedback**.

PROVIDING FOR IMMEDIATE FEEDBACK

Many procedures called "immediate feedback" do not qualify as "immediate." In PI, the learner finds out the result of each action before encountering the next task. That avoids practicing mistakes. A student who adds 19 and 12 and gets 211 needs help right away, not after completing a whole page of similar incorrectly added numbers. Grading papers just as soon as students finish all their problems does not qualify as immediate feedback.

> **Immediate feedback** requires the student learning about the success of one action before getting the next task or problem.

Giving feedback that allows for individual differences is more difficult than for group responding. As the only teacher in a classroom you cannot personally check the answers of each of your students. As Skinner said, "Teachers need help."

Help does not have to come from machines. It can come from other students. While not immediate, the use of peers for feedback is utilized in a system known as the

Personalized System of Instruction (PSI). Course material is broken down into units, each of which has text materials and essay questions at the end. Students take the quizzes at specific times and locations whenever they are ready. The quizzes are graded by proctors, students who have done well in the course in a previous semester or those who have completed previous units. Proctors both evaluate progress and also help tutor those who do not pass unit exams. PSI courses may not have lectures, though sessions with the course instructor are usually made available. While far from shaping because so much studying is done as homework, and because feedback is delayed until a test is corrected, PSI does get a lot of active responding by students.

Peers are not in a good position to teach *new* material to each other, but they can provide immediate feedback for building fluency on skills that are present but tentative. By pairing students in twos, one can perform, the other evaluate, as with TAG Teaching. For academic practice, index cards work well, with problems or questions on one side, answers on the other. A flashcard format can be used by individuals checking their own responses, but pairing students usually works better. Even at the first-grade level, pictures on the "answer" side enable peers to tell their partners whether each word read is correct or not. At the high school level, the task could be naming the more common elements of the periodic table from their atomic number or abbreviations, or capitals of countries, or any other facts used in a field. Short timings (and graphing progress as in Precision Teaching) help flashcard sessions stay fresh.

With flashcards or computer programs or the internet, instruction can be truly individualized. Each student can work on material that differs from what any other student in the class is doing.[25]

To keep students progressing, but also succeeding at each step, tasks given to students must build slowly. Successive approximation means that students progress successfully: the sequencing prevents "errors."

SUCCESSIVE APPROXIMATION TECHNIQUES: ERRORLESS LEARNING

> **Successive approximations** are student actions that come closer and closer to a goal or the steps that students are to go through to reach that goal.

You already use many successive approximation techniques. In teaching beginning reading you would start with words like "cat" and "Mom," not "through" and "though." Still, it is helpful to consider different ways to sequence steps, especially when encountering situations where a student isn't progressing.

The following methods of producing **errorless learning** can be used in any order or in any combination to suit individual needs.

Technique 1. Ask students to select among alternatives before producing from scratch.

Technique 2. Start with high contrast before moving to finer discriminations.

    2a. Begin with matching to sample.

Technique 3. Go from simple to complex and from part to whole.

    3a. Use backward chaining.

    3b. Increase the number of parts to consider.

Technique 4. Start with prompts and then vanish or fade them.
Technique 5. Gradually increase the rate of performance.

Selecting before Producing
It is easier to pick out an answer than to say or write it. Without looking back, which item is it easier for you to answer below, Item A or Item B?

Item A: What was the name of the Harvard professor who used Peer Instruction in his classes?
Item B: Which Harvard Professor used Peer Instruction in his classes?
Howard Berg   Roy Glauber   Melissa Franklin   Eric Mazur.

Most people find Item B easier to answer. When you introduce a new term, principle, procedure or skill, many of your students will require intermediate steps before supplying the term in appropriate contexts. Think of being introduced to several new people at a party. After a few minutes you may not be able to name a new acquaintance, but if asked "Is her name Janis McCorkle? or Liza Shapiro?" you can probably tell which one it is. Similarly if a student can't remember a name when you ask "What is the botanical term for the creeping rootstocks like those in asparagus or Lily of the Valley?" you can help that student answer by offering alternatives: "Is it rhizome or stolen?"

Over a century ago, Maria Montessori described teaching steps ("periods") for young children. Here is how she taught naming colors. Note which two steps illustrate selecting before producing:

Period One: Matching colors: "I had, on the table, six of the colour spools in pairs, that is two reds, two blues, two yellows. In the First Period, I placed one of the spools before the child asking her to find the one like it. This I repeated for all three of the colours, showing her how to arrange them carefully in pairs."[26]

Period Two: Presenting a red and a blue spool to the child, Montessori named each and asked the child to repeat the names.

Period Three: Then laying the spools on the table, Montessori asked the child to "Give me the red," and then "Give me the blue."

Period Four: Montessori showed the child either red or blue and asked "What (color) is this?"

The selection step (Period 3) is followed by Period Four which requires "producing" the name. Only two of the three colors are used initially, an example of Technique 3 above. Montessori's sequence also began in Period One by showing the child a sample color and asking the child to "find one like it." Being able to **match to sample** comes before picking out a color requested. A child who cannot match colors (when size and other characteristics are the same) may be color blind.

Maria Montessori

Fig. 8.7 Maria Montessori (1870–1952)
Reprinted by permission of the Archives of the Association Montessori Internationale.

Maria Montessori was the first woman in Italy to earn a medical degree, and that was in the days when women were not allowed in medical schools. In her practice, she visited Rome's "asylums for the insane" and saw children labeled "idiots." Believing that their deficiencies were more educational than medical, she looked into teaching methods. Several of her eight-year-olds did so well she had them tested and they not only passed the state tests, but scored above average. Her success led to her being asked to start a school for children from a housing project in a slum area of Rome.

In 1907 she founded the first "children's house." Over the next several years she developed the "Montessori Method." Montessori advocated careful observation of behavior and developed curricula based on skills the children lacked. Instruction centered on children's activities with many "self-correcting" activities like puzzles that gave feedback by whether or not pieces fit. Montessori attributed learning to a spirit within each child that would develop if not held back by adults. Behavior analysts would attribute her students' successes to the contingencies she set up. The contingencies Montessori designed anticipated many successive approximation techniques used today.

Provide High-Contrast Examples before Asking for Finer Discriminations
Nearly everything taught in schools involves discrimination (see Chapter 9 for a full discussion). From naming colors to identifying mammals, students must respond differently to different aspects of the environment. It helps to begin with examples that differ markedly. The colors red and blue differ more sharply than red and crimson. A first-grader will be more successful if beginning with the former pair. Matching mammals is easier with a horse and a swordfish than with a swordfish and a dolphin. While finer distinctions must be addressed, you will have more success if you ask students to make the simpler discriminations first.

With careful sequencing, a student can learn to respond to incredibly subtle differences. The task in Figure 8.8 (right side) is to touch the circle. This task was taught successfully to an institutionalized man with the label "microcephalic idiot."[27] After teaching him to press anywhere on a lighted screen, the first steps in discrimination training insured correct responding by lighting only the correct figure and making the ellipses very elongated (left side of Figure 8.8). The prompts were removed so gradually and the ellipses made circular so gradually that the man made almost no mistakes. The final discrimination, as you see, involved very subtle differences. Similar careful sequencing can eliminate or greatly reduce errors in teaching any discrimination task.

Simple to Complex and Part to Whole
In a sense, increasing the difficulty of a discrimination is a progression from simple to complex. More often, complexity involves multiple operations or the number of stimuli involved. Mathematics provides good examples. Adding single digits involves fewer operations than problems with multiple digits, and word problems requiring a single operation are simpler than those requiring several steps. In life, problems requiring mathematical solutions rarely present you with just the numbers you need to solve them. To approximate daily life, some word problems include numbers that are not

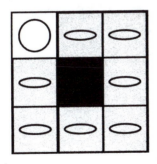 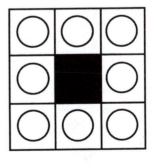

Early step: Only the circle is lit, and the ellipses are very elongated.

Final task: Touch the circle. (It is the bottom middle figure.)

Fig. 8.8 First and last steps in an errorless discrimination sequence
Adapter from B. F. Skinner, *The Technology of Teaching* (Cambridge, MA: B. F. Skinner Foundation, 2003), 77. Originally published in *Proceedings of the Royal Society*, B, 1965, Vol. 162, pp. 427–443. Used by permission of the Royal Society.

needed. They are more difficult than problems in which every number is used for a solution. The more extraneous information that is given, the more complex and difficult problem-solving becomes.

Assignments in composition, art, and in music also progress in complexity. Writing a limerick is easier than writing a sonnet. In music, students may be given three parts of a four-part chorale in the style of Bach, and asked to add the fourth line in the same style before being asked to compose an entire piece. Drawing begins with non-dimensional pictures before requiring accurate portrayal of foreground, middle ground, background, and perspective based upon vanishing points.

Backward Chaining

Many tasks start out as a sequence of steps. Again, mathematics provides a clear example. In solving the equation $2x - 4 = 24$, the first step is to get the term with the x by itself by adding 4 to both sides of the equation. Then you can divide by 2 to find x. A chain of responses is required where each step provides the task for the next step. In non-human animals long sequences of steps can be taught, but only by teaching the last step of the chain first. Once the final step is mastered, the next to last is taught. Solving the next to last step produces the now familiar last step. Completing each step in the chain sets up a situation in which the next step has already been conquered.

> **Backward chaining** is a procedure in which a sequence of steps is taught in the reverse order, starting with the last step then the next to last, and so on.

Backward chaining is also effective in teaching complex sequences to human beings. With the equation above, you could start by having students solve equations all of which have the "x" term alone on one side, like $2x = 28$. Once solving that step is fluent, you would give them equations where a simple addition or subtraction results in getting the "x" term alone on one side, like $2x - 4 = 24$. Completing the first step of adding four to each side produces familiar equations your students can already solve. Next, you could add another complication, say equations like $5(2x - 4) = 120$, and so on until your students have no trouble solving very complicated equations.

Backward chaining can be used in any sequential performance. Take writing a three paragraph essay. One chain of steps proposed is the following (here listed from first to last):

1. Write your thesis
2. Write your main points
3. Write your sub-points under each main point
4. Give examples or elaborate on your points and sub-points
5. Summarize your essay in a conclusion

If your students are having difficulty, try backward chaining. Using these same steps you could take simple essays (from the internet, newspapers, former students' essays, or your own creations) and remove the summaries or conclusions. You would give those essays to your students and have them write just the summarizing conclusion. When they get good at that, backing up one step, you would ask them to add an example or elaboration of the point in the next to final paragraph plus the conclusion. Then a final point with examples and a conclusion . . . and so on. You may be able to skip some steps depending upon your students' performance. In backward chaining each new step leads to familiar territory. Instead of getting harder and harder as students progress through the chain, the task gets easier until they end up with a complete essay. That itself is reinforcing.

The same process works well for performing a piece of music. Instead of starting with the beginning—playing until you hit trouble and then starting over (as novices usually do)—start at the end. Once the ending is fluent, back up. Now, instead of running into more difficult sections as you play, you encounter parts you already mastered. If only a few sections give you difficulty, follow the same procedure with each section. Again you would start with the end of each tough run. Once the final notes in that section are mastered, you would back up a few notes and play again to the end of that difficult spot. One benefit of backward chaining is that, instead of tightening up as you progress through a piece of music, you relax. The farther you go, the more you get to sections you have nailed with all of the practice. Relaxation, in turn, helps you perform better.

Sometimes learners require help for even a simple response. Then you can begin with a prompt.

Prompting Methods: Starting with Prompts and Then Withdrawing Them
A **prompt** is an action that assists a learner in making a first response. In the example of circles versus ellipses, to insure that the man would select the circle, a prompt consisting of lighting the circle was added.

Prompts may consist of giving part of an action, additional explanation, physical guidance, or anything else that helps the student respond correctly. In teaching Spanish, a student may hesitate when asked to translate "manzana." If you say "aaah . . ." (part of the word "apple"), that may be enough of a prompt for the student to come up with the complete word. A student faced with a math problem may be helped by a reminder to "Remember the pool problem" or some other hint about the procedure to use. Special education teachers often physically move students' hands in the initial stages of teaching a skill. Similarly, gymnastics teachers may physically guide students at the beginning of their executing a new move. Physical prompts differ from the lures discussed earlier, in that they help with execution of an action, rather than providing motivating conditions.

All prompts should be withdrawn quickly before students become **prompt dependent**. If you always say "ma" when asking for "apple" in Spanish, the student may only be able to translate the word when the prompt is also given.

Timing of Prompts
Prompting is best used *before* an error is made. If your student hesitates when asked to translate "manzana" into English, a quick "aah" *before* the student guesses "mango?" may prompt the correct response "apple." A prompt given *after* an incorrect response is a **correction procedure**. It is help that is contingent on failure (see below). Successive approximation requires correct responding, so prompts should *prevent* mistakes. One way to prevent errors involves always giving prompts, but only after a wait of a second or two.

> **A prompt** is an antecedent that enables a learner to respond appropriately. Prompts are usually withdrawn or faded quickly to prevent the student becoming **prompt dependent** which means the prompt must be given for a correct response.

Delayed Prompting

In **delayed prompting**, a question or task is presented and then after a second or two, a prompt or the complete answer is given. The student still repeats the answer which is then acknowledged as correct. You would think that if the student knew that he or she could get the correct answer just by waiting for a prompt (or the entire answer), he or she would wait. But that does not happen. A study with graduate students gave Spanish words on a computer screen for the students to translate into English. Each Spanish word was put on the screen and, after a delay of a few seconds, the English word was given for the students to copy (a prompt of the whole word). By waiting for the English word, the students could perform correctly every time. Did they wait? Only when they needed help on a particular word. As soon as they knew the English word for the Spanish given, they anticipated the prompt and typed right away.[28]

Delayed prompting is often used in one-on-one sessions especially with students with disabilities. Instructions may be given for students to wait and not to guess if they do not know the answer. They are told that the answer will be given for them. Most people prefer to respond without help if they can. Even young children will say, "Let me do it by myself."

Responding with a prompt is not the same as responding without one. In repeating what a teacher says or copying a word from a screen, the student is not answering the question. He or she is echoing what was given. Eventually control over the response must transfer from the prompts to the question or task itself. This transfer can be accomplished by gradually shortening the number of seconds before a prompt, by giving a smaller portion of the response, or by any of the successive approximation techniques above. All of these techniques have one characteristic in common: they are designed to advance skill levels with as few mistakes along the way as possible.

Why Reduce Correction Procedures, Including Prompts after Errors?

Every time you are tell a student "no," or "try again," or add a prompt after an incorrect answer, you are telling your student he or she has failed. As a correction procedure, prompting is better than most: prompts tell students what to do as well as what not to do and trials usually end with behavior that is reinforced. Problems occur, however, when errors become frequent. Then, with or without prompts, you may see some negative effects of punishment (see Chapter 11). Classroom disruption and problem behavior can usually be traced to lack of success. Frequent correction (including prompts that let students revise answers) means frequent lack of success.

Sometimes prompts that follow inappropriate responding produce a chain: wrong answer leads to prompt, leads to correct answer, leads to reinforcement. You can see this kind of chain with children who whine for a cookie (incorrect response), then are prompted "Ask nicely," say "May I have a cookie please?" (correct response), and then get the cookie (reinforcement). The goal was not for the child to whine before asking nicely, but the timing of the prompt encourages the chain. A prompt anticipating the child's whine would prevent this sequence. Better still, establishing consistent conditions where asking will and will not receive cookies prevents the whining so often seen in young children.

There is one more problem with prompting as a correction procedure. All of the time your students spend responding incorrectly takes time that would be better spent performing well. If a student gives an incorrect answer, gets a prompt, and then answers correctly, two-thirds of the instructional time involves error correction. One half of the consequences you are providing for that response are also negative. For all of these reasons, if you are going to prompt, do so *before* an error occurs.

No one can anticipate all errors. The principle of prompting *before* errors is something to work towards.

Fading and Vanishing

When prompts continue to be needed, you need to eliminate them without decreasing successful performance. Two techniques used widely in PI involve providing prompts and then reducing their intensity so they are harder to see (literally "fading"), or making them disappear bit by bit (vanishing). You may have used similar techniques yourself when memorizing vocabulary or poetry. Perhaps you "vanished" the words to learn by looking at them the first time, and then covered more and more of the material until you could say each word without help.

Fading or vanishing can be used with a whole class. In some schools, teachers are asked to teach their class a poem or school song to perform for holiday or graduation ceremonies. Fading or vanishing is supremely suited to this task. You put all the words onto the blackboard or a screen where everyone can see them. Singing or reciting the first time through is easy with all the words in view. The next time you remove a few letters or make all the words a bit grayer or fuzzier. Each time your students repeat the song, they get less and less help as the text is "vanished" or "faded." As with any shaping technique, your class must succeed at each step. If you remove too many letters at once, or fade too quickly, performance will break down and you will have to back up a step or two. But within a surprisingly short time, a class will perform beautifully without any textual help. Furthermore, the process is painless. Most students enjoy the process and they will shine when they perform for others.

GOOD SHAPING: ERRORLESS LEARNING

In "two-term" or pure shaping, there are no "errors" as such. There are just responses you do not, at the moment, reinforce. Similarly in a classroom, you do not have to respond to everything students do. Even with academic subjects, by noting and commenting on positives and not making a fuss over responses that are not yet correct, you encourage more behavior in general. In evaluating compositions, for example, if you write positive comments not only about grammar and style but about what students are saying, you will find them writing more easily. You can always fix the grammar and style problems with worksheets, or have students edit their own compositions after a first draft. Posting products on a class web page or bulletin board also gives a real reason for fixing grammar and style.

Example: Responding Only to Positives: A Suzuki Story

The founder of the Suzuki method of violin instruction was known for being positive. A violin teacher who studied with him told the following story.

Suzuki was giving a demonstration lesson for teachers who were going to teach his method. Several young students, from four to six years old, had come into the studio to perform. He had found something positive to say about each performance. Then, out came a little girl. She tucked her violin under her chin in a poor position, scraped the bow across the strings at a bad angle that made an awful screech, played "Twinkle, Twinkle, Little Star" so badly out of tune it was barely recognizable. The teacher in the audience was horrified at the performance. She wondered what on earth Suzuki could find to say that would be positive. Nothing, absolutely nothing she could think of had been done well.

The child finished and looked at Suzuki anxiously.

"Well," he said. "You played."

When you think about it, for such an unskilled performer, playing *was* an achievement. It must have taken guts knowing that everyone else played better.

What If You Get Mistakes?

Letting inferior performance go temporarily without comment does not mean that you do not address errors. Faults in performance are picked up later instead of being "corrected" at the moment. In TAG Teaching, the worst fault translates into your next TAG point. With other skills you take errors and break down performance into achievable steps, working on the most critical errors you noted. Your student's behavior will let you know when additional successive approximation techniques are needed and which procedures work best for their progress.

If you have special students in your class or in your family, or if you work with students one on one, you will encounter **Discrete Trial** instruction. A "Discrete Trial" consists of the teacher presenting a task, a student responding (or failing to respond), and the teacher giving feedback. While many practitioners of Discrete Trial instruction practice nearly errorless learning strategies, unfortunately many do not. In any case, "Discrete Trial" is *not* synonymous with behavior analysis.[29] Even the name is not appropriate. The word "trial" implies an agent making a "try." The word "discrete" implies set steps that do not exist in two-term shaping. For much of what is taught in one-on-one sessions, there are better procedures than the format called Discrete Trial.

IMPROVING ON DISCRETE TRIAL PROCEDURES WHEN WORKING ONE ON ONE

Students with special needs or those experiencing difficulty in a regular classroom are often given *one-on-one instruction*: one teacher working individually with one student. The most common format for such sessions is Discrete Trial. Tasks are presented to the student, responses evaluated, and feedback given. For students with autism or other disabilities, feedback for a correct response is usually something observed to be reinforcing, such as short verbal praise, a hug or tickle, a few seconds with a toy, or a Cheerio or other edible. Feedback for incorrect responding varies. Some practitioners follow errorless learning procedures, and change the sequence of tasks *on the spot* if an error occurs. Too often sequences are fixed once a session begins. When errors occur, the teacher may go on to the next problem, or say "Try again," once or twice with the same problem, or add prompts until the student responds correctly. Where each trial ends with the student being successful, whether or

> A **Discrete Trial** is a three-term contingency in which a task is given, the student responds, and feedback is given.

not mistakes are made along the way, trials have been named "learn units" in a system called CABAS (Comprehensive Applied Behavior Analysis for Schooling).[30]

Although the trial format is a standard procedure in Special Education, it lacks many features of shaping (see Table 8.3). Most of these disadvantages of trial formats can be reduced with fairly simple changes so that the procedures gain some of the advantages of shaping.

Adding Rate When Tutoring

Even when asking questions without hesitation, the single response for each trial reduces the opportunity for student responding and prevents getting a rate measure. Sometimes one question to one response cannot be avoided, as when teaching conversation skills. In many cases, however, a "trial" can be replaced by a fluency format permitting many responses. Chapter 5 described Discrete Trial procedures and alternatives for teaching the shapes, circle, triangle and square. Here another example is given using a format very much like Montessori's procedure: Present two colors, red and blue, and say, "Give me the red." Even assuming that the child is almost always correct, with the usual feedback and the rearrangement of objects, this restricts responding to only a few correct selections of red per minute. That can be increased at least four-fold in a fluency format.

For this example, assume you are working with a low-functioning child who requires a lot of help. First you establish a click or some other feedback as a conditioned reinforcer. You will click for each "correct" action. You would also teach the child to put objects into a can or box one by one. Now you are ready to teach color. You spread 30 red and 30 blue objects of various sizes and shapes on the table. Perhaps you put a sample of the color in a special place so the child can be reminded of the task. You say, "Put in *red.*" As the child starts reaching, you start a timer. You click each touch of a red object as it is picked up. If the child picks up other colors, even if he or she puts them in the can, you say nothing. You just do not click. At the end of the time (perhaps 15 seconds or a minute depending on the child's level), you record the number correct. If the child has not finished with the rest of the reds, fine, but they don't go into the data record. Note that you do not talk while the timing is in progress. You reserve praise,

---

Table 8.3 Disadvantages of Discrete Trial instruction (and why it is not the same as ABA or Behavior Analysis)

1. In any trial format a teacher initiates each question, so you cannot get a rate of student response. Thus you miss the most sensitive measure of student behavior.
2. Trial formats hold back the speed with which students can perform. Compare how many capitals of states a student can name using Precision Teaching flashcards with the number possible if each is presented to the student with the question "What is the capital of *this* state?
3. With a trial format, students do not *initiate* responding. They get used to waiting for a teacher before taking any action, encouraging passivity.
4. Fixed lists of tasks used in Discrete Trial instruction prevents adapting *continually* to a student's current performance so that some students may respond incorrectly or others fail to progress when they are ready for more difficult tasks.
5. Most Discrete Trial procedures include procedures for correction of errors. Correction is not part of shaping. Every failure slows down the rate of reinforced responding and dampens momentum.

hugs or other social reinforcement for the end of the child's performance. That also keeps its value higher since it isn't occurring too often.

Rate measures are very sensitive. Going from 20 correct in a 30-second timing to 25 shows substantial improvement you could never see in a series of correct trials. Not only that, the fluency format permits a much more varied presentation of objects and sizes than is possible in the time taken by a Discrete Trial format. Responding to "red" is more likely to generalize to red in other objects than when few specific objects are used during teaching. Of course, you would vary the colors requested. The next timing, you might ask for "blue."

If a student has trouble selecting colors, after making sure the child is not color blind, you could use errorless learning techniques. There are many ways to make it highly likely that the student will pick only red objects the first time. Using a red bucket, putting red objects closer, or using larger or shinier red objects than blue will encourage selecting red (see Table 8.4). When the child succeeds, the next time you gradually change location or size until it is *color* to which the child responds. Even at the beginning, errorless procedures make it possible for *any* student to be highly successful.

The one technique that will *not* teach color is to have only red objects on the table. That cannot teach a student to distinguish between colors. Differential response to properties of objects always requires having more than one property present. You must start with at least two colors.

Chapter 5 discussed the superiority of rate measures over percentage correct and over trials to criterion. When each response occurs only following a teacher question, the usual measures of student response are percentage correct or trials to mastery. Percentage correct cannot show changes in speed of performance which, along with accuracy, gives the best indication of "knowing your colors." Measuring trials to criterion is particularly to be avoided. In counting the number of "trials" it takes for a student to achieve mastery by answering correctly a set number of times in a row or by scoring at a given percentage, you are condoning errors. While in a whole classroom one cannot prevent inaccurate responses, there is little justification for allowing a student to repeatedly perform incorrectly in a tutoring session. Tolerating poor performance repeatedly is not good shaping. You must adjust tasks so nearly all responses are correct.

Some tasks cannot be adapted to a fluency format. For example in teaching conversational skills, a student response is appropriate only after another person's comment. You would not want to ask a student "How are you?" and have him or her answer "Fine, fine, fine, fine..." as fast as possible until a minute is up. For conversational skills, an analysis of verbal behavior is needed (see Chapter 10).

Table 8.4 Examples of first steps for errorless learning of colors in a fluency format

- Have all red objects bigger than the blue ones
- Place the red objects closer to the student than the blue ones
- Place all objects on a blue background, so the red objects stand out
- Use objects the student likes for the red, such as a fire truck or a ball and less desirable objects like mittens or a paperclip for the blue
- Physically guide the student's hand to the red objects (use this with caution and not for long)
- Use clapping that gets faster the closer to a red object the student's hand gets

Adding Flexibility to the Sequencing of Tasks

Shaping requires adapting *continually* to student behavior. If a first response is hesitant or incorrect, shaping requires changing immediately. Having to follow 10 or 20 set trials means that a teacher cannot adjust to the student's behavior and the student could fail to be successful more than once. Nevertheless set procedures are common in Discrete Trial instruction. Table 8.5 shows the beginning of a lesson on matching pictures. The lesson uses 3 by 5 cards with pictures of a car, dog, tree, house, cat, spoon, hat, shoe, boat, and ball. The teacher sits across the table from the student. The sample is placed in front of the teacher facing the student. The three pictures used for the student to select from are placed in front of the student. The teacher or aid records each student response. This student has a problem with "dog," but the lesson goes on without change. Some Discrete Trial procedures require stopping a session if three mistakes are made in a row, but most do not allow change otherwise: 80% correct is a standard criterion, so even with four mistakes a child goes on. Few students meet a criterion the first time they are given a set of 20 items, so the error rate is often high for each new skill. Changing to a procedure in which the child picks out dogs from a table full of objects (clicking each correct selection) shows the strength of behavior in rate measures, enabling adjustment of difficulty in the next timing. A high rate of selection of only dogs shows true mastery better than getting 10 out of 10 correct two or three sessions in a row.

As with Direct Instruction, a fixed script of steps may have arisen because many of those teaching students with disabilities have only minimal training in behavior analysis. While teachers or aids have no difficulty following scripts, they may not know how to adapt to student response during a session.[31] Whatever the reason, there is nothing in the Discrete Trial methodology that prevents adjusting at each step according to a student's response. At the very least, if the student hesitates or looks as though he or

Table 8.5 A typical Discrete Trial recording form showing repetition of student errors

Sample	For Student	Correct	Incorrect	Correct with prompt
car	tree, car, dog	✓		
car	car, house, ball	✓		
ball	house, car, ball	✓		
car	dog, ball, car	✓		
dog	ball, dog, house			✓
dog	dog, cat, car		✓	
house	tree, house, car	✓		
cat	ball, cat, dog			✓
house	cat, ball, house		✓	
car	cat, dog, car	✓		

she is not going to answer correctly, a prompt could be delivered quickly *before* the student's answer.

Eliminating the Aversiveness of "Correction" Procedures

Being told your response is incorrect is, if not punishing, at least not reinforcing. In two-term shaping, actions that are not selected do not receive any kind of feedback. You can see the difference in enthusiasm and posture of learners when correction is eliminated and only reinforcement is used. Removing materials for another "try" for incorrect responding is also aversive, usually resulting in signs of discomfort, anger, or outright crying. Errors do not have to be part of one-on-one instruction, even in a trials format. If a student is not being successful, find out whether prerequisite skills are missing or whether steps are just too large for that student. In any case, you can add prompts or additional steps to the usual progression in any curriculum until students succeed.

SUMMARY

The way in which individuals interact with each other and the natural world is not fixed. Behavior constantly shifts according to the contingencies in effect. Shaping is the process of building new behavior by selectively reinforcing properties of actions that move in a particular direction. The way in which behavior changes depends upon which actions are selected, or more precisely which properties of actions are reinforced. This chapter began with shaping jumping in a dog to illustrate the need for conditioned reinforcers and to show how more than one property of behavior is strengthened. The art of shaping lies in timing of reinforcement. Frequently reinforcing small improvements strengthens a consistent direction of change and keeps behavior going strong.

Whether planned or unplanned, shaping goes on all of the time. No one wants a screaming child, but interactions with a child may exemplify almost perfect shaping of screaming. On the positive side, without any planning, most caregivers successfully shape the beginning of clear talking in babies.

All shaping begins and ends with actions of the learner. Actions cannot be strengthened unless they occur. In the classroom, while explanation or demonstration are helpful, students must be active to learn to perform themselves. Effective teaching begins at current levels of skill and builds to more complex performances. There are many ways to break down advanced skills into successive approximations, the steps that students carry out.

In two-term shaping, behavior that does not move towards a goal is not called "wrong." It is just not reinforced. While in academic performances answers are called "right" or "wrong," what a learner does always results from current and past contingencies. The student's behavior is always "right" in that sense. Student actions follow behavioral laws just as their bodies move according to the laws of physics and gravity. There is no role for punishment or "correction" in shaping. Only reinforcement is used.

In a room full of students, one teacher cannot attend instantly and positively to each individual's momentary best actions. But even if perfect shaping is not possible, teachers can incorporate some of its most important features. This chapter has described procedures that teachers have used to increase active student responding and immediate feedback, and to build complex repertoires through a variety of successive approximation techniques. The importance of giving positive feedback rather than pointing out errors cannot be overemphasized as a way to keep behavior going and students enthusiastic. When there are "right" and 'wrong" answers to questions or problems, steps can be designed to help students answer "correctly" the first time, and to think of errors as "not getting it *yet*" rather than as "being wrong." That focuses attention on what is still needed for mastery. If a student is not behaving correctly, it is *contingencies* that have been at fault and contingencies that must be changed.

We all respond to contingencies. The procedures that teachers follow depend on the training they have received and the circumstances in which they teach. It makes no more sense to criticize teachers for failing to use good shaping techniques than for them to blame their students for failing to perform well. Teachers, like their students, need help when encountering problems they cannot solve. Principles of shaping help teachers solve behavioral problems.

Teachers enter the field of education to help students become effective citizens. All teachers thrive on student enthusiasm and achievement. They feel successful when they help a struggling student succeed or see their students continue to pursue beyond the classroom what they have taught. Shaping procedures do not guarantee ideal performance in all students, but they do improve progress and the enjoyment of instruction both for students and for their teachers.

CONCEPT CHECKS

Shaping and Conditioned Reinforcers (Objective A)

DIRECTIONS: Fill in the missing words.

1. **Shaping**: In shaping, the individual who initiates each action is the 1a. _____ . Shaping is a process of strengthening particular 1b. _____ of actions through the timing of 1c. _____ . To know which actions to select you must first know the actions you want, that is, your 1d. _____ . Paralleling the mechanism through which species evolve, the evolution of behavior through shaping is called 1e. _____ by 1f. _____ . Because the learner behaves according to the contingencies in effect, what are called "errors" in the student's behavior are due to faulty 1g. _____ .

2. **Conditioned Reinforcers**: A conditioned reinforcer is a 2a. _____ that is paired with an existing 2b. _____ . To create a conditioned reinforcer, you need something that can be activated 2c. _____ and that does not last very 2d. _____ . For non-verbal animals, you create a conditioned reinforcer by presenting first the 2e. _____ and then immediately following it with the 2f. _____ . For most students, you can make a sound a conditioned reinforcer by telling them that when they hear the sound their behavior is 2g. _____ .

Critical Characteristics (Objective B)

DIRECTIONS: Complete each sentence below with the principal reason the example fails to be a good example of the highlighted term.

1. Making sure you change visuals for your students frequently so they don't lose interest is **not** a good example of **pacing** (as in Direct Instruction) because _____ .

2. A paragraph followed by a multiple-choice question that sends the learner who picks a wrong choice to an explanation of why that answer is not right is **not** a good example of **linear Programmed Instruction** because _____

3. Grading a worksheet of 20 items as soon as a student completes it is **not** a good example of **immediate feedback** because _____.

4. A teacher sits across from a student and holds up a car. "What is this?" she asks. The boy hesitates and then says "banana." The teacher says, "no, it's a car." This is **not** a good method of prompting because the teacher should have _____.

ANALYSIS PROBLEMS

1. Shaping Pencil Position (Objective A)

You have a first-grade student who holds his pencil between his second and third fingers and at an angle that makes it difficult for him to write. You have five minutes a day when you can work individually with him alone to get him to hold the pencil with the thumb and first finger and to improve the angle of the pencil. Describe how you could shape a correct position using both modeling and a conditioned reinforcer.

2. Placement of Apostrophes (Objective C)

A teacher is introducing correct placement of apostrophes for possessives of nouns. He explains where to put the apostrophe by restating the phrase. He gives several examples like "the boy's shoes" from "the shoe of the **boy**," and "the boys' shoes" from "the shoes of the **boys**." After his presentation, the teacher asks, "Suppose you want to talk about all of the sailors' hats. How would you rephrase that? Joanie?"

Joanie says "The hats of all the sailors."

"Right. So where does the apostrophe go, before or after the s?"

Joanie: "After the s"

"Right. Like this." (The teacher writes "sailors'.")

The teacher continues: "How about the children's toys. How would you rephrase that using 'of the...?' Eric."

"The toys of the children."

"Good. So you would put the apostrophe before or after the s?"

"Before the s"

"Well done."

After five more examples done this way, the teacher hands out a worksheet with 20 apostrophes to add.

How could this teacher improve his lesson by incorporating more active responding?

ANSWERS FOR CONCEPT CHECKS

Shaping and Conditioned Reinforcers

1. Shaping

    1a. student (or learner or equivalent)

    1b. properties (or characteristics)

1c. reinforcement (or consequences or postcedents)
1d. objective (or goal or equivalent)
1e. selection
1f. consequences
1g. contingencies

2. Conditioned Reinforcers

2a. stimulus
2b. reinforcer
2c. quickly (or immediately or equivalent)
2d. long
2e. stimulus
2f. reinforcer
2g. good (or correct, right, or equivalent)

Critical Characteristics

1. For **pacing** the students must be behaving, not just the teacher. (or equivalent)

2. Linear programming requires the following: Any one of these equivalent should be considered correct. (The description is of a branching program.)
    constructed responding, not multiple-choice
    a higher density of responding than one question for a whole paragraph
    low error rates, not planning for errors by including comment for wrong answers.

3. **Immediate feedback** requires getting results for each item completed before doing the very next one.

4. The teacher should have given help before the student answered incorrectly (during the pause).

FEEDBACK FOR ANALYSIS PROBLEMS

1. Shaping Pencil Position

There are many ways to do this. Count one point for mentioning each of the following:

    establishing something as a conditioned reinforcer.
    modeling a correct hand position or physically helping the child hold the pen correctly.
    picking a first step that the student has a good chance of doing correctly.
    reinforcing often.
    adding further criteria as the student improves.

Here is an example of a five-point answer. Yours may differ, but be as good or better:

    I would get a clicker and tell my student that the click means his hand position is correct. I would demonstrate holding a pencil between the thumb and first finger and ask him to do it too, clicking when he imitates. Then I'd give him different pencils and click each time he holds each one correctly, demonstrating if needed. Next I'd ask him to draw a line or some simple figure on paper, clicking when he touches pencil to paper with the correct hand position. When this was mastered, I would watch the angle of the pencil as he copied a paragraph and every time the angle improved I would click, making sure that he got clicks often. If the hand position didn't keep the correct position as he wrote, I would go back to a previous step. I'd also ask him to put down the pencil and then start writing again, to make sure he continued to place the pencil between the thumb and finger initially. Going on to new steps would depend on his mastering the previous ones. Finally, I would mention his good hand position frequently throughout the day.

2. Placement of Apostrophes

You could arrange for every student to respond to each question by methods like the following:

a. Have everyone hold up their left hand for "before the s" or their right hand for "after the s" for each of those questions.
b. Ask each student to take out a piece of paper and to write the word with the correct placement of each apostrophe after you give each rephrasing.
c. Make a lecture fill-in sheet like the following for students to do.

      1. Rephrase: The hats of all the _____ --> The sailor_s_ hats.
      2. Rephrase: The _____ of the _____ --> The children_s_ toys.
      3. Rephrase: _____ -> The brother-in-law_s_ house.

d. Ask for choral responding for the "before" and "after" parts: "Where does the apostrophe go, before or after? Ready, set, everyone answer."
e. Pair students and have them take turns rephrasing the possessive, with the peer writing the word with the apostrophe in the right place (as you go around the room to check).
f. Make flashcards with sentences like "The three sailor_s_ hats" on the front and "before" or "after" on the back and have students do them in pairs.

9

TEACHING CONCEPTS AND UNDERSTANDING:
THE ROLE OF ANTECEDENTS

"A great part of our lives is spent in learning what behavior is appropriate in what situations."

Ellen P. Reese[1]

OVERVIEW

While operant conditioning can be described without referring to any preceding stimulus, antecedents are a major part of education. Students must respond to features of their environment and to do so in ways that will gain them entry into an enjoyable and productive life. At the basic level, they must respond appropriately to text, they must understand the concepts in a subject area, or abstractions like the number two. Understanding involves a specific kind of antecedent control. A boy who can answer "two," when shown two blue circles, but cannot identify the number when shown two red trucks or two pennies, or two of anything else, is responding to the wrong property of the circles. He is responding with the correct *form* of the answer, but for the wrong reason. It only *seems* that the boy understands "two."

This chapter introduces antecedent control with a discussion of the contingencies set by paper and pencil exercises. Most academic behavior involves attending to specific properties of objects or events. That, in turn, involves behavioral processes called induction and discrimination. Being alert to the relationship between properties of antecedents and behavior will help you better select and design exercises to teach the "understanding" and "concepts" so critical for success in school and in later life.

OBJECTIVES

By the end of this chapter you should be able to:

A. Identify whether the process illustrated exemplifies primarily induction or discrimination.

B. Fill in critical parts of definitions and examples using the following terms:

blackout technique
induction
S^D and S-delta
inappropriate antecedent stimulus control
Jabberwocky comprehension
concept
understanding
abstract concepts
equivalence relations.

C. Identify inappropriate cueing in exercises and tell how you could revise them to better teach the skills stated as their purpose.

D. Explain why "voluntary" is not a good term for emitted behavior.

E. Define "understanding" in behavioral terms and identify the induction and discrimination processes involved.

SEAT WORK, LABS, AND EXERCISES

If you are a teacher, unless you teach strictly physical activities such as sports or gymnastics, you rely on textual materials to help you teach. You may design your own materials or use products produced by others. At some point you probably give questions or problems or exercises for students to complete. Few teachers look carefully at the design of materials. Most teachers assume that exercises teach what they are supposed to teach without examining what, exactly, students actually get out of them.

It may surprise you that many publishers do not actually assess how well their materials teach. They *do* perform field tryouts. But instead of comparing the performance of students before and after completing the exercises under review, publishers are more likely to ask students and teachers how they *like* the materials. Not surprisingly, students like exercises that they can easily complete correctly, and teachers like materials that students enjoy.

As we saw in the last chapter, good shaping requires success at each step, so the fact that students correctly solve problems on a worksheet is a good feature, not a drawback. A problem occurs only when exercises permit answering "correctly" without paying attention to what the items are about. When exercises can be answered correctly for extraneous reasons, something is wrong.

GETTING THE "RIGHT" ANSWER FOR THE WRONG REASON

How can a student get a correct answer without understanding content? Suppose Pascale's paper shows the answer keyed as correct, but she has copied that answer from another student's paper. We call that "cheating." Technically it is called **inappropriate antecedent control**—behavior that has the right form, but is under the wrong controls. In this case, the form of Pascale's answer was correct, but what controlled the answer was what the peer wrote, not the question or task to which the student was supposed to respond. Pascale is not learning what the exercise was intended to teach, though she may be learning how to avoid detection or how to get close to a good student. Teachers are very sensitive to the inappropriate antecedent control called cheating.

> **Antecedent control** is the effect of an antecedent situation or event on the following behavior. **Inappropriate antecedent control** is antecedent control that differs from what is socially desirable.

Inappropriate Cueing by Pictures

Inappropriate antecedent control is not always obvious. Figure 9.1 shows an example of a poor use of pictures in teaching beginning reading. The purpose of this first-grade exercise is to "read for understanding." The questions at the end of the paragraph are intended to check that students understood the sentences they were supposed to read. The contingencies that this item sets up, however, encourage *skipping* the paragraph altogether. Students can answer the question without reading *one word* of the paragraph the question is about. All they have to do is to read the words next to the underlined spaces and look at the picture to answer.

Teachers reward finishing work quickly, so that whatever helps students work rapidly will tend to be reinforced. While your better readers may read the whole passage, slower

Jim had a ball.
He liked to throw the ball for his dog.
Jim's dog was watching.
He wanted Jim to throw the ball.

What do you think Jim will do?

___ go and eat lunch.

___ throw the ball.

Fig. 9.1 An inappropriate use of pictures to teach reading

readers will be penalized for taking the time to do so. In order to complete these kinds of pages in nearly the same amount of time as better readers, they must skip the paragraphs and go directly to the parts they need for answering. Of course, it is just these poorer readers that would benefit most from additional practice reading. Pictures should not let them avoid reading and still get "right" answers.

Pictures themselves are not bad. Figure 9.2 shows an appropriate use of pictures. In this exercise you cannot select the correct answer from the pictures alone. There is no way to answer questions one and two without the text, as you can see when the sentences are hidden.

The problem with pictures and diagrams continues through all levels of education. Most textbooks (including this one) present problems to answer at the ends of chapters. Questions with answers are designed to let students check their understanding of what they have read and also to check whether students have read the material or not. Do your students actually have to read a chapter in order to answer those questions? That depends upon the way in which the questions are designed. Here again, inappropriate cues may make it possible to answer questions quickly without reading the material they are about. If you assign a chapter to be read during class, watch how your students work. Do they first skip to the end to see what questions will be asked? That is not bad. Those questions highlight what the author thought was important. But how do your students progress from there? If you see students flipping back and forth to locate answers without reading from the beginning, you have a problem. In one high school biology text, nearly all of the questions at the ends of chapters could be answered entirely from bold print under pictures printed in the margins. Students did not need to read one word of the chapter to answer enough questions to get a high passing grade.

Which is it?

Directions: Circle the picture that shows what the underlined **word** means.

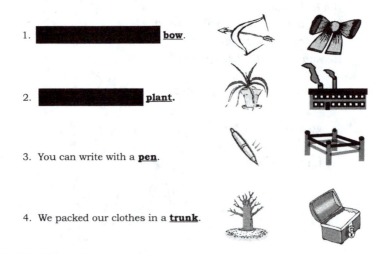

1. ▆▆▆▆▆▆▆ **bow**.

2. ▆▆▆▆▆▆ **plant**.

3. You can write with a **pen**.

4. We packed our clothes in a **trunk**.

Fig. 9.2 An appropriate use of pictures to teach reading comprehension

Inappropriate Antecedent Control in Math Word Problems
Figure 9.3 shows another kind of inappropriate cueing. What is the point of word problems? Presumably they teach students to visualize the mathematical processes needed for solving problems in daily life. The words are supposed to convey the kind of operation needed for manipulating the numbers given. Here, however, students do not have to visualize what process should be used. The items at the top show students that this is a page of multiplication: no understanding of combining equal amounts is required. Students can correctly solve every "word problem" on this page by ignoring all the words, hunting for the two numbers, and multiplying.

Some phrases also give inappropriate antecedent control. A word problem that ends with, "How many are left?" indicates subtraction. Irrelevant cues like this do not teach students problem-solving skills. Daily life does not provide tip-off words, nor will exercises or tests that vary phrasing or mix problems requiring different processes. Students who rely on inappropriate cueing will not know whether to add, subtract, multiply or divide when cues are no longer present. The badly designed exercises have not taught them which manipulations will solve practical problems.

Faulty Cueing through Position
In addition to pictures or other cues that make reading unnecessary, *position* may subvert the point of exercises. Which item in Figure 9.4 do you think students are most likely to miss? Up until item seven, all of the correct answers are the first words in the second sentence. Students who are unsure about adjectives, or who answer very quickly, may start responding to position in the sentence instead of the property of "standing in place of a noun." Thus some students circle "An" in the one example where the "right" answer is *not* the first word in the second sentence. A similar problem occurs with "main

Write each answer.

1.	1 x 3	2.	2 x 3	3.	3 x 3	4.	4 x 3	5.	5 x 3	6.	6 x 3	7.	7 x 3	8	8 x 3

9.	1 x 3	10.	2 x 3	11.	3 x 3	12.	4 x 3	13.	5 x 3	14.	6 x 3	15.	7 x 3	16.	8 x 3

17. There were 5 boxes. 3 crayons were in each box. How many crayons were there in all?

18. There were 3 pizzas. Each pizza was cut into 6 pieces. How many pieces of pizza were there in all?

19. There were 2 stools. Each stool had 3 legs. How many legs were there in all?

20. There were 6 apples. Each apple had 6 seeds. How many seeds were there in all?

Fig. 9.3 Inappropriate cueing that lets students answer without reading the problems they are supposed to solve

Directions: In the first sentence in each pair, the simple subject is underlined. Circle the pronoun in the second sentence that stands for it:

1. Sam is a ten year old boy.
   He lives in New York.

2. The students went out in the rain without umbrellas or raincoats.
   They are going to get wet.

3. Sally looked for a piece of paper.
   She needed to make a shopping list.

4. The students went to the zoo on Friday.
   They were gone all day.

5. Janet and Jean liked the red shoes in the mall.
   They both needed shoes.

6. Mom was worried that the children would be cold.
   She turned up the heat.

7. The glass vase tipped over.
   An earthquake had made it fall.

8. The river ran through the farm.
   It flowed very fast.

Fig. 9.4 A worksheet for practice in identifying pronouns

idea." When exercises put the topic sentence first in almost all practice paragraphs, students can get acceptable scores by responding entirely to position. When they hit more sophisticated tests with formats such as "Which sentence does not belong with the others," those who have responded to position will be unable to answer correctly.

Many of today's exercises are designed well. But others let students answer correctly without paying attention to the critical properties supposedly being taught. A procedure called the blackout technique helps you judge which parts of a worksheet are essential for correct responding.

THE BLACKOUT TECHNIQUE: A TOOL FOR EVALUATING INSTRUCTIONAL DESIGN

The premise of the blackout technique is very simple: if you can answer a question correctly with part of the content hidden, the blacked-out material was not needed to answer. Take the item in Figure 9.5. The left side shows an item as it was written. The right side shows the same item with the unnecessary material blacked out. A student encountering this item as part of an instructional sequence can answer correctly without understanding anything about probability that this item is supposed to teach. A fourth-grader could fill in the correct number to $3 \times 2 \times 1 = \underline{?}$.

The blackout technique is a method of identifying the parts of an exercise that are not required for correct responding. Parts of an exercise or question are hidden ("blacked out") to see how much can be removed without making it difficult or impossible to respond correctly.

The item in Figure 9.5 was part of a Programmed Instruction sequence on statistics,[2] but the same blackout test can be used for any exercises. Figure 9.6 shows examples of items where a lot of material can be hidden and where none or almost none can. In the top item, students are supposed to respond to the sequence of events in a paragraph. Most students can put the sentences in order with the text hidden. They do not have to read the paragraph that is supposed to help them complete this item.

Paragraphs for teaching sequencing must have steps or chronological events with which students are unfamiliar. Otherwise, like the item in Figure 9.1, exercises are setting up contingencies that encourage skipping material, not reading it.

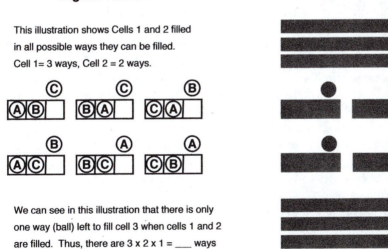

Original Version

This illustration shows Cells 1 and 2 filled in all possible ways they can be filled.

Cell 1 = 3 ways, Cell 2 = 2 ways.

We can see in this illustration that there is only one way (ball) left to fill cell 3 when cells 1 and 2 are filled. Thus, there are $3 \times 2 \times 1 = \underline{\quad}$ ways in which 3 balls can fill 3 cells.

Blacked out

$3 \times 2 \times 1 = \underline{\quad}$

Fig. 9.5 The blackout technique in use

Judith Doran and James G. Holland. "Eye Movements as a Function of Response Contingencies Measured by Blackout Technique." *Journal of Applied Behavior Analysis* 4 (1971): 13. Reprinted with permission of the Society for the Experimental Analysis of Behavior.

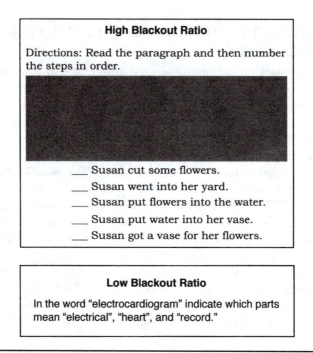

Fig. 9.6 Finding necessary parts of exercises with the blackout technique

The bottom item in Figure 9.6 shows a low blackout ratio. Except for trivial words like "the," you could not black out any part of this item and still be able to answer it. Students must respond to every part of the sentence.

The *lower* the blackout ratio, the *better* the instructional design. Low blackout ratios increase active responding because students must respond to all of the material. Anything that can be blacked out without hurting performance is material that students can ignore. They tend to do so. A study of the eye movements of students going through exercises showed that in a high-blackout version, students initially looked at the answer blank, followed by "a large number of jumps back and forth about the item in search of cues."[3] In the low-blackout version, instead of jumping around, student eye movements showed a pattern consistent with reading all of the material.

To take advantage of the blackout technique, you do not have to arm yourself with a dozen black markers and start obliterating parts of your workbooks or texts. Instead, visualize how students could respond with various parts hidden. The point is to become sensitive to the parts of exercises to which students are likely to respond.

Observing Student Behavior to Find Faulty Cueing
Watching students at work always helps identify antecedent control. If a student answers an item faster than you could yourself, that should tell you that not all of the material was needed. I was once sitting next to a student who was trying out some exercises I had written. The questions in one row had only two options "yes" and "no." The student slowly answered "yes" twice (which was correct). Then he rapidly marked "no" (which was also the correct answer.)

"How did you do that one so fast?" I asked.

"Oh, they never have three 'yesses' in a row," he said.

After that, "*they*" did. I arranged "yes" or "no" answers randomly. If three "yesses" came up in a row, that sequence stood.

Multiple-choice tests pose the same problem. Do you ever have "C" as the correct answer three times in a row? Four times? After a run of any letter, students are likely to avoid it for the next item. Students should select an answer because of content, not the letter used. You can prevent responding to sequences of letters when making tests, by putting multiple-choice options in a logical order, such as alphabetizing options and listing numbers in numerical order. Then if four "Cs" in a row are correct, so be it.

Correct answers in multiple-choice quizzes can differ from the incorrect options in many ways, including length or differing grammatical construction. One of the more bizarre examples of inappropriate antecedent control almost occurred in a final statistics exam. The professor wrote the stem of each multiple-choice item as an incomplete sentence, like "The median of a group of numbers is . . ." He then typed the correct answer to each item, adding a period as he completed each correct ending. Then he went back to the beginning of the test and added the alternatives, but he failed to add periods after the wrong answers. Fortunately for him, a proofreader discovered the faulty cues, or he would have had the most fantastic results in his entire teaching career on that final!

WHAT IS NEEDED FOR UNDERSTANDING

When you talk about "understanding," you mean more than selecting or saying something that would be marked as "correct." Had the statistics students selected every correct answer because of the periods following those options, you would not say they "understood" the problems. Understanding statistics at a basic level requires responding to quantities and

> **Understanding** means responding appropriately, that is, to those properties of an item or situation that society judges as significant.

the results that come from various manipulations of numbers. Similarly, students answering word problems by responding to multiplication signs at the top of a page do not demonstrate an understanding of the process of combining equal amounts. Understanding something means responding "appropriately," that is, to the properties that in our culture define the term or process. Understanding a word problem means visualizing how quantities must be manipulated to answer the question. In reading text, students who can tell what it says in their own words are said to understand what they read.[4] That requires responding to the *thematic elements* of content. Thematic elements are events described in a passage.

Grammatical "Give-Away" Cues: Jabberwocky Comprehension

Grammatical structure is so ingrained in our language that we respond to it without thinking. The Jabberwocky poem in Figure 9.7 does not convey information, but questions can be written on it nevertheless. Students can answer the typical "literal comprehension" multiple-choice question from grammatical cues alone. In contrast, the format at the bottom, in which options are embedded in the paragraph, prevents answering from grammatical cues. You cannot pick a "correct" answer, because there is no meaning to the passage.

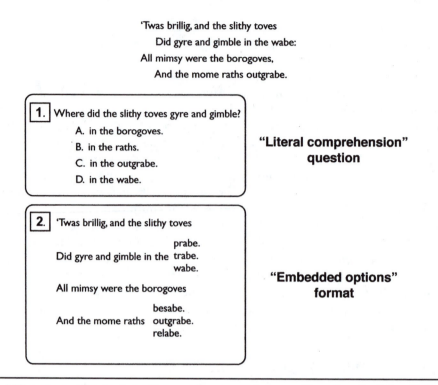

Fig. 9.7 Jabberwock comprehension: "correct" answers from grammatical cues with an alternative that avoids them
Poem by Lewis Carroll (Charles Lutwidge Dodgson). *Through the Looking-Glass and What Alice Found There*, 1871.

The **embedded options** format is used by several states as part of reading comprehension tests.[5] The words that are left out can "ask" for the same information as multiple-choice questions. For instruction, this kind of format encourages students to start at the beginning rather than hunting for answers. The embedded option format gives a higher density of student acitivity than the typical format of paragraphs followed by questions. Students make more responses per minute with blanks to fill in as a paragraph develops.

Even with the embedded option format, grammatical cues or the familiarity of phrases can give away answers. For example you can pick the "right" word to complete "down the _____ " if the options are "purple," "hall," and "zebra." You do not need to know what the passage is talking about. By making all choices grammatically correct (for example "alleyway," "ladder," and "hall"), you make it necessary to respond to the rest of the sentence and perhaps even to prior content. Students must show what we call "understanding," rather than being able to respond to inappropriate cues.

Leaving blank spaces in text instead of providing options serves the same purpose as embedded options. That format resembles the **Cloze technique** that leaves out every fifth word in text for students to fill in. The Cloze procedure does not consider meaning. Often words like "the" or "it" are omitted. To teach comprehension, the particular words left out should relate to the meaning of a passage.

If students are not responding to give-away cues or other inappropriate features of exercises, to what antecedents *are* they responding? Responding "appropriately" to meaning involves two processes, induction and discrimination. Both processes are involved in everything you teach.

INDUCTION

Induction is the name for the spread of effect from one antecedent situation to others that share similar properties. Another term describing the relationship is "generalization."[6] Induction continually occurs. If when standing in a bakery, you are told that a particular pastry is called "baklava" you can correctly identify other pieces of baklava on the

> **Induction** describes the spread of effect from one antecedent situation to others that are similar or related in some way.

same shelf without further training. Further, once you can reliably point to baklava in one pastry shop, you can identify pieces of baklava that are bigger or smaller, lighter or darker, or made in a different shape. The closer the physical resemblance, the more likely induction will occur.

Induction goes on even when two stimuli appear identical. Two instances of the printed word "Hiawatha" on the same page may look alike in every detail. But no two stimuli are ever identical. Even if two instances of "Hiawatha" are on the same part of the page and in the same font and size, subtle differences such as the angle from which the reader is viewing, lightness or darkness of print or light source, and the surrounding words or their spacing will differ. If nothing else, at least the time of viewing differs. In these cases there is not much "spread," but induction is still occurring.

The "same" words can differ markedly. Skilled readers who can pronounce "Hiawatha" in black Helvetica 12 point font can usually pronounce the same word on a billboard in six-foot-high letters in all capitals printed in blue. The defining characteristic for "sameness" of words lies in the sequence of letters, not in properties like font, size, color, or location. This "sameness" relationship must be taught. Elementary students who can pronounce "cat" may have difficulty with "cat," or with "CAT." They must be taught that the same letters have different forms. At the same time, beginning readers must learn to distinguish between similar-looking letters. Judging only by the shape of the letters, a, o, and c look more alike than A, a, and a. What you teach as "similar" or "different" is what your culture has taught you. Sometimes "sameness" can be amusing. In Victorian England, women hid their legs down to and including their ankles lest they arouse male passion. Many households also covered the legs of their grand pianos. That's induction!

Even though induction is going on all the time, we don't respond the same way to everything. A child who learns to call one fruit "apple" may initially call a pear or peach "apple" too, but soon adults will begin to teach responding differentially to different fruits.

DISCRIMINATION

Responding differently to different properties of objects or events is called **discrimination**. Along with induction, **discriminative stimulus control** is always occurring. Infants who utter "Mama" when anyone is in a room (induction) soon *restrict* "Mama" to familiar people (discrimination). The circumstance for saying "Mama" both *spreads* from one female to others, and *narrows* to familiar people. The narrowing continues when saying "Mama" receives differential consequences when the mother is around: saying "Mama" is not reinforced when another familiar person is present. When you think of it, this discrimination is tough! Babies must learn to respond to the properties that identify Mama, but not to identify her by properties that change from day to day, like clothing, hairdo, perfume, makeup, eyeglasses, which room she is in, and so on. If a mother's looks change too drastically, many babies will react as though their mother is a total stranger. If a mother appears in an unusual hat or dark sunglasses, her baby may cry. The usual properties paired with the mother are not strong enough for recognition. Talking to the child (thus adding more defining characteristics) usually helps the child see that this unsettling person is actually Mama.

Neither induction nor discrimination *explain* behavior. They merely describe the functional connections between antecedent stimuli and operants. The process by which antecedent stimuli gain control over behavior, however, has been thoroughly researched.[7]

> **Discrimination** refers to the control over responding by properties of objects or events that have been made salient through differential reinforcement of behavior in their presence.

Traditional Discrimination Training
Any feature of the environment that is correlated with reinforcement of an operant gains control over responding in its presence. Discrimination training is thus a matter of establishing relationships between properties of antecedents and the consequences for responding versus not responding in their presence. Those properties are the defining characteristics that students attend to in the better-designed exercises described above.

To illustrate classic discrimination training, imagine teaching a young boy the difference between circles and squares. The child already has experience with touching pictures on the screen, but has no experience with circles and squares. For this illustration, imagine that you cannot explain what a circle is. You must teach the discrimination solely by pairing reinforcement only with correct responding. Your goal is to get the child to touch the screen only when a circle is shown. This example follows a Discrete Trial format where only one figure is shown on the screen at a time. For the boy, when a touch is correct, two seconds of a cartoon (previously shown to be reinforcing) comes on the screen. Then the next figure is shown.

You start training: you show the circle. The child touches the screen and the cartoon excerpt is shown. The fact that the child touches the circle illustrates induction since the circle has never been a drawing the child has touched before. Prior experience of touching things shown on computer screens pretty much guarantees that the child will touch a novel stimulus.

To prevent touching the square, you must extinguish that behavior. You present the square, the child touches the screen, and you do *not* reinforce that touch. The child may quickly touch the shape again, perhaps with more force (showing an extinction burst). You catch a moment when the child's hand isn't headed for the screen, and change the shape to the circle. The child hits the screen and you reinforce the touch. Perhaps you keep the circle on for a few more trials.

The trick, as you may have realized, is to avoid extinguishing *all* touching of shapes. You must extinguish only touching *squares*. Thus you must make sure that the circle occurs often enough to keep the operant of touching strong. Soon (perhaps after only a few presentations of squares) you will note a hesitation when the square comes on the screen. That is a good time to change to the circle. As soon as you see reliable **differential responding**, you can say you have established discriminative control by shape, or a circle-square discrimination. Note that the circle has been paired with an opportunity to earn reinforcement, making it a conditioned reinforcer, like clicks that have been paired with existing reinforcers. You can now change to a circle to reinforce other behavior, such as sitting up straight. With the square on the screen, you watch the child's posture, and immediately present the circle when the child sits up a bit straighter. After the cartoon, the square again appears, and again sitting up straighter results in a change to a circle, whereupon the child touches the screen. Soon you have a chain.

The control over the child's behavior does not lie in the shape itself. The child's responding differentially to the shape results from the contingencies you set up during training. If, one day, you reverse the conditions so that only touching *squares* is now reinforced, behavior will eventually change according to the new contingencies. The power of any antecedent over operant behavior lies in its relation to past consequences for behaving in its presence versus in its absence.

The language describing discrimination is technical but, like all scientific language, precise. Before your child responds differentially to circles versus squares, shape is not a salient property of the figures. It is only when touching circles occurs at a different rate than touching squares that circles can be called a **discriminative stimulus** or S^D (pronounced "ess-dee") for touching the screen. The stimulus in the presence of which a touch does *not* occur is called an **S-delta** (S^Δ) for touching the screen (here the square). In talking about any antecedent stimulus you must include the response that is related. The square is an S-delta for *touching*, but if you shaped sitting up straight when the square was on the screen, the same square is an S^D for *sitting up straight*. In driving a car, a stoplight turning red is an S-delta for *continuing* through an intersection (we hope), but it is an S^D for *pressing* the brake. You must specify the pertinent operant when discussing discrimination.

> A **discriminative stimulus or S^D** is a stimulus in the presence of which a given response reliably occurs. A stimulus becomes discriminative through reinforcement occurring for responding in its presence but not in its absence.

Behavior analysts often define a discriminative stimulus as a "stimulus in the presence of which responding *will be* reinforced." Technically you can't call a stimulus discriminative until differential responding is shown. Usually at the beginning of discrimination training, you get an extinction burst to what will *become* the S-delta, so that there is actually more responding in the S-delta condition than during the stimulus that will become the S^D.

The Precision Teaching format that presents many of each shape, combined with a click for each one selected correctly, teaches discrimination faster than the trial format described here. But the "free operant" format does not show how changing from square to circle becomes a conditioned reinforcer in a chain.

Chains of Behavior

A discriminative stimulus serves two functions. It is an antecedent stimulus for a particular response. At the same time, the S^D becomes a conditioned reinforcer: a postcedent you can present to shape a second action. By changing the shape from a square to a circle contingent upon sitting straighter, a fine posture can be shaped within a few minutes. Of course, once you change the shape to the circle, the child will touch the screen and the cartoon will show. You thus have a **chain of behavior**: a straightening of posture produces a circle which is both a reinforcer for sitting up straight *and* an S^D for touching the shape. To get a child to first sit up straight and then touch a screen, the last response (touching) is taught first. The teaching order is the reverse of the final performance, an example of the **backward chaining** introduced in Chapter 8.

Example: Dual Functions of Stimuli in Backward Chaining of Writing the Letter K

In Chapter 8, procedures of backward chaining were illustrated with the teaching of solving equations and essay writing. Here functions of various parts of a chain will be illustrated with a simple example of a chain for teaching beginning handwriting. How would you teach, say, printing the letter "K" using backward chaining? If you write the letter, you will see that there are three strokes: first the downward back of the letter, then the top angled part and finally the line from the middle down to the bottom. Starting with the last stroke first, you give the child the first two parts already done, perhaps with a dotted line to prompt where the final stroke should go (see Figure 9. 8 Step One). By using a magic pen whose ink turns dark (or changes color) only when a line is in the correct place, you can arrange for immediate feedback for correct strokes. Completing the final line gives the dark line and also produces a complete letter, usually also reinforcing. By slowly removing the dots, very young children learn to place the last line correctly without help. They have now mastered the last step of the chain. Backing up one step you repeat the process for the second line (Step Two). At this point, completing the second line produces both a dark line *and also* produces the S^D for the last stroke already mastered. Finally the first downward stroke is added, providing an S^D for the second line which in turn is an S^D for the last link in the chain, reinforced by the complete letter. With a bit of practice, the steps in the chain flow from one to the other seamlessly.

Emitted Versus Elicited Responding

Like any operant, the response in a discrimination is "**emitted**," not "**elicited**" (see Chapter 3). Elicited responses like the blinking to a touch to the eye are controlled by antecedents, but the effect of the antecedent in respondent behavior does not depend on differential consequences for responding or not responding in that stimulus's presence. Individuals around the world inherit the same reflexes, regardless of their culture or locale. Emitted behavior differs. To explain why someone blinks when you *say* "Blink" you must look at the person's history with respect to postcedents as well as antecedents. In a non-English speaking country, saying "blink" would not produce a blink. All operants are controlled by their consequences. In operant discrimination, antecedents gain control only through their relation with the action–consequence *pairings*.

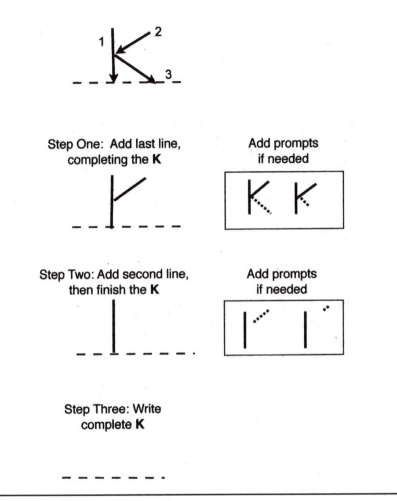

Step One: Add last line,
completing the **K**

Add prompts
if needed

Step Two: Add second line,
then finish the **K**

Add prompts
if needed

Step Three: Write
complete **K**

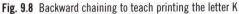

Fig. 9.8 Backward chaining to teach printing the letter K

Why "Voluntary" and "Involuntary" is Not a Good Distinction
You may hear emitted behavior described as "voluntary" and elicited behavior as "involuntary." That is a poor distinction because "voluntary" implies a conscious decision. Actions do not begin in your brain. Brain activity depends on what you are experiencing. Operant behavior is not as inevitable as respondent behavior, but it is still a result of your interactions in the world. It may be "conscious" when you can talk about alternatives and take one alternative for reasons you can identify. But everyone responds unconsciously too. You may put an object down without thinking and later not be able to find it. You may start thinking of a past experience without knowing why, perhaps due to a subtle sound, smell, or sight you cannot identify. We talk about making a decision when two or more courses of action are possible and have roughly equivalent appeal. We *feel* that we are making a decision, but what we ultimately decide depends on complex features of the situation and on our previous interactions throughout life.

Calling emitted behavior "voluntary" causes problems especially when the behavior discussed is inappropriate. It is too easy then to avoid any role in its occurrence. If you say that Bob's swearing is "voluntary" you have just put the responsibility inside Bob.

He just needs to decide to change! Acknowledging that the swearing is simply "emitted" behavior encourages looking for factors in Bob's world that can be changed to help improve that behavior. Perhaps peers are applauding his swearing in the halls, or he cannot do the work he is given. Maybe he never learned how to handle frustration. Whatever the circumstances, change is produced by changing contingencies.

Extinction and Punishment in Discrimination Training

In schools and in life in general, responding inappropriately (that is, in the S-delta condition) is rarely just ignored. It is usually punished. Discrimination training for swearing, for example, includes reinforcement from peers in the S^D situation, but in an S-delta situation, such as being in the principal's office, swearing will probably not only fail to be reinforced, but is likely to receive punishment. Similarly, writing 8 to 3+3 may get a consequence like a big red X, or an exasperated "no," or at least a "try again," instead of no consequence at all.

Some researchers recommend punishing errors in Discrete Trial formats to speed discrimination. The problem with this idea (apart from the fact that Discrete Trial is not the best format) is that to penalize errors you must be getting errors. In the classroom if you are getting a lot of errors, it is better to change your instructional sequence than to "correct" or punish mistakes. Penalizing errors is aversive for students (see Chapter 11). Even simple extinction is aversive when it follows a prolonged period of continuous reinforcement. Think of how you feel when you desperately need the internet that has never failed you and suddenly it disappears or your computer stops functioning. The emotional response that accompanies extinction and punishment makes errorless or near errorless procedures best for any teaching, including discrimination training.

TEACHING "UNDERSTANDING" OF CONCEPTS AND PRINCIPLES

> A **concept** consists of a property or set of properties shared by objects or events.

A **concept** is a collection of properties shared by objects or events. Whether or not objects are *members* or *examples* of a concept class is determined and taught by a social group. To "understand" a concept, students must respond to the defining properties and not to non-defining features. Thus the defining properties must become S^Ds for student responding.

Individual examples of any concept differ in their non-defining properties. Objects that qualify as chairs, for example, vary in shape, texture, size, color, whether they have decoration on them or not, and even their odor or whether seen in bright or dark light. An outdoor lounge chair looks very different from a four-legged chair, but both share the defining properties of being "a seat with back support designed for a single person." There is more physical resemblance between a sofa and an easy chair than between an easy chair and an outdoor lounge chair. It is not physical looks that define a chair, but its use. Calling something a "chair" is reinforced only if it is used for sitting. A child "understands" the concept of chair by responding appropriately to chairs and by differentiating between chairs and other objects (not calling a stool a "chair" or sitting on a potted plant).

When teaching a new concept, to help your students respond to defining properties, you need examples that contain those properties. Technically you cannot call members of the concept class S^Ds until differential responding occurs. That is why instances are called *examples, exemplars, members* or sometimes S^+s (pronounced Ess-Plusses). Similarly, you cannot say an object or event is an S-delta for a particular response until a specific response does *not* occur in its presence. Thus the terms *non-example, non-member* or **S-** (pronounced Ess-minus) are used. Here the terms *example* and *non-example* will be used for stimuli you *want* to become S^Ds and S-deltas.

Responding that shows "understanding of a concept" is never complete. Even the most sophisticated scientists are continually encountering new phenomena they find hard to classify. In education, the degree of understanding you teach depends on the distinctions your students need at their present level of schooling.

Introducing a New Concept

When introducing a new term, how do you make only its defining characteristics salient? In the classroom, the first step is usually to give a definition: "A fruit is a product of a tree or other plant that contains one or more seeds protected by a surrounding fleshy substance," or if you are teaching botany, "a reproductive structure of an angiosperm which develops from the ovary and accessory tissue which surrounds and protects the seed." Next, students are usually asked to tell whether or not individual items are or are not examples of the concept, starting with items in which defining characteristics are clear. The more diverse the examples and non-examples you use, the faster responses will become restricted to a concept's defining properties. If, for elementary students, you show only fruits that are located together in grocery stores, your students may fail to classify tomatoes and avocados as fruits. Put another way, to make the defining properties salient, vary as many of the non-defining properties as possible in both examples and non-examples. If students have difficulty, switch back to examples that are easy to tell apart or remind students about the definition until you advance to cases more easily confused.

Varying non-defining properties when teaching serves a second function besides helping to establish a discrimination quickly. Variation in examples promotes induction so that unfamiliar cases are more likely to be correctly classified. Students who have only seen fruits that are sitting on a table may not recognize a fruit if it is hanging from a tree branch. Teaching even such a simple concept as "fruit" requires induction from one fruit to another no matter where located, and differentiating between fruits and non-fruits regardless of size, color, or other irrelevant properties.

Abstract Concepts

The defining properties of some concepts are **abstract**. That is, they are properties that occur only *in* objects or events but never alone. While you can say of an apple, "This is a fruit," you cannot say of a red apple, "This is a red." Color is an abstract property. Even in a shining red light, red does not occur by itself. It is a property of the light not a thing or event itself.

> An **abstract concept** is a property or collection of properties that can never exist independently of objects or situations which contain them.

Another abstract concept is that of number. No number has an existence outside of a group of objects. In teaching something as seemingly simple as red or the number two, the abstract property has to be separated from the objects used as examples. Non-defining characteristics need to be varied.

Take the number *two*. Figure 9.9 shows some properties that occur in groups of two objects, but which must be separated from "two-ness." As Piaget showed, number and the space occupied by objects are often confused by young children. Youngsters are likely to say that a row of five objects spread out has "more" than a shorter row containing six objects. Many such confusions are understandable when you think of how language is acquired. When a child with a row of crackers asks for "more," the additional crackers usually lengthen the row. It is not surprising, then, that a child equates *more* with *longer.* To separate length from "more" you have to counter previous experience by making sure that a group with "more" isn't always longer than the comparison.

The same problem occurs with any abstract concept. The only way to separate an abstract property from the objects in which it is found is to vary examples. I remember teaching my daughter "red" using her red jacket as the example. When she called my green jacket, "red," smiling proudly at her accomplishment, I realized my mistake. She had paired "red" with the kind of clothing, not with the property of color.

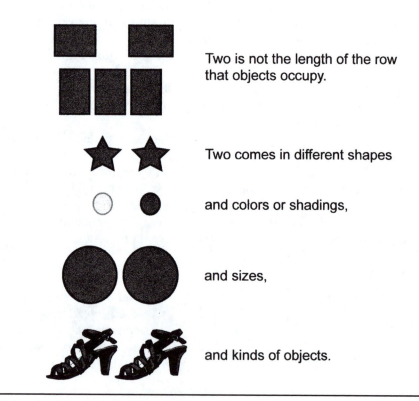

Two is not the length of the row that objects occupy.

Two comes in different shapes

and colors or shadings,

and sizes,

and kinds of objects.

Fig. 9.9 Properties that are *not* part of the abstract concept "two"

Selecting Examples and Non-Examples for Teaching Concepts and Principles
Every experienced teacher knows which discriminations students find difficult. Some difficulties can be overcome by varying examples in unfamiliar ways. Using many different examples (or **multiple exemplars** as they are also called) helps in teaching students to respond to the relevant characteristics and not to irrelevant ones.

Example: Teaching the Concept of Area
The area of a parallelogram is usually taught with figures resting on their long side. Students are told to multiply base times height. If you turn the parallelogram 90 degrees so that is it is resting on one of its points, students often have no idea of what to do (see Figure 9.10).[8] They have not learned to respond to the defining feature of area which is "number of square units a figure contains." Area is independent of position. To teach area, then, examples should be presented in various positions so that students discriminate between the measures needed and other lengths that are given. In daily life, not only do areas come in all sorts of positions, they aren't even drawn for you. That is why classroom tables and floors and bulletin boards provide better practice in calculating area than drawn figures, even when those figures are not arranged with the "base" on the bottom.

Example: Teaching the Concept of Fractions
Elementary school teachers are familiar with shaded sections of pies or pizzas to teach fractions. If only circles are presented in exercises, the defining property of "portions of a whole" may not become the property to which students respond. They may respond to the *shapes* of fractions shaded. A student who can circle 1/2 to identify a half-blackened circle may not be able to identify the fraction shaded of a half-blackened rectangle where the dividing line extends longways from end to end. To respond to fractions, students must first identify whether sections of a figure are "equal portions" or not. Then, by varying the shape of objects shaded, students will start to respond to "portions of a whole." Going from shaded fractions of a single figure to fractions of a group of objects also presents problems for many students, as does moving from two-dimensional figures on paper to three-dimensional objects in the classroom. Again

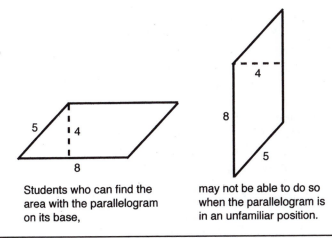

Students who can find the
area with the parallelogram
on its base,

may not be able to do so
when the parallelogram is
in an unfamiliar position.

Fig. 9.10 A test for understanding area, in this case of a parallelogram

varying everything you can think of for your examples and non-examples lets behavior come under the control of the defining features of fractions, not of irrelevant properties.

Example: Teaching the Concept of Mammal

One more example: in teaching "mammal," many students misclassify whales. Even if they learn to say "mammal" for whales, they must do so for the right reason. Just memorizing that a whale is a mammal indicates a pairing of words, not a response to the defining properties of mammals. That is why it is good to ask "why" when students give classifications of commonly taught examples. That gives them an opportunity to repeat the defining characteristics. (Even scientists must review definitions. In 2006 Pluto was reclassified as a "dwarf planet" because it did not have all the features that define "planet.")

Finding good examples is more difficult in the humanities than in mathematics and science. Clear examples of concepts such as "democracy" are tough to find. For difficult discriminations, individual cases can be used as starting points for discussions, rather than as examples or non-examples to classify. It is still important to vary the properties of cases chosen. If only the United States and Cuba are used to contrast capitalism with communism, students may miss many features of economic systems that need to be considered. Whether difficult or clearly defined concepts are taught, discrimination is only one kind of antecedent control involved. The other involves induction.

INDUCTION: PROPERTIES THROUGH WHICH INDUCTION OCCURS IN THE CLASSROOM

Induction is the spread of effect from one antecedent situation to another. One property that links antecedents is physical resemblance. If students learn to spot a "sparkly eyed" mutation in one batch of fruit flies, they can be expected to find flies with similar looking eyes in other batches of flies. Even with different microscopes, and in other labs, the faceted eye surfaces in the mutation look alike, and differ from the normal smoother eye.

Using Physical Similarity for Modeling

Physical similarity occurs in actions as well as objects. From the first days of life, youngsters learn to copy what others do. By school age, most children imitate readily. When a popular television or movie personality adopts a new hairstyle or kind of dress, it doesn't take very long before you see students sporting the same style. Students don't copy everyone, of course. They copy others who obtain the kinds of reactions they would like from others. A person that others imitate is called a **model**.[9] When you demonstrate a procedure in class, you are *modeling behavior* for your students to imitate. You are only one model that can be used in your classroom. Peers can be used as models, too. Another "model" is a student's *own* behavior.

Video Modeling of a Student's Own Behavior

To help improve performance, videos can be taken of a student's own behavior. In sports, videos taken during practice or games may be subsequently shown to the players for feedback, though often the technique is combined with punishment for mistakes, a procedure not advocated here. Video has also been used to teach contingency management to aides or caregivers.[10] The caregiver or aide may be learning how to deliver consequences appropriately. With the camera rolling, the trainee interacts with the "child" played by the session instructor. The "child" answers questions, but also provides some challenging behavior, like swearing or shouting "no." The trainee handles the situation as well as he or she can. The video of the session is then played back. Often the trainee critiques his or her own performance, with the instructor providing feedback. "Yes, you caught yourself attending to Saul's asking politely. That will strengthen good manners." Since learners are likely to be rather sensitive about how they perform, they can be asked to identify every *positive* action. For any behavior still needing improvement, a second video could be taken with a new target focusing on the behavior requiring further work, or the trainee could be given a simpler behavior to handle until ready for a more challenging situation.

Editing Video

To give a good model of one's own behavior, video can be edited. The idea behind editing a video is to show a student acting almost perfectly. Say you have a student, June, who rarely completes seat work. You video her behavior in class. She looks out the window, files her nails, makes a face at another student, arranges the paper in the middle of her desk, takes out her comb and combs her hair, shifts in her seat and completes one problem. Then she's back to grooming again. During a 30-minute session she completes only five problems. To show her working consistently, the 30-minute video is edited to remove everything except working, so that it looks like June is doing one problem after another without pausing. The video is now four minutes long. You show this video to June. She sees herself behaving perfectly! Sometimes the result of this procedure is a dramatic shift towards appropriate behavior.

Peers as Models

Peers have also been used as models. A student behaving appropriately or receiving approval encourages similar behavior from others. At a simple level, teachers attend to a peer who is exhibiting the appropriate action. Telling a first-grade student, "You are holding your pencil just right" often prompts nearby peers to correct their grips. Then you can comment right away on the imitating students' improved positions.

For high school students, consequences delivered to one student also influence others nearby, but feedback may need to be more subtle. A brief smile or approving look to a model works better than praise, especially when comments are not spontaneous and genuine. Human beings are extremely sensitive to the relation between behavior and its consequences—even when observing it in others.

Much research has been done on how induction occurs and what "transfers" from one stimulus or set of experiences to another. The properties that are similar from one situation to another do not always involve how something *looks*. Induction involves many other properties.

Induction through Relationship

An early study of induction was done with birds. Pigeons were presented with two figures, a small circle and a medium circle. Pecking the medium circle was reinforced. Soon the bird reliably pecked the medium circle and not the small one. Then the bird was presented with a large circle and the same medium circle. Which circle do you think the bird pecked? You might expect it to peck the medium circle, because pecking that circle had been reinforced. But the bird pecked the *large* circle. The bird was not responding to a particular figure, it was responding to *relative size*. It pecked whatever figure was larger.

Like birds, people often respond to relationships rather than to absolutes. For example, you recognize tunes by *relations* between notes, not by the actual notes played. Having learned "Happy Birthday" in one key, you will recognize it no matter what note it starts on. You are responding to the relations between notes. Human beings acquire a huge repertoire of relationships. Having learned one sequence of notes or "larger," we respond to other examples without having to be taught each one. Another procedure by which induction occurs has been demonstrated by research in equivalence relations.

EQUIVALENCE RELATIONS

Chapter 7 described work by Murray Sidman and his coworkers teaching reading to a handicapped boy. They demonstrated induction where no physical resemblance was involved.[11] Their work is known as equivalence relations. It involves both discrimination and induction and, as Sidman put it, "is a direct outcome of reinforcement contingencies."[12]

No one is surprised that a child who can name one cat can then name other cats or even pictures of cats that have the same overall look. While no one tries to feed a picture of a cat, a physical cat and its picture resemble each other physically, and most children easily learn to match pictures to physical objects. Cats do not share physical properties with the printed word "cat," nor do they physically resemble the sound of the spoken word "cat." Sidman and his coworkers demonstrated how stimuli that do *not* physically resemble each other can become connected so that children match them to each other. All reading requires pairing dissimilar stimuli. Words do not physically resemble the objects or animals or events to which they refer.

In teaching reading, teachers use objects or pictures of objects like "cat" with which children are already familiar. Young readers respond easily to pictures. They can pick out the correct picture when you say its name shown by Number 1 in Figure 9.11, and they can name pictures of familiar objects (Number 2 in Figure 9.11).

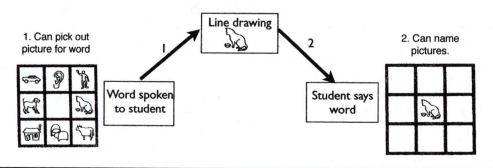

Fig. 9.11 Skills pre-readers usually already have

Adapted from Murray Sidman. *Equivalence Relations and Behavior: A Research Story.* Boston, MA: Authors Cooperative Inc., 1994, 27. Used by permission.

To say that a student can *read and understand text,* however, requires a whole lot of new behavior. For just the word "cat," the student must be able to do the following (see Figure 9.12):

- Select the printed word **cat** from different words when asked "Which word says 'cat'?" (Number 3 in Figure 9.12)
- Select the picture of the cat to match the printed word **cat**. (Number 4)
- Select the printed word **cat** to match a picture of a cat. (Number 5)

3. Touch the printed word that matches the word pronounced:

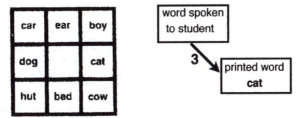

4. Touch the picture that matches the printed word:

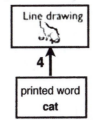
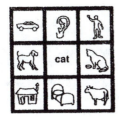

5. Touch the printed word that matches the picture:

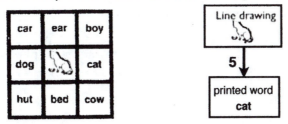

Fig. 9.12 Skills that show understanding of the meaning of the printed word "cat"
Adapted from Murray Sidman. *Equivalence Relations and Behavior: A Research Story.* Boston, MA: Authors Cooperative Inc., 1994, 27. Used by permission.

If students can do all of these, you would conclude that they can read and understand the printed word **cat**. What Sidman and his coworkers showed was that if you taught only the first of these skills shown by Line 3 in Figure 9.13, the rest of the skills shown by lines 4, 5, and 6 would "emerge." That is, induction occurred. Once the child could pick out the printed text for a spoken word, pictures, pronounced words, and printed text became paired. Any one of the stimuli was correctly matched with any of the others.[13]

In teaching any subject from beginning reading to advanced chemistry, you rely on induction to connect terms, examples, definitions, or other properties of the concepts in a field. Once one pairing is made, other connections follow. Students respond to situations that share properties with the examples you use during teaching.

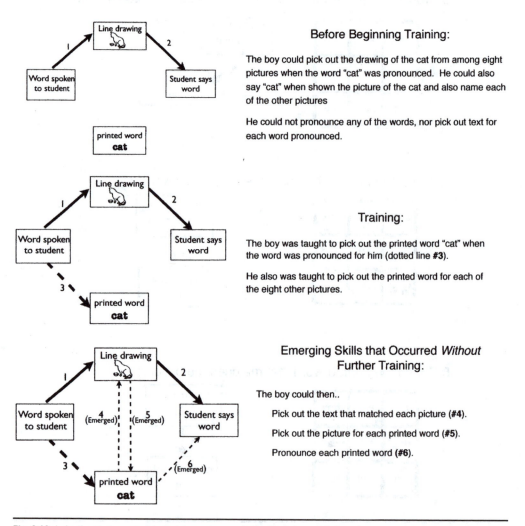

Before Beginning Training:

The boy could pick out the drawing of the cat from among eight pictures when the word "cat" was pronounced. He could also say "cat" when shown the picture of the cat and also name each of the other pictures

He could not pronounce any of the words, nor pick out text for each word pronounced.

Training:

The boy was taught to pick out the printed word "cat" when the word was pronounced for him (dotted line **#3**).

He also was taught to pick out the printed word for each of the eight other pictures.

Emerging Skills that Occurred *Without* Further Training:

The boy could then..

Pick out the text that matched each picture (**#4**).

Pick out the picture for each printed word (**#5**).

Pronounce each printed word (**#6**).

Fig. 9.13 Induction that occurred by training only one relation involving printed words
Adapted from Murray Sidman, *Equivalence Relations and Behavior: A Research Story.* Boston, MA: Authors Cooperative, 1994. 27. Used by permission.

SUMMARY

From something as simple as naming primary colors to advanced concepts taught in graduate school, induction and discrimination are part of successful performance. Induction describes the spread of effect from one antecedent situation to another. Discrimination is the narrowing of the range of control. Goals such as "understanding" or "responding appropriately" involve responding to defining *properties* of stimuli and to the contexts in which they occur. Responding to properties requires both induction from similar properties of one example to those in another, and discrimination between cases that contain defining properties and those that do not.

The design of instructional materials determines the contingencies that students encounter and thus the properties to which they respond. Some worksheets enable students to give answers that are keyed as "correct," but do not require the induction and discrimination intended. Extraneous cues permit students to avoid responding to the critical parts of an exercise and still get answers marked "right." Using the blackout technique, you can find out what parts of exercises are needed for responding. Whatever properties of exercises gain control over student responding determines the extent to which those exercises teach what they are supposed to teach. Good exercises do not enable students to get "right" answers for wrong reasons.

All concepts and principles consist of specific defining properties. In teaching a concept, you must isolate its defining characteristics so that students respond to them and not to other properties of examples. Varying as many characteristics of examples and non-examples as possible helps. All complex objectives relate behavior to antecedent properties of the world. Analyzing the precise contingencies involved lets you avoid wasting time with poorly designed activities in favor of exercises that teach the inductions and discriminations students need to learn.

CONCEPT CHECKS

Induction and Discrimination (Objective A)

DIRECTIONS: For each of the following, write I for Induction or D for Discrimination to identify the *main* process exemplified.

1. You stop for a red light and you go when the light is green.
2. You stop for a red light whether it is hung over an intersection or on a post at the right.
3. You are able to pick out the basil seedling in a pot from a number of tiny plants.
4. You name a seedling as a basil seedling whether it is in the garden or in a pot.
5. You talk more softly than usual when in the library,
6. You speak more loudly than usual when talking on your cell phone.
7. You can solve an equation like 3x = 6 no matter what letter is used for the unknown.
8. Because of riding a bike often, you find it easy to balance on a skateboard.
9. You confuse one credit card with another.
10. You answer your phone only when you recognize the caller ID.
11. The smell of a food makes a difference in how you react to it.
12. You respond in an applied situation the way you responded during training.

Terms (Objective B)

DIRECTIONS: For each of the following, fill in or select the best option.

1. The blackout technique shows the amount of material in an exercise that the student can ignore and still answer 1a. _____ . In general, the better the item, the 1b. _____ the blackout ratio.
2. Generalization is another term for 2a. _____ . It describes responding in one situation (differently than/the same way) 2b. _____ you respond in other situations.
3. Answering T for True on a test item because it followed three Fs for False is an example of _____ antecedent stimulus control.
4. A concept is a collection of 4a. _____ . An abstract concept like color (can/cannot) 4b. _____ occur by itself.
5. The term "understanding," as in understanding a joke, means responding _____ to it.
6. Sidman's equivalence relations demonstrated how, even when stimuli do not physically resemble each other, _____ can occur.
7. In distinguishing between operant and respondent behavior, the term "voluntary" (is/is not) 7a. _____ appropriate. That is because "voluntary" places the cause of behavior 7b. _____ the person behaving.
8. A student correctly distinguishes between passages written in the eighteenth century and those written in the twentieth. A twentieth-century passage is an S^D for saying 8a. _____ century, but an 8b. _____ for saying 8c. _____ .

ANALYSIS PROBLEMS

1. The Blackout Technique (Objective C)

Which of the following items will teach students the meaning of > better? How would the blackout technique reveal that fact?

 Item One: The sign for "greater than" is >.
 5 > 4 means 5 is greater than ____ .

 Item Two: The sign for "greater than" is >.
 "5 is greater than 4" is written 5 ____ 4

2. Inappropriate Antecedent Control (Objective C)

The following exercise is intended to teach classifying items as animals or plants. How could you improve it to get rid of inappropriate antecedent stimulus control?

Directions: Write "animal" or "plant" to show what each is.
A zebra is an _____ . **A rose is a** _____ .
An orchid is a _____ .   **An antelope is an** _____ .

3. Improving Exercises (Objective C)

The exercise below is intended to help students distinguish between short and long vowel sounds to aid in pronunciation. How could you improve it to require students to think of how the words are pronounced?

DIRECTIONS: Add the letter "e" to make

the word that goes with each picture:

kit __   not __

4. Teaching Concepts (Objective C)

A teacher teaches "bigger" using rectangles. What kind of induction and discriminative control is needed to make sure students understand the defining properties of the concept "bigger"?

ANSWERS FOR CONCEPT CHECKS

Induction and Discrimination

1. D
2. I
3. D
4. I
5. D
6. D
7. I
8. I
9. I
10. D
11. D
12. I

Terms

1a. correctly (or equivalent); 1b. lower/smaller (or equivalent)
2a. induction; 2b. the same way
3. inappropriate/faulty (or equivalent)
4a. properties; 4b. cannot
5. appropriately
6. induction/generalization
7a. is not;   7b. inside
8a. twentieth; 8b. S-delta (S^{Δ}); 8c. eighteenth (or anything other than twentieth).

FEEDBACK FOR ANALYSIS PROBLEMS

1. The Blackout Technique

Item Two is better because you must attend to the sign supposedly being taught. If you blacked out the first sentence in both items, you could not complete Item Two without already knowing the sign. Item One could be completed with anything replacing the > sign. You don't have to respond to the sign at all.

2. Inappropriate Antecedent Control

The "a" or "an" tells the student which word to write. The student does not need to respond to the particular item being classified. To improve it, change to "a(n)" so the answer is not given away by grammatical cues (or similar solution).

3. Improving Exercises

To read words with and without a final "e," a student must be asked to tell the difference between the pronunciations of the two kinds of words. Two options that would serve that purpose follow:

kit or kite

kit or kite

pin or pine

pin or pine

4. Teaching Concepts

The students must be able to tell which is bigger using **other** figures or objects (or equivalent answer). This shows induction from rectangles to other figures or objects and discrimination between "bigger" and not as big in objects or figures other than rectangles.

VERBAL BEHAVIOR

"Interpretation alone constitutes true reading."

Maria Montessori

OVERVIEW

As a teacher you rely on and teach verbal behavior. Through language you pass on knowledge, explain how to do things, and manage your classroom activities. At the same time you are expected to improve your students' writing, their understanding of spoken and textual material, and their ability to think clearly. As with all other behavior, a contingency analysis clarifies how verbal behavior works. This chapter shows how Skinner's analysis provides a new understanding of communication between individuals. His contingency analysis has helped teachers understand and solve problem behavior, teach reading with understanding, and help students express their ideas better on paper.

OBJECTIVES

By the end of this chapter you should be able to:

A. Classify examples of the following kinds of verbal behavior according to their primary sources of control:

>   mand
>   tact
>   echoic
>   copying text
>   textual
>   transcription
>   intraverbal

B. Identify which kind of establishing operation is illustrated in given examples.
C. Explain what determines the *meaning* of what is said or written, giving your own example.
D. Analyze examples of verbal behavior you observe in your own life according to the main sources of control over them.
E. Design an exercise for students you teach or might someday teach to incorporate natural contingencies into writing.

WHY DID SKINNER WRITE A WHOLE BOOK ABOUT VERBAL BEHAVIOR?

One of the most distinctly human kinds of behavior involves the way in which we communicate. Skinner began analyzing verbal behavior early, but it wasn't until he began work in education that he finished his book—over 20 years later.[1] The book *Verbal Behavior* uses no new principles: reinforcement, punishment, induction and discrimination work the same way for verbal behavior as they do for any other behavior. But postcedents for verbal behavior do not result directly from the actions of the person behaving. Picking up a piece of bread produces bread, but *saying* "Bread, please," may or may not result in getting bread. A "listener" is needed to *mediate* the consequences of a request. You can learn to walk without help, but there is no way you can learn a language without help from others. Skinner defines verbal behavior as behavior reinforced through the mediation of other persons.[2] (Late in the book, he discusses requirements about how those persons mediate.[3]) Adding a mediator's behavior into contingencies makes the analysis of verbal behavior a four-term analysis: For this example you have: 1) presence of bread; 2) request; 3) mediator passes; 4) bread received.

> Skinner defines **verbal behavior** as "behavior reinforced through the mediation of other persons." There are refinements to this definition.

A Functional Analysis

To understand language most people look at *what* people say or write—the words expressed and their grammatical structure. Skinner calls this the **form** or **topography** of a response. While form is important, to understand *why* people express what they do and the meaning of what is expressed, you need a **functional analysis** that looks at the contingencies responsible for the form observed. Even the meaning of a single word depends on the circumstances surrounding its expression. What is the meaning of "fire"? You cannot find the answer to this question in the sequence of letters or sounds. Nor can you find meaning in a dictionary. A dictionary gives synonyms of the word like "combustion," or "one of four medieval elements," or "to dismiss an employee," or "to discharge a gun or other weapon."

> A **formal analysis of verbal behavior** looks at **topography**—the particular words and grammatical structure of expressions. A **functional analysis** looks at the contingencies responsible for what is said, written, texted, or gestured.

These do not tell you what a person *means* when he says, "fire." Meaning lies in the circumstances under which "fire," is said and in the consequences that come from saying it. "Fire," said to a firing squad has a very different meaning than "fire" said in answer to the question, "What does the Spanish "fuego" mean in English?" The meaning of "fire" lies in contingencies over the form uttered. In the 470 pages of his book, Skinner gives a **functional analysis** of the variables that determine what is said, written, or otherwise expressed at a particular time. Skinner identifies three prime sources of control.

An analysis of contingencies considers both the specific words or phases emitted, and the variables responsible for their utterance. Two different forms may be under the same contingencies: "fire," said to a firing squad has a different topography than "shoot," but the two forms are considered equivalent if the circumstances and results of the two utterances are the same. Skinner includes both form and function in his analysis. He says that his book is "a functional analysis that sketches the topography of verbal behavior in relation to its controlling variables."[4]

Verbal Behavior analyzes the *emitting* of verbal behavior—speaking, writing, or gesturing. The behavior of the mediating "listener" is addressed only when he or she turns into a "speaker" by responding. In most verbal exchanges the same person alternates between being *speaker* and *listener*. In the classroom, teachers ask questions (speaker), hear answers (listener) and give feedback (speaker).

THE PRIMARY CONTINGENCIES OVER VERBAL BEHAVIOR

One reason people "use" language is to get others to do something: Skinner called behavior that is "under the control of deprivation or aversive stimulation" the **mand**, his first major category.[5]

The Mand

The definition of the mand is quite technical. You can think of a mand as a relation between what is expressed (the form or topography of an utterance) and the consequence that typically follows that form. Asking for pizza is a mand when under the control of getting pizza. If the source of control over what a person says is relief of discomfort (removing aversive stimulation), that too falls in the category of the mand. Skinner says of the mand, "It is sometimes convenient to refer to this relation by saying that a mand 'specifies' its reinforcement."[6] Manding "pencil" specifies pencil as reinforcement. Asking for directions specifies directions as the reinforcement for asking.

> A **mand** is "a verbal operant in which the response is reinforced by a characteristic consequence and is therefore under the functional control of relevant conditions of deprivation or aversive stimulation."[7]

The Tact

A second source of control consists of responding to stimuli or properties of stimuli that you are currently contacting, including stimuli inside your own body. You are taught to **tact** what you are

> A **tact** is verbal behavior under control of properties of objects or other stimuli with which the "speaker" is currently in contact, including stimuli inside that person's own body.

experiencing. All content areas have concepts that consist of properties or features that students need to tact in order to become competent in the field.

Control by Verbal Stimuli

The largest category of verbal behavior consists of responding to other verbal behavior. How do students respond to textual material? What do they say when answering questions? What determines the expressions they write in an essay or in creating poetry? One source of control lies in prior verbal stimuli. The response to a question about George Washington does not talk about what is for lunch, even if the student is hungry. What a student writes is largely controlled by the particular question asked (a verbal stimulus). Skinner called this category "verbal behavior under control of verbal stimuli" and subdivided it according to how the form of what is said, written, or gestured corresponds to the form of the antecedent verbal stimulus (see Figure 10.1). Several changes in Skinner's names have been proposed but Skinner's original terms are used here.[8]

That's it. There are only three *primary* sources of control. Of course the analysis gets complicated when you consider interactions between variables and the presence or absence of people (called the *audience*) as well as cultural practices that determine such basic features as which language you speak. Verbal behavior is never under a single source of control. But, as with other sciences, a few basic principles underly the complexities that occur. The *primary* sources of control over what people say, write, or gesture are 1) **deprivation** or aversive stimulation; 2) features of their current environment including the "environment" inside their own body; and 3) other verbal behavior.

The rest of this chapter looks at the implications of each kind of control for teaching.

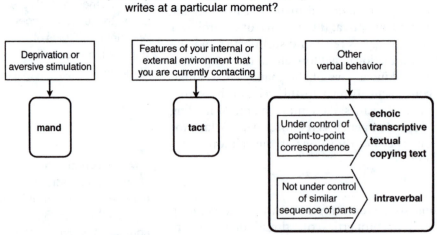

Fig. 10.1 Overview of the primary sources of control over verbal behavior

THE MAND AND ITS IMPORTANCE IN TEACHING

Imagine yourself in a hospital after an accident, unable to say anything. You are thirsty (deprivation) and the sun is hurting your eyes (aversive stimulation). You see the person in the bed next to you watching what looks like an interesting television program (which makes getting your own TV changed to that program especially reinforcing). Imagine your frustration if you could not get someone to bring you water, pull down the shade, or change your TV to the program you want to watch. It would be tempting to bang on your bed rails or otherwise make enough commotion to get the attention of a nurse or attendant. Even if an attendant came, you still could not let that person know exactly what you wanted. You would be like a youngster without a mand repertoire.

Formal Requirements for the Mand

Students who cannot effectively mand often resort to other behavior. They may disrupt class with behavior like loud noises, getting out of their seats, shoving or punching peers, or even throwing tantrums. Behavior called "challenging" or "problem" behavior usually brings teacher attention or removal from an activity. Because of predictable consequences, problem behavior often functions *like* a mand, but it does not have the form required to "specify its reinforcement." A fight or tantrum may bring many different reactions from teachers. Until a functional analysis is done, you do not know what postcedents are maintaining challenging behavior. Certainly no teachers reinforce fights or tantrums *"precisely in order to reinforce the behavior"* of fighting or throwing tantrums. This is the *further requirement* that Skinner adds late in his book for an action to be called verbal.[9] Any reinforcement of challenging behavior is unintended. Making loud noises, throwing a tantrum, fighting, and other problem behavior may produce predictable outcomes, but these behaviors lack the form that a social community requires for reinforcement with specified consequences.

Teaching Manding to Replace Problem Behavior

Clearly it is better if students mand than if they engage in challenging behavior. The time to teach manding is not, of course, in the middle of a tantrum. You would pick a time when the student is calm.

Since mands are under control of deprivation or aversive stimulation, they will not occur unless deprivation or aversive stimulation is present. To teach manding, then, you need to set up the conditions that make manding likely. You can do so in three ways: 1) by restricting access to reinforcing objects or events; 2) by using existing aversive situations; and 3) by increasing the "value" of an object or event through procedures such as advertising or modeling by others. All three of these are called **establishing operations** for the mand.[10] An establishing operation is a procedure that increases the effectiveness of an object or event as a reinforcer. It is done before using something as a reinforcer. Keeping snacks away from a child in the late afternoon is an establishing operation (deprivation) for using food as a reinforcer. Not having access to snacks makes the food you serve at dinner more

> An **establishing operation (EO)** is a procedure that increases the effectiveness of an object or event as a reinforcer. Also sometimes called a **motivating operation (MO)**.

reinforcing than it would otherwise be. The child is more likely to ask for and eat what is served. When deprivation is severe, any food may be manded, as the scene in *Oliver Twist* shows. Oliver is in a workhouse with other children who have been given a single, small basin of gruel by the master. "Child as he was, he was desperate with hunger . . . He rose from the table; and advancing to the master, basin and spoon in hand, said: somewhat alarmed at his own temerity:

"Please, sir, I want some more."[11]

Deprivation of food over many months made even gruel a powerful reinforcer.

Deprivation as an Establishing Operation (EO)

There is an old saying, "You can lead a horse to water, but you can't make it drink." If someone told you that you could earn a million dollars if you could get a horse to drink within a minute of leading it to water, I'll bet you would win your bet if you could have the horse for several days, or even just a few hours before the test. First among your procedures would be deprivation: you would restrict the horse's access to water. (There are many other procedures, such as exercising the horse in hot sun to make it thirsty [see "value altering" below], but temporary deprivation would certainly be part of your plans.) Deprivation is measured as time since last access. If the horse is kept away from water for two hours before the test, you would call that a two-hour water deprivation.

The word "deprivation" sounds mean. It certainly can be if carried to extremes. However, in the normal life of horses or people, deprivation occurs all the time. A horse ridden in a ring has no access to water during that time. Your students are "deprived" of water for many periods during the day. The number of minutes since eating is usually high just before lunch time. To take advantage of deprivation, therefore, you don't have to take anything away from your students. You can use the natural ebb and flow of access to reinforcers.

One potential reinforcer in your classroom is permission that has followed your attention, making your attention a conditioned reinforcer. If your attention *is* reinforcing, then when you are *not* attending you are creating a state of deprivation. You are setting up an establishing operation for behavior that gets your attention. Sometimes the actions that result from deprivation may be inappropriate.

Say you have a teenage boy who often gets you to answer his questions by yelling out his name. When he finally settles down, it is *very* tempting to leave him alone. At last you can interact with the rest of your students! The longer you ignore this student, however, the greater the deprivation you are creating. Most students that exhibit problem behavior get very little attention when behaving *well*. Their teachers let long periods of deprivation build up.

Asking for information is a mand when reinforced by the information you receive. If the student who calls out can get that help by quietly asking (perhaps after raising a hand or going to your desk), the appropriate action will become stronger and yelling less likely to occur.[12] When an assignment is likely to raise questions or to be difficult for a student, you need to be alert to signs like squirming or looking at peers' papers that show that deprivation of your help is building. That is the time to go over to those looking confused so that a question can be asked. The vigilance required for catching signs of deprivation can be demanding, but long term results of shaping mands are worth it.

When attending to student needs, you do not need to go overboard. A simple nod, look, or smile is usually sufficient to prompt requesting help. Giving frequent opportunities to mand for information avoids creating a deprivation state.

Aversive Stimulation as an Establishing Operation

Like the deprivation that is experienced throughout the day, aversive stimulation is also common in a normal life. Aversive situations are establishing operations for avoidance or escape behavior—any action that reduces or gets you out of the aversiveness. Behavior that *ends* an ongoing aversive situation is negatively reinforced. An itch in the middle of your back where you cannot reach it is an **aversive stimulus**. A mand, such as asking someone to scratch the spot, will reduce the aversive stimulation when reinforced by the person (the mediator) stopping the itch.

In the classroom, unfortunately, aversiveness is often present. Few students groan with disappointment when "let out" early from an academic class. While behavioral techniques make learning more enjoyable, it is difficult to eliminate all aversiveness. Acquiring new skills usually requires work and work is often aversive. This is particularly true for your least accomplished students. Day after day they see others readily completing tasks they find difficult or impossible to do. Giving an assignment that is difficult establishes the conditions for behavior that gets out of doing the work. A student can end an unfinished task by completing it, but delaying beginning to work produces more immediate reinforcement. Methods of procrastination are all too familiar. Sharpening pencils, rearranging books, or asking to go to the bathroom exemplify avoidance. Think of tasks *you* don't enjoy. Haven't you found yourself leaving your desk for a coke or another cup of coffee when faced with a task you do not enjoy doing? The next time you give a particularly difficult assignment, notice the inventiveness with which students find ways to delay starting or to escape doing the work altogether.

Much problem behavior is maintained primarily by escape. A child who cannot effectively mand a break may instead throw a tantrum that produces the same result of being removed from the classroom.

Tantrums are particularly common with students lacking verbal skills. If they have no vocal behavior, they can be taught to hand their teacher a card to indicate specific consequences like a "break." Cards developed for children or adults who cannot talk (such as cards used in the Picture Exchange Communication System or PECS) contain icons that, like Chinese characters, enable students to "ask" for specific consequences.[13] The precision of the specific consequences has been demonstrated by non-speaking students who distinguish between whether they want a temporary break or to stop an activity altogether.[14] Mands give them control over their lives, and problem behavior decreases as a result. Getting a break via verbal behavior is a lot easier than throwing yourself on the floor, kicking and screaming. Of course, as a teacher, you don't want to be handed break cards every few seconds. But teaching persistence is a different problem. Once manding a break is well established, you can address working longer at a stretch.

In addition to the deprivation created as time goes by without a particular reinforcer, and the aversiveness of a situation from which escape will be reinforcing, there is a third way to establish circumstances that encourage manding.

"Value Altering" as an Establishing Operation: Making a Reinforcer More Salient

If you are an owner of a bar, you cannot control the number of hours since your customers last had a drink. You cannot set up an aversive situation from which customers can escape by buying drinks. So how do you increase the likelihood that they will purchase more of what you have to sell? It is no coincidence that bars provide free salty snacks. Salt does not increase the number of hours since customers last had liquid, but it does make liquid more reinforcing. You may have had a glass of water just before entering the establishment, but a dozen pretzels later you probably will want something to drink. Bars use *value-altering* establishing operations to make drinks more reinforcing so their customers will buy more drinks.

An advertisement functions in a similar way to make specific items more desirable. When your students see their hero sporting a particular brand or style of shoe, for example, the ad does not increase the time they have gone without having those shoes. But the advertisement may increase the appeal of those particular shoes. In a sense, the ad creates an aversive situation of not having what others have. When "everybody else" wears an advertised article of clothing, it can become aversive to be wearing something different. Matching the appearance of a high-status figure gains social approval from peers.

On the playground, a child or teenager may not pay any attention to a ball that has been lying around until a peer picks it up. All of a sudden, the student engages in behavior to get the ball. You would say he or she now "wants" the ball: it has become a stronger reinforcer than it was a minute before.

In the classroom, this kind of establishing operation also occurs. One student's enthusiasm about an activity makes it more attractive to others. If a class leader talks excitedly about General Grant, finding out about Grant becomes more appealing. Information about Grant gains power as a reinforcer for searching the net or consulting other resources. When you give a demonstration, you expect it to help your students learn a procedure. You also probably hope for a secondary effect: that seeing what the procedure produces will make those results appeal to your students. The science demonstration where a hard-boiled egg in its shell plops into a baby food bottle, for example, may make students want to get their own eggs to plop into bottles. The result of creating a partial vacuum becomes more reinforcing than it would have been without having witnessed the demonstration first.

Special Characteristics of the Mand

The mand is the only kind of verbal behavior that produces a *specified* consequence. Manding bread produces bread, not approval or recess. Manding a break produces a break, not bread. The mand is also the only verbal operant that directly benefits the person who is engaging in the verbal behavior. Talking or gesturing gets the object or event that reinforces the form expressed. That is why the mand is the best kind of verbal behavior to teach *first* to a non-verbal child.[15] The verbal behavior specifies what he or she "wants." Neither a tact nor verbal behavior under control of verbal stimuli specifies its reinforcement.

THE TACT: RESPONDING TO FEATURES OF ONE'S IMMEDIATE WORLD

The term "tact" comes from the French and Latin words for "touch." Tacting involves responding to properties of stimuli that you are currently "touching," that is properties that are in your presence *while* you are talking or writing or thinking. A tact is "a verbal operant in which a response of a given form is evoked (or at least strengthened) by a particular object or event or property of an object or event."[16] Calling the color of a red jacket "red," is an example of a tact if the behavior is governed by the jacket's color (and not, for example, by what someone else has just said).

> The **tact** is "a verbal operant in which a response of given form is evoked (or at least strengthened) by a particular object or event or property of an object or event," one that is currently in the speaker's presence.

Like a mand, a tact must conform to the topography reinforced by a *verbal community*. A verbal community consists of the people in a social group who interact with each other. English speakers say "red" when asked the color of a red jacket. A verbal community of French speakers reinforces saying "rouge."

Teaching students to tact increases their sensitivity to the world around them. Once having learned to tact something as simple as the shapes of circle, triangle, and square, children not only can inform others about what they are seeing, they are more likely to notice the shapes of objects and to talk about shapes. Some tacts are pretty much universal. Most students learn to tact common objects like pen or pencil and abstract properties like number and color. Other tacts are content specific. The tacts you teach depend on what is important for your students. Every subject requires responding to its own special characteristics such as "offsides" in sports, "iambic pentameter" in poetry, or "mitochondria" for organelles isolated in a biology lab.

You do not need to *refer* to an object or property of an object to be under tact control. If you say "blackballed" in a class on government instead of the word "rejected" because a round black object happens to be in your peripheral vision, that utterance is under tact control. You do not even have to be aware of why you said what you said. All that is needed is control by properties of an object or event currently in your presence.

As soon as you are no longer in the presence of whatever you are describing, you cannot call your behavior tacting. Even if you are describing something you saw only a minute or two before, you are no longer tacting if you are not in its presence now. Try an experiment: ask your students to look at a bulletin board full of notices and pictures and then to turn around and sketch or describe on paper what they saw. You will be amazed at how the descriptions vary from what is actually there, and how their descriptions differ from one another. Once no longer contacting the visual stimuli, behavior is no longer under tact control. Other variables enter in, such as what you have seen on other bulletin boards, what you said to yourself as you were viewing (noting, for example, a prominent color), what interests you (versus notices about events that you would never attend), even your own wishes (misreading the date of a concert, for example, so that it isn't already over.) None of these is a property of objects you are currently "touching."

Contingencies over the Tact

The consequences that produce and maintain the tact differ from those of the mand. The tact does not "specify its consequence." Say a teenage girl says "iambic pentameter" when describing the meter of a poem being read. She doesn't receive iambic pentameter. The consequence for identifying meter lie in some kind of social approval such as "Good," or "That's right." Tacting "Mozart" for the characteristics of a piece of music you hear, or "offsides" for the configuration of team members in a game is similarly acquired and maintained by **generalized reinforcement**. Generalized reinforcement is a consequence that has been paired with many other kinds of reinforcement. The classic example is money, but praise and social approval also are paired with many other benefits. In the classroom, generalized reinforcement includes teacher approval, points towards privileges, and various indications of progress towards good grades, certificates, awards, or graduation, all of which are paired with further advantages.

Research on the Independence of Mands and Tacts

It took many years after the publication of *Verbal Behavior* for evidence to appear showing that the categories Skinner proposed were, in fact, distinct.[17] It turned out that you don't learn a "word" and then automatically "use" it under different conditions.[18] The fact that emitting a word under one set of controls doesn't make the same "word" available for other circumstances is obvious in reading and writing. No one claims that just because you can *say* "water" that you can automatically *read* "water" or *write* "water." Everyone realizes that talking, reading, and writing differ even thought the same words may be involved. But most people assume that if you can name an object (tacting) you can then automatically "use" that word to ask for an object when you want it (manding). That is not always the case. As early as 1979, a study of verbal behavior involving two teenagers who were deaf, and diagnosed as "severely retarded," revealed the differing controls. The two students could tact "spoon" when shown a spoon, but were unable to ask for "spoon" when they needed one to make soup (when no spoon was in view). Even though the word "spoon" was the same, tacting and manding were shown to be under different controls.[19]

Special Characteristics of the Tact

Tacting benefits the social community more than directly benefiting the speaker. Students learn tacts because parents and teachers consider them important. Being able to identify and talk about one's world is also useful to students themselves, but the consequences are not as immediately rewarding as those for the mand.

In teaching tacts, you must make sure that a student is responding to what he is seeing or hearing or touching. You cannot always tell by a "correct" response. In Chapter 9, a child's answering "red" when asked the color of a jacket turned out to be under the wrong controls to be a tact of color. She answered "red" no matter what color of jacket was shown to her. She may have said "red" whenever she heard "what color it this?" (see intraverbal verbal behavior below), or she may have learned to say "red" when observing any jacket. It looked as though she were tacting color when she correctly "named" the color of the red jacket, but she was responding to something else besides color. That is why you need lots of examples to make sure that it is the relevant property to which students are responding when teaching tacts.

Teaching students to tact color is straightforward. The stimuli are out in the open and you and your student are looking at the same objects. Teaching students to tact something that only *they* experience like a feeling of happiness or pain is much trickier. Yet we do teach children to tact their feelings and emotions. If you see a wound or a child doubled over holding his stomach you assume he or she is in pain. You are likely to say something like, "That must *hurt!*" The word "hurt" is thus paired with whatever feelings the child is experiencing. We describe a smiling girl as "happy," expecting that our learners pair "happy" with how they feel when *they* are smiling. Tacts of internal stimuli, however, are always imprecise. You cannot clearly communicate exactly how much pain you are feeling as accurately as you can communicate how many coins you are holding in your hand.

In order to classify verbal behavior, you have to identify the variables that are responsible for it. "I'm hungry," for example, may be a mand if under control of getting someone to bring you food, or a tact if describing what you are feeling when asked. Similarly, if you say "This garbage *stinks*," not because others are particularly interested in its odor, but because you want someone to empty it, the primary controlling variables are those of the mand. Your utterance is under control of the characteristic consequence of someone else emptying the garbage.

Whether internal or external stimuli, tacts are under control of properties that the verbalizer is *currently* contacting. It is not tacting to describe the pain you had last week, nor is it tacting to describe the garbage you smelled 10 minutes ago. Talking about past events involves a third kind of verbal behavior, control by verbal stimuli.

CONTROL BY PRIOR VERBAL STIMULI

Skinner called the chapter on his third primary source of control "Verbal Behavior under the Control of Verbal Stimuli." In private conversations, he agreed that "Intra-verbal" would have been a better name for the whole category instead of for just a part of it.[20] But so far the applied field has not shifted from Skinner's original classifications.[21]

The category of control by antecedent verbal stimuli is huge. In repeating "cat" when told to say "cat," what you said is determined by what you just heard. In answering a question, what you say is largely under the control of what was just asked. If someone asks you, "What is your name?" you do not respond "Please pass the bread," or "The apple is red." Your response is determined mostly by the verbal stimuli "what is" and "your name."

> **Verbal behavior under control of verbal stimuli** refers to verbal behavior whose form is determined primarily by immediately preceding verbal stimuli.

Intraverbal control by prior verbal stimuli can be seen when completing phrases like "George Washington was the first president of the United ____." A student's response of "States" is largely under control of "George Washington" and "first president of the United. . . ." Writing your name on paper where it says "Name" or "Name: Last, first, initial" also shows intraverbal control. What you write depends on what the prior printed verbal stimulus says.

Education relies on intraverbal behavior for most of teaching. You cannot tact events that are not currently in your presence, but students need to learn about them nevertheless. Tests and classroom questions ask students to describe events that occurred long ago or are happening elsewhere in the world now. A big difference exists, of course, between talking or reading *about* the world and directly contacting it.[22] That is the reason for simulations, lab experiments, and field trips. While you can read about the Alhambra Palace in southern Spain, you miss hundreds of aspects of walking through, such as the smells, the sounds of your footsteps and of the water spilling from the fountains, the temperature and humidity, the changes of light on the tiles at different angles, and the tiny plants struggling through cracks in the walls. What a reader gets out of reading about a place is what the writer put in, and that reflects the writer's interests. Words may not even give an accurate descriptions of what they do mention. Writers may "remember" things inaccurately, like the student describing a bulletin board after turning away from it. Intraverbal behavior, while essential for teaching, cannot substitute for direct contact with the world. But it is critical nevertheless.

There are many subdivisions of the category of verbal controls. The major ones are shown in Figure 10.2. They depend upon the relation between the form of the antecedent verbal stimulus and the form of the response.

Point-to-Point Correspondence:

Point-to-point correspondence refers to a corresponding sequence of parts. Both "pat" and "tap" are made up of the same letters, but they do not have point-to-point correspondence because of their differing order. If you were giving a spelling test and pronounced the word "pat," only p-a-t in that order would be the correct spelling. Point-to-point correspondence would be required (see Table 10.1).

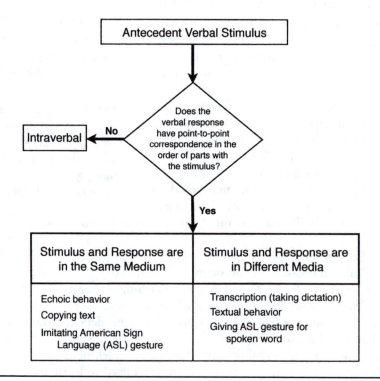

Fig. 10.2 Subcategories of control by verbal stimuli

Table 10.1 The role of point-to-point correspondence in classifying verbal operants (under "Control by Verbal Stimuli" in *Verbal Behavior*)

Point-to-point correspondence Sequence of parts of antecedent verbal stimulus and parts of verbal response match.	Intraverbal: No point-to-point correspondence Verbal response does not share the same sequence of parts as the stimulus.
Same medium SOUND: Auditory stimulus, ORAL response: **echoic**. *Example*: Student repeats "bonjour" after the teacher says "bonjour." TEXT: Printed stimulus, WRITTEN response: **copying text**. *Example*: Student writes "Wednesday" from word on the board. PHYSICAL MOVEMENT: GESTURAL stimulus, GESTURAL response: *Example*: Student imitates the finger spelling for car.	**Same medium** All are called **intraverbal**. SOUND: *Example*: Teacher: "How do you say 'hello' in French? Student: "Bonjour" TEXT: *Example*: Student writes "Wednesday" in the blank shown: "The day that follows Tuesday is _____." PHYSICAL MOVEMENT: *Example*: In response to teacher's signing "driving" student signs "car."
Different media: AUDITORY stimulus, WRITTEN response: **transcription** *Example*: Student writes spelling words dictated by the teacher. PRINTED stimulus, ORAL response: **textual** *Example*: Student pronounces each word printed on paper. AUDITORY stimulus, GESTURAL response: *Example*: Teacher says, "car" and student shows the sign language for "car."	**Different media:** All are called **intraverbal** by Skinner. AUDITORY stimulus, WRITTEN response. *Example*: Teacher says: "Write a word that rhymes with each word as I say it . . . . . . '1. red' (pause) '2. pop'. . ." Student writes 1. bed 2. stop
(Many other combinations exist of matching sequence but not matching media, but they don't have separate names.)	(There are many other combinations of media possible for intraverbal behavior.)

Skinner does not specify what constitutes the parts that must correspond in "point-to-point correspondence." Even in copying *one* letter there are parts that need to match. Students just learning to copy the capital letter M, for example, often end up with a W if they don't lift the pencil after the initial downwards stroke for the left part of the letter.

Point-to-point correspondence also occurs in speech. Repeating what is said (**echoic** behavior) requires point-to-point correspondence. Students with autism often exhibit echoic behavior where it is socially inappropriate. For example, when asked "What is your name," they may answer "What is your name?" This echoic response has a **formal** similarity to the antecedent stimulus: it matches the question point-to-point both in order and in medium (sound as opposed to print). To teach a child to give his or her name when asked, teachers have to establish different controls.

Copying printed text also shows formal similarity. Sometimes the proximity of the stimulus makes a difference in performance. A student in a first grade could not copy words from a blackboard. He was given an intermediate step—a paper with the word to copy printed in large letters at the top. He copied the word well enough on the first line, but the form of his response deteriorated as he went down the page. His letters matched the sample letters at the top only when he wrote right next to them.[23] Practice in copying increasing distances from the sample was needed before he could duplicate words written on the board.

Not all point-to-point correspondence requires the same medium for stimulus and response. When you take dictation, your product appears on paper but the stimulus is auditory. Skinner called this transcription. It has point-to-point control in the sequencing of parts, but not in medium. The response is *written*, the stimulus *spoken*. Similarly, pronouncing printed text (textual behavior) involves different media. The text is *printed*, pronouncing *oral*. Textual behavior requires uttering sounds that follow the same sequence of letters and words appearing on a page. Textual behavior thus shows point-to-point correspondence in serial order, but not a match in media.

Textual behavior differs from "understanding" what is read. A student can pronounce "zolk" by saying the word phonetically without responding in ways called "understanding." You may be able to pronounce Spanish words correctly, but not know what a passage is talking about.

Non-Point-to-Point Correspondence: The Intraverbal

In his book, *Verbal Behavior*, Skinner offers no subcategories for verbal behavior that is under verbal control but that lacks point-to-point correspondence with the prior verbal stimulus. He calls this whole category the **intraverbal**.[24]

> The **intraverbal** is a verbal operant in which a response of given form is under the control of a prior verbal stimulus with which it shares no point-to-point correspondence.

The intraverbal category looks small in Figures 10.1 and 10.2. In fact, most of the talk about the world that a school or community teaches has no matching physical properties between stimuli and responses. The intraverbal category includes much of the control over answering questions, solving problems, and creative behavior in addition to more simple completion of sequences (such as saying "3" to "1, 2, . . ." or "go" to "ready, set, ... "). The critical part of student answers to questions is the intraverbal part. If you were grading the answer to "What is Skinner's definition of 'verbal behavior'?" you would ignore any copied part ("Skinner's definition of verbal behavior (is)..") and go straight to the rest. Of course what then follows is not all intraverbal. It will be under multiple control.

MULTIPLE CONTROL OVER VERBAL BEHAVIOR

Verbal behavior is always under the control of more than one source of control. We may ask for something when we see it, combining the relations of mand (asking) with tact (responding to properties of the object seen). Answering "What is that?" when pointing to a pencil is under both intraverbal control (the verbal stimulus "What is that?") and tact control (the physical looks of the pencil). "What do you want?" usually produces a combination of mand and intraverbal control. The answer is under both deprivation (of what is "wanted") and control by the specific question. One kind of control nearly always present in addition to those already described is audience control.

Audience Control

"Audience," in verbal behavior, does not mean a group of people assembled for a performance. *Audience control* consists of the control that one or more "listeners" exert over verbal behavior. Most talking occurs when a conducive audience is present. Audience control shows when students ask for things from a substitute teacher that they would not ask of their own teacher. Tacting, too, is largely restricted to suitable circumstances. You would think students crazy if they came into a classroom and began tacting "Desk, pencil, teacher, blue, round, window..." and everything else in the room. Tacting is reinforced by an audience only under appropriate conditions, for example when answering "What is that?" or "What do you see?" The audience also partly controls the response in intraverbal behavior. Completing "red, white, and ..." produces "blue" with an American audience, but when talking about the Mexican flag the response reinforced would be "green."

Audience control also often determines *when* we talk. Students rarely ask for information when alone in a classroom. If another teacher or student enters, however, the likelihood of talking increases. That shows audience control.

The presence of a listener not only affects whether or not people talk, but also the language they speak and what they talk about. Bilingual individuals talk in the language that will be understood by the person they are addressing. At a party, you may start to talk about a football game only to find out that your listener is looking around for someone else to talk to. If you wish to continue the conversation, you will shift to another topic. Most people swear at some time or other, but not with all audiences.

Important as the audience is, having someone present is not a necessary condition for talking at a particular time. People sometimes talk when no one is around to hear.

Talking when an Audience is Not Present

Verbal behavior follows the same principles of reinforcement, induction, and discrimination as non-verbal behavior. Like physical actions, talking can become very persistent through intermittent reinforcement. Very early on, children learn that they don't always get everything they ask for. A mand for "Mommy," doesn't always bring Mommy, even if she is in sight, nor does "cookie" always produce a cookie. But both occasionally "pay off," thus creating intermittent reinforcement and making verbal behavior persistent so that it often occurs when no reinforcement follows. Thus people mand when alone, talk to themselves, or speak to inanimate objects. You may tell your computer to hurry up when it is responding slowly. Saying "hurry up" has been established by getting people to hurry, at least some of the time. (If a web page just happens to load as you say "hurry up," your talking to your computer may be further strengthened, even though you know perfectly well that there is no connection between saying "hurry up," and the web page appearing.) There is no requirement that a given instance of verbal behavior is mediated by other people every time.

THE AUTOCLITIC

During the 20 years from the time Skinner first started writing about language and the publication of his book, he gave talks and courses on verbal behavior. Students must have asked all sorts of challenging questions such as, "How come children say, 'he runned,' meaning 'he ran?'" Towards the end of the book, Skinner answers questions about "special arrangements of responses," where part of verbal behavior "becomes in turn one of the variables controlling another part."[25] He calls this **autoclitic behavior**.

> **Autoclitic behavior** is verbal behavior "which is based upon or depends upon other verbal behavior,"[26] and does so in ways that enhance the effect upon a listener, including the "speaker" him or herself.

Before uttering phrases or sentences, children learn primary verbal operants: mands, tacts, and various kinds of control by verbal stimuli. The mand "cookie" may, at first, be all that is required to get a cookie. A tact, "doggie," is likely to gain approval; "Yes, that's a doggie." A child may say "Bye, bye," as an echoic following a parent's "Say 'bye-bye'." Simple mands, tacts, and verbally-controlled utterances, Skinner calls "raw" verbal operants.

By the time a child enters school, these primary verbal operants are arranged into phrases even before a complete phrase is uttered. Skinner has three chapters on how people manipulate their own verbal operants in ways that make a complete phrase more effective for a listener. The process is like editing a sentence you have just written, except that you "edit" quickly even before beginning to speak.

Grammar as Autoclitic Behavior

One of the chapters on autoclitics addresses grammatical structure. An example is given here to give the flavor of the analysis. Skinner often uses examples of "incorrect" verbal behavior to reveal particular sources of control. Suppose a child says "He runn*ed*." What contingencies would be responsible for such a construction? In English-speaking communities, adding "-ed" for past tense is reinforced, as in "walk*ed*, talk*ed*, cri*ed*, touch*ed*," and so on. Adding "-ed" involves the primary operant "*run*," plus an autoclitic "-ed" that is under control of being in the past. Just as induction occurs in non-verbal behavior (for example kicking a new kind of ball for the first time), induction occurs in verbal behavior. Saying "runn*ed*" when talking about past running shows induction from other autoclitic verbal behavior, in this case induction of the grammatical structure "-ed" for past tense. If "runned" is then corrected to "ran," the new form eventually replaces the old. If not, "runned" will remain.

The power of contingencies over speaking shows in the differing "languages" of different verbal communities. Although students may hear "standard" English, the contingencies over their inflection, their grammar, and their vocabulary are local. Schools provide a set of "local" contingencies, too, but they may differ from those at home or with peers. Conflicting contingencies make the teaching of "standard English" difficult. That is why it is so critical to adopt effective methods of instruction based on an analysis of the contingencies over behavior.

IMPLICATIONS OF *VERBAL BEHAVIOR* FOR TEACHING READING COMPREHENSION

There are two components to beginning reading: pronouncing words (textual verbal behavior), and responding to their meaning (understanding). Meaning has typically been thought of as being a property of words and their grammatical structure. As mentioned at the beginning of this chapter, meaning does not reside in the *form* of expression as much as in the variables responsible for their expression. Misunderstanding can occur when you hear sounds correctly, but infer different contingencies from those controlling what was said, as the following incident illustrates:[27]

> A four-year-old girl named Laura came into the room where her mother was sitting. The girl asked a question. What the mother heard was, "Mom, what is sex?"
>
> "Oh boy," she thought. "Has Laura's older sister, Amy, been talking about sex? It is better Laura hears the explanation from me."
>
> So she began, "Well, to make a baby you need two parts, one from the Daddy and one from the Mommy. Here, I'll show you." She got a book showing animals copulating and explained that that was how the two parts got together. The little girl stood patiently by. After several minutes the explanation was finished.
>
> "Why did you ask?" Laura's mother asked.
>
> "Oh," Laura replied, "Amy said she'd be back in a couple of secs."

The meaning the mother gave to the question came from talking or reading about questions children often ask. The meaning of *Laura's* question come from different contingencies—her sister's talk.

Teaching Reading with Understanding

Textual verbal behavior, as any teacher knows, is not the same as reading "with understanding." Understanding does not even require correct pronunciation, as an undergraduate applicant to a psychology department discovered when talking about "Frood" in an interview. He had learned about Freud only from reading. He was accepted because he could talk effectively about what Freud had to say even with his incorrect pronunciation.[28]

Since meaning lies in contingencies, not just in the form of expressions, to understand the meaning of a passage you must respond appropriately to contingencies you infer from the words you read. Teachers do not assume that just because students can repeat a definition, they understand what was written. Understanding requires students to respond as though they are expressing the same themes or ideas themselves. Saying something in your own words has been acquired mostly through intraverbal control. Once having learned the pairing of "humungous" with "huge," students can rephrase a sentence containing "humungous." Restating in a student's own words shows a first level of comprehension. Students must still respond to the contingencies in which the large object or person was involved for a more profound level of comprehension. Understanding meaning also involves emotions. A student who responds with fear or anxiety to a scary passage is responding appropriately to the contingencies described. As Skinner put it, "***Meaning** is not properly regarded as a property either of a response or a* *situation but rather of the contingencies responsible for both the topography of behavior and the control exerted by stimuli.*[29]

To teach students to understand what they read, you need to emphasize the described contingencies more than pronunciation. In a conversation, you do not correct every word said incorrectly. But interrupting a reader in the middle of a sentence is recommended by many educators (Table 10.2 top). The "word attack hierarchy" procedure, for example, gives excellent suggestions for helping students *pronounce* individual words with which they are having trouble. But phonics are best taught separately from reading passages if your goal is for students to understand and to enjoy what they read.

Try reading the next sentence. It has italic "correction" procedures interspersed.

Stopping at each incorrectly proposed... *You mean pronounced, say pronounced...* **pronounced.** . . . *Yes that's right. Now go on.* . . **word makes it difficult to extort.** . . . *Look at the ending and try again.* . . **extract** . . . *good.* . . . **meaning from what you read.**

Students find it difficult to understand text with similar interruptions. Most of the components of comprehension, such as answering who, what, where and why questions, can be taught orally. Talking about events described can be taught to children before they can pronounce a single printed word. Children who have been read to and asked questions have a head start in understanding *printed* text. They already have acquired the skills of responding to elements of what is described in a passage. Part of that control is the intraverbal control of the specific question asked, but answering also requires responding to inferred contingencies.

Table 10.2 Teaching reading: effects of procedures for students reading aloud

Procedure	Example	Effect on Comprehension
Word attack hierarchy In this approach, the instructor prompts the student to apply a hierarchy of word attack.	Before the student begins to read, tell the student, "*If you come to a word that you do not know, I will help you with it. I will tell you the correct word while you listen and point to the word in the book. After that, I want you to repeat the word and continue reading. Try your best not to make mistakes.*"	Interrupts the flow so that it is difficult for the reader to follow what is happening.
Contingencies to promote reading for "understanding" In this approach, the instructor ignores mispronunciations and engages the student in talking about the characters or events depicted in the story.	The student mispronounces "Hangletons" in the sentence, "The Little Hangletons all agreed that the old house was 'creepy'." The teacher says, "*Would you want to go into that old house?*"	Focuses the reader's attention on the events in the story, not on pronunciation.

Comprehension is taught best by asking students to respond to the overall meaning of uninterrupted text rather than concentrating on pronunciation. Even with mispronouncing a few words, you can respond to "meaning," as the following sentence shows:

Stopping at each incorrectly proposed word makes it difficult to extort meaning from what you read.

Well, it's not perfect. Still it is easier to respond to the "uncorrected" version's meaning than to the one with "corrections" interrupting the flow. When listening to students read aloud, let mispronunciations go. (You can teach phonics later.) Instead, have readers respond to what they are saying. If you concentrate on interpretation, your students will too. Talking about what is happening also makes reading more pleasant. Instead of a time where students have to be careful not to make mistakes, it is a time for them to share their thoughts and ideas about the events described.

In addition to your asking questions about a passage, your students can ask questions too.[30] In thinking about what to ask, students respond to what interests them. It frees their attention from the narrower control of answering a specific teacher's question. For students, forming their own questions promotes thinking about what they are reading *as they are reading*, which is a critical part of the behavior of reading with understanding.

It isn't even necessary to pronounce every word when reading silently. I remember reading *Great Expectations* aloud to my 12-year-old daughter. There were words in that book that I knew the meaning of perfectly well, but I had never said them aloud. I found myself stumbling over their pronunciation. Similarly you may read about a character with a difficult name in a novel and understand the story without being able to pronounce the character's name.

In any setting you get the behavior your contingencies produce. Chapter 9 described how teaching comprehension primarily with passages followed by multiple-choice "literal comprehension" questions encourages poor readers to skip reading the paragraphs, go to the questions at the end and then hunt for matching phrases. A change to a format with blanks throughout was suggested as a way to encourage reading from the beginning, as well as requiring responding to the content of each sentence. As with oral reading, reading silently requires responding to what a passage is about.

The contingencies that basal readers set up may produce amusing results. A teacher was working with a student who didn't seem to understand passages on a worksheet. The boy could pronounce individual words without hesitation. But when the student read the passage to the teacher, this is what she heard:

The dog ran down the.
Street he got to.
Tom near the school.

The printed text *looked* like this:

The dog ran down the
street. He got to
Tom near the school.

The reading series the boy had been using had stories with each sentence printed on a separate line. The boy had learned to respond to each line as a complete sentence. No wonder he could not understand the passages on the worksheet! Once the problem was identified, it was solved with an explanation about periods, plus practice with an intermediate step that had each sentence start on a new line, but not end on the same line (see Figure 10.3). Soon, continuing to the next line became part of the child's usual procedure. If that hadn't worked, further steps shown in Figure 10.3 could have been taken.

Grades Four On: The Role of Intraverbal Behavior in Comprehension

Beginning reading comprehension involves teaching students to respond to words most of which they already know and to actions and events with which they are already familiar. By the fourth grade, however, students may not have information that is assumed in the text they read. Take, for example, "It was the top of the ninth and the bases were loaded." These words make absolutely no sense without connecting them to baseball. Top of the ninth *grade*? Ninth *building*? Bases of *columns*? *Military* bases? Bases loaded with what, *soldiers*? Intraverbal control is needed to connect "bases" and "ninth" with baseball, so that readers can visualize a game and what is happening in it.

Textual material in the higher grades relies increasingly on assumed knowledge like that needed to understand the baseball sentence. Unfortunately not all students have the required cultural background. Teaching cultural information is a daunting task and no easy solution is offered here. At least, by helping students become fluent, and by making reading a positive experience, students are more likely to read outside of school, and that will gain them some of the knowledge that textual materials take for granted.

First approximation: To teach continuing to the next line to finish the sentence.

> The dog ran down the
> street.
> He got to Tom near
> the school.

Second approximation: To teach paying attention to periods

> The dog ran down the
> street●   He got to
> Tom near the school.

Third approximation: Fading large periods and decreasing extra space before new sentences.

> The dog ran down the
> street. He got to Tom
> near the school.

Fig. 10.3 Successive approximations to teach responding to periods in reading text

IMPLICATIONS OF *VERBAL BEHAVIOR* FOR TEACHING CREATIVE WRITING

Writing is behavior that is shaped and maintained like any other behavior except that the contingencies are mediated by other people and are less reliable than those coming from the physical environment. In *Verbal Behavior* Skinner looks at *why* people write what they do, instead of only at *what* people write. "What" involves a structural analysis like analyzing grammar. "Why" involves contingencies that teachers can use to help students better express and develop their own ideas

Like reading, writing is usually taught by correcting technical details. Students rarely get much feedback on the ideas they express. Figure 10.4 shows an example of a

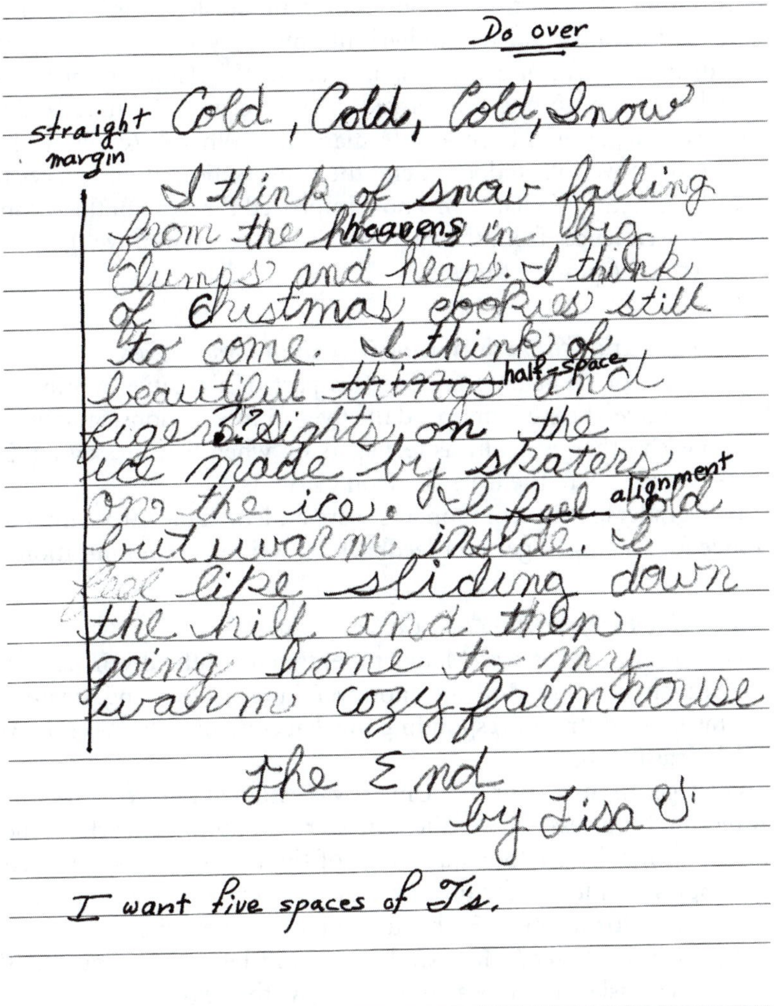
Do over
straight margin
Cold, Cold, Cold, Snow
I think of snow falling from the heavens in big clumps and heaps. I think of Christmas cookies still to come. I think of beautiful ~~things~~ half-space and figures sights on the ice made by skaters on the ice. I feel alignment cold but warm inside. I feel like sliding down the hill and then going home to my warm cozy farmhouse
The End
by Lisa V.
I want five spaces of T's.

Fig. 10.4 A "corrected" composition

fifth-grade girl's composition. Her teacher (and this was a *good* teacher) has not responded to one point that Lisa made. How would you feel if you greeted someone by saying, "How're ya doing?" and received the reply, "The word is 'you', not 'ya.' Say 'you' correctly five times." Talk about putting a stop to conversation! Yet that is exactly what we do to writers. Then we are surprised when they have nothing to say or cannot put into words what they want to express.

Looking at the function of writing rather than just at its form suggests a different approach. One way is to set up contingencies that arrange for writers to get responses to the meaning of what they write rather than to its form.

Example: Communicating through Writing in Second Grade

Chapter 1 described a five-minute silent session in second grade where students could pass notes to anyone they could reach without getting out of their seats. While the original intent of this was to quiet a rowdy class, it soon became clear that the students' writing improved. Of course, the second-graders misspelled words, used incomplete sentences and wrote with scrawly handwriting, but they *communicated*. Their notes included mands in the form of questions, tacts about the classroom or other students, and intraverbal responses to questions asked. If the receiver of a note couldn't understand it, the writer would get back a note manding "What?" Receiving the response "What?" in an oral conversation doesn't end the conversation. It just makes the speaker talk more clearly. Similarly "What?" on a note improved the form of the second-graders' messages. The consequences from their readers did more to improve their writing than copying a "corrected" form five times.

Example: Communicating through Writing in a Sixth-Grade Class

The same procedure of silent note passing was part of a creative writing project in a sixth grade.[31] Of course, the students loved the five-minute sessions. Students responded intraverbally to each other as avidly as teenagers do when text messaging. During one session, a note was passed to the teacher, "Don't stop us."

For the sixth-graders, other components were added. Table 10.3 shows a few other ways to arrange for writing to get peer feedback on written communication.

Example: Improving Essay Writing in a College Course

Few students love to write essays. Many students have difficulty in coming up with things to say. Students have no difficulty, however, in text messaging. If you can capitalize on the intraverbal control of responding to what someone else has said, you will get your students' ideas flowing.

In a Texas college, an instructor, Mr. Unger, was assigned to teach a freshman writing course that required four essays over the semester.[32] Adapting a teaching methodology from his mentor,[33] Mr. Unger took advantage of the internet. First he offered his students several topics in internet forums, like "gun control," about which he was pretty sure they would have strong ideas. Each student picked one topic.

What is the usual next step? Most students would be asked to outline their ideas. Maybe they would be asked to draw a "mind map" with the main topic in the middle of a page and words written all over the page with lines to show relationships.[34] Students who have difficulty writing outlines may produce many words when what they write

Table 10.3 A few examples of ways to provide immediate (or almost immediate) peer feedback for the *content* of student writing

Writing Assignment	Peer's Response
Set aside a few minutes at the beginning of the day or the start of a period. During that time, no one is to say a word, including the teacher. Students can pass notes to anyone they can reach without getting out of their seats. They can also pass a note to someone nearby with a request to pass it on to someone farther away.	Answers what was said in writing or initiates another topic of "conversation."
Draw a name from a box of names of your classmates. Make sure it is not your own name. Describe as many good things about that person as you can think of.	Names the person described. This can be done with the teacher reading the description (to make sure that only positive things are said) or descriptions can be numbered and swapped with peers who guess who was described and hand back the description to the original writer to check if the person was the one the writer had in mind.
Add on to a story. One person starts a story but stops after writing a sentence or two and passes it to a peer. Most students stop in the middle of a sentence to make it more challenging for the next person. Ghost or space stories are popular.	Adds on to what has been written so far and returns the story to the original writer or to another peer to continue the story.
Cut out pictures of popular figures and give one to each student to describe. This can be made simple or difficult depending on how similar the pictures are.	Picks out which figure matches the student's description using three or more of the cutouts.
Describe something scary on one side of the paper and something sad on the other. Variations include describing two fictional people, one generous, one selfish. The discriminations can be easy or more difficult such as "sad" versus "depressed."	Reads both sides and at the top of each write how it makes them feel, or what kind of a person is described, or whatever other property is contrasted. The paper is then returned to the original writer.
Set up internet pen pals from around the world to find out how life at school differs in the US from that in schools in other countries.	Depending on what the pen pal says, asks further questions, or gives information about his or her school.

will not be "corrected." Still, a "mind map" does not receive the feedback of a peer's response, and that was what Mr. Unger arranged.

To get interaction, Mr. Unger asked students to sign on to an internet news discussion forum and to post an opinion on their topic. A student might type, "Nations are better off when you have a right to own a gun." Someone in England might jump in with homicide statistics showing that they are lower in countries with gun control. That might prompt the student to search the internet for contrary statistics, or to shift to another argument for owning guns. Each week, students emailed their teacher a summary of their interactions. Mr. Unger, in turn, checked that they had completed the required discussions, but he did not respond to what either side said.

As in a conversation, students had no reluctance to express their ideas. When they received comments back, some phrase or sentence in the reply would exert intraverbal control and start a whole new line of argument. Instead of rewriting to please a teacher, students revised what they wrote to better state and defend their position. Students also enthusiastically sought facts or authority to substantiate their points, something it is often difficult to get students to do for an essay. They were even careful about their grammar and spelling, editing their own messages before sending them out to the world. When the time came for writing each essay, students wrote their papers, bolstered by weeks of discourse. By then, they had *plenty* to say.[35]

As with reading where concentrating too much on pronunciation interferes with understanding, worrying over structural details while writing interferes with thinking about what one has to say. Professional writers talk of "releasing the critic," during the initial act of writing. They suggest not criticizing your own writing as you compose, saving editing for later. This is another way of removing the effects of the punishment most of us have received when our compositions were "corrected" in writing classes. Exploring your own ideas requires capitalizing on weak intraverbal behavior and that happens best when writing is free of other concerns. Form *does* need to be addressed, just not during the process of creating. Spelling, grammar, and the structure of writing paragraphs are better taught with textbook examples, or paragraphs saved from prior student papers, or later with students' own first drafts.

Moving from Instructional Contingencies to "Natural" Contingencies

Many of the situations and consequences used to teach a skill differ from those that will maintain that skill later in life.[36] The latter are called **natural contingencies** (or sometimes "automatic" or "intrinsic" reinforcers).

> **Natural contingencies** are those that occur in daily life, in contrast to **instructional contingencies** which are special arrangements of both consequences and settings specifically designed to establish skills.

Performance is useful only if it will occur under ordinary conditions where consequences coming from the behavior itself maintain performance. Natural contingencies may be verbal as well as physical. In learning to talk, children may initially have to be prompted to say "thank you." Eventually thanking should occur without the prompt. In workshops, teachers may be taught to avoid using "I" when giving instructions: instead of saying "*I* want you to finish this by Friday," they are prompted to say something like, "You will reach your goal if you finish this by Friday." The instructional contingencies effective in training must carry over to the situations in which the behavior will eventually occur.

Some skills are acquired without help. Youngsters can learn to ride a bike by getting on and experiencing the forces of gravity and the bike's movement.[37] Training wheels, or helpful suggestions like "keep pumping when you change gears so the chain doesn't come off" are instructional contingencies designed to speed mastery. They also reduce the frustration that comes from frequent falling or from chains repeatedly falling off the gears. Some students like to try to master tasks by themselves. If they succeed, fine. If not, they may give up in frustration. Instructional contingencies can subsequently be added. Instruction is nearly always needed for non-physical skills.

There is no way children can learn to read entirely on their own. At the very least they need someone to read to them. Imagine yourself being given books in a language you have learned to speak, but whose symbols are totally unfamiliar (like Arabic or Japanese). Without any help, how successful would you be in figuring out which symbol corresponds to which pronunciation? How long would it take for strings of symbols to make enough sense to give you enjoyment, thrills, or information? Intraverbal prompting is needed to tell you what the printed squiggles say.

In mathematics, everything from counting to differential equations requires teaching, either by a live teacher or by a book or instruction designed by a teacher. In science, many exercises are based on the "discovery method" that provides "natural" consequences for manipulating objects. No student could discover all the important scientific principles useful for adult life. The principles that students are to "discover" are carefully programmed. Instructional contingencies inevitably involve the various kinds of verbal behavior described above.

SUMMARY

The book *Verbal Behavior* presents a whole new way to look at communication. Traditional approaches to language focus on the form or topography of what students write or say, such as grammatical structure or pronunciation. The contingency analysis outlined in this chapter shifts the analysis to controlling variables. Skinner's analysis looks not only at *what* students say or write, but also at *why*. Three examples of implications of a functional analysis for instructional practices were presented in this chapter: handling challenging behavior, teaching comprehension in reading, and teaching "creative writing." These examples give only a glimpse of the power of a contingency analysis.

Applications based on the book *Verbal Behavior* have been growing steadily as the effectiveness of the analysis has yielded results previously thought unobtainable, especially with children with autism.[38] With any student population, understanding the "why" of verbal behavior relations helps you and your students avoid wasting time on work with little payoff. A contingency analysis locates where controls over verbal behavior come from. That helps in designing contingencies that are effective in producing the complicated verbal repertoires demanded by our complex society.

CONCEPT CHECKS
Kinds of Verbal Behavior (Objective A)[39]

DIRECTIONS: Name the action according to its controlling variables. Anything in "quotes" indicates a verbal stimulus heard or printed. The first one is done for you. The categories are:

1. **Mand**
2. **Tact**
3. **Echoic**
4. **Copying text**

5. **Textual**
6. **Transcription**
7. **Intraverbal**
8. **Not Verbal if the action is not an example of verbal behavior**

Action . . .
say "reinforcement"

Mainly as a result of . . .
hearing "reinforcement"

Answer: **Echoic**. Explanation: Saying "reinforcement" mainly as a result of hearing "reinforcement" is echoic verbal behavior: An *oral* response matches *point-to-point* the *auditory* stimulus.

Action . . .		**Mainly as a result of . . .**
_____	1. write "help" in the snow	being lost and hoping a plane would come rescue you
_____	2. say "stand up"	seeing the words "stand up"
_____	3. open a window	someone saying "please open the window"
_____	4. say "Fine" when in pain	hearing "How are you?"
_____	5. write "red"	seeing an apple
_____	6. saying "I won't do it"	seeing "I won't do it"
_____	7. say "dog"	hearing a dog's bark
_____	8. say "operant"	hearing "operant"
_____	9. write "operant"	seeing the word "operant"
_____	10. say "chair"	seeing a chair
_____	11. write "chair"	seeing a chair
_____	12. write "tap"	hearing "tap"
_____	13. write "bed"	Seeing a bed
_____	14. smile	being happy
_____	15. say "happy"	seeing someone smiling
_____	16. say "please"	seeing the text "please"
_____	17. calling out "dodge ball"	to increase the chances of the gym teacher letting you play dodge ball
_____	18. say "pencil"	hearing "pen and. . ."
_____	19. say "describe"	hearing "describe"
_____	20. saying "you're welcome"	hearing "thank you"

Establishing Operations (Objective B)

DIRECTIONS: Identify the kind of establishing operation that makes or has made each bolded item effective as a reinforcer.

D for deprivation (specify the article or activity withheld)
A for aversive stimulation (specify the aversive stimulus)
S for procedures that make something more salient or potent as a reinforcer

1. You show all the things an **electronic gadget** that has been sitting at the side of the room can do to encourage learning how to use it.
2. You use getting to **lunch** early as a consequence.
3. Your school room is too hot so you consider **opening windows**.
4. You put a paste of **baking soda** on a student' s poison ivy to reduce the itching.
5. Finally, you get a day without rain so recess can be **outside**.

ANALYSIS PROBLEMS

1. Classify Observed Verbal Behavior (Objective D)

This week, carry a notebook (paper or electronic) and record interesting bits of verbal behavior and then analyze the controls over them. If you have difficulty finding examples, you can set up a mini-experiment. Vary the way you greet people before they speak to you. For example, say "Hi" to some, "Hello," or "Good morning (or "afternoon") to others or "What's up?" to others. Note what *you* said when you talked first and what the other person *replied*. Then classify their responses into Skinner's categories of verbal behavior.

2. Incorporating "Natural" Contingencies into Teaching Creative Writing (Objective E)

Design an exercise to incorporate peer response to what is written ("natural" contingencies) for students you teach or might someday teach.

ANSWERS FOR CONCEPT CHECKS

Kinds of Verbal Behavior (Explanations Added to Answers for Your Information)

1. **Mand**. This is under the establishing operation of aversive stimulation and probably also deprivation.
2. **Textual** behavior. Printed stimulus, oral response with point-to-point matching of the order of corresponding parts.
3. **Not Verbal**. Your action of opening a window operates directly on the environment. The form of your behavior in opening it is determined by the kind of window it is, not by a verbal community. Of course, you must have acquired verbal behavior in order to "understand" the request, but your actions in opening the window depend on the kind of latch, whether the window sticks or not, the direction it opens, etc., all of which depend on mechanical action. The postcedents over your opening of the window come from the window physically opening, not from a mediator.
4. **Intraverbal**. If there were a strong tact component you would mention not feeling well.
5. **Tact**. This is a tact of a property (color).
6. **Textual**. Point-to-point match in the order of corresponding parts of the printed text and oral response.
7. **Tact**. This is a tact of a characteristic of dogs. You are in contact with the sound that is usually paired with them.
8. **Echoic**. The oral response matches both the sequence and medium of the auditory stimulus point-to-point.
9. **Copying text**. Printed response corresponding point-to-point to the ordering of parts of the printed stimulus.

10. **Tact**. Your verbal behavior is under direct visual contact of the chair.
11. **Tact**. The writing is under control of the presence of the chair. Tacts do not have to be oral.
12. **Transcription**. Point-to-point correspondence of the order of parts of the oral stimulus and written response.
13. **Tact**. The bed is in your presence.
14. **Not Verbal**. Smiling seems to be part of our inheritance. No mediator is required to establish smiling as a result of being happy.
15. **Tact**. Smiling is a property paired with being happy. Although some inference is involved, society considers smiling a property of happiness.
16. **Copying text**. Point-to-point correspondence in order of parts of the printed stimulus and printed response.
17. **Mand**. The response specifies its reinforcement. It is also at least partly under control of deprivation—the number of hours since last playing. The response would have been less likely had the student been playing non-stop for a long time.
18. **Intraverbal**. "Pencil" is under control of verbal stimuli, but is not under control of a point-to-point correspondence with the stimulus.
19. **Echoic**. Point-to-point matching of oral response and auditory stimulus.
20 **Intraverbal**. No point-to-point correspondence, but the verbal response is under control of a prior verbal stimulus.

Establishing Operations (Explanations Added to Answers for Your Information)

1. **S** If the gadget has been around, there is no deprivation. Your demonstration, however, makes playing with it more reinforcing.
2. **D** Near lunch time food deprivation is high. You are taking advantage of that deprivation to use access to food (a bit early) as a reinforcer.
3. **A** "*Too* hot," indicates that the high temperature was an aversive situation.
4. **A** An itch is an aversive stimulus. The paste of baking soda relieves the itch.
5. **D** The run of days of rain produces a deprivation of outside play. (This assumes that outside recess is more reinforcing than inside recess.)

Part IV

Ethical Practices and Ultimate Goals

11

PUNISHMENT AND WHY TO AVOID IT

"You can't shake hands with a clenched fist."

Indira Gandhi

OVERVIEW

Education has traditionally relied on punishment as a technique of control. By the turn of the twenty-first century verbal chastisement and "time out" had replaced the rod for most of America's students, but punishment still is a major method of controlling behavior in schools. That needs to change. Aversive methods of control do not benefit anyone. At best they lead to escape or apathy in the person or group punished, at worst to counter aggression such as vandalism or violence. In contrast, control based upon positive contingencies leads to a social climate in which everyone prospers, including you the teacher.

This chapter looks at punishment, why it is harmful to the recipient, to peers who observe it, and to the person doing the punishing. While the rest of this book addresses positive contingencies that make problems less likely, it is unrealistic to imagine that you will never encounter behavior that needs to be decelerated. Suggestions are thus also given about what to do when you *feel* like punishing or need to stop some ongoing behavior *right now*.

OBJECTIVES

By the end of this chapter you should be able to:

A. Describe the harmful effects of punishment on the person punished, on onlooking peers, and on the person doing the punishing.
B. Identify or describe situations that exemplify the following:

punishment	reinforcement
extinction	response cost
avoidance	escape

---

time out   escalation of treatment
"natural" versus "added" consequences
differential reinforcement procedures
>   Differential Reinforcement of Incompatible behavior (DRI)
>   Differential Reinforcement of Alternative behavior (DRA)
>   Differential Reinforcement of "Other" behavior (DRO)

C. Using a contingency analysis, explain why people punish and continue to punish.
D. Select from several situations, the ones for which extinction alone would work best.
E. For a given punishment you personally experienced or observed, describe how the person punishing could have handled the situation with positive procedures.

Ms. Rennix's Story[1]

It was one of those days. I had lunch duty, and Sybil, one of my third-graders, was acting up again. A likable tomboy with pigtails, Sybil could have stepped out of an advertisement for children's clothes, except for her energy. Today, for example, Sybil would not stay sitting at her lunch table and, as if that weren't bad enough, other students were following her example. I had to take action. "Sybil, come here," I said as she ran past my table. No response. I got up and went after her. Seeing me following, Sybil disappeared under a lunch table. I cleared the kids and chairs away from one side of the table to talk to her, but she squiggled out and ran under the next table. In exasperation, I left her there. When all the children but my third grade had left the lunch room, Sybil finally came out, grinning.

When we got back to the classroom, Sybil was still grinning. I turned to the third-graders and asked, "What did Sybil do wrong today?"

"She crawled under all the tables. Look, she got spaghetti all over her tights."

The children giggled.

"She shouldn't be out of her seat."

"She didn't come when you said."

The accusations came thick and fast. I began to feel better. "And what should we do about it?" I asked.

"Make her stay in for recess for the rest of the year."

"Make her eat alone up in the classroom."

Sybil stopped grinning.

"Send her to the principal's office."

"She should do spelling all day and get no art."

"Don't let her eat lunch for a year."

I was surprised at the severity of the punishments and, from her look, so was Sybil. Turning to Sybil, I asked, "What do *you* think we should do, Sybil?" Sybil's face turned red. She was silent. Then—and I never thought I'd live to see that day—Sybil cried.

PUNISHMENT IN AMERICA'S SCHOOLS: A TRADITION IT IS TIME TO REPLACE

Did Sybil deserve this treatment? Tradition would say "yes." In the United States, punishment is sanctioned as a method of control. Even corporal punishment as of the year 2007 was permitted in some school districts in 21 of the 50 United States. In the 2006–07 academic year, 223,190 public school students received corporal punishment at least once.[2] It is ironic that guards in United States prisons are not allowed to hit prisoners, but state laws prevent only "unreasonable" physical punishment of children and teenagers. Actions that are "presumed unreasonable" when used to correct or restrain a child include:

> Throwing, kicking, burning, cutting, striking with a closed fist, shaking a child under 3, interfering with breathing, threatening with a deadly weapon, any other act likely to cause and which does cause bodily harm greater than transient pain or minor temporary marks.[3]

If 29 states can manage behavior without inflicting "transient pain or minor temporary marks," why is physical punishment needed in the others? It is not. Spanking is a primitive method of control. When corporal punishment is banned, teachers must adopt alternative procedures.

Unfortunately banning physical punishment does not end punishment in classrooms. Teachers still punish behavior by yelling, humiliating, taking away privileges, sending to the principal's office, keeping after school, making the student write "I will not . . . " over and over—the list goes on and on. Why are these so familiar? Why is punishment so common? Teachers resort to punishment, corporal or otherwise, when they have lost control and don't know what else to do.

Why Do People Punish?

To understand why any behavior occurs, look at the contingencies over it. People punish in situations where behavior is occurring that is aversive for them. It doesn't take any training to come up with some kind of punitive consequence. Everyone knows how to yell, hit, or take away privileges. What is the immediate effect of this treatment on the undesirable behavior? It almost always stops it dead. The act of punishing is thus (negatively) reinforced. Regardless of the effect on the person receiving the treatment, the effect on the behavior of *punishing* is to increase it. When again faced with behavior the punisher does not like, the probability of punishing is high. Punishment as a technique interrupts ongoing behavior, at least temporarily, and seems to "work." Unfortunately problems that punishment *creates* tend to make future behavior worse, not better. That is why it is important to design classroom environments where students behave well, so that punishment is rarely used.

Rationalizations You May Hear

Most teachers know they should be able to handle behavior problems without using punishment, so rationalizations are common. In class and in daily life, you will hear statements like, "I had to do *something* to stop him," or "I'm just using natural consequences." A **natural consequence** of behavior is something that *behavior itself* produces. Injuring your thumb from holding a nail incorrectly while hammering is a natural consequence, or getting burned by touching a hot object. The breaking of a china dish is a natural consequence of dropping or throwing it. Having to clean up the resulting mess is *not* a natural consequence. Cleaning up the mess is under contingencies set by other people. Similarly, being made to apologize for an insult, or to scrub walls as a consequence of writing graffiti may partially make up for damage caused, but they are consequences imposed by an authority figure not by "nature." They are *not* natural consequences. They are still teacher- or administrator-added punishments.

Because punishment is frowned upon, most of us would like to think that we are not using it even when we are. If people claim that a treatment they are using is not punishment, ask them "What is the intended effect of the procedure?" If the answer is to decrease the behavior, then the treatment is expected to function as punishment.

PUNISHMENT: WHAT IT IS AND WHEN IT "WORKS"

Punishment is a postcedent event that decreases the behavior on which it is made contingent. The postcedent can be an added stimulus, like a spanking, or the removal of a reinforcer like a fine. The loss of reinforcers contingent upon an action is called **response cost**.

Like reinforcement, punishment is defined not by a subjective feeling about a procedure, but by its effect on behavior (Table 11.1). Punishment is any event that decreases the frequency or intensity of the operant it immediately follows. The "event" can be something added or something removed, leading to the adjectives "positive" and "negative." Positive punishment sounds like something beneficial and will not be used in this book. "Negative" isn't much better. Instead of "negative" a better term for taking away reinforcers like money, points, or privileges is **response cost**.

Punitive consequences must be connected with behavior to have a decelerating effect. Verbal statements of later consequences are often given, as in "You will be *staying in* from recess today," or "no pizza party for *you* this Friday." In the example of Sybil, she did not receive any punitive consequences in the lunch room. The statements by her classmates were linked to her earlier behavior in the lunch room only verbally. Still Sybil's teacher addressed her behavior as soon as was feasible. The teacher did not wait until the end of the day.

Contrast with Extinction

Punishment is not the only procedure that weakens operant behavior. The other procedure is extinction. Operant extinction is the process of no longer immediately delivering reinforcement that has previously followed the behavior in question. (Pavlovian extinction is a different procedure).[4] The effect of withholding reinforcement depends on how reinforcement has been contingent on behavior in the past. Extinction occurs very rapidly when only one or two responses have been reinforced. If pushing a button on a toy has produced a nice sound only a few times, a child will soon stop pressing the button when it stops working. With a longer history of playing with the toy under continuous reinforcement (all presses reinforced), behavior differs. When pressing no longer results in sound, you may see an **extinction burst**: button pushing

Table 11.1 Forms punishment can take (To be punishment, the procedure **must** immediately decrease the frequency or intensity of the operant the consequence is contingent upon.)

Added stimuli	Examples of consequences added by the behaving individual	Examples of consequences added by others
Physical	burning (added from putting a finger in a candle flame)	hitting, jerking, or shaking
Verbal	saying "no" to oneself	shouting, insulting, or embarrassing
Tasks	picking up stack of scattered cards (after dropping them)	writing of "I will not throw spit balls in class" 100 times or scrubbing graffiti off school walls
Over-correction		requiring student to make 1000 spitballs and number each one

Removed reinforcers	Reinforcers removed by the behaver	Reinforcers removed by others
Response cost	dropping money where it cannot be retrieved or breaking a favorite object	taking away money or a favorite object
Time out or suspension	staying away from friends or a favorite band's concert	removing student from friends or preventing from attending a concert

increases in speed or force, and emotional responses like pounding or throwing the toy may occur before behavior stops.

Extinction bursts are common occurrences at all ages. Think about how you respond when an action that has always worked stops working. Or watch someone trying to open a door that has always opened before, but is now stuck fast. You are likely to witness harder pushes, jerks or kicks before attempts at opening stop.

Following intermittent reinforcement, extinction takes longer than after continuous reinforcement. When reinforcement has occurred very infrequently (especially if unpredictably), behavior can become *very* resistant to extinction. Skinner and his colleagues were able to shape such persistent pecking in a pigeon that after disconnecting the food magazine (an extinction procedure), the bird pecked over 6,000 times before quitting.[5] The bird did eventually stop, but with its history of a high **variable ratio schedule** of reinforcement, extinction took a *very* long time. Much classroom behavior that interferes with instruction has been intermittently reinforced, often by peers as well as the teacher. That makes extinction as a sole treatment less than

> **Operant extinction** is a process in which reinforcement that has previously followed an operant is no longer forthcoming. The word **extinction** is also applied to the resulting behavior, as in "The child's swearing underwent extinction when no one responded to it any more."

ideal for eliminating behavior. When extinction by itself does not work, too often teachers fall back on punishment.

Time Out: Extinction or Punishment?

One procedure that has become popular for reducing behavior is time out. Removing a misbehaving student from activities is hardly new: students have been sent to corners, or to stand in halls, or to a principal's office for hundreds of years. What is new is the name.[6] Time out is often mislabeled as an "extinction" procedure. It is not extinction. Extinction requires withholding former reinforcement so that *nothing* happens, but in time out an action is taken. Removing a person from a reinforcing activity, like removing a reinforcing activity from a person, takes away the opportunity to participate. Both processes are contingent consequences, not a lack of effect. Say a teenage girl on the playground calls her teacher "stupid" to his face. Extinction would require nothing to happen, as if the behavior had never occurred. Whatever was maintaining calling names, such as the teacher's outrage or minor facial expressions of disapproval, would be withheld, along with any peer's reactions (clearly difficult to arrange). Time out, in contrast, would require an *action* such as asking the girl to leave the playground for a few minutes. Time out thus *adds* a consequence, in this case an order to leave.

> **Time out** is a procedure for decelerating behavior by removing a student from a reinforcing activity for a limited period of time. Also called **time out from positive reinforcement**.

Whether a time-out procedure is punishment depends on its effect on behavior. Being removed from class activities may, or may *not*, decrease the rate of the behavior on which removal was contingent. In some cases, removal from an activity may reinforce "problem" behavior. The *procedure* may be the same, but how it affects behavior reveals whether it is reinforcement or punishment.

> **Punishment** is any event that reduces the frequency or intensity of the operant it follows. Punishment differs from extinction in that punishment is a contingent event. In **extinction** whatever has maintained an operant no longer occurs.

Punishment is often said to "suppress" behavior, not to directly weaken it. The problem with assessing effects of punishment, even in a controlled laboratory setting, is that you have to have ongoing behavior in order to assess the effect of a procedure on that behavior. But if an operant is strong enough to judge the effect of punishment, that operant must have been firmly established, probably by intermittent reinforcement. Behavior that has been intermittently reinforced is likely to come back once punishment is removed: hence the description of punishment as "suppressing" behavior.

The Problem of Concurrent Reinforcement

Any operant that occurs repeatedly in a classroom is being reinforced. Otherwise it would die out. So when some kind of punishment is added, two contingencies conflict: you have reinforcement *and* punishment of the same operant. Reinforcement keeps the behavior going, punishment weakens it. When both contingencies are strong, behavior continues but with an added action: watching out so as not to get caught! The failure of punishment to deter behavior can be impressive. In the early nineteenth century in

England, hangings were a popular public event and many people, rich and poor, turned out to watch. Gatherings were good opportunities for thieves to relieve onlookers of their money—in plain view of the punishment they would receive if caught![7] Even such a dire consequence as hanging did not eliminate stealing, though it undoubtably did suppress it, especially when London Bobbies were in view. The reinforcing contingencies for stealing were powerful enough to risk death.

In any classroom where an inappropriate behavior occurs repeatedly, you have a similar problem: somewhere, somehow, that operant is being reinforced. Adding punishment, then, is unlikely to stop the behavior if the reinforcement also continues at least intermittently. The added punishment may suppress the behavior, driving it "underground," or it may make little change in the overall frequency. In certain circumstances, however, punishment "works."

Conditions for Punishment to "Work" in Eliminating an Operant

You can probably remember a time when something you did was punished and you never did it again. In my case, the behavior was swinging my violin bow back and forth while riding my bicycle home from a violin lesson. All of a sudden, the tip of the bow caught in the rear spokes and snapped. I stopped immediately and looked at my beautiful bow. The bow's hair hung limply from the inch-long piece of wood left in my hand. The rest of the wood lay on the ground, splintered into an amazing number of pieces. I felt terrible. I *liked* that bow. Although I didn't get any additional punishment from my parents, I never again carried a violin bow outside of its case while riding a bicycle. The punishment of its breaking was plenty enough to stop that behavior forever.

The conditions for punishment needed to eliminate a behavior were just right in this instance. Optimal conditions include the following (see Table 11.2):

1. The punished behavior is occurring for the first time.
2. Punishment is inevitable, that is, it always follows the action and does not require another person to catch the behavior.
3. Nearly the same or stronger reinforcement can be obtained from alternative behavior.
4. Alternative behavior is no more effortful than the punished action.

For my bow swinging all were met:

1. This was the first time I had ridden with the bow swinging from my hand.
2. The bow would always break if it caught in the wheel. (Of course, I might have gotten away with swinging the bow without catching it in the wheel, but at least no one had to be around for the punishment to occur if the bow did catch.)
3. Riding without swinging a bow was nearly as reinforcing as riding with swinging a bow (and I could always swing a stick rather than a bow).
4. Putting the bow in the violin case did not require a lot more effort than leaving the bow out of the case to be carried separately.

These four requirements—1) first time occurrence; 2) inevitability of immediate punishment; 3) equivalent reinforcement for alternative actions; and 4) ease of executing

Table 11.2 Optimal conditions for punishment to eliminate an operant (whether a desirable operant or undesirable operant)

Contingency	Example	Comments
Punishment follows immediately from the behavior itself, AND there is no strong reinforcement maintaining the behavior.	Touching a candle flame *always* produces pain AND there is no particular payoff (such as peer approval for showing off) for putting a finger in flames.	There is no "getting away with it" when punishment immediately results from your own action.
Punishment given by someone else ALWAYS follows the operant AND there are no strong contingencies maintaining the action.	Class "bully" always hits you if you grab something from him AND the object is not something of very high value to you.	Punishing individual must *always* be present, a problem for many situations.
Aversive consequence is physiological but delayed AND there are no strong immediately reinforcing effects.	Eating a food that tastes good, but causes vomiting later.	No strong reinforcement must be present. (Delayed consequences of binge drinking or smoking or eating bad food when starving do not counter the immediate benefits.)
Alternative, less effortful operant produces the same or an equivalent consequence as the punished operant.	Handing a "take a break" card to a teacher (instead of banging one's head on the desk).	The alternative operant must be in the individual's repertoire or has to be shaped.

alternative actions—rarely exist for behavior likely to be punished in a classroom. Actions that interfere with instruction are usually firmly in the repertoire of the individual exhibiting them: they are not always "caught;" they are often more immediately reinforcing than instructional activities; and finally, most disruptive actions require less effort than the educational tasks assigned.

Take, for example, talking to a friend during seat work. Talking to peers is a well established behavior. It is not always caught. Alternative actions (i.e. working) probably do not produce as immediately reinforcing feedback as the response by peers, and talking requires much less effort than completing algebra problems, or grammar exercises, or whatever work has been assigned. Adding punishment for talking does nothing to reduce the *tendency* to talk to peers. It just adds a second contingency. The student will still "want" to talk and will talk whenever there is no likelihood of it being punished.

Because of these conflicting contingencies in schools, "problem behavior" rarely disappears with the application of punishment. If you look at the records kept on disciplined students, you usually find the same students receiving the same disciplinary actions week after week. If a behavior reoccurs, punishment has not solved your problem. Period.

What Punishment Can Never Do
Punishment can never build behavior. Eliminating Paul's swearing will not automatically result in his suddenly taking an interest in trigonometry. Education is about building behavior. In addition to improving classroom performance, building skills has an additional benefit. In any time period, students who are actively working cannot at the same time be disrupting class (see specific strategies below). Building any skill is done through reinforcement and thus avoids all of the destructive side effects of punishment that run counter to the goals of education.

UNDESIRABLE SIDE EFFECTS OF PUNISHMENT

Many of the problems that teachers face result from punishment. Students who come to school hostile or aggressive, or suspicious of authority, or sullen and withdrawn, show a prior history of punishment. For these students, more punishment only makes the situation worse. For many of these students, schools serve as a refuge, a further reason for arranging a positive experience for them.

Harmful Effects of Punishment on the Future Behavior of Students Punished
Although individuals differ in how they react to punishment, respondent reactions inevitably occur. Remember that in respondent conditioning, a "neutral" stimulus occurs before or at the same time as a stimulus that already elicits a response. After pairing, the formerly neutral stimulus by itself elicits the response. If a student is embarrassed by her teacher when she answers a question, the unconditioned reflex consists of the teacher comment producing respondents like flushing and discomfort. Answering comes just before the teacher's comment and that pairing produces a new reflex: answering questions (the conditioned stimulus) now produces embarrassment (the conditioned response) as shown in Figure 11.1. Embarrassment is intended to decrease *incorrect* responding, but answering questions *in general* is likely to be affected. Whether those reactions are strong enough to decrease classroom participation altogether depends on many factors such as the student's past experiences with teachers. But in all cases, whenever an aversive stimulus occurs, you can expect some spread of

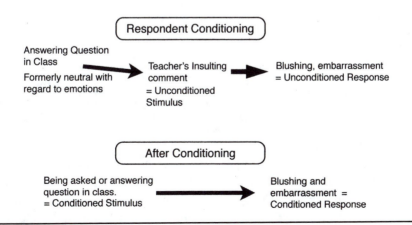

Fig. 11.1 Respondent conditioning to an aversive stimulus

effect. Physiological respondents like increased heart rate and rapidity of breathing typically occur when errors are made during instruction.[8]

Many aspects of a class situation are part of the antecedents paired with a particular punishment: the presence of an authority figure, the subject matter under discussion, the kind of question, even school itself. Needless to say, creating negative reactions to authority figures, to the subject-matter taught, or to school in general runs counter to the goals of education.

Escape and Avoidance as a Side Effect of Punishment

Respondent reactions to stimuli paired with punishment provide an establishing operation for operant behavior of escape or avoidance. **Escape** is an action that reduces or gets the behaver out of an aversive situation. **Avoidance** refers to behavior that postpones or prevents encountering an aversive situation. Escape and avoidance can be remarkably persistent. Once escaping from a situation where someone threatens you, you may **avoid** the location where the incident occurred, even if the threatening person is *never there again.*

> **Escape** refers to behavior that ends or gets out of an existing aversive situation already present. In **avoidance** the behavior prevents or postpones an aversive situation from occurring.

Students experiencing punishment often exhibit escape or avoidance behavior. Mathematics provides a prime example. In almost any college class of 30 or more students you will find at least one student who has avoided taking math courses because of a bad experience in a math class. Even if future experiences with math would never again be aversive, unless that student again must take math, he or she will not find out. The student is avoiding situations that have been paired with punishment.

Actions in schools that we label as sneaky, deceitful, dishonest, cheating, or truant also exemplify avoidance of punishment. Punishing smoking cigarettes may not eliminate smoking, but smokers hide behavior from those likely to punish it. Saying your dog ate your homework shows avoidance of consequences of failing to hand in homework. Cheating avoids bad grades. Truancy avoids school altogether. While punishment does not directly *cause* any of these actions, it sets up circumstances for them to be reinforcing.

Not everyone responds to punishment with avoidance. One other common response is aggression.

Counter Aggression as a By-Product of Punishment

To illustrate the "fight" effect, an early study put two non-aggressive rats in the same cage. They showed no signs of aggression. When, however, one rat was shocked, it immediately attacked the other rat who then retaliated.[9] Punishment begets punishment. The next time a student in your class responds angrily or aggressively, note the circumstances surrounding that behavior. Chances are good that something aversive has just happened to him or her. Individuals punished exhibit a heightened predisposition to act violently. You may yourself have kicked objects, shouted, slammed doors, thrown objects or otherwise acted aggressively when experiencing a punishing event. Hitting your fist on a table is "safe." It doesn't really hurt you, and tables don't hit back. Unfortunately not all violence is harmless: it may be directed towards others as

Figure 11.2 shows. Here counter aggression is aimed towards someone who has less power, like students who pick on weaker students on the playground. Counter aggression against more powerful figures occurs, too, often out of their hearing in such actions as hostile comments, unflattering caricatures, or symbolic representations of hate posted in the dead of night. And, of course, direct counter attacks also occur. Slashed tires, vandalized school property, and shootings occur in American schools. It is no coincidence that those who commit school violence have a history of punishment. Corporal punishment is particularly harmful, especially when frequent or when severe enough to leave marks: Interviews of individuals imprisoned for murder, rape, or other violent crimes inevitably reveal a history of corporal punishment.[10]

The relationship between corporal punishment and later aggression shows in state statistics. Table 11.3 shows how many of the top 10 and bottom 10 states that permit paddling fare on various indices.[11] Among states with the highest murder rates, eight permit paddling. Only one paddling state falls among the 10 states with the lowest murder rates. Of course, this relation does not prove cause and effect: you can see that other factors, such as per pupil spending and "overall well-being" also favor states with no paddling. At the very least, however, these statistics do not support claims that paddling prevents violence or encourages high graduation rates. The statistics favor the opposite conclusion.

Fig. 11.2 Punishment begets punishment

Table 11.3 Relationship between permitted paddling in schools and a few sociological indices

Index	Number in Top Ten States That Permit Paddling	Number in Bottom Ten States That Permit Paddling
Murder rate	8	1
Incarceration rate	9	0
Percentage of births to unwed mothers	9	2
Overall well-being of children in terms of poverty, education, health, etc.	0	10
Average proficiency in math 8th-grade	1	10
High school completion rate	1	7
Spending per pupil	1	7

Source: From Congressional Quarterly State Fact Finder, 2002

A study of discipline methods in Australian schools found that the classes with the best behaved and most responsible students had teachers who were the least punitive.[12] Again, correlation does not prove cause and effect. After all, classes that had more unruly students could encourage harsher discipline methods. However, the teachers who used aggressive tactics also failed to acknowledge the *appropriate* behavior of their "unruly" students when it did occur, in contrast to the more positive teachers. In all classes, "misbehaving" students responded better to less aggressive tactics from teachers. This is exactly what an analysis of contingencies would predict.

When a student's behavior is making your life difficult, you may *feel* like punishing. That provides a good opportunity to model handling a difficult situation calmly, preferably with the student alone. If specific infractions have specific penalties, you need to adhere to the rules, but you can do so without any show of anger. Public punishment with a raised voice or angry tone has a "ripple effect" on onlooking students. The same principles apply to a business setting or to the home.

Harmful Effects of Punishment on the Behavior of Onlooking Students

Punishing one student often affects other students who observe the teacher's action. The Australian study mentioned above found that at both the elementary and secondary level, students witnessing another student being ridiculed or embarrassed sympathized with the punished student and felt embarrassed themselves. This "ripple effect" was first reported in a classic study done in 26 kindergartens in Detroit. In this study, undergraduate observers went into the classrooms at the beginning of the school year. They recorded each time a student was "corrected" for "misbehavior" and wrote down how students who observed that "correction" responded. They found that when the teachers specified the behavior expected, such as "Tommy, in kindergarten we ask for things. We don't grab," onlookers tended to respond positively, paying more attention to what they were supposed to be doing. In contrast, when teachers said things like

"Tommy, stop that" with an angry tone or a rough touch, onlooking children tended to show anxiety, become confused or restless, or stop participating in class activities. It was this effect on onlookers that the researchers called the "ripple effect." Although the effects of the teacher's actions wore off after only a few days, the researchers concluded, "What a teacher does to control children's behavior affects the children who watch as well as the children who are corrected."[13]

Another effect of aggressive methods of control lasts longer than the "ripple effect." Yelling at students or insulting them models behavior you do not want to see in your students. It is far better to demonstrate appropriate ways of handling problems. If you establish the social climate with proper conduct, students will tend to follow your lead.

The effects of observing violence does not depend on viewing a live model. Exposure to violence in videos, games, and television has been shown to predict not only increased violence in childhood, but also later aggression as a young adult, regardless of socioeconomic background, even when the level of aggressiveness as a preschooler is controlled.[14] By the turn of the twenty-first century, the average child in the United States spent three to five hours a day watching television, 60% of which depicted violence. Add to that the hours playing violent games and the exposure reaches very high levels.[15] Not all who watch violence or play violent games respond the same way, of course. Large individual differences exist, both in the amount of violence viewed and in the way in which a child reacts to exposure. But no study has shown that exposure to violence shown in television or games *decreases* later aggression! Today's games and media are increasing in the degree of violence shown, making it increasingly important for schools to teach alternative ways of handling conflict.

Harmful Effects of Punishment on the Behavior of the Person Punishing

What about the effects of using punishment on *you* when you punish? They are not good either. When your interactions with students consist largely of reprimands, your attention becomes something to avoid. The value of your attention diminishes and, with it, the effectiveness of your approval as a reinforcer. Far better to pair your attention with all things positive, including help when students encounter difficulty with their work.

Those who rely on punishment as a technique of control often succumb to escalation. Effects of a particular punishment tend to wear off with repeated use. The first reaction to a harsh reprimand is greater on the punished student than the second time the same punishment is applied. The third is less effective than the second. Soon the original level is pretty much ignored by the recipient. To get the same effect, then, the teacher has to give a stronger reprimand, escalating the level of aversiveness.

Without positive alternatives, the only option for controlling behavior when mild sanctions don't work is to increase the level of punishment, If, in a normal voice a teacher asks students to stop shoving and they don't stop, the tendency is to repeat, only louder. Then, the next time that teacher needs to stop students shoving, the tendency is to *start* at the louder volume. This cycle sometimes escalates until yelling can be heard from one end of a school to the other. Needless to say, this does not help one's relationships with students, nor does it model appropriate behavior.

Other punishments tend to escalate, too. A two-minute time out becomes five minutes, an in-school study hall grows into suspension, and swats on the behind become full scale paddlings. With all of the disadvantages of punitive procedures, alternative ways of decelerating behavior are always preferable. The first step is prevention: you can decrease the number of infractions you will have to deal with by your handling of school rules at the beginning of each term.

ALTERNATIVES TO PUNISHMENT: PREVENTION

All contingencies that you set up to shape beneficial behavior will help prevent problems during the school year. Still, inappropriate behavior not allowed in your school needs to be specifically addressed. All schools have rules. How those rules are stated and explained affects much of the behavior of students.

Establishing Rules of Conduct

Don't you find it unfriendly when you visit a national park to be greeted with a sign that says:

- No fires except in grills provided.
- No smoking anywhere in the park.
- No camping. Park closes at 6:00 PM.
- Do not litter.
- Do not feed any wildlife.
- Do not pick or disturb flowers or plants.
- Violators will be fined.

How about this instead?

- Welcome. Help us keep the park for everyone to enjoy.
- Take only photographs: leave only footprints.
- Feed only yourself. Human food makes wild animals sick or aggressive.
- Prevent forest fires by keeping fires to grills provided.
- Smoke *only* when you leave the park.
- You may stay until 6:00 PM when the park closes.

Well, they are not all positive, but they give a better "feel" than the original. Rules are statements of contingencies—if you do action X, then consequence Y follows. Stating rules as appropriate behavior reduces their punitive overtones. Of course, if you are given school-wide rules of conduct you may not wish to rephrase them. But you can make sure that students know their positive counterparts, as well as going over consequences for infractions. Especially for non-English speaking students, lack of understanding of rules causes confusion about exactly what conduct is expected. To clarify distinctions between approved and prohibited behavior, some schools have found role-playing helpful.

In general, the fewer rules in writing the better. Students remember them better, and you can monitor compliance more easily. Pick the most important rules to put into writing or to emphasize: many policies, such as procedures for fire drills, can be explained without an "if you don't" part of rules.

Ownership: Involving Students in Setting Rules of Conduct
When students help set up class rules, they not only understand them better, they are more likely to follow them. Rules are seen as *their* rules, not those imposed upon them by others. That "ownership" encourages peer support, thus requiring fewer reminders by you. Rules to which students contribute are also more likely to be seen as fair, so that consequences for infractions don't cause as much resentment as penalties designed by a teacher or other authority figures.[16]

If you and your class feel a penalty should not be imposed, change the rule for everyone. If two students miss a deadline for a report or paper, and you feel they make a good case ("the internet was down"), extend the deadline for everyone. Of course, changing rules should not be done lightly. In a large college class, one student came in to the professor's office the day after a big football game to ask for an extension of a deadline. He thought he had an infallible excuse. He couldn't finish his assignment, he said, because he had celebrated the win too hard and had spent the night in jail! The professor explained that giving one person an extension would be unfair to all the other students who had managed to finish their work *before* the game began. The professor then added ways the student could make up lost points to improve his grade. By explaining rules as a matter of fairness to others, and by giving alternative positive actions, some of the harmful effects of punishment can be softened.[17]

Involving students in phrasing rules does not mean giving up the final say. Like any ideas expressed by students, you can accept proposals or not accept them. Here, too, positives work better than negatives: starting off discussing what behavior your students like in others helps build consensus before addressing the more controversial topic of penalties.

Turning Negatives into Positives
To emphasize behavior expected you can often turn statements of what not to do into statements of positive actions. Instead of penalties for infractions, how about bonuses for behaving well? Most people toilet train their children by punishing accidents. How about checking pants frequently and praising a child when pants are *dry*? Combined with other behavioral procedures potty training has been done in "less than a day."[18]

Example: Getting Teenagers to Pick Up Trash in a Common Room
A counselor at a residential prison for young male offenders had a problem with littering in the TV room that was shared by everyone in the residential unit for which he was responsible. The prison had a point system where points could be exchanged for privileges or for purchasing small items at the institution's store. At first, the counselor used fines. When he entered the TV room, he counted the number of items left on the floor and docked points from everyone according to the degree of the mess in the room. As you can imagine, this did not make anyone happy. Everyone protested: "I didn't leave that there. He did." "Hey, that's not fair. I just got here," and so on. So the counselor changed to a positive system: whenever he came by the room, if there was no trash on the floor, everyone in the room got a bonus point! Rapid improvement: when the teenagers entered the room, they checked for trash and picked up any that was laying about.[19]

Example: Bonuses Instead of Fines

Grading is another area that often relies on fines. Say an assignment is worth 10 points with a fine of one point for handing it in late. The exact same numbers can be stated as a nine-point assignment, with a bonus point for getting it in on time. Students catch on fast, and soon will begin to expect the extra point, turning it back into a 10-point assignment. To prevent that, make a bonus unexpectedly contingent. When all assignments (or more than usual) come in on time, everyone who has handed in homework that day gets an extra point. You can set your grading scale to allow for several bonuses, so you can give them often. From the students' point of view, any day might be the one where it will be especially important to complete homework.

Well-stated, clearly explained rules help start students on the right track, but not even the most experienced teacher goes through a school year without encountering some behavior that should be eliminated. Even then, minor inappropriate actions can usually be handled without punishment.

ALTERNATIVES TO PUNISHMENT OF BEHAVIORAL "EXCESSES": EXTINCTION PLUS

Many actions of students interfere with instruction, but are not serious and can be ignored. Whenever teacher attention is the primary source of reinforcement of a behavior, extinction should be considered. Misbehavior often draws teacher attention to the *offender*. In a kindergarten, if Billy shoves Patrick on the playground, who does the teacher address? Typically Billy: "We don't push in school, Billy. Come over here and sit down until you are ready to play nicely. . . ." Instead, if you ignore Billy and direct all your attention to Patrick ("You're not hurt are you? Come on, we'll go play ball"), Billy is left standing alone.[20]

Since extinction often produces an "extinction burst," you cannot just ignore inappropriate behavior without building alternatives. As you walk off with Patrick, you need to watch Billy for any kind of acceptable interaction. That then is rewarded. Combining extinction of inappropriate behavior with reinforcement of appropriate behavior works better than punishment.

Punishment can be avoided in other situations, too. Say, you give an assignment to be done in class, and one or two of your students keep talking to each other. Now what? If you "remind" them that they should be working, you risk the "Criticism Trap" of reinforcing their behavior. Punishment, such as taking away recess or sending to the principal's office, is too extreme. But extinction by itself will not work: most of the reinforcement of talking isn't coming from you, but from the peer.

With younger students, giving approval for appropriate behavior to a nearby student provides both a prompt and a model. "Jaime, you remembered to put your name at the top. Good for you." High school students, too, often respond when a working peer is addressed: "Jaime, this is a tough chapter. Do you understand what to do?" As soon as the talkative students start working, their behavior, too, gets recognition. A class-wide reminder can also serve as a prompt without singling out anyone: "Class, you have 17 more minutes."

Another option for decelerating non-academic chatting is to channel interaction into productive activity. Good friends who chat non-stop through a lecture may turn their talk to educational topics if given an assignment that requires their interaction, such as

BILLY

Fig. 11.3 What could teacher attention be reinforcing?

constructing a web page or designing a presentation. Restless students often benefit from activities built around movement, such as representing the planets and sun of the solar system or making models of soil erosion. Even such minor activity as popping up and down for rapid short presentations to the rest of the class helps utilize excess energy. Since all shaping depends upon student activity, the more you involve students in active work, the better.

When Ignoring Inappropriate Behavior Will "Work"

In general, if a student does something improper you must immediately decide whether to respond or not. If the action ends quickly and does not leave others upset or angry, you can safely ignore it when it occurs. If a student swears to herself, or spits gum into the wastebasket from five feet away, why turn it into a federal offense? It may never occur again. If you think it *will* reoccur, remind the student quietly about proper conduct at another time. Comments that provoke student irritation right after an episode often receive embarrassed apologies when given at a later time.

Sometimes *your* actions maintain inappropriate behavior. A common example is responding to comments called out by students who have not raised hands or been called upon. If your response to what they say is the critical consequence, extinction is all that is needed. For best effect, you must *consistently* acknowledge only raised hands, and *never* respond to called-out comments. This assumes, of course, that it is not laughter or reactions of peers that is reinforcing talking out.

Some students (especially those who have had a history of punishment) may exhibit some of the verbal aggression mentioned above. Verbal aggression is reinforced by signs that the comments have hit home. If verbal aggression is directed towards you, your reactions may be maintaining the verbal comments.

Example: Eliminating Insulting Comments through Extinction

In a high school, an older teacher, Ms. Spangler, had a very bright male student who made quiet, but insulting comments about her intelligence. He never made the comments directly to her. He would quietly mutter things like "How can they keep these stupid teachers?" just within her hearing as he walked by. It was driving his teacher crazy. Deciding to do a project on this problem, Ms. Spangler borrowed a golf counter to wear on her wrist like a watch. Every time the student made an insulting comment she would push the button to increase the tally by one. Watching her on the first day of the project, you would have thought she was intent on breaking the counter. The student would pass by and Ms. Spangler would grit her teeth and push the button with all her might. You could imagine her thinking, "That's one, you snob." By the third day, all of that frustration had disappeared. All you could see was a subtle movement of the hand to the wrist. At the end of the week, when data were to be reviewed, Ms. Spangler announced that the student had quit altogether. When his comments no longer got a rise from his teacher, he stopped: extinction had occurred.[21]

Handling Non-Compliance: What to Do about Sybil

Teacher reactions may also support non-compliance. You give an instruction and a student refuses, like Sybil refusing to come out from under the lunch room table. If the refusal causes no harm, let it go at the moment. By repeating instructions, perhaps more insistently or with added threats, you risk showing exasperation that can keep refusals going. Being under a table wasn't all that much fun for Sybil, but the game of chase was. After asking Sybil to come out, if the teacher had ignored her, eventually Sybil would have come out on her own.

The incident above was the first time Sybil had left her table in the lunch room. *Persistent* non-compliance ("No, I'm not doing it and you can't make me") requires a different approach: that of shaping successive approximations to obeying requests (see Chapter 8). Non-compliance may be maintained by avoiding an aversive task like a difficult assignment. Perhaps prerequisite skills are lacking, or directions are confusing. Students do need to learn to tackle unpleasant jobs and difficult assignments, but they won't learn by failing. Like any other behavior, persistence and compliance are shaped by increasing difficulty levels slowly enough so that successful behavior is guaranteed all along the way.

Most of the misbehavior of students is non-critical and can be handled without assistance. In today's schools, however, you may be confronted with more serious behavior problems.

HANDLING SERIOUS BEHAVIOR PROBLEMS

Serious problems are actions that endanger health, destroy school property, or interrupt class to such an extent that further instruction is impossible.

Handling Situations That Have to be Stopped NOW

Because of school shootings and gang violence, schools today have procedures for emergency situations. Reviewing your school's procedures periodically will help you respond calmly if a confrontation erupts. Whatever your school's procedures, speaking slowly without raising your voice helps to de-escalate any situation. Similarly, moving slowly and deliberately prevents escalation better than rushing towards a fight. In any case, before you encounter problems, make sure you know your school's procedures and how to get help if it is needed.

Violence is not born full-blown. There are always precursors that warn about impending trouble. Where gangs exist, you can expect hostility between members. Preventing violence is easier than stopping an ongoing fight, but someone needs to see the precursors to a fight to stop confrontation from escalating. Since teachers can't be everywhere at once, some schools train peers to help in conflict resolution.[22] Without training, most students do not have any idea of what to do when in a conflict situation, other than shouting or fighting. Ways to resolve differences have to be taught. In peer mediation, a representative group of students receives training and assumes some of the responsibility for keeping peace within the school, supported by one or more experienced teachers.

In your classroom you can probably sense when trouble is brewing. If one of your students comes into class more agitated than usual, a quiet comment like "Are you OK?" shows concern rather than annoyance, and may help a student settle down, preventing an outbreak. Taking an upset student or students aside also helps. It changes the setting, avoids the effect of peer onlookers, and helps get the student talking rather than solving matters aggressively.

Offering Alternatives When Trouble Erupts

Sometimes, when a situation erupts you may feel compelled to resort to punishment. Even here, you can reduce the aversiveness of your actions by giving alternatives. If you are about to keep John in from recess because he has thrown trash on the floor as a protest, and a polite request to pick it up has not worked, try "John, you can pick up your trash now or you can stay in from recess." Even when giving penalties it helps to offer alternatives: "Are you going to sit on the bench or stand by the fence?" Alternatives give some control to the recipient—a way to save face.

Example: Cheating at a University

The "choices" strategy was used by a young female instructor who taught a large required class at a state university. Grading one of the two forms of a midterm, the instructor noticed that three students had written R and O where the choices were A or B. The other form of the test asked for R or O. The instructor checked the pattern of letters with the key to the R and O form. Sure enough, all three students would have scored 100%. It was a clear case of cheating. The penalty for cheating at that school was automatic expulsion, much too harsh for a behavior that was known to be fairly common. But action did need to be taken. The three students were called into the instructor's office. They towered over her and aggressively challenged her assertion that they had cheated. Without arguing, she said, "OK. You have a choice. You can take an incomplete this semester and take the whole course over again next semester, or you can have me take your case to the college committee on cheating." The course was a required course for the students. They "chose" to retake it without further protest.

Is Punishment Ever Justified?

Punishment always reveals lack of control. Any action punished would better have been prevented. Not every action can be prevented, however, and if consequences stated in rules are not applied, whatever deterrent power they have is undermined. When punishment is overly harsh, like expulsion which would have been disastrous for the three students caught cheating, most people avoid using it. It is far better for schools to have rules with penalties that have been agreed upon by administration and students alike. Then punishment is seen as "justified."

Even "fair" punishment is not a good method of control. Whenever you find yourself using the same penalties for the same infractions week after week, remember that whatever your student is doing (or not doing) is being reinforced by something going on in your classroom. If you cannot figure out what the relevant contingencies are, or if you see behavior deteriorating from week to week, you can request help. For special students or for those who have received "suspensions beyond 10 days in a school year or placements in interim alternative educational settings" an IEP meeting is required by law.[23] Part of the role of the IEP team is to identify contingencies responsible for troublesome behavior. A functional behavioral assessment or functional analysis identifies those contingencies so that they can be changed.

Functional Behavioral Assessment and Functional Behavioral Analysis

Functional behavioral assessment procedures come directly from behavior analysis—a recognition that all behavior, including challenging behavior, is maintained by existing contingencies in settings where the behavior occurs. Rather than punishing behavior that current contingencies support, a functional assessment identifies those contingencies. As the student's teacher you will be asked to provide information on what specifically a student does, when it occurs and does not occur, and what happens when it occurs. You may be asked to give descriptive information, an *indirect* assessment based on questionnaires or interviews, or you may be asked to record actions while you are observing the student, a *direct* assessment (see Table 11.4).[24] The resulting descriptions of contingencies help a student's IEP team make a conjecture about variables responsible for the student's actions. Because escape from a task is so often the consequence maintaining challenging behavior, the tasks given to the student are also reviewed as part of the antecedents considered.

Functional behavioral *analysis* goes further. With preliminary descriptions in hand, brief changes in contingencies are tried to see their results. Because alterations in procedures (like extinction) may temporarily make a behavior worse, such procedures are best carried out by a skilled behavior analyst. The resulting data identify critical factors and clarify what contingencies need to be changed.

Whether from an assessment or analysis, positive behavioral interventions include the same kinds of procedures involved in any good teaching, such as building missing

Table 11.4 Functional behavioral assessment

A functional assessment includes four parts. Teachers are usually asked to provide information on numbers one through three using forms such as the one below. A form may be filled out after school, or used to record behavior as it occurs.

1. A clear behavioral specification of the behavior that is impeding learning.
2. Identification of the settings in which it is most likely and least likely to occur (antecedents).
3. A description of what happens when the problem behavior occurs (postcedents).
4. One or more hypotheses specifying the contingencies probably maintaining the behavior.

Student _____   Teacher _____

Date filled out: _____

What is going on when the problem behavior occurs?	What, specifically, does the student do?	What happens when the student engages in this behavior?	In what situations in the behavior *unlikely* to occur?	Comments

prerequisites, adapting instructional materials or formats to the student's level, and shaping appropriate behavior. Although functional behavioral assessment and functional behavioral analysis usually target behavior to decrease, solutions lie in procedures that address behavior to *increase*. Many of those contingencies can be set up before problems occur and before an IEP team is needed.

GUIDELINES FOR RESPONSIBLE CONDUCT

Any time punishment is part of a *planned* IEP (Individualized Educational Plan), federal law requires concurrently building alternative actions. That requirement is also part of the Behavior Analysis Certification Board (BACB) Guidelines for Responsible Conduct. The BACB Guidelines say, "The behavior analyst recommends reinforcement rather than punishment whenever possible. If punishment procedures are necessary, the behavior analyst always includes

Functional Behavioral Assessment is a description of contingencies surrounding a specified behavior, with a hypothesis about which factors are most likely to be functionally related to its occurrence. **Functional Behavioral Analysis** is an experimental procedure in which contingencies are altered to determine which antecedents or postcedents exert the most functional control over a specified behavior.

reinforcement procedures for alternative behavior in the program."[25] Adding reinforcement for an alternative behavior to the one to be decreased involves differential reinforcement.

Differential Reinforcement Procedures (DRI, DRA, and DRO)

There are many ways to reinforce one behavior as a way to decelerate other behavior. They depend on what is reinforced to "replace" the challenging behavior. **Differential Reinforcement of Incompatible behavior (DRI)** works at building behavior that cannot be done at the same time as the behavior to be decreased. Shaping writing answers to "replace" doodling is an example because you cannot write answers and draw doodles at the same time. **DRA (Differential Reinforcement of Alternative behavior)** sets up contingencies for reinforcing an alternative action that may not be incompatible. Reinforcing writing answers will probably reduce making loud noises, but writing and making noises could both be done at the same time. They are not incompatible.

For a DRO procedure (**Differential Reinforcement of Other behavior**), reinforcement is made contingent upon *zero* occurrence of the specified behavior during a set period of time (interval DRO), or during spot checks at particular times (momentary DRO). In *interval DRO*, a student is usually told that he or she will receive a particular reinforcer if the specified behavior has *not* occurred before a timer goes off. For *momentary DRO*, the directions say that reinforcement will occur *when* a timer rings *if* the specified behavior is not occuring. The "other" behavior reinforced in both DRO schedules is whatever the student happens to be doing as the timer rings, which may or may not be something that should be strengthened.

In setting up a DRO schedule, initial intervals are usually based upon the student's recorded behavior. Setting intervals about half as long as the time between recorded incidents of the behavior makes it likely the student will be successful. If a slip occurs during an interval in interval DRO, the timer is reset and the time period begins again—a punishing event. For momentary DRO, nothing happens if the student is engaging in the problem behavior when the timer rings and the scheduled spot checks are not affected.

Times in either kind of DRO can be equal (all five minutes long, for example), or unpredictable (randomly varying between two and seven minutes, for example). In either case, as behavior improves, intervals are gradually lengthened until behavior does not occur at all.

During DRO procedures the time signal for reinforcement may inadvertently strengthen undesirable behavior, a disadvantage of DRO as a deceleration procedure. Furthermore, no *appropriate* actions are specifically reinforced, and therein lies a problem with DRO procedures. Refraining from behavior is much harder than engaging in alternatives.

Suppose you are hungry and at a gathering where your favorite snack is available right in front of you. Let's assume you want to refrain from eating. Wouldn't it be easier to *not* eat if you were busy talking or singing (DRI) or if you were listening to an interesting conversation (DRA) than if you were sitting alone by the food? For most students concentrating on what *to* do is easier than resisting temptation.

If you work with individuals with difficult behavior, specifically targeting appropriate actions has three benefits. First, it requires reinforcement instead of punishment. Second, it pairs you with positive actions or benefits. Third, it improves your own feelings towards the individual involved. When you look for and record only problem behavior, you are pairing behavior you do not like with the student. In contrast, recording actions to build makes you aware of what the student does that you like, positive actions that can otherwise go unnoticed. It is easier to appreciate or like someone when you are conscious of all the positive things they do than if you are constantly reminded of their faults. Giving punishment to decelerate behavior never improves the overall life of the student punished. There is always a better way.

Positive Behavior Support

Positive Behavior Support (PBS) originated in the 1980s for procedures designed to help students with special needs without using punishment. It arose as a reaction to early punishment methods such as shock or cold water sprayed in the face for severe behavior such as biting or head banging. Instead of punishing behavior that is, after all, supported somehow by existing contingencies, PBS practitioners recommend functional analyses to find all relevant variables, so that precipitating events and postcedents can be changed as well as missing repertoires shaped, all *without* using punishment. In practice this means more emphasis on antecedents.[26] For example, an early study found a girl's behavior worse in the morning. Further questioning revealed that she often had not been given any breakfast. Sending her to the school cafeteria in the morning improved her behavior.[27]

PBS is built on operant conditioning and the derivative engineering practices of Applied Behavior Analysis. The only difference you may see at an IEP meeting between traditional behavior analysts and those advocating positive behavior support is that the latter are more likely to address all of the settings a student encounters. PBS advocates include caregivers as well as school personnel in programs for change. Consistent procedures based on reinforcement improve the overall life for the student. That, in turn, decreases the likelihood of "problem behavior" in your classroom.

Moving in a Positive Direction

When control has depended on threat and punishment, you cannot just stop cold and expect students to behave well. Positive contingencies must be put in place before or while punitive ones are eliminated. While you cannot ignore all misbehavior, any time you resort to punishment it is time to examine your own behavior. How could you handle similar situations better in the future? Each time you replace a punitive contingency with one based upon reinforcement, you take a big step towards a more positive educational experience for yourself and for all of your students.

SUMMARY

Teachers today face problems that were rare or unknown a generation or two ago. In the middle of the last century you did not hear of students coming to school high on drugs, or homes lacking supervision, or students bringing guns to school, or violent games and television programs, or internet sites that exploit children. As the potential for abuse and danger increases in our society, so too must the sophistication with which we handle problems.

Punishment is not a solution for society's ills. It can never build skills that citizens need, nor does it model effective handling of conflict. Fortunately the science of behavior offers ways to decelerate problem behavior by building alternative behavior that will serve students and contribute to society at large. The strategies given here as examples will not work in all situations. But the science will. By analyzing contingencies you see what needs to be changed to improve behavior, *any* behavior. Only reinforcing contingencies build academic and social skills while at the same time improving student attitudes and the overall climate of a classroom or school. When you replace punishment with more positive approaches everyone benefits.

CONCEPT CHECKS

Kinds of Consequences (Objective B)

DIRECTIONS: For each action below:

FIRST, write the letter for the kind of consequence *italicized*.
SECOND, write the operant affected.
THIRD, describe how the behavior is most likely to change.
(Assume that consequences work as they usually do, and that attention is reinforcing.) The first one is done for you. Use:

R for "reinforcement" or "reinforcing"
E for "extinction" or "extinguishing"
P for "punishment" or "punishing"

Sample: After always recognizing waving hands, you *no longer call* on students when they wave their hands.

Kind of consequence: _E_ Behavior affected: _waving hands_
Likely result? _E_ Behavior affected: _Waving will occur more at first, then gradually decrease_

1. Pressing a combination of keys *works faster* than using a trackpad on your computer.
   Kind of consequence: ____ Behavior affected: _____
   Result?: _____

2. You *eliminate a homework assignment* when students groan about it.
   Kind of consequence: ____ Behavior affected: _____
   Result?: _____

3. You *stop reacting* when a student mutters within your hearing that you are stupid.
   Kind of consequence: ____ Behavior affected: _____
   Result?: _____

4. You *take away pizza party points* when students talk while you are talking.
   Kind of consequence: ____ Behavior affected: _____
   Result?: _____

5. You *withhold your attention* when a student says "over here, come over here."
   Kind of consequence: ____ Behavior affected: _____
   Result?: _____

6 You *call on a different student* when a student stands up to answer.
   Kind of consequence: ____ Behavior affected: _____
   Result?: _____

7. You *announce a field trip* to spark interest when your students put their heads on their desks.
   Kind of consequence: _____ Behavior affected: _____
   Result?: _____

8. You *tell a student to sit on a time-out chair for five minutes* when she bites a peer during recess.
   Kind of consequence: _____ Behavior affected: _____
   Result?: _____

9. You *let class out early* when you notice students looking at their watches.
   Kind of consequence: _____ Behavior affected: _____
   Result?: _____

10. You *read a short chapter of a favorite book* when your students get in on time from recess.
    Kind of consequence: _____ Behavior affected: _____
    Result?: _____

Terms (Objective B)

DIRECTIONS: Match each of the following terms with the italicized example that illustrates it, using the following. Each term is used only once.

avoidance   **escape**
time out   **escalation of treatment**
side effects of punishment   **response cost**
DRI (Differential Reinforcement of Incompatible behavior)
DRA (Differential Reinforcement of Alternative [but not incompatible] behavior)
DRO (Differential Reinforcement of Other behavior not specified).

1. A student is *sent from a game to sit on the bench* until he quiets down.
2. Saying "no" quietly doesn't work any longer. Now you need to *shout.*
3. Instead of replying when her student shouted, the teacher *responded to her only when her hand was raised.*
4. Instead of replying when her student shouted, the teacher *responded to her quiet voice.*
5. The teenager didn't *bully others* until after getting humiliated in class.
6. By complaining of cramps a student can *skip gym.*
7. A teacher says a cellular call is urgent in order to *get out of* a boring faculty meeting.
8. "You may be first in line for lunch if you don't grab anything from others during recess."
9. "Each time you grab a pencil from others you will *lose one point.*"

Extinction (Objective D)

DIRECTIONS: Circle the numbers of the **FOUR** situations below in which extinction alone could eliminate the behavior specified. For the others, specify the most likely source of reinforcement.

1. **groaning** to get out of a gym exercise
2. **coming to your desk** during seat work
3. **painting fingernails** during class

4. **text messaging** (instead of doing a lab assignment)
5. **asking for extra time** on a test
6. **throwing paper airplanes** in class
7. **carving a girlfriend's name** on school property
8. **whining** for the privilege of passing out paper

ANALYSIS PROBLEMS

1. Harmful Effects of Punishment (Objective A)

Name at least one harmful effect of punishment on the person punished, on onlooking peers, and on the person doing the punishment, giving your *own* example.

2. Harmful Effects of Punishment (Objective A)

A fifth-grade English teacher grabbed a student's paper and tore it up in front of the class. What kinds of side effects might this consequence produce if it was very punishing?

3. Classifying Examples of Terms (Objective B)

A student swears in Spanish class. Her teacher tells her to stand in the hall until class is over. How would you know what kind of consequence this is?

4. Classifying Examples of Terms (Objective B)

A website says: "If a student is disruptive and does not complete an assignment within the allotted time, then that student may have to stay in at recess or after school to complete the work. This is a natural consequence of his actions, not a punishment of his behavior." What would a behavior analyst say about this analysis?

5. Why People Punish (Objective C)

If punishment has so many undesirable side effects, why do people punish?
Explain the contingencies over the behavior of punishing, using technical terms.

6. Alternatives to Punishment (Objective E)

A teacher put the phrase "Popcorn party" on the board and erased a letter for each misbe-havior in his classroom. How would you change this procedure into a more positive one?

ANSWERS FOR CONCEPT CHECKS
Kinds of Consequences

(Parts in parentheses are optional.)

1. Kind of consequence: *R* Behavior affected *Using key combinations*
   Result? *Using key combinations increases (and replaces some use of the trackpad).*
2. Kind of consequence: *R* Behavior affected *Groaning (about homework)*
   Result? *An increase in groaning when (similar) homework assignments are given.*

3. Kind of consequence: _E_ Behavior affected: _Comments about your intelligence._
   Result? _A decrease, perhaps after an initial increase (in frequency or volume or both)._
4. Kind of consequence: _P_ Behavior affected _Talking while you are talking._
   Result? _An immediate decrease in talking, but talking is likely to reoccur in the future._
5. Kind of consequence: _E_ Behavior affected: _Saying "over here, come over here."_
   Result? _Repeating "over here" louder and more urgently at first and then less and finally quitting._
6. Kind of consequence: _E_ Behavior affected: _Standing when answering a question._
   Result? _Standing (and perhaps jumping up and down) will increase at first, then decrease. If combined with a DRI procedure of calling on the student when the student is sitting (and perhaps raising his hand) you might eliminate standing to answer questions._
7. Kind of consequence: _R_ Behavior affected: _Putting heads on desks._
   Result? _The likelihood of students putting their heads on their desks in the future increases._
8. Kind of consequence: _P_ Behavior affected: _Biting a peer (during recess)._
   Result? _No more biting that recess, but biting may return especially when a teacher is not looking._
9. Kind of consequence: _R_ Behavior affected: _Looking at watches._
   Result? _More looking at watches at the end of periods._
10. Kind of consequence: _R_ Behavior affected: _Coming in on time._
    Result? _The likelihood of coming in on time increases._

Terms

1. **time out**
2. **escalation of treatment**
3. **DRA (Differential Reinforcement of Alternative behavior)** You can shout and raise your hand at the same time, so this is not DRI.
4. **DRI (Differential Reinforcement of Incompatible behavior)**
5. **side effects of punishment**
6. **avoidance**
7. **escape**
8. **DRO (Differential Reinforcement of Other behavior not specified)**
9. **response cost**

Extinction

The **FOUR** situations are **1**, **2**, **5**, and **8**. They are the only ones where reinforcement of behavior is most likely to be coming from you. Comments on the others follow:

3. **Painting fingernails** during class is reinforced first by changing the look of the nails. Past peer reaction for specific looks makes particular looks conditioned reinforcers.

4. **Text messaging** (instead of a lab assignment) is reinforced immediately by seeing letters on the screen and later (even if only a few seconds) by replies from peers. Seeing your message appear as you type is a conditioned reinforcer because of having been paired with replies. We all find ourselves smiling at the thought of how a recipient will react to what we are typing.

6. **Throwing paper airplanes** in class not only produces interesting flight patterns, but also usually peer attention.

7. **Carving a girlfriend's name** on school property is reinforced by the look of the carving first, and by its connection with peer comments that have followed other carvings.

COMMENTS ON ANALYSIS PROBLEMS

1. Harmful Effects of Punishment (Objective A)

Harmful effects of punishment on the person punished include (any of the following) *fear, escape, avoidance, hostility (or equivalent).*

Harmful effects on onlooking peers are similar. *(Good for you if you added the effect of peers modeling undesirable control methods.)*

Harmful effects on the person doing the punishing include *the tendency to escalate punishment. (A more subtle point is the negative effect of your feelings when concentrating on behavior you don't like.)*

2. Harmful Effects of Punishment (Objective A)

A fifth-grade English teacher grabbed a student's paper and tore it up in front of the class. What kinds of side effects might this consequence produce if it was very punishing?

Answers will, of course, vary. Here are a few criteria with which to judge your answer. You should have mentioned at least one:

Hostility: *Hostility comes in many forms. You could have mentioned an action like sticking out your tongue or giving someone the finger, posting or making negative comments, and so on.*
Escape: *Such as leaving the classroom or getting out of a writing assignment already in progress, or just by daydreaming.*
Avoidance: *The student might avoid anything paired with the punishing situation, like the teacher, the subject (English), or even school.*
Aggression: *No problem coming up with examples here.*

3. Classifying Examples of Terms (Objective B)

A student swears in Spanish class. Her teacher tells her to stand in the hall until class is over. How would you know what kind of consequence this is?

You must observe the effect on behavior. Perhaps it is reinforcing to be out in the hall: it avoids any aversiveness of classwork, and there may be alternative benefits such as interacting with a friendly janitor or teacher or boyfriend (who might be making a trip to the bathroom or doing an errand for his teacher). The only way to know is to record swearing and see whether it increases or decreases in frequency following the teacher's action.

4. Classifying Examples of Terms (Objective B)

A website says: "If a student is disruptive and does not complete an assignment within the allotted time, then that student may have to stay in at recess or after school to complete the work. This is a natural consequence of his actions, not a punishment of his behavior." What would a behavior analyst say about this analysis?

Staying in from recess or after school is a consequence given by a teacher and is not, therefore, a "natural" consequence. Furthermore it is a consequence that students normally avoid. If so, it is an example of a punishment procedure.

5. Why People Punish (Objective C)

If punishment has so many undesirable side effects, why do people punish? Explain the contingencies over the behavior of punishing, using technical terms.

The problem with punishment is that it stops (at least at the moment) a situation that is aversive for the punisher, and thus the act of punishing is negatively reinforced (thus making it likely to be repeated as a way to stop behavior in the future).

6. Alternatives to Punishment (Objective E)

A teacher put the phrase "Popcorn party" on the board and erased a letter for each misbehavior in his classroom. How would you change this procedure into a more positive one?

Instead, add a letter for some positive action, for example everyone handing in assignments done in class or students raising their hands before speaking, or students getting ready for class quickly after entering your room. An added advantage of adding letters rather than erasing them is that by not telling what the word or phrase will be, you add a positive element of surprise. Students like to try to guess what the reward will be. If you write letters often, you would want to vary big events like a pizza party with smaller events like "conversation break" where students could talk with friends for five minutes.

12

BEYOND TESTING: REACHING THE ULTIMATE GOALS OF EDUCATION

"We are not born with imagination. It has to be developed by teachers, by parents."
Kurt Vonnegut[1]

OVERVIEW

The passage of the No Child Left Behind Act increased testing in America's schools. While few people doubt that these tests sample performance on useful skills, they constitute only a part of the behavior needed by high school graduates and by our society. Focusing on a narrow set of skills risks losing the broader picture. America needs citizens who not only *can* read, but *do* read, who not only know *how* to solve math problems, but who put math into operation in their daily lives so that they can, for example, understand what adjustable mortgage rates mean. And what about science, or the humanities, or the arts, or interpersonal relations and judgment? The goal of education is to prepare students for a future that requires much more than the skills assessed on a test.

OBJECTIVES

After reading this chapter, you should be able to:

A. Identify examples of state curriculum goals that can and cannot be measured by paper and pencil tests.
B. Identify the sources of control over specific actions seen in classrooms or skills specified in state standards.
C. Select the best ways to increase "motivation" from a list of procedures.
D. For a given area, describe procedures to transfer control from reinforcement provided by a teacher to reinforcement that comes from students' actions.

E. For a topic or skill that has little interest for most students, design an activity or suggest procedures that would give students more immediate reasons for working.

F. Explain how poor contingencies involving material rewards produce undesirable behavior, and suggest a change in contingencies that would avoid that effect.

G. Analyze the features that promote divergent actions in an exercise, worksheet, or lesson plan designed to promote "creativity."

Testing as the primary assessment of the quality of schooling diverts effort and resources into preparing students to take tests. There is nothing wrong with teaching the kinds of skills tested, but they need to be taught efficiently rather than consuming the majority of class time. The procedures discussed in the former chapters of this book should help students master those skills. This chapter looks at aspects of behavior not addressed by standardized testing.

CURIOSITY AND MOTIVATION FOR CONTINUED LEARNING OUTSIDE SCHOOL

One skill that tests cannot measure is motivation: the reasons for acting in a particular way. Two students can both be working away at solving problems or answering questions. If one works to avoid punishment, and the other for the pleasure in finding out information, they are working under very different contingencies. To understand why a student is doing what he or she is doing in class, you must find the sources of control over that behavior.

Two contrasting sources of control are those coming from authority figures and those following directly from the results of one's own actions (see Figure 12.1).[2]

Top-Down Systems: Control by Authority Figures

When the consequences for behavior come primarily from authority figures in a school, control comes from "above." In a teacher-controlled classroom, the teacher makes the rules and enforces them. Phrases such as "*I* want you to sit down" or "*I* need you to get away from the window" are frequent. Reinforcement, too, comes from the teacher. A supporter of "teacher-controlled" classrooms might advocate giving points when the class as a whole has been respectful and attentive. Who determines whether the class has been respectful and attentive? The teacher, of course.

When the teacher provides most of the benefits and penalties over classroom existence, students become very sensitive to what the teacher is doing. Instead of working to develop skills, to find solutions to problems, or to develop their own creative ideas, students under strong teacher control keep a watch on the teacher. They concentrate on what will gain teacher approval or disapproval.

The classroom management approach called "Assertive Discipline" promotes teacher-centered control that includes punitive sanctions. In Assertive Discipline, consequences for failing to obey rules are given immediately after every infraction, starting with mild sanctions, such as a warning, and moving up a "Discipline Hierarchy." A first

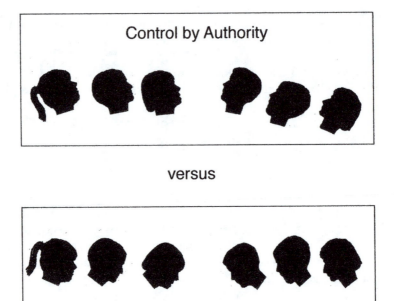

Fig. 12.1 Control by authority versus control by the results of one's own efforts
Adapted from Julie S. Vargas and Hank Pennypacker, "Using Student Performance to Evaluate Teaching." Paper presented at the National Council on Measurement in Education, San Francisco, CA, 1976.

consequence might be "Bob, the direction was to work without talking. That's a warning."[3] Bob's second or third violation receives a stronger postcedent, like a brief time out, being told he will have to stay in the classroom an extra minute after the class bell, or writing in a log what he did wrong and what he should have done instead. A fourth infraction might result in his parents being contacted and a fifth in being sent to the principal's office (assumed to be punishing). Most Assertive Discipline authors have shifted recently to stressing more positive than negative sanctions. Still, the critical consequences lie in doing what the *teacher* wants: control lies in teacher authority.

The control-by-authority often extends to an entire school. When a supervisor enters the classroom under these contingencies, teacher attention is drawn to the supervisor. Classroom activities may be put on hold while the teacher finds out what the supervisor wants. Of course, supervisors and principals have responsibility to give feedback to subordinates, but there are better ways to help teachers improve than enforcing compliance with the "wants" of those above.[4]

Carrying top-down control to extremes runs counter to the values of a democratic society. Enforcing strict obedience to authority, especially when no options exist for challenging that authority, is called authoritarianism. Teaching students to obey authority *without questioning* encourages a docile citizenry; exactly the kind that can be easily manipulated by a dictatorial leader. Strong top-down control by an authority figure thus runs counter to the kind of behavior that enables a democratic society to function well. Of course, control is required in any social group, including the classroom. A better kind of socially appropriate control, however, comes from the bottom up.

Bottom-Up Control: Consequences that Come from Students' Own Actions

Identifying the sources of "bottom-up" control is much more difficult than in a top-down-oriented classroom. This kind of control goes by many names (see the right side of Table 12.1.) When the consequences for each individual's behavior lie in the direct results of that behavior, they do not come from a single source. They derive from many sources, including peers and the physical environment. In bottom-up control, finding the solution to a problem becomes more important than the grade the teacher gives for the "right" answer. Recording progress or seeing how your action benefits peers supersedes the approval you get from an authority.

For students, concrete evidence of their own improvement motivates continued effort better than being *told* they are improving. Beating a timer, for example, qualifies as bottom-up control even when a teacher sets the timer, because the consequences of finishing before the time is up depends on the student's own effort, not on someone else's judgment. Social behavior, too, can be maintained by behavior-generated consequences when, for example, a person shares with others because of enjoying their pleasure.

Reasons for an action may not be obvious, but everyone makes inferences about where control lies. An action like grabbing may be seen as *selfish* if the grabbing solely benefits the grabber, but as *kind* or *heroic* if the object grabbed is dangerous or about to explode. It all depends upon where control lies.

Consequences that result from tangible achievement avoid prejudicial treatment. Students cannot say they did badly because "The teacher doesn't like me." Prejudice, whether real or imagined, does not determine how much students improve on a timed Precision Teaching quiz or whether they solve a problem of meter in writing a poem. Rewards that come from a student's own behavior are independent of a teacher's likes and dislikes. They rest on the effort the student makes.

Educators have always argued for bottom-up control under one or more of the names at the right of Table 12.1. This kind of control is essential for the ultimate goals of our educational system.

Table 12.1 Names for top-down control by authorities versus bottom-up control by effectiveness

Names for contingencies controlled by authority figures	Names for contingencies controlled by a student's own behavior
artificial consequences	natural consequences
extrinsic rewards	intrinsic rewards
extrinsic motivation	intrinsic motivation
teacher-provided reinforcement	automatic reinforcement
external control	self-control
imposed discipline	self-discipline
grades "given" by a teacher	grades earned
requirements	electives
pleasing a teacher	enjoying work
holding accountable	taking responsibility

Why the Sources of Consequences Matter for the Future

The educational system was designed to build behavior needed by individuals and by our society *after* students leave school. Top-down control may help students pass tests, even when the controlling techniques are largely punitive. But tests cannot capture life-long motivation for self-improvement, or kindness or tolerance of others, or creativity, or many other kinds of behaviors needed for society to function well.

The transitory nature of top-down control is revealed when students act differently in one class than in others, even when dealing with the same subject matter. Consequences delivered by a specific teacher do not follow students when they leave that teacher's class. To produce lasting repertoires, instructional control must transfer to consequences that always accompany the actions that produce them. Of course, there is no guarantee that any behavior will continue after school, but if, as a teacher, you can shift control to the direct consequences of behavior, you increase the likelihood of it continuing. You can see the lasting effects of your influence, for example, when your students go on to major in a subject they first studied with you.

In addition to surviving after the school years, behavior-produced consequences lead to emotions that in turn encourage more effort. Students are said to "want" to do what they are doing, not to "have to." They behave "well" because behaving well works for them, the **self-control** of Table 12.1. They get caught up in their work even to the point of losing awareness of what their teacher is doing. Independence—being successful from your own efforts and able to provide for yourself what you value—*feels* good. Controlling contingencies over your life, the "ownership" of Table 12.1, also encourages commitment to the social group to which you belong. Ultimately society benefits.

The goal of establishing student-generated reinforcement does not mean relinquishing control or abandoning what you usually teach. Quite the contrary. *You* still have the final say on classroom procedures and on instructional goals. But unless students come into your classroom eager to work on whatever assignments you give them, you need first to get behavior going and then to make working itself reinforcing.

We all want our students to enjoy the subjects we teach. The issue goes beyond *what* our goals are to *how to achieve them.* How do students learn to enjoy a subject, or education in general? What can teachers do to help?

INCORPORATING "NATURAL" CONSEQUENCES INTO TEACHING THROUGH ACTIVE PARTICIPATION

Some activities produce results that are themselves interesting or rewarding. To let consequences come from behavior you must, of course, arrange for behavior to occur. No student would enjoy volley ball if it were taught entirely by lecture. Schools recognize the importance of direct participation in many subject areas. There are labs for science, staged performances for music or dance or plays, and student newspapers for writing and editing. All of these provide real consequences. Students work more intently on them than on assignments where little or no results accrue from the activity itself.

Bringing Daily Life into the Classroom

Many activities can be simulated in the classroom. Setting up a real store stocked with second-hand items brought in by students (using special school "money") gives a reason for calculating change, or giving discounts, or learning the real costs of buying on time with interest. At the high school level, how can you help students take an interest in problems they will encounter only after graduation?

Example: Simulating Personal Finances after Graduation

One teacher was concerned about the unrealistic expectations of many of her twelfth-grade students. They did not plan to go to college, but talked about houses and cars they would buy that cost far more than they could possibly earn without further education. The teacher planned a simulation of managing finances after graduation. She gathered photographs of houses for sale from local realtors and asked students to bring in catalogs for clothes, furniture, and other items. Students calculated their net incomes based on professions open to them with their planned level of education. Couples could work together, deciding on a house to buy and calculating monthly mortgage payments. They could "buy" furniture or items like cars if they had the money, or on credit if they did not, but they would have to make payments. The students calculated eagerly. The resulting numbers, unlike the answers to textbook problems, were of interest to them. For many students, the results were a shock. Realistic financial dealings gave these students a more compelling picture of the importance of continued education than any exhortation a teacher could have provided.

Some subjects are not very amenable to participatory activity. Even there, however, you can think of what professionals enjoy about their work. In history, for example, professionals enjoy discovering sources of new information or documents that challenge prevailing thought. With the internet, students can research historical figures or events, or find out about the history of their own city or town or school building. Projects like this also give opportunities to teach the difference between reputable and untrustworthy sources of information. When students search the internet, often what one student discovers is of interest to peers, adding that consequence to the rewards of finding out something new. In general, the more students work in a field rather than talking about a subject, the more natural consequences they will experience.

It takes time to set up procedures that let students work actively in a field. Once designed, however, a unit usually needs only a bit of updating for the next class. The high school teacher that did the project on financial life after school realized that her project lacked the use of a checkbook. That needed to be added the next time around.

Not everything can be transformed into an approximation of daily or professional life. Most teaching involves written assignments or worksheets that talk *about* a subject. Some worksheets are best put into a timed practice format where beating one's own record serves as motivation. For other worksheets, approval, a grade, or whether an answer is judged as "right" depends on your reaction as a teacher. Even then, you can add a bit of fun to finding answers by making them rewarding in some way.

Adding "Easy" Or "Fun" Problems to Worksheets

By the time a student comes to school, being "right" and finishing work are both positive consequences. Students like easy items they can do quickly. You can improve the appeal of worksheets by including some simple items along with the rest, as in worksheets A through C in Figure 12.2. These exercises teach basic processes and at the same time they give everyone problems that can be done correctly in a hurry. Not only do students enjoy these items, but they learn not to be threatened by big numbers.

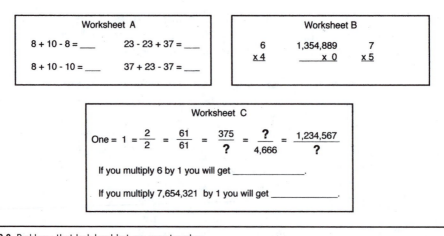

Fig. 12.2 Problems that look hard but are easy to solve
Worksheet A is based upon R. S. Siegler, and E. Stern. "Conscious and Unconscious Strategy Discoveries: A Microgenetic Analysis." *Journal of Experimental Psychology: General* 127 (1998): 377–397.

Progress as a "Natural" Consequence of Practice

To become competent at any skill requires practice and repetition that few students enjoy for itself. The "natural" consequence of practicing is improvement, but progress must be visible to be reinforcing. Improvement in academic skills shows most clearly when performance is timed and progress graphed. As Chapter 5 describes in more detail, short, frequent, timed practice sessions let your students see change that is invisible in the usual untimed seatwork. All students can be given worksheets at their level where they, too, can work quickly and accurately, seeing improvement from day to day. The usual charts of student performance posted in classrooms show *level* of performance and make only superior students look good. Chapter 6 shows how graphing *gain* with Standard Celeration Charts equalizes the upward slope of percentage improvement. All students can look good when their charts show the same percentage of gain.

For any of the direct products of active engagement, success is critical. An athletic tennis player invited to try handball will not enjoy the new game if barely able to return the ball. You can imagine her saying, "I'm just no good at handball. I like tennis better." Similarly, students gravitate to fields in which they have had success. Consequences that flow from successful performance maintain interest in sports without much help from teachers. But most subjects cannot be taught by counting entirely on natural consequences to keep activity and interest flowing. In fact, the most important goal of teaching may be creating *new* interests where none existed before. Behaviorally speaking that means creating new conditioned reinforcers and new sources of reinforcement.

WHERE NEW INTERESTS COME FROM

Some activities and objects seem to be reinforcing at birth. The taste of milk, physical comfort, and moderate motion reinforce behavior in newborns worldwide. As a child grows up, genetic predispositions interact with social consequences that soon come to control behavior. Even in eating, tasting "good" only partly determines what you eat. Few Americans drink the blood of cattle, though if they didn't know what they were tasting, bovine blood probably would taste good. In other societies people drink it mixed with milk or even straight.[5]

An early interaction occurs between innate skill and social approval: a preschooler whose drawings impress others is likely to draw more frequently, thus gaining additional expertise. From being paired with social rewards, their own pictures become **conditioned reinforcers**. Chapter 8 described how conditioned reinforcers are created by pairing stimuli like clicks with already existing reinforcers. When a student's performance or products are paired with real social approval, new conditioned reinforcers are created. Control passes from consequences provided by others to consequences stemming from their own actions. At that point we say that the child *enjoys* drawing.

Budding artists' drawings won't all receive approval. The properties of drawings paired with the greatest social approval are those most likely to become conditioned reinforcers, pleasing the artist him or herself. Of course, not all drawings will please others or the person who drew them. Drawing is thus *intermittently* reinforced, making it more persistent (see below). The child who draws whenever possible is then described as "intrinsically" motivated. **Intrinsic motivation** describes *the end product of the creation of new conditioned reinforcers and an intermittent schedule of reinforcement.*

> **Intrinsic motivation** is the control over behavior that comes as a result of behaving. Other than biological reinforcers such as food and comfortable temperature, "intrinsically" reinforcing effects of behavior come from contingencies: Social interactions have created new conditioned reinforcers or have made behavior persistent through intermittent reinforcement.

Intrinsic motivation does not originate inside a person. Nothing in our genes makes English words on paper important in a person's life. Nor is there any inborn reinforcing power of numbers. Nothing in our genetic endowment makes scientific or historical information automatically reinforcing. If it did, everyone would be interested in science and history. Reinforcement from other people must *initially* be added by others to make subjects "intrinsically" reinforcing. How ironic that to produce "intrinsic" rewards, "extrinsic" rewards must first be used.

Take reading: books are not automatically reinforcing when presented to very young children. Books become reinforcing when they are paired with hugging, laughing, and attention—all consequences added by others. Children with such experiences are more motivated to find out what all that print reveals than those from homes where there are no books or where books have not been paired with positive social interactions. Once in school, instructional consequences must be added by teachers to shape the textual behavior and comprehension that makes reading itself reinforcing. For all academic subjects "intrinsic motivation" requires consequences initially provided by others, especially teachers.

Creating new reinforcing (or punishing) consequences does not always require pairing existing reinforcers with consequences from a child's own behavior. A study of babbling in a baby girl showed how parental pairing of sounds with different postcedents affected which syllables the baby uttered.[6] The researcher (who was the father) began by recording all of the sounds uttered by his baby. A phoneme that the baby didn't utter often ("Da") was identified as the "target" and it and all other syllables were recorded for about five minutes both before and after the treatment period. Three treatments were employed:

1. Neutral Condition: The father randomly said "Da," about every four seconds but did not follow it with any known source of reinforcement.
2. Positive Condition: The father said "Da", then immediately followed it with tickling or blowing bubbles (activities the baby liked).
3. Negative Condition: The father said "Da", followed by a stern "Bad girl." Because this condition was aversive, it lasted only 20 seconds, and the pairing of "Da" with "Bad girl" was done only five times.

Figure 12.3 shows the results on the baby's uttering of "Da" compared to other syllables as a result of each procedure. Just hearing the sound in the neutral condition didn't affect the child's verbalization of "Da." "Da" remained at a low rate while other syllables bounced around. After pairing "Da" with tickling or bubbles, "Da" initially jumped up as did babbling in general, but then all syllables settled down to a level barely above that before any pairing. Saying "Bad girl" just after saying "Da" had a big effect. In the

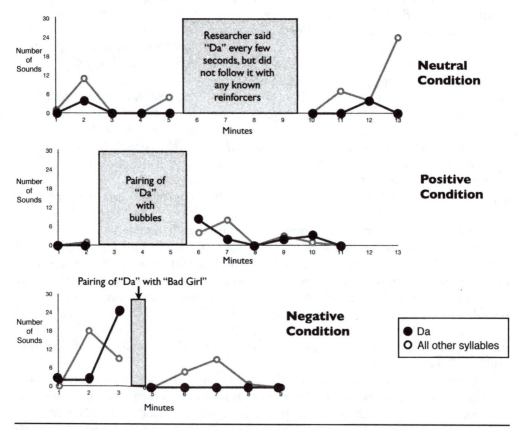

Fig. 12.3 "Automatic" reinforcement and "automatic" punishment

Adapted from Rick Smith, Jack Michael, and Mark L. Sundberg. "Automatic Reinforcement and Automatic Punishment in Infant Vocal Behavior." *The Analysis of Verbal Behavior* 13 (1996): 39–48. Association for Behavior Analysis International. Adapted with permission.

minute before that pairing the baby had said "Da" 24 times, but afterwards didn't utter "Da" at all for the next five minutes. Of course, the father then went back to making that syllable reinforcing not punishing.

The authors concluded that the sounds of the baby's own babbling had picked up reinforcing or punishing power just from having been paired with relationships the father had established. The sound of the baby's own syllables had become "automatically reinforcing" or "automatically punishing." Just like clicking paired with reinforcers, sounds paired with reinforcement became conditioned reinforcers whether said by others or by the baby herself.

A similar result of the power of observation for creating new reinforcers was obtained in a preschool. Plastic discs about the size of quarters were first shown to have no effect as consequences for the behavior of four children. After they watched another child receive the plastic discs for performing a task, the plastic discs gained the power to reinforce behavior in the observers. The effect occurred even though the observing children saw only the receiving of the discs. They could not see the task their peer performed, nor the teacher who was giving the discs.[7]

The effect of increasing reinforcing effects from observing others continues throughout life. Billions of dollars are spent pairing products with positive scenarios. Everyone knows that the attractive woman standing next to a particular brand of automobile does not guarantee that by driving that automobile a driver will attract similar females. Still, pairing the two alters the behavior of enough potential buyers to make advertisements pay off. Ads create new conditioned reinforcers, making advertised brands more reinforcing than before pairing occurred.

While observation can create new reinforcers, pairing existing reinforcers with the products of students' own behavior is more reliable. That requires, of course, student activity. Lectures are notorious for producing sleeping, not new sources of reinforcement. Fortunately most elementary and secondary classroom instruction involves student activity as well as listening. Thus the best opportunities for creating conditioned reinforcers occur when approval or praise or grade points or privileges or tangible rewards are paired with progress.

Automatic Reinforcement as a Concept

The term **automatic reinforcement** refers to consequences that follow as a result of behavior itself. It is not helpful to say that a behavior occurs *because* it is automatically reinforced. In the absence of other consequences, *everything* you do is maintained by "automatic" reinforcement. Whatever you do that is never reinforced undergoes extinction and thus does not become part of your repertoire. As mentioned above, except for what you inherit or develop physiologically, all reinforcing consequences are *conditioned* through pairing with other positive consequences. Calling a consequence automatic reinforcement hides the history that has made it a conditioned reinforcer, and thus diminishes the importance of the instructional reinforcement that created it. "Automatic reinforcement" does not explain behavior. Like "intrinsic reinforcement" it describes postcedents that come from an action itself rather than being added by others.

THE POWER OF PAIRING: APPROVAL, GRADES, AND OTHER TEACHER-ADDED CONSEQUENCES

Some educators believe that students should work without added incentives. I would agree. They *should*, but what do you do if they don't? If you don't add positive consequences to shape new behavior, your alternative methods of control are punitive—more aversive control from authority above. Fortunately positive contingencies are powerful when paired with behavior to be strengthened. Consequences you have at your disposal include your attention or approval, grades, privileges, and tangible items. The way in which you make these postcedents contingent on behavior determines how your students will react.

Teacher Approval or Praise

The most common consequence teachers "add" is their own attention, approval, or praise. Teacher attention *usually* reinforces ongoing actions even when the intent is to reduce a behavior. Approval is even more reliable than attention as a strengthening consequence. Teacher approval is usually paired with desirable consequences and thus usually is a conditioned reinforcer. Added reinforcement does more than just strengthen the action occurring: It also improves emotions. Pairing is enhanced by stating explicitly the action to be strengthened. "That's good *that you showed the steps*" will strengthen writing down steps better than "Good job. You are so smart." The "TAG points" of TAG Teaching discussed in Chapter 8 make it clear exactly what action is paired with the reinforcement of the clicking sound.

Since frequency of reinforcement builds behavior faster than quantity, it is better to acknowledge actions often with brief comments, smiles, or other subtle signs than to go overboard with praise. Too much praise can satiate, making each instance less effective or, in some cases, aversive. At the high school level, no one wants to be labeled a teacher's pet. Subtle approval is also more likely to be, and to be seen as, sincere. Especially for your less skilled students, by commenting on *progress* rather than on *level* of performance you pair approval with success they have earned and can feel good about.

In all cases, the behavior you strengthen depends upon the actions or their products with which you pair your attention and approval. Each pairing affects student behavior. That makes it especially important to be aware of the contingencies you are establishing.

As students begin to show satisfaction with what they have achieved, your approval is needed less often. By slowly reducing the frequency of your comments, being careful to keep the behavior going, you create persistence. When students almost totally ignore you as they concentrate on their work, you have shifted control successfully to the products of their own actions.

The Role of Schedules of Reinforcement in Persistence and Motivation

A motivated individual works persistently when no visible consequences are present. Seeing persistent behavior, however, does not tell you how it came about. Take, for example, a pigeon in an operant chamber. If it pecks rapidly with no sign of any reinforcement, you might call it a motivated pigeon. But the persistent pecking you observe does not occur without careful programming of contingencies: after shaping a first key peck, a second peck is required for reinforcement, then slowly the number of pecks required per bit of food is increased. The bird's final behavior will depend on how you make reinforcement contingent on pecking (see Figure 12.4). The relation between the way in which reinforcement is based on responding and the resulting behavior has been extensively researched.[8] By varying the *number* of actions required per reinforcement so that sometimes only a few are needed, sometimes many, you create rapid and persistent behavior. Watching a bird working away, you see only the *result* of its training. Of course, since the bird is in an operant chamber you would assume that reinforcement has been occurring at some point. However, a bird on such a schedule also pecks in other places such as the sides of its home cage where pecking has *never* been reinforced with food. Most people seeing the activity outside the teaching situation would say that the bird "likes" to peck or that pecking is "automatically reinforcing." What they don't see is how that behavior developed.

Of course students are not birds. But just as principles of genetics discovered in fruit flies show how genes work in human beings, the schedule effects researched in pigeons also occur in human beings. Schedules are carefully programmed in such

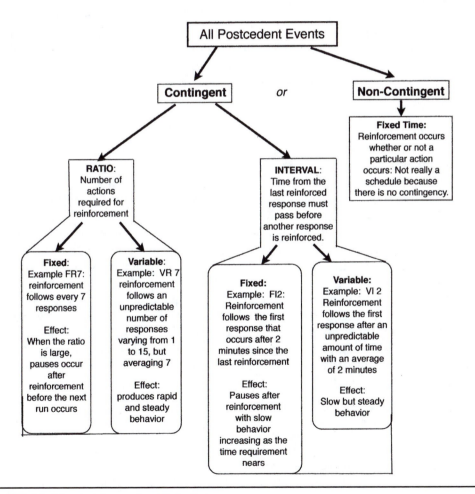

Fig. 12.4 Schedules of reinforcement and their effects

establishments as gambling casinos and they produce the same behavior in people except when social contingencies interfere, like a peer's urgent request to leave. Even then a "win" may keep a gambler playing. Intermittent reinforcement in human beings, just as in non-human animals, makes behavior more persistent.

Intermittent reinforcement is best begun once an operant is established. During the shaping process, you try to catch *every* "best" action, thus shifting the entire range of behavior towards your objective. During initial shaping, if you wait for two or three responses at a particular level, you strengthen performance at that level, making it more difficult to move on. If you wait too long for a second "best" action and fail to reinforce anything, you risk losing momentum or worse, extinguishing responding altogether. Once a goal is met, however, and the behavior reliably occurs, you can safely move to intermittent reinforcement. *After* standards are met, gradually "thinning" reinforcement makes an action persistent.

Most teachers "thin" the schedule of reinforcement without thinking about it: you praise the first successful execution of a new skill, but pay less attention as the same operant occurs more often. The trick is to keep behavior going, especially at the beginning. That is where reducing the frequency of your approval needs to be done carefully. As behavior occurs with less attention from you, it not only becomes more persistent, but other consequences begin to take over. Intermittent reinforcement thus helps transfer control from your approval to the student's own successful performance. Even then, you may need to intervene from time to time. Until students learn not to give up when dissatisfied with their own performance, your support is still needed.

Using Grades Wisely

Each reinforcing consequence strengthens an operant. For consequences you provide, frequency is more critical than size. An A grade, or a field trip, or party will have more of an effect on behavior if broken down into parts that can be earned bit by bit. Most teachers are required to assign grades, so you might as well make the most of them. In college courses, basing a grade on one or two exams rarely produces much studying until just before an exam. Further, particularly if graded on a curve, a grade based on a single test will be punishing to many, if not most students. Even for those getting an A, any positive influence on studying occurs too late to strengthen working during the weeks preceding.

By dividing tests into several shorter and more frequent quizzes you not only create more student effort, you can spot places where students are having difficulty while you can still provide help. Small assignments also reduce the aversiveness of a single poor grade. One failure does not doom students to a bad final grade if they can make up lost points. Small frequent successes make academic work more rewarding than studying done frantically for a good grade on a big test.

Grade Inflation

Some administrators feel uncomfortable when nearly everyone in a course earns an A grade. It seems as though they think that only a few students can succeed. That is not really their fear. Administrators are concerned with **grade inflation.** Grade inflation is increasing the percentage of students scoring "well" by *lowering standards.* Want more students to pass? Make your tests easier. Of course, students are not performing better.

Your test is just measuring simpler skills. This kind of "improvement" justifies the discomfort with large proportions of A grades.

When an A grade reflects a high level of student performance, however, no grade inflation has occurred. An A grade represents what it is supposed to represent. You can alleviate concerns if your supervisor complains about grade inflation by showing the quizzes, assignments, and all the other criteria students have to meet to earn an A grade. That demonstrates that the grades your students received reflect their mastery of the material (and your success as an instructor!) not the lowering of standards.

Do You Have to Grade Everything?

The simple answer is "no." Some of the products on which students work hardest are not graded, such as stage performances or student newspapers or brochures or websites, or performance in after-school clubs, sports, or community service.

USE AND MISUSE OF TANGIBLE REWARDS, ACTIVITIES, AND PRIVILEGES

The use of tangible items as consequences requires more care than the giving of approval or praise. Small tangible items like gold stars or stickers indicate little more than success or approval. They are conditioned reinforcers, not valuable in themselves. When you offer more valuable items, however, you need to be careful in how you set up contingencies.

Tangible Rewards in Behavioral Contracts

Teachers (and parents) often make rewards part of a **behavioral contract**. A contract states contingencies: if you do X, you will get Y. Novices at using tangible rewards usually offer too valuable items as consequences for too little behavior. You do not need expensive items or events for reinforcers. Even consequences worthless in themselves, like clicking sounds or progress shown in graphs of daily timed performance, reinforce behavior. Inexpensive items work as well as expensive items in contracts if made contingent on points easily earned. Tangible rewards are frequently found as part of IEPs, so they will be discussed here.

Material goods such as CDs or special activities like a visit to a favorite restaurant may be part of a contract. Obviously the reward is not given for one action. Usually it is earned bit by bit, giving teachers many opportunities to reinforce behavior. Contracts should not permit students to "blow it" by one poor performance. A contingency that requires homework to be handed in every day in order to earn a prize will no longer have an effect once one day is missed. Instead by setting a number of points to be earned, a lapse in performance only delays earning the reward.

Tangible Rewards and Bribery

You may hear the use of tangible rewards called "bribery." A bribe is an inducement to behave illegally or dishonestly. In bribery, benefits go to the person bribing, not to the ultimate advantage of the person bribed or to society as a whole. Payment for work does not constitute bribery. No one considers a salary a bribe. Calling inducements for academic behavior "bribes" is also inappropriate. Rewards themselves, even material items, are not necessarily good or bad. What they are given *for* determines their moral status. *How* they are given determines their effect on behavior.

Contingencies to Avoid

Stating contingencies can itself be a consequence. Being offered payment for behavior is typically reinforcing, especially if the reward is great or the behavior easy. The moment that you *offer* an incentive, then, you may be reinforcing whatever behavior is going on. Say you ask a student to help clean up around the school during recess, but she refuses. If you then tell her, "I'll give you a new pencil if you help," she may comply. But what have you just reinforced? Your offer followed *refusing*. If a new pencil is reinforcing for her, your offer was too. You may have just increased the likelihood that she will refuse requests more often in the future. The more valuable the consequence, the more likely the paired offer is also reinforcing.

This problem is made worse when the reinforcers that come from offers or contracts follow behavior *only* when offered ahead of time. If the *only* time students get rewards is when a promise is made beforehand, you risk producing a discrimination: doing what is asked gets rewards if they are offered beforehand (S^D). Doing what was asked doesn't get rewards if they aren't promised beforehand (S-delta). Behavior will tend to occur when rewards are offered and not otherwise (see Figure 12.5). The tip-off that this kind of discrimination has occurred is students asking, "What will you give me if I do it?" This is not desirable.

Giving a new pencil is not bad or good as a consequence. It is how tangible items are made contingent on behavior that determines outcomes. Rarely are tangible rewards needed anyway. Far more common are activities or privileges.

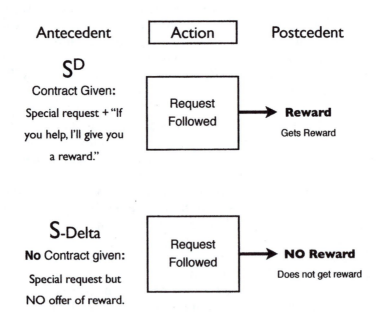

Fig. 12.5 Classic discrimination training

Activities and Privileges as Consequences for Behavior
Activities and privileges may involve an individual or a whole class. Like all consequences, the contingencies you arrange will determine the resulting behavior. If your intent is to shape behavior in your least successful students, rewards should be earned by them as often as by their more advanced peers. Competition can be a problem. If you want to use competition, base postcedents on *improvement* rather than on level of performance and keep an eye out for overall effects. The power of gaining a competitive advantage depends at least in part on lowering an advantage for others. Competition can create resentment rather than a positive atmosphere.

Cooperative contingencies in contrast encourage (surprise!) cooperation. Activities that involve a whole class are usually earned gradually by members of the group. As usual, the more clearly specified the actions that qualify, the more likely you are to produce the desired behavior. The only danger in group activities occurs when one student's behavior can ruin everyone's chances. An event contingent on 100% homework being turned in can turn a class against the student who forgets. This problem can be avoided like the "blow it" contingencies in behavioral contracts. It is easy to set up a system where each acceptable action adds to the sum required, but a single lapse does not ruin everything. A forgetful student's lapse would delay the desired activity by an insignificant amount.

Activities and privileges usually involve a prior contract, and the same principles apply to their use as with contingencies involving tangible rewards. If procedures you set up don't work the way you hoped, change the contingencies. By being sensitive to the relation between consequences and behavior, you will see why your students are behaving as they do. As a teacher, you can always experiment, going back to an analysis of contingencies for ideas on how to improve your own effectiveness and thus that of your students.

Not all rewards need to be contingent. Non-contingent reinforcement like bringing brownies to class for no reason, or surprising a class with a homework-free weekend boosts classroom morale and pairs good things with school in general.

Research on "Extrinsic" Versus "Intrinsic" Rewards
Many research studies have been done on the effect of *extrinsic* rewards on **intrinsic motivation**. Extrinsic rewards are rewards like praise or trinkets supplied by others. Intrinsic rewards are those that result from one's own behavior like enjoying what you find out by reading, or hitting a perfect serve when practicing tennis alone. Praise typically increases later enjoyment of an activity, making it more "intrinsically" rewarding. Praise is never promised beforehand and thus does not set up a discrimination, as in the example of offering a new pencil for helping out. You don't say, "If you finish this task, I'll give you praise." Approval is implied whenever you ask others to do something, but the actual receiving of it is unpredictable and is never dependent on a prior contract. In general, students whose work receives approval are *more* likely, not less, to continue working after praise is no longer given. They are also more likely to express positive attitudes towards the activity for which they received praise. You don't have to worry that your approval or praise will decrease so-called intrinsic motivation. Research says quite the opposite.[9]

The effect of tangible rewards is more complex and shows the need for considering the contingencies discussed above.[10] A review of 145 studies showed undesirable effects

Table 12.2 Impact of teacher rewards on later behavior without rewards

Rewards generally **increased** future time spent, or interest expressed, in an activity when:
• the "rewards" consisted of verbal approval or praise.
• the "rewards" were material objects and the task rewarded was a low-interest activity.
• the "rewards" were material objects and the requirements for earning them were clearly defined.

Rewards generally **decreased** future time spent, or interest expressed, in an activity when:
• the "rewards" were material objects and given for an activity already in high strength.
• the "rewards" were material objects promised beforehand for behavior without any criteria, and were given once at the end of the work session.

only under special circumstances. Here is a representative format for the studies: Children were asked to wait in a waiting room equipped with materials for drawing. Then they were taken into a different "experimental" room. In one condition the children were offered a "Good Player Award" for drawing. Others were given a Good Player Award when they had finished drawing (without any prior promise), and still others were asked to draw without any awards being given or mentioned. Then they were taken back to the waiting room, and their play observed. The amount of time children from each group drew after being taken back to the waiting room was used for the measure of "intrinsic" motivation.

The only results showing a decrease in the measure of "intrinsic motivation" were when three conditions occurred together: 1) The action (drawing) was already in high strength, that is, the child already drew a lot before the experimental procedure, 2) the reward was a material item (like the Good Player Award), and 3) it was promised for behavior without any criterion ("You will get a reward for drawing"). The combination of a promise of a tangible reward for engaging in a general activity that the child already enjoyed had a dampening effect on the time they drew afterwards. Even then, no decrease occurred when a reward was unexpected. Table 12.2 summarizes the results of the 145 studies.[11]

Just as positive consequences tend to enhance intrinsic motivation, punishment paired with specific actions transfers some of that aversiveness to the subject involved or to school in general. You cannot avoid punishment entirely. When students violate school rules, you are bound to administer the specified consequences. But if you find yourself punishing the same behavior in the same student more than one or two times a month, look for alternatives. If you can't shape better behavior on your own, don't hesitate to request help. Repeated punishment may hold down the punished behavior temporarily, but the side effects are never good.

Mild punishment slips into many schools for behavior that differs from the norm. Divergence, however, is one property of creative behavior. To give creativity more than lip service, unique behavior needs to be strengthened, not weakened.

CREATIVE BEHAVIOR AND CREATIVE PROBLEM-SOLVING

To be considered creative, actions or their products must differ from those of others. Not all unique behavior qualifies. Social utility enters into the definition. People who behave too idiosyncratically are put into institutions, not celebrated as creative. In creative problem-solving, an approach that fails to produce a useful solution is judged "wrong," not "creative." The source of control over behavior matters, too. You would change your opinion about a wonderful and imaginative product or solution if you found out that it was copied.

Fluency as Part of Measuring Creative Behavior

With these rather vague requirements, measuring creative behavior is a challenge. A popular measure, one of the Torrence Tests of Creative Thinking, asks for short, timed sessions where you write down all the uses you can think of for an object like a brick. At the end of the timing, your suggestions are compared with uses written by others. Using a brick for building occurs commonly, so does not qualify as creative. Grinding the brick up and using the powder as rouge, however, is unusual, so that use adds to your creativity score.

Scores on the Torrence test improve if you ask students to "write uses no one else would think of." Similarly, by teaching students to consider different *properties* of whatever object is given, they come up with more imaginative ideas. Considering a brick's color, or porosity, or smell, or taste, or texture, suggests uses you would otherwise not consider.

Helping students score better on one test does not, of course, mean you have taught students to be more creative in other arenas. But, like any other behavior, creative actions adjust to the contingencies you set up in your classroom.

Removing Punitive Contingencies

The first step in producing creativity is to remove punishment for divergent actions. School is so oriented to "right" and "wrong" that it is easy to dismiss answers that don't match conventional patterns. A kindergarten student coloring sky green will probably be told that sky should be blue. Disapproval of divergent actions can be found throughout the educational system. The daughter of Richard P. Feynman, the Nobel Prize winner in physics, describes the result of her father's help as follows:

> "When I was in high school, he started showing me shortcuts in my math homework that diverged from the teacher's methods. I was subsequently scolded by my Algebra II teacher for not solving the problem in the right way."[12]

It is no more helpful to blame teachers than to blame a student for lack of creativity. In the often hectic atmosphere of a classroom, taking a moment or two to seriously consider a novel idea or method can be as difficult as it is important. Novelty doesn't occur all the time (or it would not be novel), so you have to remind yourself to treasure it when you have a chance.

The Importance of Basic Skills in Creating

You cannot help students become more creative by abandoning practice in basic skills. In fact, basic skills provide the tools needed for creating. Try writing an English haiku (a poem with three lines of five, seven, and five syllables per line) without a good vocabulary and knowledge of syllables. Chapter 4 described short fluency drills that improved the quality of students' subsequent writing of haiku. Whenever skills are fluent, students can concentrate on what they have to express. Attention isn't siphoned away from their train of thought by concern with mechanics.

Throughout life, skills remain important components of creativity. A study of nearly 100 creative artists, educators, engineers, politicians, scientists, religious leaders and writers in the 1990s showed that a major characteristic differentiating them from their peers was mastery of their content area.[13] The importance of practice is illustrated by the following story:

> A Chinese emperor loved the work of a particular artist who lived way up in the hills. The emperor sent a messenger to order a horse drawing for his palace. The artist said he would be honored. A year went by. Three months into the next year, the messenger was sent back into the hills.
>
> "Where is the Emperor's drawing?" the messenger asked.
>
> "I'm ready," replied the artist. He took a fine sheet of the best paper, and then and there painted a fine painting of a horse.
>
> While the painting was being wrapped for carrying, the messenger ventured a question.
>
> "If it only took you one minute to make the painting," he said. "Why did it take you so long to make this for the Emperor?"
>
> "Aah," replied the artist. "Come. I'll show you."
>
> He led the messenger to a huge storeroom and opened the door. There spilling over from stacks 10 feet high, stood thousands of horse paintings, filling the entire room.
>
> "I wasn't yet ready," the artist said.

Prompting Unique Responses

To set up contingencies that encourage creativity you need to find assignments that encourage unique products. Asking for personal experiences or "your own" examples prompts individual responses. Everyone has a different life history and all students are "experts" about their own history, their own emotions, their own fantasies, and their own goals. Furthermore, what students have to say about their lives often interests other students, gaining some of the attention needed to build behavior. As an added advantage, it is more interesting to read unique assignments than essentially the same answer over and over. Try asking students to think of unlikely scenarios, like a dog on the ceiling, and ask them about what they imagine: "What color is your dog? How big is it?" and so on.[14] If you give a part of a story to finish,[15] or a squiggle to turn into a picture, you will get individual products with features worthy of comment.

Another vehicle for promoting creative products is to impose limits on what is to be done. Structure is often seen as the enemy of creativity, but it can also promote novel actions. Given a task, restrictions mean that you cannot respond as you usually do. You have to come up with something different. Thus, for example, musicians may compose a piece using unfamiliar scales or instruments that prevent their usual style of composition. Some of the new sounds created will be pleasing enough to be kept for a composition that will be judged creative.

In a classroom, structure similarly encourages new actions. Try writing an essay without the verb "to be," or a story set in the seventeenth century, or a personal experience from the point of view of an adversary. Of course, not all novel productions "work," but such exercises help students generate new ideas, the better of which can be encouraged.

Because so often novelty is dismissed or criticized, you may need to specifically identify times when novelty will be welcome. American business loses many innovations because of employee suggestions being ignored or punished. To counter those contingencies, businesses use "brainstorming" sessions where every idea, no matter how odd or ridiculous, is accepted. Later good suggestions are separated from the impractical. By setting sessions in a classroom with the same rules as brainstorming, you can draw out students who hesitate to venture original opinions.

Creative Problem-Solving
It takes a good bit of thinking to design assignments that encourage unique problem-solving skills. One might think that nothing creative could be done in an area as cut and dried as beginning mathematics. Even there, however, problems can require a variety of procedures or "right" answers. Figure 12.6 shows two examples. Try answering Exercise

---

Exercise A: Which item does not belong with the others?

Tell why. 2 6 5 10

> **Sample student answers for Exercise A:**
>
> 5 is the wrong number because all the others are even.
>
> 10 is the wrong number because the rule is "single-digit numbers."
>
> 6 is the wrong number because the rule is "factors of 10."

Exercise B: This is an In and Out Machine. What is the "out number" for 7? How did you find it?

IN	OUT
1	0
2	3
3	8
4	15
5	24
6	35
7	??

> **Sample student methods for Exercise B:**
>
> Square the "in" number and subtract 1
>
> Each "out" goes up 2 more, 3, then 5, then 7. For 7 you need to add 13.
>
> Add the "in" number 7 to the previous "in" number, then add the previous "out" number.

Fig. 12.6 Creativity in mathematics problems

A yourself before reading some of the answers given by students. Note that this kind of problem challenges advanced students without discouraging their less skilled peers. Similar items can be made for any subject area at any level of education. For example, for the four words cat, boy, horse, and dog, one student noted that only one of them spelled backwards makes a real word.[16]

Can Creativity be Taught?

As the previous section illustrated, the answer is "yes." Just as history, or science, or any other subject matter is taught by establishing appropriate contingencies, so, too is creative behavior. You teach creative actions by prompting and reinforcing responding that is novel and useful.

No behavior is immutable. Everything students do continually changes from interacting within the multiple environments they encounter each day. Each setting comes with its own conditions, prompting behavior that has adapted to the contingencies of that setting. That includes not only academic behavior, but social behavior as well.

SOCIAL BEHAVIOR

Much social behavior has to be taught. The "natural" consequences of good social behavior are usually costly when they require putting the welfare of others ahead of one's own immediate gain. An action that benefits others often results in a loss of material goods, less access to activities, loss of time, or amount of power. The "others" whose welfare is important to your students may extend only so far as a particular group, and that may not include you or many of their peers in your classroom. Conflict between individuals and between groups often occurs. To handle disagreements before they escalate into chaos or violence, special procedures may need to be added to the positive classroom contingencies for academic work.

Schools that serve neighborhoods where gang violence is common cannot expect those alliances to disappear once members enter the school doors. While handling this problem is beyond the scope of this book, it is important to realize that no behavior originates full-blown. Teachers and school personnel need to be on the lookout for precursors to serious behavior problems so they can be handled *before* a crisis occurs. The U. S. Department of Justice provides resources for schools.[17] In addition, reducing the side effects generated by punitive classroom procedures decreases hostility that can spill over onto the playground or the school halls.

Self-Control and Anger Management

Like "intrinsic motivation" the term "self-control" refers to actions without noticeable control by others. One kind concerns handling respondents like anger.

Anger consists of a combination of respondents including increases in heart rate, blood pressure, adrenaline, and overall energy level. These respondents are often accompanied by aggressive operant behavior such as swearing, slamming doors, throwing objects, or attacking others. You cannot eliminate all situations that make students angry, but both respondents and their accompanying operants can be reduced. The time to work on anger management is not in the middle of an explosion, but when a student is calm.

Working directly on respondents is called **systematic desensitization**, and is usually done by counselors. Students identify situations that trigger their anger. They are taught to relax to descriptions of situations that gradually come closer and closer to the circumstances that are most troublesome.[18] Operant procedures include a variety of approaches, including teaching ways to avoid trouble in the first place and actions that avoid escalation when trouble begins.

A combination of procedures was used with a 14-year-old student who was placed in a special school after being released from jail. The youth violently reacted to any request or criticism. Working first in a separate room, a counselor told him that he would hear insults, each of which would be preceded by the word "barb." His job was to "take" the criticism. The first comments were pretty mild: "Barb. You aren't sitting up straight." As the youth succeeded in holding back his overt reactions, the insults grew stronger. When he no longer reacted to the counselor's insults, the procedure was transferred to school. His teachers were told to precede any comment that could possibly upset the youth with the word, "barb." As the youth's anger and violence no longer occurred, the word "barb" was faded until it was no longer necessary. The antecedents that had produced both anger and aggression were no longer problems.

We tend to think of "self-control" as requiring observable effort to control an equally visible physiological anger. If a student no longer *looks* angry, is he or she exhibiting "self-control"? One could claim that by not showing anger you have better "self-control" than when your anger is visible. It may be preferable to teach not just how to handle anger, but how not to *feel* angry in situations that are aversive.

A frustrating event is less likely to produce feelings of anger or of operant outbursts if, in general, life is going well. Students are more likely to tolerate aversive events in positive classrooms than in classrooms where punishment is common. Behavioral procedures thus not only give a boost to academic success, they make life more positive especially for students from dysfunctional homes or dangerous neighborhoods. You can probably handle occasional outbursts calmly, but if they occur frequently or are severe, ask for help. Self-control skills are easier to teach when a student is separated from situations that trigger strong emotions.

Self-Management of One's Own Environment

A second kind of "self-control" applies to behaving for long-term payoffs rather than for short-term consequences. The lack of this kind of control shows in the pervasiveness in American society of such problems as procrastination, obesity, alcoholism, risky sexual practices, drug use, smoking, failure to exercise, escalating personal credit card debt . . . the list is long indeed. The "natural" consequences of all of these actions, being immediate, conspire against behavior that results in a better future. Countering immediate benefits requires another "self," that is, other behavior that can be learned. Preschoolers who waited 15 minutes to receive five pretzels rather than immediately taking one pretzel placed in front of them have been shown to cope better with frustration and stress later as adolescents than their more impulsive peers.[19] Strategies included putting pretzels out of sight or imagining them as something other than food, such as small logs.

Many procedures for self-control involve engineering one's own environment the way you would if you were working on someone else's behavior (see Table 12.3).

Table 12.3 Parallels between control of behavior in oneself and in others

Antecedents for behavior:

For others: You phone a friend to get him out of bed.
For yourself: You set an alarm clock to get yourself out of bed

For others: You stop peer talking in class to make it easier for students to work.
For yourself: You go to a quiet place to make it easier to get your work done.

Postcedents to strengthen behavior:

For others: You tell your roommate how nice she looks when she dresses appropriately.
For yourself: Looking in the mirror you think to yourself you look pretty sharp.

For others: You ask students to record their time each week to run a mile, applauding improvement.
For yourself: You record your own time to run a mile, appreciating your own improvement.

For others: You take your spouse or friend out to her favorite restaurant as a reward for completing a project.
For yourself: You wait until you finish your project before going out to dinner at your favorite restaurant.*

---

* Note that this is not a real contingency since you *could* go even before finishing, but when held until finishing, it may strengthen project completion in the future.

A simple example of managing one's own behavior occurs with **precurrent behavior**, that is, acting at the moment to produce behavior later. Students set up an alarm clock at night, perhaps placing it across the room, so that they will get up on time the next morning. They write down an assignment or a shopping list in order to remember it later. They may shut the door to their room or silence their cell phone to avoid distractions that will interrupt studying. Creating a tidy living space, as implied in the saying "a place for everything and everything in its place," is precurrent behavior when it helps in locating items later. Creating labeled folders encourages filing papers rather than letting them pile up. Putting a box of a favorite candy out of sight decreases reminders of its presence. Victorian ladies who did not want to eat more heartily than was socially appropriate would stuff themselves before going out to a dinner party.

In addition to setting up antecedents for future behavior, people supply consequences following their own behavior. Small children praised for picking up or sharing often say "good boy" or "good girl" to themselves following those actions. Similarly, when as a teacher you have rewarded student achievement, similar accomplishments produce students' own rewarding thoughts. More overt consequences also support otherwise weak behavior. As a consequence for finishing a difficult task, people may "reward themselves" with an activity they particularly enjoy. Of course, if a person can "cheat" and engage in the activity without completing the task, the consequence is not really contingent. Nevertheless when people adhere to their resolution, the timing is right for strengthening behavior.

A consequence students can provide for their own behavior is a record of progress.

When in your classroom you pair approval with recording of data, you help make those records reinforcing. Of course, not all records show improvement. Teaching students to treat disappointing data as a problem to solve helps them learn strategies for self-improvement. As an added benefit, students who graph their progress also learn to read and interpret graphs, a valuable skill.

While these are simple examples, all the principles can be taught. Take, for example, precurrent behavior like getting students to take home everything they need to do their homework. Initially you need to check that they write down and understand the assignment, and assemble needed books and supplies. To get students to check by themselves, you must fade your reminders, but spot check to make sure all the behavior has occurred. When your students routinely write down assignments and pack all necessary materials, you have taught one instance of "self-control." Another strategy teaches students to plan and follow schedules for accomplishing tasks. Even special students can learn to make and follow a list of activities and the times at which they are to be done.[20]

Teaching acceptable social behavior early prevents problems later. In kindergarten, teaching children to mand appropriately reduces grabbing and screaming. Hand-raising is a universal alternative to calling out answers, effective when consistently followed. Where fights break out frequently, alternative ways of settling differences need to be instituted, perhaps with the help of classroom discussions or cooperative projects. As mentioned earlier, in difficult cases, especially where gangs are involved, school-wide student committees have been set up and trained to handle disputes. Of course, specific procedures need to be adapted to each local school and community. The point here is that the "self" in "self-control" or "self-discipline" is one repertoire of behavior that interacts with other repertoires within the same individual. Society has to teach the behavior attributed to the "self." That is fortunate, since that responsibility can be taught by following the principles that behaviorology has made available to us.

Self-Esteem

The role played by teachers in creating what is attributed to the "self" is most acknow-ledged in "self-esteem." Teachers have been encouraged to raise student self-esteem in order to improve academic performance. A thorough review of studies on self-esteem, however, concluded that "efforts to boost the self-esteem of pupils have not been shown to improve academic performance and may sometimes be counterproductive.[21] Research does show a connection between self-esteem and achievement, but it goes in the other direction: improving academic performance improves self-esteem.

SUMMARY

The future of our country rests in our most valuable resource: the repertoire of our next generation. Broken homes and poverty shift the responsibility for producing that reper-toire increasingly to schools. The goals demanded for tomorrow's citizens go far beyond skills measured by high school graduation tests. A healthy society requires individuals described as motivated, rational, reasonable, and kind. These are not easy objectives to meet, but everything that goes on in every classroom in the country affects them. No behavior is caused by a "self" or "agent" inside the behaving individual. The behavior attributed to a "self" consists of many different repertoires, each of which is shaped and maintained by complex contingencies. Many of those contingencies require support that you, as a teacher, initially contribute. To enable behavior to carry into later life, however, you must transfer the control you initially provide to contingencies that come from a student's own behavior.

All behavior continually changes through interactions in the world. Shifting the definition of teaching from presenting information to shaping behavior focuses attention on factors responsible for repertoires that exist, and on changes needed for better forms of behavior and the kinds of controls to maintain them. Using behavioral principles means setting up appropriate contingencies for the interlocking forces that surround and affect all aspects of behavior. Positive reinforcement added or "extrinsic" to behavior is paired with students' effectiveness to produce conditioned "intrinsic" reinforcers that carry on after a class is over. Reinforcing contingencies give teachers power to build behavior and at the same time model positive ways of interacting with others. While no one can avoid punishment altogether, any tiny shift that replaces force and threat with approval and success moves one step toward creating a better society for all.

CONCEPT CHECKS

Objectives That Tests Cannot Measure (Objective A)

DIRECTIONS: Which four of the following state standards could LEAST easily be evaluated with paper and pencil tests?

1. Recognize "how many" in sets of objects.
2. Evaluate conclusions and recognize that arguments may not have equal merit.
3. Determine sequence of events after reading a short story.
4. Apply self-monitoring strategies.
5. Identify four major historical developments of language and literature in America from 1900 to the present.
6. Use tables and graphs to represent data.
7. Understand the ethical and human issues related to using technology.
8. Diagram the components of a specified system.
9. Select appropriate measuring instruments based on the degree of precision needed.
10. Demonstrate respect for other students while using technology.

Sources of Control (Objective B)

DIRECTIONS: For each of the following descriptions:
First, identify whether the contingencies describe control by an authority (A) or control by the products of student actions themselves (P), and
Second, name likely postcedents.

1. Jack completes his homework to please his teacher.
2. Luke concentrates hard when making free shots in basketball.
3. Peter reads only stories about horses.
4. "If everyone sits down in three seconds, you will all get an extra 10 minutes of recess."
5. By starting quickly, students can beat their own records

Motivation (Objective C)

DIRECTIONS: Which three of the following are most likely to have a positive effect on future studying (especially when the teacher is no longer around)?

1. Giving an inspiring lecture showing how interesting the subject is that students are about to study.
2. Pointing out the increased future earnings of students who finish high school.
3. Providing big rewards for achieving good grades.
4. Adding ways for students to see small improvements in their performance.
5. Giving abundant praise to each student whenever he or she is attentive.
6. Pairing approval with achievement frequently at first, then intermittently.
7. Providing activities in which students can experience the results of their efforts.

ANALYSIS PROBLEMS

1. Goals That Paper and Pencil Tests Cannot Measure (Objective A)

Print out your state's objectives for one of the subjects and grade level(s) you teach. What percentage of them can be assessed by paper and pencil tests?

2. Transferring Control and Making Behavior Itself More Reinforcing (Objectives D & E)

2a. You want to make identifying local plants by name and/or species rewarding to a child or to your students. How could you do that?

OR

2b. Describe specific contingencies you could set up in a class you teach or might some-day teach, so that students that are not initially interested in a subject will find activity in that area rewarding.

3. Contingency Mistakes With Tangible Rewards (Objective F)

A boy usually refuses to do simple tasks like taking out the garbage or putting his dirty clothes in the laundry. His parents start offering a special treat to get him to do tasks when he refuses to do them. Soon, whenever he is asked to do a new task, the boy asks, "What will you give me if I do?" Describe the discrimination training responsible for this inappropriate behavior.

4. Promoting Creativity (Objective G)

Find or try out an exercise, worksheet, or lesson plan designed to promote "creativity" in your subject area. How does the activity encourage divergent actions?

ANSWERS FOR CONCEPT CHECKS

Objectives That Tests Cannot Measure

The most difficult (or impossible) to measure with paper and pencil tests are numbers 2, 4, 7, and 10. (Note that you must restate most of these behaviorally to see how they would be measured. Also note how many state goals cannot be measured by test items.)

Sources of Control

1. A. Teacher approval (or equivalent).
2. P. The ball going in the hoop, and perhaps social approval by peers.
3. P. Since Peter reads only about horses, finding out about horses or what happens to them is the relevant consequence.
4. A. Extra recess
5. P. Seeing progress or beating one's own record.

Motivation

The three procedures most likely to have a positive effect on future studying are numbers 4, 6, and 7.

1. Inspiring lectures reinforce listening, but rarely affect studying afterwards.
2. Money earned for finishing high school is much too far in the future to influence what a student does on any particular day.
3. Big rewards for good grades are too delayed and based on too big a step for all but those students who are likely to earn them anyway.
4. Abundant praise for attentive behavior centers control in authority rather than in the rewards of working.

NOTES

Chapter 1

1   http://en.wikipedia.org/wiki/Discovery_of_Neptune. (Accessed December 8, 2008.)
2   B. F. Skinner, *Science and Human Behavior* (New York: Macmillan, 1953), 14.
3   B. F. Skinner, *Particulars of My Life* (New York: Alfred A. Knopf, 1976), 154.
4   Jerome D. Ulman and E. A. Vargas, "Behaviorology," in *Encyclopedia of Behavior Modification and Cognitive Behavior Therapy Vol. I: Adult Clinical Applications*, Michael Hersen and Joan Rosqvist (Eds.) (Thousand Oaks, CA: Sage Publications, 2005), 175–176.
5   B. F. Skinner, *The Technology of Teaching* (New York: Appleton-Century-Crofts, 1968), 5. (Reprinted: Cambridge, MA: B. F. Skinner Foundation, 2003.)
6   Tony Perry, "Zoo Spares Rod with Elephants," *Los Angeles Times*, July 26, 2004. (Reprinted on the *Boston Globe* website: http://www.boston.com/news/nation/articles/2004/07/26/zoo_spares_rod_with_elephants/. Accessed November 6, 2008.)
7   Patricia Wen, January 10, 2005, http://www.boston.com/news/local/articles/2005/01/10/campaigner_targets_spanking_tools_sale/ (Accessed March 11, 2008.)
8   ACLU and Human Rights Act Report: A Violent Education: Corporal Punishment of Children in U.S. Public Schools (August 19, 2008). http://hrw.org/reports/2008/us0808/. (Accessed September 4, 2008.)
9   Connie C. Taylor and Jon S. Bailey. "Reducing Corporal Punishment with Elementary School Students using Behavioral Diagnostic Procedures," in *Positive Behavior Support: Including People with Difficult Behavior in the Community*, Lynn Kern Koegel, Gobert L. Koegel, and Glen Dunlap (Eds.) (Baltimore, MD: Paul H. Brookes Publishing Co, 1996), 207–225.

Chapter 2

1   *Poor Richard's Almanack* (1745).
2   H. Allen Murphy, J. Michael Hutchison, and Jon S. Bailey, "Behavioral School Psychology Goes Outdoors: The Effect of Organized Games on Playground Aggression," *Journal of Applied Behavior Analysis* 16 (1983): 29–35.
3   When neither experimenter nor participant knows what treatment is occurring, the procedure is called a *double blind* experiment.
4   See http://www.ed.gov/policy/speced/reg/regulations.html for the latest version.
5   R. Douglas Greer et al., "Acquisition of Fluent Listener Responses and the Educational Advancement of Young Children with Autism and Severe Language Delays," *European Journal of Behavior Analysis* 2 (Winter 2005): 88–126.
6   Paul Lichtenstein et al. (2000), "Environmental and Heritable Factors in the Causation of Cancer," *The New England Journal of Medicine* 343 (2000): 78–85.

7 See, for example, Mario F. Fraga et al., "Epigenetic Differences Arise During the Lifetime of Monozygotic Twins," *Proceedings of the National Academy of Sciences* 102 (July 26, 2005): 10604–10609. (Also available at http://www.pnas.org/cgi/content/abstract/102/30/10604.)

Chapter 3

1 Ivan Petrovich Pavlov (Translated and edited by G. V. Anrep), *Conditioned Reflexes: An Investigation of the Physiological Activity of the Cerebral Cortex* (Oxford: Oxford University Press, 1927).
2 In his writings, Pavlov emphasized that after their lab experiences, his dogs lived "without the slightest deviation from normal health." Ivan Pavlov, Nobel Prize address delivered in Stockholm, December 12, 1904. In Michael Kaplan (Ed.), *Essential Works of Pavlov* (New York: Bantam, 1966), 50.
3 The terms "conditional" and "unconditional" were mistranslated as "conditioned" and "unconditioned." The more accurate terms are used here.
4 Respondent conditioning is also sometimes called "classical conditioning" or "Pavlovian conditioning."
5 I. P. Pavlov *Conditioned Reflexes*.
6 John B. Watson, *Behaviorism* (New York: W. W. Norton & Company, Inc., 1925).
7 Bertrand Russell, *Philosophy* (New York: W. W. Norton & Company, Inc., 1927). (Published earlier in Great Britain as *Outline of Philosophy*.)
8 John B. Watson, *Behaviorism*, 19.
9 B. F. Skinner, *The Shaping of a Behaviorist* (New York: Alfred A. Knopf, 1979), 35.
10 Originally it moved down, but Skinner reversed the direction so that each response moved the pen up.
11 B. F. Skinner, *The Shaping of a Behaviorist*, 59.
12 B. F. Skinner, "A Case History in Scientific Method," *American Psychologist* 11 (1956): 221–233. (Reprinted in B. F. Skinner, *Cumulative Record* (Cambridge, MA: B. F. Skinner Foundation, 2004), 108–131.)
13 B. F. Skinner, *The Shaping of a Behaviorist*, 95.
14 F. S. Keller to B. F. Skinner, Letter dated October 2, 1931 refers to Skinner's "brand new theory." Harvard University Archives.
15 Everyone else calls an experimental space that includes a way to provide reinforcement contingent on the operation of a lever or something else the animal can manipulate, a "Skinner Box."
16 For suggestions to drop the "positive" and "negative" qualifiers for "reinforcement" see the following two articles: 1) Jack Michael, "Positive and Negative Reinforcement: A Distinction that is No Longer Necessary; or a Better Way to Talk about Bad Things," *Behaviorism* 3 (1975): 33–44; and 2) Alan Baron and Mark Galizio, "Positive and Negative Reinforcement: Should the Distinction be Preserved?," *The Behavior Analyst* 28 (2005): 5–98.
17 Wesley C. Becker, Siegfried Engelmann, and Don R. Thomas, *Teaching I: Classroom Management* (Chicago, IL: Science Research Associates, 1975), 67–68.
18 Ibid.
19 Paige M. McKercar and Rachel H. Thompson, "A Descriptive Analysis of Potential Reinforcement Contingencies in the Preschool Classroom," *Journal of Applied Behavior Analysis* 37 (2004): 431–444.
20 Like "reinforcement" some behavior analysts distinguish between "positive punishment" which is *adding* something, like a spanking, and "negative punishment" which is *removing* something like grade points or privileges. The term "positive punishment" sounds like a positive procedure, which it is not. Like "positive" and "negative" reinforcement, you may encounter these terms, but they will be used as little as possible in this book.
21 A good source for the harmful effects of punishment is Murray Sidman, *Coercion and its Fallout* (Boston, MA: Authors Cooperative, Inc., 1989). Available from www.behavior.org.
22 Robert Dietiker, "Decreasing a Fifth Grade Boy's 'I Can't Do It' Responses to Written Assignments," *School Applications of Learning Theory* 3 (1970): 30.
23 Behavior that needs to be decreased has many names like "inappropriate," "problem," or "challenging." These terms will be used interchangeably.
24 Kent R. Johnson and T. V. Joe Layng, "Breaking the Structuralist Barrier: Literacy and Numeracy with Fluency," *American Psychologist* 47, 11 (1992): 1475–1490.

Chapter 4

1 Carolyn S. Ryan and Nancy S. Hemmes, "Effects of the Contingency for Homework Submission on Homework Submission and Quiz Performance in a College Course," *Journal of Applied Behavior Analysis* 38 (2005): 79–87.

2   See the website http://idea.ed.gov.

3   Search for Individualized Education Program under the Federal Government's website http://idea.ed.gov. This quote was taken on April 18, 2008 from http://www:ideapartnership.org/oseppage.cfm?pageid=45.

4   R. Douglas Greer and Dolleen-Day Keohane, "The Evolution of Verbal Behavior in Children," *Behavioral Development Bulletin* (2005): 31–47. Reprinted 2006 in *Journal of Speech and Language Pathology: Applied Behavior Analysis*. Volume 1(2). www.behavior-analyst-today.com.

5   The term "frequency" is preferred by Precision Teachers who insist upon a time component in measurement.

6   Kent R. Johnson and Layng, T. V. Joe. (1992), "Breaking the Structuralist Barrier: Literacy and Numeracy with Fluency," *American Psychologist* 47, 11 (1992):1475–1490.

7   http://www.ascd.org/terminology link (October 2005), section called "The Lexicon of Learning."

8   J. Lynn McBrien and Ronald Brandt (Eds.), *The Language of Learning: A Guide to Educational Terms* (Baltimore, MD: Association for Supervision and Curriculum Development, 1997). Accessed through www.ascd.org, October 2005, in a section called "Lexicon of Learning."

9   See Kent Johnson and Elizabeth M. Street, *The Morningside Model of Generative Instruction*. Concord, MA: Cambridge Center for Behavioral Studies, 2004.

10 Based on Ernest A. Vargas, "The Triad Model of Education (II) and Instructional Engineering," *The Spanish Journal of Psychology* 10 (2007): 314–327.

11 B. F. Skinner called this "rule-governed behavior," but it goes well beyond following rules, so the term proposed by E. A. Vargas is used here. See E. A. Vargas, "Verbally-Governed and Event-Governed Behavior," *The Analysis of Verbal Behavior* 6 (1988): 11–22.

12 Behavior to decrease has many names. The term "challenging" will be used here as the least pejorative.

13 Project completed in a graduate class taught by the author at West Virginia University, 2003.

14 For guidelines on confidentiality as well as for other ethical questions, see Jon S. Bailey and Mary R. Burch, *Ethics for Behavior Analysts* (Mahwah, NJ: Erlbaum, 2005).

15 A book based on the BCBA task list for certification is John O. Cooper, Timothy E. Heron, and William L. Heward, *Applied Behavior Analysis: Second Edition* (Upper Saddle River, NJ: Pearson Education, 2007).

Chapter 5

1   Sidney W. Bijou and Donald M. Baer, *Child Development: Readings in Experimental Analysis* (New York: Appleton-Century-Crofts, 1967), 156–157.

2   As was mentioned in the last chapter, different words are used for count divided by time. B. F. Skinner used "rate." Ogden Lindsley, Skinner's student and the originator of Precision Teaching, used "frequency" for actions per unit of time. Both words can be found in the literature, and both appear in dictionary definitions of each other. Both will also be used in this book.

3   See, for example, Carl V. Binder, Eric Haughton, and D. Van Eyk, "Increasing Endurance by Building Fluency: Precision Teaching Attention Span," *Teaching Exceptional Children*, 22 (1990): 24–27.

4   S. Brown, D. Churella, J. Lyonett, K. Oyster, and D. Petrovich, "The Effects of Behavior Specific Praise on Task Completion," Final report for an Educational Research Class at West Virginia University, November 2001.

5   Both latency and duration of a single action can be converted into rate (one action divided by the number of minutes it took for the action to occur).

6   Ogden R. Lindsley, "What We Know That Ain't So." (Paper presented at the annual meeting of the Midwestern Association of Behavior Analysis, Chicago, IL, May 27–30, 1977.)

7   The word "data" is plural. "Datum" is the singular. More technical publications make the distinction and, except for quotations where the single is used, data will be used as a plural.

8   A measure called a "learn unit" has been proposed by Douglas Greer in his CABAS instructional system. Each interaction is called a "learn unit" when the student correctly responds with or without additional help and is given feedback. The size of a learn unit can vary, however, so that it is not standard. See R. Douglas Greer, *Designing Teaching Strategies: An Applied Behavior Analysis Systems Approach* (San Diego, CA: Academic Press, 2002), 28.

9   Maeve G. Meany-Daboul et al., "A Comparison of Momentary Time Sampling and Partial-Interval Recording for Evaluating Functional Relations," *Journal of Applied Behavior Analysis* 40 (2007): 501–514.

10 In the "learn unit" Discrete Trial format designed by R. Douglas Greer, a failure to respond or an incorrect response results in a prompt or other help so that the correct "answer" is always given and reinforced. Each trial ends in reinforcement. When a student responds to prompts or other help, however, the antecedent control differs from that of the initial task given.

11   The consequence is usually determined beforehand to be positive reinforcement, often through a functional analysis.

12   See R. Douglas Greer, *Designing Teaching Strategies: An Applied Behavior Analysis Systems Approach*, 28.

13   This description is based upon an algebra class in Martinsville, West Virginia.

Chapter 6

1   Data are taken from John E. Humphrey, "A Comparison of how Paced and Unpaced Problems Affect Learning During CAI Math Drills" (EdD diss., West Virginia University, 1983).

2   Darrell Huff, *How to Lie with Statistics* (New York: W. W. Norton & Company, 1954).

3   Paige M. McKerchar and Rachel H. Thompson, "A Descriptive Analysis of Potential Reinforcement Contingencies in the Preschool Classroom," *Journal of Applied Behavior Analysis* 37 (2004): 436.

4   Robert G. Wahler, Gary H. Winkel, Robert F. Peterson, and Delmont C. Morrison, "Mothers as Behavior Therapists for Their Own Children," in *Child Development: Readings in Experimental Analysis*, Sidney W. Bijou and Donald M. Baer (Eds.) (New York: Appleton-Century-Crofts, 1967), 247.

5   Journal articles usually put actual numbers somewhere in the body of the text since it is important to know what the numbers were.

6   Graphs of the Dow Jones Industrial average over time use ratio graphs for this reason.

7   Robert Bower and Ken Meier, "Will the Real 'Slow Learner' Please Stand Up?," *Journal of Precision Teaching* 2 (1981): 3–12. The students labeled "gifted" are numbers 1, 2, 11, and 13. The students labeled "resource" are numbers 12, 19, and 21.

8   Standard Celeration Chart paper can be ordered from http://www.behaviorresearchcompany.com.

9   Carl H. Koenig, "Charting the Future Course of Behavior" (EdD diss., University of Kansas, 1972).

10   Ogden Lindsley et al., *Handbook of Precise Behavior Facts: Listings of the First Twelve Thousand Published Precise Behavior Management Projects* (Kansas, MO: Precision Media, 1971). Two volumes.

11   Steve Graf and Ogden R. Lindsley, *Standard Celeration Charting 2002* (Poland, OH: Graf Implements, 2002), 24A.

12   The full Standard Celeration Charts can be obtained from http://www.behaviorresearchcompany.com.

13   Pat McGreevy, *Teaching and Learning in Plain English* (Kansas City, MO: Plain English Publications, 1983).

14   Graf and Lindsley, *Standard Celeration Charting 2002*, 31.

15   See http://www.aimchart.com/.

16   Terry J. Knapp, "Behavior Analysts' Visual Appraisal of Behavior Change in Graphic Display," *Behavioral Assessment* 5 (1983): 161.

Chapter 7

1   It is conceivable, of course, that among the hundreds of facilitated communication projects, somewhere some student actually began to respond without needing a facilitator's guidance. Even with that remote possibility, however, there are better ways to teach students beginning communication.

2   B. Dickerson, "How to Wreck a Boy's life (Part I of II)," *Detroit Free Press,* March 16, 2008, Sections 1A, 8A. Also B. Dickerson, "A Legal Horror Show Tears Oakland Co. Family Apart, (Part II of II)," *Detroit Free Press,* March 17, 2008, Sections 1A, 11A.

3   For directions for one form of SAFMEDS, see http://www.tuccionline.com/dl/SampleMaterials/SAFMEDsInstruction.pdf.

4   Benjamin Thompson (Count Rumford). "Heat is a Form of Motion: An Experiment in Boring Cannon," *Philosophical Transactions,* 88 (1798). Also see http://dbhs.wvusd.k12.ca.us/webdocs/Chem-History/Rumford-1798.html. (Accessed December 8, 2008.)

5   Murray Sidman, *Equivalence Relations and Behavior: A Research Story* (Boston, MA: Authors Cooperative Inc., 1994), 34. Also available from www.behavior.org.

6   Ms. Miller. Class project for Dr. Roy Moxley, West Virginia University.

7   D. R. Carrigan, K. C. Kriby, and D. B. Marlowe, "Effect of Dispenser Location on Taking Free Condoms in an Outpatient Cocaine Abuse Treatment Clinic," *Journal of Applied Behavior Analysis* 28 (1995): 465–466.

8   Elizabeth M. Goetz and Donald M. Baer, "Social Control of Form Diversity and the Emergence of New Forms in Children's Blockbuilding," *Journal of Applied Behavior Analysis* 6 (1973): 213.

9   Matthew Porritt, Andrew Burt, and Alan Poling, "Increasing Fiction Writers' Productivity Through an Internet-based Intervention," *Journal of Applied Behavior Analysis* 39 (2006): 396.

10   Ron Van Houten and Joy Van Houten, "The Effects of Breaking New Spelling Words into Small Segments

on the Spelling Performance of Students with Learning Disabilities," *Journal of Behavioral Education* 1 (1991): 399–411.

11   Jerome D. Ulman and Beth Sulzer-Azaroff, "The Multi-Element Baseline Design in Educational Research," in *Behavior Analysis: Areas of Research and Application*, E. Ramp and G. Semb (Eds.) (Englewood Cliffs, NJ: Prentice-Hall, 1975), 371–391.

12   Brent Rushall, "The Restoration of Performance Capacity by Cognitive Restructuring and Covert Positive Reinforcement in an Elite Athlete," in Joseph R. Cautela and Albert J. Kearney (Eds.), *The Covert Conditioning Casebook* (Pacific Grove, CA: Brooks/Cole Publishing, 1993).

13   Tiffany Kodak, John Northup, and Michael E. Kelley, "An Evaluation of the Types of Attention that Maintain Problem Behavior," *Journal of Applied Behavior Analysis* 40 (2007): 169.

14   Matthew P. Normand and Jon S. Bailey, "The Effects of Celeration Lines on Visual Data Analysis," *Behavior Modification* 30 (2006): 295–314.

15   Roy F. Baumeister, Jennifer D. Campbell, Joachim I. Krueger and Kathleen D. Vohs, "Does High Self-Esteem Cause Better Performance, Interpersonal Success, Happiness, or Healthier Lifestyles?," *Psychological Science in the Public Interest* 4, Issue 1, (2003): 1–44. Published online April 10, 2003 12:00AM. (Accessed December 8, 2008 at http://www3.interscience.wiley.com/journal/118855650/abstract.)

16   B. F. Skinner, *Science and Human Behavior* (New York: Macmillan 1953). (Reprinted 1965. New York: The Free Press. Available free online at http://www.bfskinner.org.)

Chapter 8

1   B. F. Skinner, *The Shaping of a Behaviorist* (New York: Alfred A. Knopf, 1979), 242.

2   Companies supported the war effort. General Mills, headquartered in Minneapolis, sponsored Skinner's work.

3   B. F. Skinner, "Reinforcement Today," *American Psychologist* 13 (1958): 94.

4   Gail B. Peterson, "A Day of Great Illumination: B. F. Skinner's Discovery of Shaping," *Journal of the Experimental Analysis of Behavior* 82 (2004): 317–328.

5   Even though giving a perfect demonstration in which his pigeon accurately tracked an image of a ship the way it would look from a falling missile, Washington discontinued Skinner's project. It would work only in the daytime and, unknown to Skinner, radar was under development. The technology was later used in peace time to help locate survivors at sea. Pigeons are better than humans at spotting a human form in the vastness of the ocean.

6   B. F. Skinner, *The Shaping of a Behaviorist* (New York: Alfred A. Knopf, 1979) 275.

7   Francis Mechner, "What are the Effects of Reinforcement Presentations?" Chapter 9 in *The Revealed Operant: A Way to Study the Characteristics of Individual Occurrences of Operant Responses* (Cambridge, MA: Cambridge Center for Behavioral Studies Monograph Series, 3rd ed., 1994).

8   "Harvard Trained Dog," *Look Magazine*. March 10, 1952. Photographs taken by Douglas Jones, photographer, Look Magazine Collection, Library of Congress, Prints & Photographs Division.

9   Michael H. Goldstein, Andrew P. King, and Meredith J. West, "Social Interaction Shapes Babbling: Testing Parallels Between Birdsong and Speech," *Proceedings of the National Academy of Science*s 1200 (June 24, 2003): 8030–8035. Also available at http://www.pnas.org/content/100/13.toc.

10   Amy Sutherland, "What Shamu Taught Me About a Happy Marriage," *New York Times*, Modern Love, June 25, 2006.

11   Two classroom systems worth mentioning are Vicci Tucci's Competent Learner Model (http://www.tuccionline), and the Morningside Model (http://www.morningsideteachers.org).

12   R. Allan Allday and Kerri Pakurar, "Effects of Teacher Greetings on Student On-task Behavior," *Journal of Applied Behavior Analysis* 40 (2007): 317–320.

13   If a click has been paired with something aversive, for example used to indicate mistakes, pick a different sound.

14   http://www.tagteach.com, home page. (Accessed January 16, 2007.)

15   To demonstrate shaping, instructors have played what is known as the "shaping game." A student is sent out of the classroom while students decide upon a behavior to shape (like standing on a chair). The student is called back in and, without any words, the instructor shapes successive approximations to the final performance using claps or a click as feedback.

16   These characters mean "pajamas."

17   Skinner did not know it, but Sidney Pressey had designed a "testing machine" like Skinner's first efforts. Pressey's machine did not use shaping, just repetition of problems but with immediate feedback.

18   Nancy A. Neef, Brandon E. McCord, and Summer J. Ferreri), "Effects of Guided Notes Versus Completed

Notes During Lectures on College Students' Quiz Performance," *Journal of Applied Behavior Analysis* 39 (2006): 123–130.

19   See Siegfried Engelmann and Douglas Carnine, *Theory of Instruction: Principles and Applications* (New York: Irvington Publishers, Inc., 1982).

20   The revised DISTAR materials for math and reading are now available from SRA under other titles.

21   Gary Adams, "Project Follow Through: In-depth and Beyond," ESP 15(1) Project Follow Through and Beyond. From summary at http://darkwing.voregon.edu~adep/ft/adams.htm. (Accessed July 19, 2008.)

22   Eric Mazur, *Peer Instruction: A User's Manual* (Upper Saddle River, NJ: Prentice-Hall, Simon & Schuster, 1997), 4.

23   Erick K. Marmolejo, David A. Wilder, and Lucas Bradley, "A Preliminary Analysis of the Effects of Response Cards on Student Performance and Participation in an Upper Division University Course," *Journal of Applied Behavior Analysis* 37 (2004): 405–410.

24   Linda L. Davis and Robert E. O'Neil, "Use of Response Cards with a Group of Students with Learning Disabilities Including Those for whom English is a Second Language," *Journal of Applied Behavior Analysis* 37 (2004): 219–222.

25   See http://www.headsprout.com for an example.

26   Maria Montessori. *The Advanced Montessori Method, Volume 2*, John J. McDermott (Ed.) (New York: Schocken, 1973), 178.

27   Lawrence T. Stoddard and Murray Sidman, "Programming Perception and Learning for Retarded Children," in B. F. Skinner, *The Technology of Teaching*, 77 (Cambridge, MA: B. F. Skinner Foundation, 2003). (Originally published in *International Review of Research in Mental Retardation* 2, 1966, 151–208.)

28   Mark R. Clingan and Ernest A. Vargas, "Nonrestricted Operant Prompting in Sequelic Instruction," *Behaviorology* 5 (2000): 110–127.

29   See the website of Christina Burke at http://www.christinaburkaba.com for more on Discrete Trial versus nonrestricted operant procedures.

30   R. Douglas Greer, *Designing Teaching Strategies: An Applied Behavior Analysis Systems Approach* (San Diego, CA: Academic Press, 2002).

31   Randi A. Sarokoff and Peter Sturmey, "The Effects of Behavioral Skills Training on Staff Implementation of Discrete-Trial Instruction," *Journal of Applied Behavior Analysis* 38 (2005): 23–37.

Chapter 9

1   Ellen P. Reese, *Experiments in Operant Behavior* (New York: Meredith Publishing Company, 1964), 125. Ellie taught at Holyoke College in Massachusetts from to 1954 to 1994, and introduced many professionals to behavior analysis through her books, videos, and laboratory manual.

2   Judith Doran and James G. Holland, "Eye Movements as a Function of Response Contingencies Measured by Blackout Technique," *Journal of Applied Behavior Analysis* 4 (1971): 11–17.

3   Ibid., 17.

4   In the early twentieth century Maria Montessori recommended telling or dramatizing a story as the best way for a child to assess "understanding" of material read.

5   California and Connecticut, for example.

6   Both "induction" and "generalization" describe a relation between responding and antecedents. Because "generalization' sounds more like a process inside the person responding, induction will be used here.

7   See, for example, Charles B. Ferster and B. F. Skinner, *Schedules of Reinforcement* (Cambridge, MA: B. F. Skinner Foundation, 1997). (Originally published by Prentice-Hall, 1957.)

8   Max Wertheimer, *Productive Thinking* (New York: Harper & Row, 1959), 13–24.

9   Not all models need be people. Objects, such as a sculpture or web page layout, may be models too. All models, however, provide antecedents that set up situations where producing something similar is likely to be reinforced.

10   John V. Stokes, John Randall, Julie Lomartire, and Michelle Graham, "Becoming Measurable and Observable: Performance Feedback and Video Modeling in Training Clinical Competence and Vocational Skills." (Paper presented at the annual national meeting of the Berkshire Association for Behavior Analysis and Therapy, Amherst, USA, October 12–13, 2006).

11   Murray Sidman, "Reading and Auditory-Visual Equivalences," in Sidman, *Equivalence Relations and Behavior: A Research Story* (Boston, MA: Authors Cooperative, Inc., 1971).

12   Murray Sidman, "Equivalence Relations and the Reinforcement Contingency," *Journal of the Experimental Analysis of Behavior* 74 (2000): 127–146.

13   Ibid., 362.

Chapter 10

1   B. F. Skinner, *Verbal Behavior* (New York: Appleton-Century-Crofts, Inc., 1957). (Reprinted 1992 Cambridge, MA: B. F. Skinner Foundation.), vii.

2   Ibid., 2.

3   Those ways differentiate between mediation that is social but *not* verbal and mediation that has been shaped "precisely in order to reinforce the behavior of the speaker." Ibid., 224–226.

4   Ibid., 11.

5   Ibid., 35–36.

6   Ibid., 36.

7   Ibid., 35–36.

8   See, for example, Jack Michael, "Skinner's Elementary Verbal Relations: Some New Categories," *The Analysis of Verbal Behavior* 1 (1982): 1–4, and Ernest A. Vargas, "Intraverbal Behavior," in *Psychological Aspects of Language*, Phillip N. Chase and Linda J. Parrott (Eds.) (Springfield, IL: Charles C. Thomas, 1986), 128–151.

9   Skinner, *Verbal Behavior*, 225.

10 Skinner, in his first publications, talked about a "third variable" in addition to antecedents and consequences, giving deprivation as an example. Fred S. Keller and William N. Schoenfeld coined the term "establishing operations" for these procedures in their 1950 book, *Principles of Psychology* (New York: Appleton-Century-Crofts, 1950). (Reprinted 1995 Cambridge MA: B. F. Skinner Foundation, 1995), 273.

11 Charles Dickens, *The Adventures of Oliver Twist* (New York: The Heritage Press, 1939), 26.

12 Anne K. Overcash, Andrew S. Bondy, and Todd A. Harris, "Comparing the Effects of Three Communication Strategies upon Spontaneous Requesting of Preschoolers with Autism" (Paper presented at the annual convention of the Association for Behavior Analysis, San Francisco, United States, June, 1996).

13 Lori Frost and Andy Bondy, *The Picture Exchange Communication System Training Manual, Second Edition* (Newark, DE: Pyramid Educational Products, Inc., 2002).

14 Holly Almon-Morris and Michael Fabrizio, "Teaching Assent Withdrawal and Self-Advocacy Skills to Persons With Autism" (Paper presented at the annual convention of the Association For Behavior Analysis International, Chicago, IL, May 27, 2008).

15 Mark L. Sundberg and Jack Michael, "The Benefits of Skinner's Analysis of Verbal Behavior for Children With Autism," *Behavior Modification* 25 (2001): 698–724.

16 Skinner, *Verbal Behavior*, 81–82.

17 Genae Hall and Mark L. Sundberg, "Teaching Mands by Manipulating Conditioned Establishing Operations," *The Analysis of Verbal Behavior* 5 (1987): 41–53; Jennifer Lamarre and James G. Holland, "The Functional Independence of Mands and Tacts," *Journal of the Experimental Analysis of Behavior* 43 (1985): 5–19.

18 Sundberg, Mark, "Should We Stop Doing Mand and Intraverbal Training? What Do the Data Tell Us?" (Keynote address presented at the annual conference of the California Association for Behavior Analysis, February 18, 2006).

19 Hall and Sundberg, "Teaching Mands by Manipulating Conditioned Establishing Operations," 41–53.

20 Conversation between Ernest A. Vargas and B. F. Skinner, 1988 or 1989.

21 For example, see Mark L. Sundberg, *The Verbal Behavior Milestone Assessment and Placement Program: (The VB-MAPP)* (Concord, CA: Advancements in Verbal Behavior Press, 2008).

22 Ernest A. Vargas, "Verbally-Governed and Event-Governed Behavior," *The Analysis of Verbal Behavior* 6 (1988): 11–22.

23 This occurred in a first grade in West Virginia where the author was observing a handwriting class.

24 Skinner, *Verbal Behavior*, 71–80.

25 Ibid., 313.

26 Ibid., 315.

27 This incident was reported by a student in a verbal behavior class taught by the author.

28 The applicant was Jack Michael.

29 B. F. Skinner, *About Behaviorism* (New York: Alfred A. Knopf , 1974), 90.

30 Having students ask questions is sometimes called "reciprocal teaching."

31 This project was conducted in a public school in Morgantown, West Virginia.

32 The course was called "Essentials of College Rhetoric," taught in 1993 at Texas Tech University.

33 Fred O. Kemp, "Computer-Mediated Communication: Making Nets Work for Writing Instruction," in *The Dialogic Classroom: Teachers Integrating Computer Technology, Pedagogy, and Research*, Jeffrey R. Galin and Joan Latchaw (Eds.) (Urbana: National Council of Teachers of English, 1998), 133–150.

34 Tony Buzan, *Use Both Sides of Your Brain: New Mind-Mapping Techniques,* 3rd ed. (New York: Penguin Plume Paperback, 1991).

35 Joseph P. Unger, "Widening the Classroom's Horizons: Using the Internet's Usenet News as an Intervention Heuristic" (Paper presented at the eleventh annual Computers and Writing Conference, El Paso, TX, May 1995), http://english.ttu.edu/KAIROS/1.3/news/UsenetPaper.html. (Accessed August 30, 2008.)

36 Vargas, "Verbally-Governed and Event-Governed Behavior," 11–22.

37 This is often called "contingency-shaped" behavior. Since all behavior is shaped by contingencies, the critical distinction involves the source of the contingencies in effect.

38 R. Douglas Greer and Denise E. Ross, *Verbal Behavior Analysis: Inducing and Expanding New Verbal Capabilities in Children with Language Delays* (Boston, MA: Allyn and Bacon/Pearson Education, 2008).

39 This quiz is in a format originally designed by Jack Michael.

Chapter 11

1   Ms. Rennix is the author of this book.

2   ACLU and Human Rights Act Report: A Violent Education: Corporal Punishment of Children in U.S. Public Schools (August 19, 2008), http://www.hrw.org/en/reports/2008/08/19/violent-education. (Accessed December 4, 2008.)

3   Assembly Bill No. 755: An act to amend Section 273a of the Penal Code, relating to corporal punishment.

4   In respondent or Pavlovian extinction, the conditioned stimulus is repeated many times without any further pairing with the unconditioned stimulus until the conditioned stimulus no longer elicits the response.

5   B. F. Skinner, *Schedules of Reinforcement* (New York: Appleton-Century-Crofts, 1957), 411.

6   The name appeared in the 1960s. According to Wikipedia it was coined by Arthur Staats, http://en.wiki pedia.org/wiki/Child_time-out. (Accessed September 4, 2008.)

7   Personal email from Richard Clark, February, 2008, who also recommended the website http://www.oldbaileyonline.org.

8   Ellen P. Reese, "Learning About Teaching from Teaching About Learning; Presenting Behavioral Analysis in an Introductory Survey Course," in *The G. Stanley Hall Lecture Series, Volume 6,* Vivian Parker Makosky (Ed.) (Washington, D.C.: American Psychological Association, 1986), 85.

9   Roger E. Ulrich and Nathan H. Azrin, "Reflexive Fighting in Response to Aversive Stimulation," *Journal of the Experimental Analysis of Behavior* 5 (1962): 511–520.

10 See, for example, Richard Rhodes, *Why They Kill: The Discoveries of a Maverick Sociologist* (New York: Random House, 1999).

11 Taken from *Congressional Quarterly's State Fact Finder,* 2002.

12 Ramon Lewis, "Classroom Discipline in Australia," in Carolyn M. Evertson and Carol S. Weinstein (Eds.), *Handbook of Classroom Management: Research, Practice and Contemporary Issues* (Mahwah, NJ: Lawrence Erlbaum Associates, 2006), 1193–1213.

13 Jacob S. Kounin and Paul V. Gump, "The Ripple Effect in Discipline," *The Elementary School Journal* 59, 3 (December, 1958): 158–162.

14 L. Rowell Huesmann, Jessica Moise-Titus, Cheryl-Lynn Podolski, and Leonard D. Eron, "Longitudinal Relations between Children's Exposure to TV Violence and their Aggressive and Violent Behavior in Young Adulthood: 1977–1992," *Developmental Psychology* 39 (2003): 201–221.

15 Report of the Surgeon General: *Media Violence: Exposure and Content.* http://www.surgeongeneral.gov/library/youthviolence/chapter4/appendix4bsec2.html/. (Accessed December 4, 2008.)

16 Lewis, "Classroom Discipline in Australia," 1193–1213.

17 This occurred in a large undergraduate education class taught by E. A. Vargas at West Virginia University.

18 Nathan Azrin and Richard Fox, *Toilet Training in Less Than A Day* (New York: Simon & Schuster Pocket Books, 1976).

19 John Minor designed this procedure in his unit at the Kennedy Youth Center in Morgantown, WV.

20 This is not a pure case of "extinction" because, in addition to withholding attention from Billy, your walking Patrick away is an added postcedent.

21 The teacher taught at University High School, Morgantown, WV. Her name has been changed.

22 Rita Cantrell Schellenberg, Agatha Parks-Savage, and Mark Rehfuss, "Reducing levels of elementary school violence with peer mediation," *Professional School Counseling* June, 2007.

23 Department of Education Federal Register, "Assistance to States for the Education of Children With

Disabilities and Preschool Grants for Children With Disabilities: Final Rule" (August 14, 2006), 71, 156, 46539–46845.

24   See, for example, New York State's requirements: vesid.nysed.gov/specialed/publications/policy/function-behav.htm (Accessed February 26, 2008).

25   Section 4.02 of the BACB Guidelines for Responsible Conduct.

26   Edward G. Carr, Christine E. Reeve, and Darlene Magito-McLaughlin, "Contextual Influences on the Problem Behavior in People with Developmental Disabilities," in Lynn Kern Koegel, Robert L. Koegel, and Glen Dunlap (Eds.), *Positive Behavioral Support: Including People with Difficult Behavior in the Community* (Baltimore, MD: Paul H. Brookes Publishing Co., 1996) 403–423.

27   Deanne A. Crone and Robert H. Horner, *Building Positive Behavior Support Systems in Schools* (New York: Guildford Press, 2003) 14.

Chapter 12

1   Kurt Vonnegut, *A Man Without a Country* (Random House Trade Paperback NY, 2005), 132.

2   Hank Pennypacker, and Julie S. Vargas, "Using Student Performance to Evaluate Teaching" (Paper presented at the annual meeting of the National Council on Measurement in Education, San Francisco, 1976).

3   Lee Canter and Marlene Canter, *Lee Canter's Assertive Discipline: Positive Behavior Management for Today's Classroom* (L. and M. Canter, 1992), 84–85.

4   E. A. Vargas, "The Triad of Science Foundations, Instructional Technology, and Organizational Structure," *The Spanish Journal of Psychology* 7 (2004): 141–152.

5   http://www.madsci.org/posts/archives/2000–06/962288811.Me.r.html. (Accessed July 23, 2008.)

6   Rick Smith, Jack Michael, and Mark L. Sundberg, "Automatic Reinforcement and Automatic Punishment in Infant Vocal Behavior," *The Analysis of Verbal Behavior* 13 (1996): 39–48.

7   Greer, R. Douglas, Jessica Singer-Dudek, and G. Gatutreaux, "Observational Learning," *International Journal of Psychology* 41 (2006): 486–489; Greer, R. Douglas and Jessica Singer-Dudek, "The Emergence of Conditioned Reinforcement from Observation," *Journal of the Experimental Analysis of Behavior* 89 (2008): 15–39.

8   Charles B. Ferster, and B. F. Skinner, *Schedules of Reinforcement* (Cambridge, MA: B. F. Skinner Foundation, 1997). Originally published by Appleton-Century-Crofts, NYC, 1957.

9   Judy Cameron, "The Detrimental Effect of Reward Hypothesis: Persistence of a View in the Face of Disconfirming Evidence," in W.L. Heward et al. (Eds.), *Focus on Behavior Analysis in Education: Achievements, Challenges, and Opportunities* (Upper Saddle River, NJ: Merrill/Prentice-Hall, 2005) 304–315.

10   David W. Pierce, Judith Cameron, K. M. Banko, and S. So, "Positive Effects of Rewards and Performance Standards on Intrinsic Motivation," *Psychological Record* 53 (2003): 561–579.

11   Judy Cameron, "The Detrimental Effect of Reward Hypothesis: Persistence of a View in the Face of Disconfirming Evidence," in W.L. Heward et al. (Eds.), *Focus on Behavior Analysis in Education*, 304–315.

12   Michelle Feynman (Ed.), *Perfectly Reasonable Deviations: The Letters of Richard P. Feynman* (New York: Basic Books, 2005).

13   Mihaly Csikszentmihalyi, *Creativity: Flow and the Psychology of Discovery and Invention* (New York: Harper-Collins, 1996).

14   This was taken from the ideas in Richard de Mille, *Put your Mother on the Ceiling* (New York: Viking, 1973).

15   This is like the campfire activity of each person adding a bit to an ongoing tale.

16   Robert R. Lawler, "Math at Shady Hill: How Does the Shady Hill Math Program Add Up?" From a school newsletter, 2006.

17   Also see http://www.safeyouth.org/scripts/faq/prevgangs.asp.

18   Larry L. Mullins and Sharon M. Simpson, "Systematic Desensitization with Children and Adolescents," in *Encyclopedia of Behavior Modification and Cognitive Behavior Therapy, Volume Two*, Michael Hersen, Alan M. Gross, and Ronald S. Drabman (Eds.) (Thousand Oaks, CA: Sage, 2005), 1061–1064.

19   Walter Mischel, Yuichi Shoda, and M. L. Rodriguez, "Delay of Gratification in Children," *Science* 244 (1989): 933–938. (B. Bower from *Science News*.)

20   Lynn E. McClannahan and Patricia J. Krantz, *Activity Schedules for Children* (Bethesda, MD: Woodbine House, 1999).

21   Roy F. Baumeister, Jennifer D. Campbell, Joachim I. Krueger, and Kathleen D. Vohs, "Does High Self-Esteem Cause Better Performance, Interpersonal Success, Happiness, or Healthier Lifestyles?", *Psychological Science in the Public Interest* 4 (2003): 1–44.

GLOSSARY

AB design. A repeated measures (also called single-subject) design consisting of a baseline phase followed by one change in procedures. With only the one change for comparison, demonstration of functional relations between dependent and independent variables is weak or non-existent.

ABA design. A design consisting of an initial baseline phase followed by the implementation of experimental procedures, and then followed by either 1) a return to the baseline conditions, or 2) a change to the opposite procedure to that in the B phase. The latter is called a reversal phase.

ABC (Antecedent–Behavior–Consequence). A three-term contingency analysis: Behavior (B), what immediately follows (C), and the antecedent situation (A) in which the behavior-consequence pair usually occurs. Popular because of the alphabetic sequence ABC. ABP (Antecedent–Behavior–Postcedent) is more logically consistent in the naming of parts.

Abstract concept. A property (or collection of properties) that exists only in objects or situations, never alone. For example, the abstract concept of "two" can never be shown alone. It is a property that occurs only with two *things*. In contrast, concepts that are not abstract like "leaf" have concrete examples. You can say of a leaf, "This is a leaf," but it makes no sense to say "This is a two."

Action, an action. A single instance of behavior. Preferable to the term "response" because "action" does not imply an initiating stimulus. In operant behavior many actions have no particular initiating prior stimulus.

Active responding. A feature of instruction that requires students to answer questions or otherwise respond to content at each step of instruction. Moving to different pages by clicking on arrows or links in a computer program is *not* active responding because anyone could do that without any understanding of the content presented.

ADHD (attention deficit hyperactivity disorder). A diagnostic classification of levels of activity ("overactivity"), impulsivity, and lack of concentration that are higher than those characteristic of typically developing peers and that interfere with classroom activity.

Alternating treatment design. See **Multielement design**.

Antecedent control (antecedent stimulus control). The control of a situation or event over the following behavior. **Inappropriate antecedent control** describes features of a situation that are different from those approved of by a social group.

Applied Behavior Analysis. The application of the science of contingency relations to practical problems especially those of social significance. Behavior analysts adjust contingencies to improve behavior.

Attitude. A predisposition to act in certain ways. Like any "predisposition" the only evidence of an attitude is what a person does, including facial expressions and other overt activities. A student is said to have a positive attitude towards science when selecting science books to read, watching science shows rather than other shows, spending money on science projects or museums or games, and otherwise engaging in scientific activities.

Autism (Autism spectrum disorder). A diagnostic classification of behavior based upon deficits in language, lack of responding to one's environment or to other persons, and repetitive stereotyped actions that have persisted for a specified period of time.

Autoclitic behavior. Verbal behavior "which is based upon or depends upon other verbal behavior," and does so in ways that enhance the effect upon a listener, including the "speaker" him or herself.

Automatic reinforcement. Reinforcement that follows directly from an action itself, rather than being added by others. Automatic reinforcement is the behavioral equivalent of what others call intrinsic rewards or natural consequences. Except for consequences that are reinforcing genetically (such as water, comfortable temperature, food, and sexual contact), all other "automatic" reinforcers are conditioned through pairing with existing reinforcers. For example when looking at books is paired with parental pleasure and affection, books become conditioned reinforcers and looking at books becomes "automatically" reinforcing even when a parent is not around.

Aversive stimulus. A stimulus that reduces behavior on which it is made contingent and that is avoided or that produces behavior that eliminates it. What is aversive varies from person to person and from situation to situation. Loud music may be aversive to one person but not to another. The same music may be aversive to the person who often plays it when that person is trying to hear a friend on a cell phone. The only way to be sure about the effect of a stimulus in a particular situation is to make it contingent on behavior and see what happens. If the behavior decreases, you have an aversive stimulus. Also called a "negative reinforcer" or "punisher."

Avoidance. Behavior that prevents or postpones coming in contact with an aversive stimulus or situation. Unlike escape, the stimulus is not encountered during avoidance behavior.

Backup reinforcer. An object or event that follows a conditioned reinforcer to maintain the effectiveness of the conditioned reinforcer. Backup reinforcers are often exchanged for a given number of points or stars or other conditioned reinforcers.

Backward chaining. A procedure in which the last of a series of steps is taught first, the next to last step taught next, and the remaining steps taught in reverse order as soon as each following step has been mastered.

Bar graph. A graph that represents values with rectangular bars. Used with young children who can color bars to the height specified. Also good for comparing two numbers side by side, or for showing proportions where part of a bar is shaded to show how many of the problems given or completed were done correctly or how many of those assigned were completed.

Baseline. Measures taken prior to implementing a change in procedures (the treatment). Also the time period over which those measures are taken. Baseline measures are also called the "operant level," "initial level," or "pretreatment level." Baselines are used as a measure of performance against which to judge the impact of procedures that follow.

Baseline phase. A period of time during which data are taken before a procedure is implemented.

Behavior. Action of an individual including actions that take place inside the individual, such as thinking, breathing, or holding one's breath. Behavior is a process that changes the behaver's immediate environment in some way. Thinking and breathing alter the immediate circumstances of the individual who does them. (See **Operant** and **Respondent** for the two kinds of behavior.)

Behavior analysis. The study of relationships between behavior and environmental variables, especially those that can help change behavior in socially desirable ways. See also **Behaviorology**.

Behavioral assessment. The gathering of information about specific actions of an individual (usually ones that cause problems), and possible controlling variables, especially immediate antecedents and postcedents that usually occur. See also **Functional behavioral assessment**.

Behavioral contract. A statement of contingencies that specifies behavior to be performed and the rewards that will follow. Contracts are set in advance of the opportunity for the behavior to occur, in contrast to lures which are rewards offered during training.

Behavioral deficits. Specific actions that a person lacks that are needed for functioning successfully in school or other settings. Behavioral deficits usually consist of specific academic skills that have not been mastered, or social skills that, once acquired, would improve relations with peers or adults.

Behavior modification. Procedures for changing behavior including 1) the explicit use of reinforcement or punishment, or 2) respondent conditioning as in "desensitization" where clients are taught behavior like relaxing when exposed to stimuli that come closer and closer to the stimuli that are causing problems. The term is used more by clinical psychologists than by educators.

Behavioral objective. A goal stated in terms of what students should be able to do as a result of instruction. Behavioral objectives state observable and measurable actions, a level of difficulty of tasks or materials, and the level of performance required. Also called **performance objectives**.

Behavior therapy. Application of operant or respondent conditioning to improve the life of persons with behavioral or emotional problems. Assumes that behavioral problems are maintained by factors currently operating in the person's life, and that they can be changed by altering those contingencies.

Behaviorism. The philosophy of the science of human behavior. It addresses questions like whether a science of behavior is possible and what role it plays in daily life. Radical behaviorism ("radical" meaning "root") was coined by B. F. Skinner for his philosophical position that thinking, feelings, and verbal behavior are all legitimate parts of a science of behavior.

Behaviorology. The science of relations between behavior and the contingencies that affect any of its properties, such as rate, magnitude, or quality. Refers especially to the principles and philosophical positions of B. F. Skinner.

Blackout ratio. See **Blackout technique**.

Blackout technique. A method of identifying the parts of an exercise to which students are likely to attend when responding. Parts of an exercise or question are hidden ("blacked out') to see how much can be removed without making it difficult or impossible to respond correctly. Since students generally ignore parts they do not need to answer correctly, *low* blackout ratios are a feature of good instructional design.

Causes (of behavior). One or more factors upon which behavior depends in a lawful way. Suspected causes are called independent variables when their effects are assessed through experimentation. Scientists prefer to talk of functional relations instead of using the word "cause."

Celeration. A change in the rate (speed) of a specific action over time. The term was introduced by Ogden Lindsley in connection with Precision Teaching. The most common Precision Teaching celerations are recorded as changes in actions per minute per week. Both acceleration and deceleration are recorded as ratios of change. For example, a celeration of x 2 (times two) per week means that performance is doubling each week. Deceleration is calculated by dividing: a celeration of ÷ 2 (divide by two) per week would occur if saying a swear word in gym went down from 10 a minute to 5 a minute a week later. See also **Precision Teaching**.

Chaining. The process of linking steps so that they are emitted in sequence. The performance of each step sets up antecedents for the next step. For example, in tying a bow, each manipulation of the laces sets the position of the laces needed for the next step. Where a student has difficulty with a chain, the steps are best taught in reverse order with the last step first. See **Backward chaining**.

Challenging behavior. An alternative term for **problem behavior**: any kind of action that endangers the student or others, or that interrupts ongoing activities frequently enough to hinder student progress.

Circular explanation (of behavior). A statement that has the form of an explanation, but which gives as the cause a restatement of the behavior to be explained. Circular explanations go round and round with different ways of describing behavior without identifying any independent variable that can be changed to see its effect. Circular explanations are also called **explanatory fictions**.

Classical conditioning. See **Respondent conditioning**.

Clicker training. Shaping with an auditory conditioned reinforcer. Used especially where verbal instruction is not possible, as when training non-human animals. See also **TAG Teaching—Teaching with Acoustical Guidance**.

Cloze technique. A technique of testing or teaching reading comprehension by asking students to fill in missing words in a paragraph. The words to fill in are selected statistically (such as every fifth word), in contrast to the **embedded options format** that asks students to select or fill in words that relate to the meaning of a passage.

Competent Learner Model (CLM). A system of instruction primarily for learners that lack skills for success in school and community settings. The system includes 1) a specific curriculum to teach communicating, observing and listening skills, and the prerequisites for reading and writing, 2) staff training in behavioral procedures, 3) continual supervision of staff and student progress, and 4) a placement and overall evaluation system. Developed and supervised by Vicci Tucci (http://www.tuccionline.com).

Concept. A property or set of properties shared by objects or events that distinguish between *members* or *examples* of the concept and *objects or events* that do not have those defining properties. Both induction and discrimination are involved: for example, the concept "red" is a property shared by all of the things called "red" (induction from one red to others) and that differs from other colors (discrimination between red and other colors). In both cases, responding must be under the control of the defining properties of the concept (in this case color) and not to other features (such as size or shape).

Conditioned reinforcer. A stimulus that reinforces behavior on which it is contingent because of prior pairing with an already existing reinforcer. When the original reinforcer continues to be needed, it is called a **backup reinforcer**. When a backup reinforcer is no longer needed, the conditioned reinforcer may be called "automatic reinforcement" or an "intrinsic reward" or "natural reinforcement."

Conditioning. The strengthening or weakening of the likelihood of a particular behavior in similar situations through the addition of reinforcement or punishment. See **Operant conditioning** and **Respondent conditioning**.

Consequence. A postcedent that depends on an action occurring, as opposed to something that follows behavior in time but may not depend on behavior occurring.

Contingency. The relation between an operant and features of the environment that come before or come after. **Two-term contingencies** specify behavior and postcedent events (events that immediately follow). **Three-term contingencies** include the antecedent situation in which behavior–postcedent pairings usually occur. Contingencies can include even more terms, as is necessary in analyzing verbal behavior. The term "contingency" specifies pairings that are likely but not inevitable. Whether a contingency has an effect on behavior must be further determined. See **Reinforcement**, **Schedules of reinforcement**.

Contingency analysis. An examination of the contingencies over a specific behavior usually in order to change how often that behavior occurs.

Contingencies of reinforcement. The interrelationships among the settings or occasions where an action occurs, the action itself, and the reinforcement that follows. There are also contingencies involving punishment.

Contingency management. The arrangement of contingencies to produce specified behavior.

Contingent reinforcement. Reinforcement that depends upon the occurrence of an action. When reinforcement occurs randomly or without any relationship to whether or not an action occurs, it is called **non-contingent**.

Continuous reinforcement (abbreviated crf). A schedule of reinforcement where reinforcement follows every response of a given kind. Reinforcement that follows only some actions is called **intermittent reinforcement**.

Contract. See **Behavioral contract**.

Convergent goals. Objectives for behaviors that students need to perform similarly, such as pronouncing words correctly or doing a handstand with straight legs. Convergent goals differ from *divergent* goals where the aim is for differing performances, as in writing creative compositions or inventing new dance routines.

Counting period ceiling. The limit imposed in a timed exercise by the number of available opportunities to respond. When only 10 problems are given for a one-minute timing, no one can correctly complete more than 10 problems. A student who could have completed 20 problems is limited to 10 per minute by the counting period ceiling. Ceilings are calculated by dividing the total number of problems or tasks given by the number of minutes used.

Counting period floor. The minimum rate possible to record in the time used. Calculated as one divided by the number of minutes in the counting period.

Correction procedure. Any action taken by an instructor immediately following an incorrect response to prompt a correct response.

Creative behavior. Behavior that is unique and that meets social standards for usefulness or beauty. Not all unique behavior is considered creative. A student who suddenly puts glue all over her clothing would rarely be called creative, although her behavior would certainly differ from the norm. To be judged creative, behavior must be valued by others.

Criticism Trap. A situation where criticizing a behavior to decrease seems to work because it temporarily halts the behavior, but the criticism actually makes the behavior occur more frequently in the future.

Cue. A stimulus to which a particular response is to be made. When the response reliably occurs, cue is equivalent to a **discriminative stimulus** or S^D.

Cumulative record (graph). A graph that adds each response as it is made in real time to a slowly moving line. Each response moves the line up a small amount, so that the faster the responding the steeper the slope of the line. If responding stops, the line is flat (horizontal). Typically, reinforcement is indicated by a short slash mark on the line where each reinforced response occurred.

Curriculum alignment. The matching of objectives, instructional activities, and evaluation methods. When all three address the same behaviors, the curriculum is said to be "aligned."

Delayed prompting. A technique where prompts are withheld for a few seconds after a task is given, but then automatically given whether or not the student responds. Students can avoid answering incorrectly by waiting for the prompt. Usually, as soon as students can answer correctly, they anticipate prompts.

Dependent variable. Behavior or a property of behavior that you are trying to explain or to change. A researcher looks for **independent variables** that, when manipulated, determine how often the behavior of interest (the dependent variable) occurs.

Deprivation. The reduced availability of a reinforcer usually measured as the time since the last availability. Often used as an **establishing operation** to make a particular postcedent a reinforcer. When someone is food deprived, that is, when an individual has not eaten recently, food can be used as a reinforcer.

Desensitization. See **Systematic desensitization**.

Differential reinforcement. Reinforcement of only some actions or properties of actions, usually those closest to a specified behavior.

Differential Reinforcement of Alternative behavior (DRA). Reinforcement of a behavior different from one to be decelerated as a way to decrease or "replace" it.

Differential Reinforcement of Incompatible behavior (DRI). Reinforcement of behavior that cannot occur simultaneously with a behavior to be decelerated.

Differential responding. A difference in the rate of a particular kind of behavior depending on which antecedent stimuli are present.

Direct Instruction (DI). A teaching format that involves student responding in planned incremental steps. DI usually involves a script for the teacher. It can be done individually or with a group in a choral responding format.

Direct measures. Numbers that indicate how many times or how rapidly a particular action occurred, or its latency or duration. Direct measures are obtained by "directly" observing behavior *as it occurs* or counting some property of the products of those actions. (Contrast Indirect measures.)

Discrete Trial Training, Discrete Trial Teaching (DTT). A three-term contingency teaching format usually used with one teacher and one student in which the teacher asks a question, the student responds, and the teacher gives feedback or additional prompts. Usually the sequence of tasks is set beforehand and the teacher records each student response.

Discrimination. Responding differently to different objects or events or to their properties. Established by reinforcing responding differentially according to which stimuli are present when responding occurs.

Discriminative stimulus or S^D. A stimulus in the presence of which a given response reliably occurs. A stimulus becomes discriminative through reinforcement having been contingent on responding in its presence and not in its absence. The stimulus "2 + 2" is a discriminative stimulus for the answer "4" once the answer "4" reliably occurs.

Divergent behavior. Behavior that differs from individual to individual, such as creating a product that is unique. It is contrasted with convergent behavior where student responses are the same such as all students giving the correct date of an historical event.

Duration. The length in time from the start to the completion of an action.

Echoic. Oral verbal behavior that matches, in point to point correspondence, a prior oral stimulus. Imitating the pronunciation of a word is echoic behavior.

Elicit. Produce a reflex response to an antecedent stimulus. Respondent behavior is elicited. An elicited eye-blink is controlled (and explained) by its relation to the prior stimulus such as a touch to the eye. Elicited behavior is contrasted with **emitted** behavior controlled by postcedents. When asked to blink an emitted eye-blink may or may not occur, depending on its relation to past consequences of blinking versus not blinking when asked.

Embedded options format. An instructional format to teach reading comprehension in which important words or short phrases in a paragraph are replaced with two to four alternatives from which the student selects the option that makes most sense.

Emit. To execute a particular operant action. Control over emitted behavior lies in its relation to postcedents, in contrast to **elicited behavior** which is controlled by an antecedent stimulus.

Emotional side effects of punishment. Emotional behavior that is elicited by punishment. Punishment elicits responses such as fear or anger. Through respondent conditioning those responses can be later elicited by whatever preceded the punishment, such as a teacher's question, making mistakes, a particular subject matter, or school in general. Any such reactions that came from the punishment are called emotional side effects. Emotional side effects also occur from reinforcement, but they are seldom problems.

Entering behavior. What a student does or can do prior to instruction, especially that part of his or her repertoire relevant to the skills to be taught.

Equal interval graph. A graph which has lines equally spaced up and down the vertical axis so that when you *add or subtract* a certain amount, you move up or down the same distance, no matter where you start. Improvement on an equal-interval graph shows in the number increased, not the ratio of change. Thus a student who goes from two to four (adding two) shows less improvement than one going from 20 to 40 (adding 20), although both doubled their performance.

Equal-ratio graph. A graph with a ratio (logarithmic) scale on the vertical axis. The horizontal lines are spaced so that multiplying (or dividing) by any value (such as two for doubling) moves up or down the same distance no matter where you begin. Going from two problems correct one Monday to four correct a week later moves up the same vertical distance as going from 20 to 40. Equal-ratio graphs standardize ratios of change.

Equivalence relations. Induction where different stimuli produce the same or equivalent matching responses, although no physical resemblance is involved. A direct outcome of special reinforcement contingencies in which some pairings are taught to mastery, thus enabling other pairings to emerge.

Errorless learning. The mastering of new skills by taking steps that increase in such small increments of difficulty that mistakes are rarely if ever made.

Escape. Getting out of or removing an aversive stimulus situation. Escape differs from avoidance in that in escape the aversive situation is already present, while in avoidance the aversive situation is postponed or does not occur at all. One escapes smoky environments by leaving. One avoids smoky environments by not entering places that are smoky.

Establishing operation. A procedure that affects the ability of a particular object or event to function as a reinforcer. One establishing operation is deprivation. When someone is deprived of liquids, a drink is more likely to reinforce behavior than when liquid has been readily available. The ability of a drink to reinforce behavior can also be enhanced by eating salty foods, an establishing operation often taken advantage of by bars.

Event-governed. Behavior under control of environmental contingencies in contrast to **verbally-governed** behavior that is mediated by rules or instructions. A competent driver responds to traffic conditions and the feel of the car (event-governed behavior). In contrast, the behavior of a learner is largely governed by the instructions of an instructor (verbally-governed behavior).

Exemplar. An exemplar is an object or event that illustrates a concept or principle. It has the properties that define the concept or principle. See also **Multiple exemplar**. May also indicate a person who serves as a role model.

Explanatory fiction. An explanatory fiction is a statement that has the form of an explanation, but in which the "cause" is essentially a restatement of the behavior to be explained. For example, the statement "Jack doesn't work because he is lazy," is an explanatory fiction. The "cause" (being lazy) is merely another way of saying that Jack doesn't work. Such statements are also called **circular**.

Extinction. Operant extinction. The procedure of withholding the reinforcement that has previously followed a particular operant. Responding occurs, but without reinforcement. Operant extinction differs from forgetting in that the latter refers to a decrease in the strength of a behavior over time when it has *not* been emitted. In addition to describing the procedure of withholding reinforcement, the term extinction is also used to describe the resulting behavior, as in "flipping the (broken) light switch underwent extinction."

Extinction. Respondent extinction. The procedure of repeating the conditioned stimulus without pairing it with the unconditioned stimulus until responding no longer occurs. The term extinction in respondent extinction also describes the result of the procedure, as in "Drooling to the bell underwent extinction."

Extinction burst. An initial sharp increase in the rate or intensity of responding following the withholding of reinforcement. Extinction bursts occur most often following continuous or nearly continuous reinforcement schedules that have occurred for a long time. Extinction bursts often include emotional responding as well as an increase in the operant no longer reinforced.

Fading. The gradual decrease in visibility or clarity of a prompt as student responding continues to be successful.

Feedback. A postcedent that indicates the accuracy or effectiveness of an action. Unlike "reinforcement" or "punishment," the term "feedback" does not specify the effect on behavior of the postcedent event. See also **Immediate feedback**.

Fixed-interval schedule (abbreviated FI). A schedule of reinforcement in which reinforcement follows the first action to occur after a fixed time since the last reinforced response. Responding that occurs before the time interval ends is neither reinforced nor penalized. After the time is up nothing happens until a response occurs. Responding in fixed-interval schedules tends to be slow, rising towards the end of the time period.

Fixed-ratio schedule (abbreviated FR). A schedule in which the nth response is reinforced. In a fixed-ratio 5 (FR5), the fifth action is reinforced. In a fixed-ratio 10, 10 responses are required for reinforcement to occur. Assuming that gold stars are reinforcing, a star following the 10th problem completed would be a FR10 schedule. Responding under fixed-ratio schedules may be slow after reinforcement, but speeds up as the required number is approached.

Fluency. The combination of consistent speed and accuracy of performance, usually recorded in count of actions per minute. Fluent behavior is not only rapid and accurate, but it is also smooth and automatic in the sense of not requiring much thought. Fluency is also called "automaticity."

Forgetting. A decrease in the strength of behavior over time when the behavior has not been emitted. Forgetting differs from extinction where an operant continues to be emitted but is no longer reinforced.

Formal analysis of verbal behavior. An analysis of the structure of language that considers particular words and grammatical forms, in contrast to Skinner's **functional analysis** that looks at the contingencies responsible for the various forms said, written, texted, or gestured.

Free operant behavior. Behavior that can occur at any time. Responding does not have to wait for a task or question to be asked. When actions can occur repeatedly without restriction, rates of behavior can be obtained.

Frequency graph. A graph in which a measure of frequency is shown on the vertical axis. In behavior analysis, "frequency" usually means a simple count. However, "frequency" can also mean "rate" or "count per unit of time," and is used in that sense by Precision Teachers. Graphs of just the number of problems correctly completed, of questions asked, or the number of students attending after school sports practice without a time dimension would be called frequency graphs by most behavior analysts.

Functional analysis (1). A procedure for finding out what controls behavior by altering antecedents or postcedents and measuring any change in the behavior. Usually done in order to decelerate problem behavior.

Functional analysis (2). An analysis of the contingencies responsible for behavior of a particular kind. Especially in talking about verbal behavior, a functional analysis is contrasted with a **formal analysis** that looks at the form or structure of expressions, rather than at their effects or controls.

Functional behavioral assessment. A procedure that identifies antecedents and postcedents of specific actions to locate factors likely to be related to the occurrence of a behavior of concern.

Functional relation. A systematic relationship between dependent and independent variables. The functional relations of interest to teachers involve behavior and variables that reliably produce it.

Generalization. See **Induction**.

Grade inflation. An increase in the percentage of students receiving high grades due to a *lowering of standards* rather than improvement in performance.

Group design. A research design that compares groups that receive different treatments. Analysis of results usually depends on one or more tests given at the end of the experiment. Differences in performance between groups are statistically evaluated to see whether they are large enough to have resulted from the treatment rather than from the random differences between groups. Group designs do not provide information on individual performance.

Guided notes. Outlines with critical terms and definitions missing. They are given to students to fill in while listening to lectures.

Hypothetical construct. An explanatory variable which is not directly observable and cannot therefore be directly manipulated to see its effect. For behavior, hypothetical constructs, like "intelligence" are usually assumed to exist inside individuals whose behavior is to be explained. When hypothetical constructs use the same evidence for their existence as the behavior they are said to explain, they are classic examples of explanatory fictions.

IDEA (Individuals with Disabilities Education Act). "A law ensuring services to children with disabilities throughout the nation. IDEA governs how states and public agencies provide early intervention, special education and related services to more than 6.5 million eligible infants, toddlers, children and youth with disabilities" (http://idea.ed.gov/).

IEP (Individualized Educational Plan). An educational program meeting federal requirements for free and appropriate education to a child with a disability. Also refers to the written document that describes that educational program.

Immediate feedback. A consequence that is delivered for one answer or action before the next question or task is begun.

Incompatible actions. Two actions that cannot be done at the same time. Walking and riding a bike are incompatible actions.

Independent variable. A condition or procedure that is systematically varied to observe its effect on behavior.

Indirect measures. Measures of behavior in which counts of actions are converted into percentages, relative standing (standard scores), or other scales that require interpretation to understand. The SAT is an indirect measure. The number of items a student answers correctly is converted into numbers that compare that student's standing to the performance of all the others in a large comparison group.

Induction (also called **generalization**). The spread of effect from one situation to other situations that are similar or related in some way. Identifying a new leaf as a "sugar maple" after having identified examples in class is an example of induction.

Informed consent. A written agreement to participate in a study including a statement that the participant is participating willingly, understands what will happen, has been informed of any disadvantages of participating, and knows that he or she can withdraw at any time. Where necessary, a legal guardian signs the document.

Intermittent reinforcement. Reinforcement that follows only some actions but not all, in contrast to **continuous reinforcement** where every instance of an operant is reinforced.

Intraverbal. A verbal operant in which a response of given form is under the control of a prior verbal stimulus with which it does not share similar sequence or form. Saying "four" when asked "What is three plus one?" is intraverbal behavior. Intraverbal behavior is a very large part of what is taught in homes and schools.

Intrinsic motivation. The control over behavior that comes from postcedents of one's own actions rather than being added by other people. Other than biological reinforcers such as food or water, the reinforcing effects of behavior come from contingencies that create new conditioned reinforcers or make behavior persistent through intermittent reinforcement. See also **Natural consequences**.

Latency. The time from the presentation of a task to the beginning of a response. If a student is asked to give her phone number and takes four seconds to begin, the latency would be four seconds.

Learning picture. The pattern made with two lines on a graph; one drawn through data points showing correct responding over a number of days and the other through points for incorrect responding on the same days. Usually counting period floors are also shown.

Lecture fill-in sheets. Pages given to students with blanks to fill in as a presentation progresses. They may include quiz items or, like guided notes, may consist of an outline with critical parts missing.

Level (of data on a graph). The general height (numeric value) of a group of data points on a graph: how high or low they fall on the y-axis. Often recorded as an average over the days on which the data were taken.

Lure. A reward offered or shown *just before* a behavior in order to attract behavior towards it. A hotdog held over a dog to get it to jump is a lure. Lures differ from prompts in that prompts help in the execution of performance but are not themselves reinforcers. Lures differ from behavioral contracts that specify contingencies but do not present the rewards until after the specified behavior occurs.

Magnitude. The size, force, or intensity of an action. A yell has a higher magnitude than a whisper.

Mand. "A verbal operant in which the response is reinforced by a characteristic consequence and is therefore under the functional control of relevant conditions of deprivation or aversive stimulation." Mands "specify" their reinforcement and are the only verbal operants that do so. A mand for milk is reinforced by milk, not approval.

Match to sample. An instructional format that requires a student to select among objects or pictures of objects the one(s) that match some property of the sample presented. In a match to sample format for color, a red truck might be presented as the sample and the student asked to pick out from objects of different colors those that are red. Match to sample is the format usually used to demonstrate equivalence relations.

Meaning. Contingencies under which specific verbal behavior is emitted. Meaning does not reside in the specific words, phrases or gestures, but rather in the circumstances under which they are expressed. "Hello" means one thing if said when discovering something unexpected, but has a different meaning when said on a telephone, even when the word and the way it is said are similar.

Measurement. The process of assigning numbers for equivalent units to specify extent or other properties of an action or event.

Mentalistic construct. A hypothesized internal structure proposed as a cause of behavior. Mentalistic constructs, like short-term or long-term memory, are explanatory fictions when evidence for the "cause" is the same as for the behavior to be explained.

Model (as used in behavior analysis). A person, object, or action that provides an antecedent stimulus for imitation.

Motivating operation. A procedure that increases the likelihood that a particular postcedent will function as a reinforcer, for example timing the use of snacks before rather than after a meal, or increasing the effectiveness of water as a reinforcer by making salty food freely available, or showing a model working for or expressing delight with a token to make it more reinforcing for others.

Multielement design. An experimental format in which one or more conditions are rapidly alternated to see which conditions most affect behavior. For example, to find out which discussion format produces more participation, the two formats would be rapidly alternated, for example by using one method for the first 10 minutes of class and the other for the second 10 minutes. Which procedure would be used first each class period would be decided randomly, for example by a flip of a coin.

Multiple baseline. An experimental design in which baselines are taken for more than one behavior, individual, or group, followed by implementing procedures with one of them at a time (one of the behaviors, individuals, or groups). Used especially where treatments (like teaching mnemonics) cannot be withdrawn or where a return to baseline conditions would be undesirable.

Multiple exemplars. A large number of different examples of a concept or principle. Use of multiple exemplars facilitates responding to the defining properties of the concept or principle and not to irrelevant features of specific examples. For example, using many different shapes to teach the concept of one half helps students respond to "portion of a whole" rather than to the shape of half a pizza. Using multiple exemplars also promotes induction. The student working with many shapes is more likely to identify one half of new examples than one taught only with halves of circles.

Natural consequences. Consequences that follow directly from behavior itself, not postcedents given by another person. A natural consequence of throwing a fragile dish is that it breaks. Breaking results directly from the action of throwing. It is not a natural consequence to be made to clean up the mess. That consequence is added by someone else. It is not a result of the act itself.

Natural contingencies. Contingencies that occur in daily life, in contrast to *instructional contingencies* which are special arrangements of both consequences and settings specifically designed to establish skills.

Negative reinforcement. A procedure in which a stimulus is removed or decreased in intensity, with the result of an increase in rate of the operant on which the procedure was contingent. Covering one's ears when a jackhammer begins drilling reduces the stimulus of the noise. It is an example of negative reinforcement if covering ears occurs more often in the future in similar circumstances.

Negative reinforcer. A stimulus or event that increases the rate (likelihood) of the operant that reduces or removes it.

Occam's razor. The principle that explanation should make as few assumptions as possible, and use only factors that predict outcomes. Occam's razor recommends parsimony of explanation, often stated as "The simplest explanation is the best."

Operant. A class of actions defined by their effects. Operants are defined *functionally*, that is by how they change the immediate environment of the person behaving. The operant "opening a door" may have many different forms, but in all cases results in an open door. Unlike respondent behavior, there need be no particular antecedent stimulus preceding an operant. We do not open every door we see. Opening is controlled by the consequence of a particular door being open at a particular time.

Operant behavior. Behavior that operates on the environment and is controlled by its immediate effects, in contrast to **respondent behavior** that can be explained as the response to a stimulus.

Operant conditioning. The process of altering the frequency and/or strength of behavior through reinforcement or punishment procedures. A special case of operant conditioning is called **shaping**, where the reinforced actions gradually change as they increasingly approximate a final performance.

Peer Instruction. An instructional format where students are paired and one serves as a tutor or teacher, the other as a student. Usually the roles are switched back and forth. The term has also described a format in which students sitting next to each other in an auditorium discuss answers to questions asked at intervals during a lecture.

Percentage. Conversion of direct counts to a scale of 100, that is to what an equivalent proportion of 100 would be. Percentage hides how large or small the original numbers were.

Performance domain. A classification of skills into hierarchies. Typically the categories range from convergent skills which have one "right" answer or "correct" performance to divergent skills like creative performances that differ from person to person. The basic performance levels in this book are Knowledge (or Knowing), Problem-solving, and Creating.

Performance objective. See **Behavioral objective**.

Permanent product. A relatively stable result of behavior, like the marks that come from the action of writing. In schools, permanent products are considered equivalent to direct observations of behavior, so long as it is clear that the students produced the permanent products themselves.

Personalized System of Instruction (PSI). A system designed by Fred S. Keller in which course material is broken down into units, each of which has text materials and essay questions at the end. When ready, students take each quiz which is graded on the spot by "proctors" who are usually students who have done well on that unit earlier in the term or in a previous semester. Remediation is also done by proctors. Students cannot progress until they master each unit.

Phase. A period of time in an experimental study during which similar conditions are in effect. See also **Baseline**.

Positive Behavior Support. A system for remedying problem behavior that begins with a functional assessment to find possible controlling variables, makes changes in precipitating events and postcedents as well as building missing repertoires, using positive reinforcement instead of punishment.

Positive reinforcement. A postcedent addition of a stimulus that increases the frequency or strength of the operant on which it is made contingent. (See also **Negative reinforcement**.) All reinforcement is defined by its effects. Saying, "Very good," or handing someone a "good behavior" sticker qualifies as positive reinforcement *only* if the postcedent increases the frequency or strength of the behavior it immediately follows.

Precision Teaching. A system in which frequent (usually very short daily) measures of fluency of behavior are plotted on a special graph called a Standard Celeration Chart (SCC) to aid in making instructional decisions. Fluency is measured as counts per unit of time (usually actions correct per minute). The Standard Celeration Chart shows proportion of change in equal distances, so that doubling performance looks the same whether beginning at a slow rate or at a faster rate. Developed by Ogden Lindsley in the 1960s.

Precurrent behavior. Actions taken at one time to prompt a specific action later, like setting an alarm clock so you will get up on time.

Probing. A technique of checking the performance on a new skill by interspersing test items into a sequence of instruction.

Problem behavior. Any action that is severe enough or frequent enough to endanger or hinder academic or social progress of the student involved or of others in the class. Also called **challenging behavior**.

Programmed Instruction (PI). An instructional format consisting of a series of increasingly difficult sequential steps that students take to master skills they could not perform at the outset. The steps are presented as **frames** that require student responding to the material presented. Responding is designed to demonstrate understanding of content. Pressing arrows for more information is not Programmed Instruction.

Project Follow Through. A half-billion dollar project in which nine major models of preschool education for at-risk students were implemented in over 180 sites and their results over 20 years compared against each other and against non-participating schools.

Prompt. Antecedent help that enables a learner to respond correctly. Prompts may be suggestions, additional instructions, parts of the response, or physical guidance. They are usually withdrawn or faded quickly to prevent the student becoming **prompt dependent**.

Prompt dependence. Responding that occurs only when a prompt has been given, rather than in the situation for which the behavior was taught.

Property of behavior. The strength, form, duration, or rate of behavior.

Punishment. A postcedent event that decreases or weakens behavior upon which it is made contingent. The postcedent can be an added stimulus, like a spanking, or the removal of a reinforcer like money (called a "fine"). Punishment is defined by its effect not by how you think it should work. If sending a student to suspension hall does not decrease the behavior on which it was contingent, it is not punishment. In addition to decelerating behavior, punishment usually produces undesirable emotional side effects like anger and hostility.

Rate. A count of actions divided by the time period over which the count was taken. The term "frequency" is also used for count per unit time by Precision Teachers, but not by most behavior analysts.

Reinforcement. Any change in the environment that strengthens behavior on which it is contingent. Reinforcement is defined by its effects. There is no such thing as reinforcement that doesn't "work." Reinforcement may be a direct result of an action, like the change in location that results from walking, or it may be provided by others, like getting an answer when asking a question. In all cases it must increase the magnitude or rate of the behavior it follows. Reinforcement differs from "reward" in that a reward is a tangible item or privilege whose relation to behavior is often delayed or imprecise.

Reinforcer. A postcedent event that increases (positive reinforcer) or decreases (negative reinforcer) the future probability of behavior on which it is made contingent.

Repertoire. All of the behavior that a person has emitted or is likely to emit. Usually assessed by actions that have been observed or that are assessed by tests.

Replacement behavior. Behavior specified as an alternative action to build in order to decrease behavior that is considered a problem.

Respondent behavior. Behavior that is controlled by a prior stimulus. Many respondents, like blinking when the eye is touched, are part of inherited reflexes. Other respondents, like anxiety before a test, are acquired through respondent conditioning. Respondent behavior is **elicited** in contrast to **operant behavior** that is **emitted**.

Respondent (Pavlovian) conditioning. The process of pairing a "neutral" stimulus that does not elicit a particular response with one that does until the previously neutral stimulus alone elicits that same response. The neutral stimulus is then called a "**conditional (or conditioned) stimulus**," and the response a "**conditional (or conditioned) response**."

Response. A single action, especially the reaction to an antecedent in respondent conditioning. Also used for a single instance of operant behavior. Not all operant actions have an initiating stimulus, so "action" is a better term unless a specific discriminative stimulus is present.

Response cost. The loss of reinforcers contingent upon an action. A form of punishment.

Response generalization. See **Induction**.

Response latency. See **Latency**.

Response to Intervention (RtI) (also called Response to Instruction). A system for identifying behavior problems and skill deficits, primarily in at risk students, designing instruction to address the problems, and assessing progress frequently to make sure that the intervention or instruction is helping. RtI is part of an **Individualized Educational Program (IEP)** required for students who qualify for special services.

Return to baseline research design (ABA). A research design with a phase after the treatment phase that returns to the original conditions before treatment.

Reversal design. A research design where, after a treatment phase, procedures are implemented that are opposite to the treatment strategies. A study of blockbuilding in kindergarten reinforced placing blocks to make new shapes for the treatment phases. In the reversal phase, placing blocks to create old shapes was reinforced. The reversal in behavior provides strong evidence that the contingencies were responsible for changes observed. Usually a reversal phase is ended once behavior changes, and the treatment is reinstated.

Reward. A tangible item or privilege given for performance. In contrast to reinforcement, the effect of a reward is assumed not demonstrated, and the relation to behavior is often delayed and imprecise.

Rubric. A description of performance levels from low quality to high quality. Rubrics are more general than scoring keys that assign points for each criterion met.

Satiate. Providing so much of an event or material goods that no more is taken when available.

Schedules of reinforcement. A specification of the way in which reinforcement is made contingent on behavior. Schedules specify the conditions under which reinforcement occurs and which actions in a string of actions get reinforced.

Science. The systematic study of relations between phenomena, and the formulation of those relations into **scientific laws** that predict when events occur and the conditions required.

S-delta or S^Δ. A stimulus in the presence of which a particular response does not occur because of being extinguished when that stimulus was present.

Scoring key. A list of characteristics a student product should contain, usually with points indicating relative importance. When given at the beginning of an assignment, scoring keys serve as performance objectives for the task.

Selection by consequences. The process by which operant conditioning occurs: some actions are "selected" by consequences and become part of an individual's repertoire. Other actions fail to be reinforced and no longer occur.

Self-control. One set of actions taken to alter another set of actions of one's own behavior. Includes, 1) verbal behavior said to oneself (usually covertly) to control one's current behavior, like telling oneself to keep calm or counting to 10 in anger, 2) actions taken at the moment to control one's own behavior later, like setting an alarm clock to make sure one wakes up on time later, and 3) giving up short-term rewards or engaging in aversive activities for long-term benefits, like resisting fattening foods or exercising now for physical benefits later.

Self-management. Designing contingencies over one's own behavior following the same procedures one would propose for managing someone else's behavior.

Shaping. The process of building new behavior by reinforcing the form, direction, or intensity of existing actions that most closely approximate or will lead to the final action. Learner actions that come closer and closer to the goal are called **successive approximations**.

Stability. Consistency of performance or lack of change over time.

Stimulus equivalence. See **Equivalence relations**.

Social validity. The degree to which a behavior taught has a direct benefit to society and to the individuals involved. Behavior that enables a student to interact more effectively both in and out of school has social validity.

Stimulus. An action or event to which an animal responds in some way. You must specify which action is under consideration. Background music playing when a person is asked about the weather is not a stimulus for talking about weather, but it is a stimulus for thinking about the music.

Successive approximations. Student actions that come closer and closer to a goal or the steps that students are to go through to reach that goal.

Systematic desensitization. A procedure for reducing maladaptive respondent behavior. Clients are taught to relax when presented with stimuli that do not elicit the target respondent and then to relax to stimuli that increasingly resemble the situation that originally caused problems. A person afraid to talk to an audience, for example, may be given scenarios that start with talking to a good friend, and then asked to relax to increasingly threatening scenarios until the fear disappears.

Tact. Verbal behavior under control of properties of objects or other stimuli with which the "speaker" is currently in contact, including stimuli inside that person's own body. Tacts are reinforced by generalized reinforcers like social approval.

TAG Teaching (Teaching with Acoustical Guidance). A behavioral system of instruction that uses an audible click or other brief sound as a conditioned reinforcer to strengthen specific actions or properties of behavior. TAG Teaching includes 1) picking one immediately achievable target at a time, 2) using only reinforcement (no "correction" is used; errors are ignored), 3) providing high rates of practice often with peers tagging each other, and 4) adjusting procedures according to individual moment to moment progress.

Target behavior. The behavior specified for a student or students to achieve.

Teaching. The arrangement of contingencies that facilitate learning. Presenting or demonstrating is not teaching unless student behavior shows change. Both socially desirable and undesirable behavior can be taught.

Three-term contingency. The relationship between an operant, what results from or follows it, and the antecedent situation in which that behavior–postcedent pairing usually occurs.

Time on task. The time that a student is judged to be working or paying attention, often converted to percent of time available.

Time out. A punishment procedure to decelerate behavior in which a student is removed temporarily from a presumably reinforcing situation to a different location for a short time.

Time sampling. Recording of whether or not a specific behavior occurs 1) at specific times (momentary time sampling), or 2) at all during specified short intervals (partial-interval recording), or 3) during the whole of each short time interval (whole-interval recording).

Topography of behavior. The physical properties of an operant; its form or magnitude or other features of how it looks, sounds, smells, or feels. Topography of behavior is contrasted with **function** which takes into consideration the contingencies that control the likelihood of behavior occurring. Extending a hand palm out (as in a policeman's stop signal) has a very different topography than calling out "Stop," or blowing a whistle. But if both are done in order to get someone to stop, the three are under the same functional controls.

Trial. A single presentation of a question or task to which a student is to respond. See **Discrete Trial Training/Teaching**.

Trials to criterion. A count of how many times a student responds to a question or task before responding in a way that meets a pre-established criterion.

Trend. The degree to which data points on a graph are rising or falling over time; the direction in which behavior is heading.

Two-term contingency. An operant and the immediate consequences that control the likelihood of its occurrence.

Two-term shaping. Shaping that is not in a trial format. Two-term shaping does not have an antecedent stimulus for each opportunity to respond, but rather reinforces whatever actions come closest to a goal. Also called "free operant" shaping.

Understand. To respond "appropriately" to a situation. "Appropriately" is judged by the common practices of a social group. A person blushing at a compliment would be said to understand what was said. A person who looks confused when insulted with a slang term would be said not to understand what was said.

Vanishing. The removal of parts of a prompt bit by bit while insuring that student performance continues to be successful.

Variable. A variable is something that can take on different values. Aspects or properties of behavior to be explained or changed are called "dependent variables." Instructional procedures that are altered to assess their effects are called "independent variables."

Variable-interval(VI) schedule. A schedule in which reinforcement occurs for the first response that follows varying periods of time since the last reinforced response. An action must take place in order for reinforcement to occur. Actions before the time is up go unreinforced and do not lengthen or shorten the set times. Checking mail for a package is on a VI schedule. Checking frequently does not hurry delivery, but as soon as delivery has occurred, the next check will be reinforced. VI schedules usually produce slow but persistent responding.

Variable ratio (VR) schedule. A schedule in which reinforcement follows a number of actions that vary between set values. Responding faster produces reinforcement sooner, and this schedule produces a high, steady rate of responding.

Variability. The up-and-down bounce of values of data points on a graph. High variability is the opposite of stability of performance over time.

Verbal behavior. Behavior reinforced through the mediation of other persons. Different words or phrases may be under the same functional controls, but the consequences delivered by mediating persons reinforce only forms that conform to the practices of their social group.

Verbally-governed behavior. Behavior that is under the control of instructions or rules that mediate interactions within one's world. Also called *rule-governed*. Verbally-governed behavior is contrasted with event-governed behavior that is controlled directly by environmental contingencies. New skills (such as driving a car) usually begin largely as verbally-governed behavior ("put your turn signal on"), and then move to event-governed controls as the driver responds to road conditions without thinking of instructions.

Withdrawal (experimental design). A repeated measures research design in which, after adding a procedure for the "treatment" phase, the procedure is withdrawn, resulting in a return to the baseline condition.

BIBLIOGRAPHY

Adams, G. L., and Siegfried Engelmann. *Research on Direct Instruction 25 Years Beyond DISTAR.* Seattle, WA: Educational Assessment Systems, 1996.

Allday, R. Allan, and Kerri Pakurar. "Effects of Teacher Greetings on Student On-task Behavior." *Journal of Applied Behavior Analysis* 40 (2007): 317–320.

Almon-Morris, Holly, and Michael Fabrizio. "Teaching Assent Withdrawal and Self-Advocacy Skills to Persons With Autism." Paper presented at the annual convention of the Association For Behavior Analysis International, Chicago, IL, May 27, 2008.

Azrin, Nathan, and Richard Fox. *Toilet Training in Less Than A Day.* New York: Simon & Schuster Pocket Books, 1976.

Bailey, Jon, and Mary R. Burch. *Ethics for Behavior Analysts.* Mahwah, NJ: Erlbaum, 2005.

Baron, Alan, and Mark Galizio. "Positive and Negative Reinforcement: Should the Distinction be Preserved?" *The Behavior Analyst* 28 (2005): 85–98.

Baumeister, Roy F., Jennifer D. Campbell, Joachim I. Krueger, and Kathleen D. Vohs. "Does High Self-Esteem Cause Better Performance, Interpersonal Success, Happiness, or Healthier Lifestyles?" *Psychological Science in the Public Interest* 4 (2003): 1–44.

Becker, Wesley C., Siegfried Engelmann, and Don R. Thomas. *Teaching I: Classroom Management.* Chicago, IL: Science Research Associates, 1975.

Behavior Analysis Certification Board. http://www.bacb.com.

Bijou, Sidney W., and Donald M. Baer. *Child Development: Readings in Experimental Analysis.* New York: Appleton-Century-Crofts, 1967.

Bijou, Sidney W., and Donald M. Baer. *Behavior Analysis of Child Development.* Englewood Cliffs, NJ: Prentice-Hall, 1978.

Binder, Carl V., "Behavioral Fluency: Evolution of a New Paradigm." *The Behavior Analyst* 19 (1996): 163–197.

Binder, Carl V., Eric Haughton, and D. Van Eyk. "Increasing Endurance by Building Fluency: Precision Teaching Attention Span." *Teaching Exceptional Children* 22 (1990): 24–27.

Bjork, Daniel W. *B. F. Skinner: A Life.* New York: Basic Books/Harper Collins Publishers, Inc., 1993.

Bondy, Andy S., and Beth Sulzer-Azaroff. *The Pyramid Approach to Education in Autism.* Newark, DE: Pyramid Educational Products, Inc., 2002.

Bower, Robert, and Ken Meier. "Will the Real 'Slow Learner' Please Stand Up?" *Journal of Precision Teaching* 2 (1981): 3–12.

Brown, S., D. Churella, J. Lyonett, K. Oyster, and D. Petrovich. "The Effects of Behavior Specific Praise on Task Completion." Final report for an Educational Research Class at West Virginia University, November 2001.

Buzan, Tony. *Use Both Sides of Your Brain: New Mind-Mapping Techniques, Third Edition.* New York: Penguin Plume Paperback, 1991.

Cameron, Judy, David Pierce, and Charles Greenwood. *Rewards and Intrinsic Motivation: Resolving The Controversy.* Westport, CT: Bergin & Garvey, 2006.

Canter, Lee, and Marlene Canter. *Lee Canter's Assertive Discipline: Positive Behavior Management for Today's Classroom.* L. and M. Canter, 1992.

Carr, Edward G., Christine E. Reeve, and Darlene Magito-McLaughlin. "Contextual Influences on the Problem Behavior in People with Developmental Disabilities." In *Positive Behavioral Support: Including People with Difficult Behavior in the Community*, Lynn Kern Koegel, Robert L. Koegel, and Glen Dunlap (Eds.), 403–423. Baltimore, MD: Paul H. Brookes Publishing Co., 1996.

Carrigan, D. R., Kimberly C. Kirby, and D. B. Marlowe. "Effect of Dispenser Location on Taking Free Condoms in an Outpatient Cocaine Abuse Treatment Clinic." *Journal of Applied Behavior Analysis* 28 (1995): 465–466.

Catania, A. Charles, and Stevan Harnad (Eds.). *The Selection of Behavior: The Operant Behaviorism of B. F. Skinner: Comments and Consequences.* Cambridge: Cambridge University Press, 1988.

Cautela, Joseph R., and Albert J. Kearney. *The Covert Conditioning Casebook.* Pacific Grove, CA: Brooks/Cole Publishing Company, a division of Wadsworth, Inc. Belmont, CA: Wadsworth, a part of Cengage Learning, Inc., 1993.

Clingan, Mark R., and Ernest A. Vargas. "Nonrestricted Operant Prompting in Sequelic Instruction." *Behaviorology* 5 (2000): 110–127.

Cooper, John O., Timothy E. Heron, and William L. Heward. *Applied Behavior Analysis: Second Edition.* Upper Saddle River, NJ: Pearson Education, 2007.

Critchfield, Thomas S., and Vargas, Ernest A. "Self-recording Instructions, and Public Self-graphing: Effects on Swimming in the Absence of Coach Verbal Interaction." *Behavior Modification* 15 (1991): 95–112.

Crone, Deanne A., and Robert H. Horner. *Building Positive Behavior Support Systems in Schools: Functional Behavioral Assessment.* New York: Guildford Press, 2003.

Csikszentmihalyi, Mihaly. *Creativity: Flow and the Psychology of Discovery and Invention.* New York: Harper-Collins, 1996.

Davis, Linda L., and Robert E. O'Neil. "Use of Response Cards with a Group of Students with Learning Disabilities Including Those for whom English is a Second Language." *Journal of Applied Behavior Analysis* 37 (2004): 219–222.

de Mille, Richard. *Put your Mother on the Ceiling.* New York: Viking, 1973.

Dickens, Charles. *The Adventures of Oliver Twist.* New York: The Heritage Press, 1939.

Dietiker, Robert. "Decreasing a Fifth Grade Boy's 'I Can't Do It' Responses to Written Assignments." *School Applications of Learning Theory* 3 (1970): 30.

Doran, Judith, and James G. Holland. "Eye Movements as a Function of Response Contingencies Measured by Blackout Technique." *Journal of Applied Behavior Analysis* 4 (1971): 11–17.

Engelmann, Siegfried, and Douglas Carnine. *Theory of Instruction: Principles and Applications.* New York: Irvington Publishers, Inc., 1982.

Eshleman, John W. "Quantitative Trends in the History of Verbal Behavior Research." *The Analysis of Verbal Behavior* 9 (1991): 61–80.

Ferster, Charles B., and B. F. Skinner, *Schedules of Reinforcement.* Cambridge, MA: B. F. Skinner Foundation, 1997. Originally published by Prentice-Hall, 1957.

Feynman, Michelle (Ed.). *Perfectly Reasonable Deviations: The letters of Richard P. Feynman.* New York: Basic Books, 2005.

Fraga, Mario F., Esteban Ballestar, Maria F. Paz, Santiago Ropero, Fernando Setien, Maria L. Ballestar, Damia Heine-Suñer, Juan C. Cigudosa, Miguel Urioste, Javier Benitez, Manuel Boix-Chornet, Abel Sanchez-Aguilera, Charlotte Ling, Emma Carlsson, Pernille Poulsen, Allan Vaag, Zarko Stephan, Tim D. Spector, Yue-Zhong Wu, Christoph Plass, and Manel Esteller. "Epigenetic Differences Arise During the Lifetime of Monozygotic Twins." *Proceedings of the National Academy of Sciences* 102 (July 26, 2005): 10604–10609. (Also available at http://www.pnas.org/cgi/content/abstract/102/30/10604.)

Frost, Lori, and Andy Bondy. *The Picture Exchange Communication System Training Manual, Second Edition.* Newark, DE: Pyramid Educational Products, Inc., 2002.

Gardner, Ralph, Diane M. Sainato, John O. Cooper, Timothy E. Heron, William L. Heward, John W. Eshleman, and Teresa A. Grossi (Eds.). *Behavior Analysis in Education: Focus on Measurably Superior Instruction.* Pacific Grove, CA: Brooks Cole, 1994.

Graf, Steve, and Ogden R. Lindsley. *Standard Celeration Charting 2002.* Poland, OH: Graf Implements, 2002.

Goetz, Elizabeth M., and Donald M. Baer. "Social Control of Form Diversity and the Emergence of New Forms in Children's Blockbuilding." *Journal of Applied Behavior Analysis* 6 (1973): 209–217.

Goldstein, Michael H., Andrew P. King, and Meredith J. West. "Social Interaction Shapes Babbling: Testing Parallels Between Birdsong and Speech." *Proceedings of the National Academy of Sciences, 1200* (June 24, 2003): 8030–8035.

Greer, R. Douglas. *Designing Teaching Strategies: An Applied Behavior Analysis Systems Approach*. San Diego, CA: Academic Press, 2002.

Greer, R. Douglas, and Dolleen-Day Keohane. "The Evolution of Verbal Behavior in Children." *Behavioral Development Bulletin* (2005): 31–47.

Greer, R. Douglas, Mapy Chavez-Brown, Anjalee S. Nirgudkar, Lauren Stolfi, and Celestina Rivera-Valdes. "Acquisition of Fluent Listener Responses and the Educational Advancement of Young Children with Autism and Severe Language Delays." *European Journal of Behavior Analysis* 2 (Winter 2005): 125–144.

Greer, R. Douglas, and Denise E. Ross. *Verbal Behavior Analysis: Inducing and Expanding New Verbal Capabilities in Children with Language Delays*. Boston, MA: Allyn & Bacon/Pearson Education, 2008.

Hall, Genae A., and Mark L. Sundberg. "Teaching Mands by Manipulating Conditioned Establishing Operations." *The Analysis of Verbal Behavior* 5 (1987): 41–53.

Hersen, Michael, George Sugai, and Robert Horner (Eds.). *Encyclopedia of Behavior Modification and Cognitive Behavior Therapy, Volume Three: Educational Applications*. Thousand Oaks, CA: Sage Publications, 2005.

Heward, William L. *Exceptional Children: An Introduction to Special Education* (8th ed.). Upper Saddle River, NJ: Merrill/Prentice-Hall, 2006.

Heward, William L., Timothy E. Heron, and Nancy A. Neef (Eds.). *Focus on Behavior Analysis in Education: Achievements, Challenges, and Opportunities*. Upper Saddle River, NJ: Merrill/Prentice-Hall, 2005.

Huesmann, L. Rowell, Jessica Moise-Titus, Cheryl-Lynn Podolski, and Leonard D. Eron. "Longitudinal Relations between Children's Exposure to TV Violence and their Aggressive and Violent Behavior in Young Adulthood: 1977–1992." *Developmental Psychology* 39 (2003): 201–221.

Huff, Darrell. *How to Lie with Statistics*. New York: W. W. Norton & Company, 1954.

Iwata, Brian A. "On the Distinction Between Positive and Negative Reinforcement." *The Behavior Analyst* 29 (2006): 121–124.

Johnson, Kent R., and T. V. Joe Layng. "Breaking the Structuralist Barrier: Literacy and Numeracy with Fluency." *American Psychologist* 47 (1992): 1475–1490.

Johnson, Kent, and Elizabeth M. Street. *The Morningside Model of Generative Instruction*. Concord, MA: Cambridge Center for Behavioral Studies, 2004.

Johnston, James M., and Pennypacker, H. S., *Strategies and Tactics of Human Behavioral Research* (2nd ed.). Hillsdale, NJ: Erlbaum, 1993.

Kaplan, Michael (Ed.). *Essential Works of Pavlov*. New York: Bantam, 1966.

Kazdin, Alan E. *Behavior Modification in Applied Settings* (6th ed.). Belmont, CA: Wadsworth, 2001.

Keller, Fred S. *Summers and Sabbaticals; Selected Papers on Psychology and Education*. Champaign, IL: Research Press Co. 1977.

Keller, Fred S., and William N. Schoenfeld. *Principles of Psychology*. New York: Appleton-Century-Crofts, 1950. (Reprinted by the B. F. Skinner Foundation, 1995.)

Kemp, Fred O. "Computer-Mediated Communication: Making Nets Work for Writing Instruction." In *The Dialogic Classroom: Teachers Integrating Computer Technology, Pedagogy, and Research*, R. Galin and Joan Latchaw (Eds.), 133–150. Urbana: National Council of Teachers of English, 1998.

Knapp, Terry J. "Behavior Analysts' Visual Appraisal of Behavior Change in Graphic Display." *Behavioral Assessment* 5 (1983): 155–164.

Kodak, Tiffany, John Northup, and Michael E. Kelley. "An Evaluation of the Types of Attention that Maintain Problem Behavior." *Journal of Applied Behavior Analysis* 40 (2007): 167–171.

Koegel, Lynn Kern, Robert L Koegel, and Glen Dunlap (Eds.). *Positive Behavioral Support: Including People with Difficult Behavior in the Community*. Baltimore, MD: Paul H. Brookes Publishing Co., 1996.

Koenig, Carl K. "Charting the Future Course of Behavior." EdD diss., University of Kansas, 1972.

Kounin, Jacob S., and Paul V. Gump. "The Ripple Effect in Discipline." *The Elementary School Journal,* 59 (1958): 158–162.

Lamarre, Jennifer, and James G. Holland. "The Functional Independence of Mands and Tacts." *Journal of the Experimental Analysis of Behavior* 43 (1985): 5–19.

Laties, Victor, G., and A. Charles Catania. "A Matter of Record." *Introduction to Cumulative Record: Definitive Edition* by B. F. Skinner, xiii–xxvi. Cambridge, MA: B. F. Skinner Foundation, 1999.

Lichtenstein, Paul, Niels V. Holm, Pia K. Verkasalo, Anastasia Iliadou, Jaakko Kaprio, Markku Koskenvuo, Eero Pukkala, Axes, Skythe, and Kari Hemminki. "Environmental and Heritable Factors in the Causation of Cancer." *The New England Journal of Medicine* 343 (2000): 78–85.

Lindsley, Ogden R. "What We Know That Ain't So." Paper presented at the annual meeting of the Midwestern Association of Behavior Analysis, Chicago, IL, May 27–30, 1977.

Lindsley, Ogden R. "Precision Teaching's Unique Legacy from B. F. Skinner." *Journal of Behavioral Education* 1 (1991): 253–266.

Lindsley, Ogden R. "Precision Teaching: Discoveries and Effects." *Journal of Applied Behavior Analysis* 25 (1992): 51–57.

Lindsley, Ogden R. "Skinner on Measurement." 2001. Unpublished MS. Copies may be obtained by emailing admin@behaviorresearchcompany.com/

Lindsley, Ogden R. "Studies in Behavior Therapy and Behavior Research Laboratory: June 1953–1965." In *A History of the Behavioral Therapies: Founders' Personal Histories*, William T. O'Donohue, Deborah A. Henderson, Steven C. Hayes, Jane E. Fisher, and Linda J. Hayes (Eds.), 125–153. Reno: Context Press, 2001.

Lindsley, Ogden R., Carl H. Koenig, J. B. Nichols, D. B. Kanter, and N. A. Young. *Handbook of Precise Behavior Facts: Listings of the First Twelve Thousand Published Precise Behavior Management Projects*. Kansas: Precision Media 1971. Two volumes.

Lewis, Ramon. "Classroom Discipline in Australia." In *Handbook of Classroom Management: Research, Practice and Contemporary Issues*, Carolyn M. Evertson and Carol S. Weinstein (Eds.), 1193–1213. Mahwah, NJ: Lawrence Erlbaum, 2006.

Lowenkron, Barry. "Meaning: A Verbal Behavior Account." *The Analysis of Verbal Behavior* 20 (2004): 77–97.

Malott, Richard W., and Elizabeth A. Trojan. *Principles of Behavior* (5th ed.). Upper Saddle River, NJ: Prentice-Hall, 2004.

Marmolejo, Erick K., David A. Wilder, and Lucas Bradley. "A Preliminary Analysis of the Effects of Response Cards on Student Performance and Participation in an Upper Division University Course." *Journal of Applied Behavior Analysis* 37 (2004): 405–410.

Martin, Gary L., and Joseph Pear. *Behavior Modification: What it is and How to Do it*. Upper Saddle River, NJ: Prentice-Hall, 2006.

Mazur, Eric. *Peer Instruction: A User's Manual.* Upper Saddle River, NJ: Prentice-Hall, 1997.

McBrien, Lynn J., and Ronald Brandt (Eds.). *The Language of Learning: A Guide to Educational Terms*. Baltimore, MD: Association for Supervision and Curriculum Development, 1997.

McClannahan, Lynn E., and Patricia J. Krantz. *Activity Schedules for Children*. Bethesda, MD: Woodbine House, 1999.

McGreevy, Pat. *Teaching and Learning in Plain English*. Kansas City, MO: Plain English Publications, 1983.

McKerchar, Paige M., and Rachel H. Thompson. "A Descriptive Analysis of Potential Reinforcement Contingencies in the Preschool Classroom." *Journal of Applied Behavior Analysis* 37 (2004): 431–443.

Meany-Daboul, Maeve G., Eileen M. Roscoe, Jason C. Bourret, and William H. Ahearn. "A Comparison of Momentary Time Sampling and Partial-Interval Recording for Evaluating Functional Relations." *Journal of Applied Behavior Analysis* 40 (2007): 501–514.

Mechner, Francis. "What Are the Effects of Reinforcement Presentations?" In Mechner, *The Revealed Operant: A Way to Study the Characteristics of Individual Occurrences of Operant Responses*. Cambridge, MA: Cambridge Center for Behavioral Studies Monograph Series (3rd ed.), 1994.

Michael, Jack. "Positive and Negative Reinforcement: A Distinction that is No Longer Necessary; or a Better Way to Talk about Bad Things." *Behaviorism* 3 (1975): 33–44.

Michael, Jack. "Skinner's Elementary Verbal Relations: Some New Categories. *The Analysis of Verbal Behavior* 1 (1982): 1–4.

Miltenberger, Raymond G. *Behavior Modification: Principles and Procedures* (3rd ed.). Belmont, CA: Wadsworth/Thomson Learning, 2004.

Mischel, Walter, Yuichi Shoda, and M. L. Rodriguez. "Delay of Gratification in Children." *Science* 244 (1989): 933–938.

Montessori, Maria. *The Advanced Montessori Method, Volume 2*. John J. McDermott (Ed.). New York: Schocken, 1973.

Moran, Daniel J., and Richard W. Malott. *Evidence-Based Educational Methods*. San Diego, CA: Elsevier Academic Press, 2004.

Morris, Edward K., and Smith, Nathaniel G. "Bibliographic Processes and Products, and a Bibliography of the Published Primary Source Works of B. F. Skinner." *The Behavior Analyst* 26 (2003): 41–67. Also available at http://www.bfskinner.org

Mullins, Larry L., and Sharon M. Simpson. "Systematic Desensitization with Children and Adolescents." *Encyclopedia of Behavior Modification and Cognitive Behavior Therapy, Volume Two*. Michael Hersen, Alan M. Gross, and Ronald S. Drabman (Eds.), 1061–1064. Thousand Oaks, CA: Sage, 2005.

Murphy, H. Allen, J. Michael Hutchison, and Jon S. Bailey. "Behavioral School Psychology Goes Outdoors: The Effect of Organized Games on Playground Aggression." *Journal of Applied Behavior Analysis* 16 (1983): 29–35.

Neef, Nancy A., Brian A. Iwata, Robert H. Horner, Dorothea Lerman, Brian A Martens, and Diane S. Sainato (Eds.). *Behavior Analysis in Education: Second Edition: 1968–2002.* Lawrence, KS: Society for the Experimental Analysis of Behavior, 2004.

Neef, Nancy A.. Brandon E. McCord, and Summer J. Ferreri. "Effects of Guided Notes Versus Completed Notes During Lectures on College Students' Quiz Performance." *Journal of Applied Behavior Analysis* 39 (2006): 123–130.

Normand, Matthew P., and Jon S. Bailey. "The Effects of Celeration Lines on Visual Data Analysis." *Behavior Modification* 30 (2006): 295–314.

Overcash, Anne K., Andrew S. Bondy, and Todd A. Harris. "Comparing the Effects of Three Communication Strategies upon Spontaneous Requesting of Preschoolers with Autism." Paper presented at the annual convention of the Association for Behavior Analysis, San Francisco, United States, June, 1996.

Pavlov, Ivan Petrovich. Translated and edited by G. V. Anrep. *Conditioned Reflexes: An Investigation of the Physiological Activity of the Cerebral Cortex.* Oxford: Oxford University Press, 1927.

Pennypacker, Hank, and Julie S. Vargas. "Using Student Performance to Evaluate Teaching." Paper presented at the annual meeting of the National Council on Measurement in Education, San Francisco, 1976.

Pennypacker, H.S., Anibal Gutierrez, Jr., and Ogden R. Lindsley. *Handbook of the Standard Celeration Chart.* Gainesville, FL: Xerographics, 2003. Available from the Cambridge Center http://www.behavior.org.

Peterson, Gail B. "A Day of Great Illumination: B. F. Skinner's Discovery of Shaping." *Journal of the Experimental Analysis of Behavior* 82 (2004): 317–328.

Pierce, David W., Judith Cameron, Katherine M. Banko, and Sylvia So. "Positive Effects of Rewards and Performance Standards on Intrinsic Motivation." *Psychological Record* 53 (2003): 561–579.

Pierce, David W., and Carl D. Cheney. *Behavior Analysis and Learning, Third Edition.* Mahwah, NJ: Erlbaum, 2004.

Porritt, Matthew, Andrew Burt, and Alan Poling. "Increasing Fiction Writers' Productivity Through an Internet-based Intervention." *Journal of Applied Behavior Analysis* 39 (2006): 393–397.

Pryor, Karen. *Don't Shoot the Dog: The New Art of Teaching and Training (rev. ed.).* New York: Bantam, 1999.

Pryor, Karen. *On Behavior: Essays and Research.* Waltham, MA: Sunshine Books, Inc., 2004. www.clickertraining.com

Reese, Ellen P. *Experiments in Operant Behavior.* New York: Meredith Publishing Company, 1964.

Reese, Ellen P. "Learning About Teaching from Teaching About Learning: Presenting Behavioral Analysis in an Introductory Survey Course." In *The G. Stanley Hall Lecture Series, Volume 6,* Vivian Parker Makosky (Ed.), 69–127. Washington, D.C.: American Psychological Association, 1986.

Rhodes, Richard. *Why They Kill: The Discoveries of a Maverick Sociologist.* New York: Random House, 1999.

Ryan, Carolyn S., and Nancy S. Hemmes. "Effects of the Contingency for Homework Submission on Homework Submission and Quiz Performance in a College Course." *Journal of Applied Behavior Analysis* 38 (2005): 79–87.

Rushall, Brent. "The Restoration of Performance Capacity by Cognitive Restructuring and Covert Positive Reinforcement in an Elite Athlete," in *The Covert Conditioning Casebook,* Joseph R. Cautela and Albert J. Kearney (Eds.), 47–57. Pacific Grove, CA: Brooks/Cole Publishing Company, a division of Wadsworth, Inc. Belmont, CA: Wadsworth, a part of Cengage Learning, Inc., 1993.

Russell, Bertrand. *Philosophy.* New York: W. W. Norton & Company, 1927.

Sarokoff, Randi A., and Peter Sturmey. "The Effects of Behavioral Skills Training on Staff Implementation of Discrete-Trial Instruction." *Journal of Applied Behavior Analysis* 38 (2005): 23–37.

Schellenberg, Rita Cantrell, Agatha Parks-Savage, and Mark Rehfuss. "Reducing Levels of Elementary School Violence with Peer Mediation." *Professional School Counseling* June, 2007.

Sidman, Murray. *Tactics of Scientific Research: Evaluating Scientific Data in Psychology.* New York: Basic Books, 1960. Available at www.behavior.org

Sidman, Murray. "Reading and Auditory-Visual Equivalences." *Journal of Speech and Hearing Research* 14 (1971): 5–13.

Sidman, Murray. *Coercion and Its Fallout.* Boston, MA: Authors Cooperative, Inc., 1989. Available at www.behavior.org

Sidman, Murray. *Equivalence Relations and Behavior: A Research Story.* Boston, MA: Authors Cooperative, Inc., 1994. Available at www.behavior.org

Sidman, Murray. "Equivalence Relations and the Reinforcement Contingency." *Journal of the Experimental Analysis of Behavior* 74 (2000): 127–146.

Siegler, R. S., and E. Stern. "Conscious and Unconscious Strategy Discoveries: A Microgenetic Analysis." *Journal of Experimental Psychology: General* 127 (1998): 377–397.

Skinner, B. F. "Two Types of Conditioned Reflex: A Reply to Kororski and Miller." *The Journal of General Psychology* 16 (1937): 272–279.

Skinner, B. F. *The Behavior of Organisms.* New York: Appleton-Century-Crofts, 1938. (Reprinted by the B. F. Skinner Foundation, 1991.)

Skinner, B. F. *Science and Human Behavior.* New York: The Macmillan Company, 1953. (Reprinted 1965. New York: The Free Press. Available online at bfskinner.org)

Skinner, B. F. "A Case History in Scientific Method." *American Psychologist* 11 (1956): 221–233. (Reprinted in B. F. Skinner, *Cumulative Record: Definitive Edition.* Cambridge, MA: B. F. Skinner Foundation, 2004, 108–131.)

Skinner, B. F. *Schedules of Reinforcement.* New York: Appleton-Century-Crofts, 1957. (Reprinted by the B. F. Skinner Foundation, 1997.)

Skinner, B. F. *Verbal Behavior.* New York: Appleton-Century-Crofts, 1957. (Reprinted by the B. F. Skinner Foundation, 1992.)

Skinner, B. F. "Reinforcement Today." *American Psychologist* 13 (1958): 94–99.

Skinner, B. F. *The Technology of Teaching.* New York: Appleton-Century-Crofts, 1968. (Reprinted by the B. F. Skinner Foundation, 2003.)

Skinner, B. F. *About Behaviorism.* New York: Alfred A. Knopf, 1974.

Skinner, B. F. *Particulars of My Life.* New York: Alfred A. Knopf, 1976.

Skinner, B. F. *The Shaping of a Behaviorist.* New York: Alfred A. Knopf, 1979.

Smith, Richard, Jack Michael, and Mark L. Sundberg. "Automatic Reinforcement and Automatic Punishment in Infant Vocal Behavior." *The Analysis of Verbal Behavior* 13 (1996): 39–48.

Stebbins, L. B. R. G. St. Pierre, and E. C. Proper. *Education as Experimentation: A Planned Variation Model Effects of Follow Through Models.* Vol. IV-A & B. Cambridge, MA: Abt Associates, 1977.

Stewart, Bernice, and Julie S. Vargas. *Teaching Behavior to Infants and Toddlers: A Manual for Caregivers and Parents.* Springfield, IL: Charles C. Thomas, 1990.

Stoddard, Lawrence, T., and Murray Sidman. "Programming Perception and Learning for Retarded Children." In B. F. Skinner, *The Technology of Teaching,* 77. (Reprinted by the B. F. Skinner Foundation, 2003. Originally published in *International Review of Research in Retardation,* 151–208.)

Stokes, John V., John Randall, Julie Lomartire, and Michelle Graham. "Becoming Measurable and Observable: Performance Feedback and Video Modeling in Training Clinical Competence and Vocational Skills." Paper presented at the annual national meeting of the Berkshire Association for Behavior Analysis and Therapy, Amherst, USA, October 12–13, 2006.

Sundberg, Mark L., *The Verbal Behavior Milestones Assessment and Placement Program: The VB-MAPP.* Concord, CA: Advancements in Verbal Behavior Press, 2008.

Sundberg, Mark L., and Jack Michael. "The Benefits of Skinner's Analysis of Verbal Behavior for Children with Autism." *Behavior Modification* 25 (2001): 698–724.

Sutherland, Amy. "What Shamu Taught Me About a Happy Marriage." *New York Times,* Modern Love, June 25, 2006.

Sutherland, Amy. *What Shamu Taught Me about Life, Love, and Marriage.* New York: Random House, 2008.

Taylor, Connie C., and Jon S. Bailey. "Reducing Corporal Punishment with Elementary School Students Using Behavioral Diagnostic Procedures." In *Positive Behavior Support: Including People with Difficult Behavior in the Community,* Lynn Kern Koegel, Gobert L. Koegel, and Glen Dunlap (Eds.), 207–225. Baltimore, MD: Paul H. Brookes Publishing Co., 1996.

Thompson, Benjamin (Count Rumford). "Heat is a Form of Motion: An Experiment in Boring Cannon." *Philosophical Transactions* (1798), 88.

Thorndike, Edward L. "Animal Intelligence." *Psychological Review Monograph Supplement* (1898) (Serial N. 8).

Tu, Joyce C. "The Role of Joint Control in the Manded Selection Responses of Both Vocal and Non-Vocal Children with Autism." *The Analysis of Verbal Behavior,* 22 (2006): 191–207.

Ulman, Jerome. D., and Sulzer-Azaroff, Beth. "The Multi-Element Baseline Design in Educational Research." In *Behavior Analysis: Areas of Research and Application,* E. Ramp and G. Semb (Eds.). Englewood Cliffs, NJ: Prentice-Hall, 1975.

Ulman, Jerome D., and E. A. Vargas. "Behaviorology." In *Encyclopedia of Behavior Modification and Cognitive Behavior Therapy, Vol. 1, Adult Clinical Applications,* Michael Hersen, and Joan Rosqvist (Eds.), 175–176. Thousand Oaks, CA: Sage Publications, 2005.

Ulrich, Roger E., and Nathan H. Azrin. "Reflexive Fighting in Response to Aversive Stimulation." *Journal of the Experimental Analysis of Behavior* 5 (1962): 511–520.

Unger, Joseph P. "Widening the Classroom's Horizons: Using the Internet's Usenet News as an Intervention Heuristic." Paper presented at the 11th annual Computers and Writing Conference, El Paso, TX, May 1995. http://english.ttu.edu/KAIROS/1.3/news/UsenetPaper.html

Van Houten, Ron, and Joy Van Houten. "The Effects of Breaking New Spelling Words into Small Segments on the Spelling Performance of Students with Learning Disabilities." *Journal of Behavioral Education* 1 (1991): 399–411.

Vargas, Ernest A. "Intraverbal Behavior." In *Psychological Aspects of Language*, Philip N. Chase and Linda J. Parrot (Eds.), 128–151. Springfield, IL: Charles C. Thomas, 1986.

Vargas, Ernest A. "Verbally-Governed and Event-Governed Behavior." *The Analysis of Verbal Behavior* 6 (1988): 11–22.

Vargas, Ernest A. "Explanatory Frameworks and the Thema of Agency." *Behaviorology* 4 (1996): 30–42.

Vargas, Ernest A. "Verbal Behavior: Implications of its Mediational and Relational Characteristics." *The Analysis of Verbal Behavior* 15 (1998): 149–151.

Vargas, Ernest A. "The Triad of Science Foundations, Instructional Technology, and Organizational Structure." *The Spanish Journal of Psychology* 7 (2004): 141–152.

Vargas, Ernest A. "The Triad Model of Education (II) and Instructional Engineering." *The Spanish Journal of Psychology* 10 (2007): 314–327.

Vargas, Julie S. *Writing Worthwhile Behavioral Objectives*. New York: Harper & Row, 1992.

Vargas, Julie S. "B. F. Skinner's Contribution to Therapeutic Change: An Agency-less, Contingency Analysis." In *A History of the Behavioral Therapies: Founders' Personal Histories*, William O'Donohue, Deborah A. Henderson, Steven C. Hayes, Jane E. Fisher, and Linda J. Hayes (Eds.), 59–74. Reno, NV: Context Press, 2001.

Vargas, Julie S. "Improving Teaching Performance." In *Teaching Tips for College and University Instructors: A Practical Guide*, David Royse (Ed.), 254–280. Needham Heights, MA: Allyn & Bacon, A Pearson Education Company, 2001.

Vargas, Julie S. "Precision Teaching and Skinner's Legacy." *European Journal of Behavior Analysis* 4 (2003): 80–86.

Vargas, Julie S. "Contingencies over B. F. Skinner's Discovery of Contingencies. *European Journal of Behavior Analysis* 5 (2004): 137–142.

Vargas, Julie S. "Skinner, Burrhus Frederic." In *Encyclopedia of Behavior Modification and Cognitive Behavior Therapy; Volume Three: Educational Applications*, Michael Hersen, George Sugai, and Robert Horner (Eds.), 1526–1531. Thousand Oaks, CA: Sage Publications, 2005.

Vonnegut, Kurt. *A Man Without a Country*. New York: Random House Trade Paperback, 2005.

Wahler, Robert G., Gary H. Winkel, Robert F. Peterson, and Delmont C. Morrison. "Mothers as Behavior Therapists for Their Own Children." In *Child Development: Readings in Experimental Analysis*, Sidney W. Bijou and Donald M. Baer (Eds.), 240–255. New York: Meredith Publishing Company, 1967. Originally published in *Behavior Research and Therapy* 3.

Watson, John B. *Behaviorism*. New York: W. W. Norton & Company, Inc., 1925.

Wertheimer, Max. *Productive Thinking*. New York: Harper & Row, 1959.

Index